The Playful Crowd

The Playful Crowd

Pleasure Places in the Twentieth Century

Gary S. Cross & John K. Walton

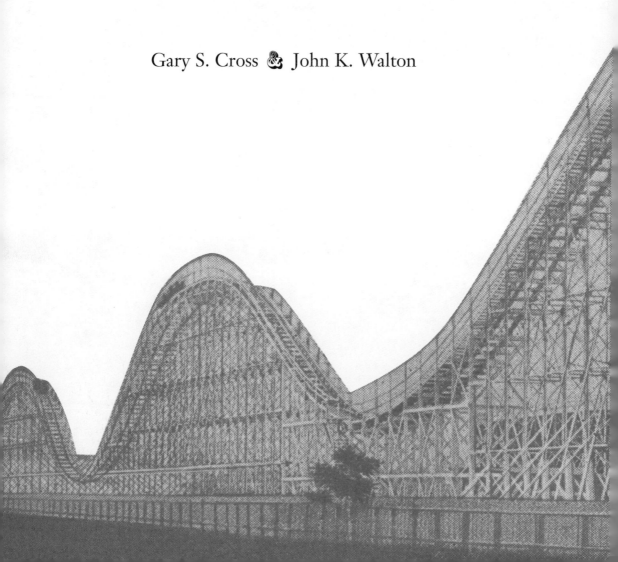

COLUMBIA UNIVERSITY PRESS   NEW YORK

Columbia University Press
Publishers Since 1893
New York, Chichester, West Sussex
Copyright © 2005 Columbia University Press
All rights Reserved

Library of Congress Cataloging-in-Publication Data

Cross, Gary S.
The playful crowd : pleasure places in the twentieth century /
Gary S. Cross, John K. Walton.
p. cm.
Includes bibliographical references and index.
ISBN 0–231–12724–3 (cloth : alk. paper)
 1. Amusement parks—Social aspects—United States—History—20th century.
 2. Amusement parks—Social aspects—England—History—20th century.
 I. Walton, John K. II. Title.

GV1851.A35C76   2005
791'.06873'0904—dc22   2005045786

Columbia University Press books are printed on permanent and durable
acid-free paper
Printed in the United States of America

c 10 9 8 7 6 5 4 3 2 1

References to Internet Web Sites (URLs) were accurate at the time of writing. Neither the author nor Columbia University Press is responsible for Web
sites that may have expired or changed since the book was prepared. Every
effort was made to obtain permission to publish copyrighted images and to
acknowledge their authors and we will endeavor in future printings to correct
any errors or omissions.

Contents

Preface

John Walton and Gary Cross met for the first time on a rainy June day in 1987 at the Preston (England) train station. They had arranged to rendezvous there on their way to Blackpool where John would show Gary this extraordinary relic of the Victorian seaside, on which John was already the leading authority. Gary had journeyed up from Brighton where he was working in the Mass-Observation archive on a book based on reports of Blackpool crowds in the 1930s, which he found while writing a book about the reduction of worktime in Britain and France. They had a wonderful day despite the heavy rain as John told amazing stories about the piers, Tower, shops, and Blackpool landladies and as Gary with his generic American accent amused elderly couples at the Tower Ballroom asking them about their experiences there in the 1930s.

This was the beginning of an enduring transatlantic friendship, with intermittent meetings in Preston, Lancaster, and at various conferences in England. In 2000 and 2001, John arranged for Gary to be a "Leverhulme Visiting Professor" at the University of Central Lancashire in Preston, and Gary spent two late springs and early summers in Lancashire, taking part in two international conferences at Preston and being introduced to some of the finer points of cricket. In turn, in the spring of 2003, Gary persuaded John to come over for a visit to Coney Island and showed him around Victorian Bellefonte in rural Pennsylvania near where Gary lives. Over these years, they shared stories of life changes and new projects. Gary raised a family and went on to publish broad comparative histories of leisure and consumption, eventually shifting from European to American topics. John lived through challenging times with partners in Preston, Lancaster, and the old industrial town of Accrington, and developed interests in the early Spanish seaside and the comparative history of tourism. Although their interests diverged as Gary got involved in the consumer culture of children and John's interests became more

European in scope, they kept a lot of common ground. Neither got bitten by the postmodernist bug, but they both moved on from the social history of the 1970s and 1980s to ask new questions.

Despite their very different approaches, backgrounds, and personalities, they decided in 2001 to write what became this book. They came upon the idea of a comparing American and British pleasure places and the crowds that they gathered across the twentieth century. This was a natural given Gary's growing fascination with fresh thinking on Disney and Coney Island, and John's interest in the Beamish Open Air Museum and why Blackpool survived the twentieth century when so many of its rivals faltered. They shared ideas across the Internet and made joint visits to the sites they were to write about.

Historians do not usually write books together. As a group, they learn to be original by working on their own. It is not so much that John and Gary are so different, although both are experienced in the art of the joint literary enterprise. Writing this book at this time brought new challenges, not least in reconciling contrasting academic cultures. Although many may refuse to believe this, they enjoyed the experience and had no disagreements worth mentioning. To be sure, pace and styles of writing clashed a bit at points. John had to put up with a lot of "translating" his British prose into American English, for example. But, in the end, this did not matter. This is not because they are particularly selfless and saintly (as anyone who knows them will attest), but because they appreciated how they complemented each other and simply would not let anything get in the way of the pleasure of the project and their friendship. They also began with a strong outline, clear division of labor, and a willingness to accept each other's editing as they passed drafts back and forth by e-mail, with layer upon layer of rewrites in contrasting colors.

Not only has their friendship survived and been enhanced by the experience, but the resulting book also stretched them both as historians. *The Playful Crowd* may or may not be a model of historical collaboration for other historians, but it is a rare example of a genuine and sustained transatlantic collaboration on a transatlantic theme, and neither of the authors could have written it without the other.

The Playful Crowd

Introduction

About 1,500 New Yorkers gathered in the dead of winter on January 3, 1903 to witness the "execution" of Topsy, the elephant. A 28-year veteran of the traveling American circus, Topsy had for two previous years developed a mean streak, killing three trainers (the last after he "fed" her a lighted cigarette). Topsy's current owners, Skip Dundy and Frederick Thompson of Coney Island's newest amusement park, Luna Park, had finally had enough of the temperamental beast. They decided to make a moral lesson of her and win in the process valuable publicity by "executing" the elephant.

At a time when public hangings were being banished from most of the civilized world, the spectacle of hanging the elephant first caught the promoters' fancy. But it was not merely the logistics of such an act that frustrated them but the objections of the American Society for the Prevention of Cruelty to Animals. Instead Luna Park teamed up with Thomas Edison to electrocute the offending pachyderm. Edison, who had only recently promoted the electric chair as a humane form of capital punishment, found Luna Park's offer an opportunity to once again show the "dangers" of alternating current (a rival to his preferred form of electricity, direct current) by arranging for the execution. As significant, a team from Edison's movie studio eagerly filmed the event for the millions who could not attend. Luna Park staff secured the beast and fitted her with wooden sandals lined with copper to which they attached electrodes. On a signal, "a current of 6,600 volts was sent through her body. The big beast died without a trumpet or a groan." While the *New York Times* described it as "a rather inglorious affair," Topsy's execution fascinated Americans at the time when crowds no longer could enjoy the morality play and gruesome thrill of the public executions of people. The sight of a six-ton beast at the mercy of the silent and still mysterious power of electricity brought the crowd to this death scene. This spectacle was memorialized and moralized a century later in 2003 with a sculpture of Topsy at the Coney Island Museum where Edison's film could be seen through a vintage coin-operated mutoscope. Most Americans today find this event disgusting and especially object to its public character, but in 1903 it was fascinating, even amusing, and suitable for the hoopla of an amusement park.[1]

Twenty years later the popular British resort of Blackpool put on its version of the age-old festival of Carnival. Yet this was hardly the ancient custom of festivities taking place the week before the solemnity of Christian Lent. Instead, it was a promotion of the local government from June 9 to 16, 1923 to stimulate the tourist industry in the lull before the start of the holiday season in July. This commercialized saturnalia imitated a successful tourist attraction, the Carnival of Nice on the French Riviera, which was in turn based on the pre-Lenten traditions of Catholic Europe. Carnival was thus transplanted in space and time, and visitors were urged to lay aside their English inhibitions and embrace the "glorious exhilaration in giving rein to folly" that the "Carnival spirit" entailed. Huge processions snaked along the town's long sea-front promenade, featuring special carriages containing strangely dressed music-makers and dancers, and accompanied by giants wearing enormous papier-mâché heads constructed in the municipal workshops by craftsmen imported from Nice itself. Solid Lancashire citizens did circle dances on the beach; Carnival officials obliged plump traffic policemen to run races along the shore and encouraged visitors to cavort around striking each other with inflated pigs' bladders. As the official souvenir programme enjoined, "There'll be laughter for all these eight days, the merriest, maddest laughter that even Blackpool, the home of mirth, has ever heard. So get merry. Join in it."[2]

But there were limits to how far this could go in Northern England in the 1920s. Everything stopped on Sunday, where preachers at the churches and chapels were expected to "speak on the spirit of Carnival and the value of healthy enjoyment"; extra police were brought in to control the crowds, catch pickpockets, and enforce the car parking regulations; and there were complaints that the "bladder biffing" had got out of hand. Blackpool would enjoy only two Carnivals; after complaints about rowdyism at the 1924 event and about the disruption caused to production in Lancashire's mines and factories, the town sought other means of extending its season. It was all very well to shed inhibitions and give way to absurdity and self-indulgence, however self-consciously; but in the end British reserve had to prevail over Continental relaxation.[3]

How different from this version of Carnival were the orchestrated Electric Parades of Disneyland! Thousands lined Main Street U.S.A. at nightfall on June 17, 1972 to witness the debut of Disneyland's latest spectacle. It ran daily from June 17 through September 9, the height of the summer vacation crowds, so popular that it ran twice nightly by the end of July. The quarter mile procession lasted exactly 30 minutes and over the years was performed approximately 3,600 times to 75 million visitors. This spectacle was reminiscent of old-time American regional gatherings in small cities that featured high school bands, baton-twirling teams, and colorful floats built by members of small town grange halls. However, instead of featuring the local court of kings and queens of the parade, the floats were tableaux of Disney cartoon characters and the music was piped in from hidden speakers along the procession. Instead of lighted torches, Disney's parade glowed from hundreds of thousands of colored electric lights. The Grand Marshal was no longer a regional hero or politician, but the Blue Fairy from Disney's cartoon version of "Pinocchio." Notable floats included the Casey Junior Circus Train (from "Dumbo") with Goofy at the controls of the engine. Instead of a single annual event timed to the blossoming of apples or lilacs, the parade was to the 100 performers an everyday thing, shown to Americans on vacation on that special day when they entered the paradise of Disney nostalgia. Though discontinued in 1996, it had already been copied and sent to Walt Disney World in 1977 and thereafter to EuroDisney, transcending completely its American small town roots.[4]

The North of England Open Air Museum at Beamish, County Durham, also celebrates the regional and presents itself as a small town; but its opening on August 30, 1971 was a much less choreographed affair. There were five volunteers manning a makeshift car park, and the arrival of several hundred curious visitors created two-hour queues at the main entrance.[5] This was a controversial new kind of regional museum, dedicated to bringing the distinctive recent past of northeastern England back to life, reconstructing old home interiors, and making old machines work. It wanted to make history fun without compromising academic standards of accuracy and, as far as possible, authenticity. Its ideals were democratic and participatory as well as educational, and by 1991 it was drawing in over half a million visitors per year: small change compared with the Disney enterprises, but very impressive for an educational facility established and backed up by local government. But Beamish found that there were limits to spontaneity, as it ran on a shoestring in its early years. In 1973 the Newcastle *Journal* urged local people to go to Beamish and let their kids run wild until they were "brought up short". by the wonder of what was on display. However, two months later staff threatened to walk out as hundreds of under-supervised schoolchildren did run wild, producing "absolute chaos." Five years later organized theft by school parties led Beamish to replace its volunteer staff in the shopping areas with trained full-timers, and detectives were employed. Here was a loss of innocence even though the museum kept on trying to find its way between spontaneity and order and to create a distinctive version of the "playful crowd."[6]

Across the twentieth century, masses of pleasure-seeking humanity gathered on both sides of the Atlantic to interact with each other and to react to spectacles. And yet how much these throngs and the things that attracted them have changed! The crowd that gawked at the silent horror of the "execution" of Topsy had little in common with the families who lined the manicured "streets" of Disneyland to smile and coo at life-sized Mickey Mouse figures. The revelers at Blackpool's version of Carnival seem a world away from the people from northern England who came to contemplate and enjoy their own past at the Beamish open air museum. Someone who witnessed the death of Topsy or watched the Carnival parades at Blackpool might also have been present in adulthood or old age at the Disneyland spectacle or in the opening seasons of Beamish; but a great deal had happened in between. Part of the attraction of Beamish and Disney was that grandparents could explain what was presented as a living past to their grandchildren: and even though they may have conjured up or recalled different things (and forgotten still others), Beamish and Disney were, like this book, to lay claim to being exercises in recovered memory.

These playful crowds reflected their times and places, and comparisons between them help us to understand how the world has changed across the century and between the Atlantic's opposite shores. This book tells the story of how and why Americans and Britons gathered at such sites as Coney Island, Blackpool, Disneyland, and Beamish, especially at the height of their popularity. In the sheer contrast and diversity of these settings and the crowds that they attracted, we see the playfulness of modern humanity across an astonishingly wide range of contrived and mostly commercial, but still intensely appealing, settings and experiences.

In contrast to so many other throngs (from shoppers on main streets or malls to gatherings at political rallies), our crowds were engaged in the unalloyed pursuit of pleasure. As sites of outdoor spectacle that invite crowds to interact with each other and with the sites themselves, to participate actively as well as to gaze and listen, to move, mingle, compete for attention and put the self on show, all four places created crowds distinct from sports or staged entertainment spectators. Their pursuits were distinctly complex—seeking the novel as well as the nostalgic, the thrill of the mechanical ride as well as the majesty of the sea, both the gaudy and the sublime. And, in their inherent structure as artificial, but relatively open environments, they created a flowing, even potentially promiscuous, crowd that required special efforts to regulate and control and frequently raised the question of whether these throngs threatened rational self-restraint and other prized values of modern industrial civilization.

Most of all these four sites fostered crowds very different from those gathered to witness human executions (in contrast to the mockery of Topsy's demise) or in anger or frustration at a riot or political demonstration. These resorts and theme parks promised experiences and meanings that contrasted with, relieved, and yet often confirmed the ordinary work-a-day lives of their paying visitors. This liberation from and yet reconciliation with the everyday is what made their visitors into playful crowds. Human culture has produced many versions of playful crowds—on feast days and holidays, in lulls in the hunting or agricultural work cycle, in religious, political, or military celebrations. Temporarily "turning the world upside down" has taken many forms from the ancient Roman saturnalia to the modern New Orleans Mardi Gras. Each reflected and reinforced a particular society and culture. One of our goals is to explore that distinctive version of the playful crowd that came to culminate in the early twentieth century—what we call industrial saturnalia—and how it was transformed across the course of that century.

We begin our panorama of the playful crowd with the two most popular resorts at the dawn of the twentieth century: Blackpool, the holiday destination first of the wage earners of England's Lancashire cotton towns and eventually of most of the British Isles; and Brooklyn's Coney Island, southeast of Manhattan, the model of the popular American amusement resort/park for a half century. These were the first great popular playgrounds for the industrial working class in the modern world.[7] Although the working classes at play never completely dominated their beaches, streets, and fairgrounds, they quickly came to provide the images that overrode all others, and Blackpool and Coney Island became indelibly associated with crowded, noisy, vulgar, unbuttoned, uninhibited enjoyment, for better and worse. They epitomized the suspension of dignity and inhibitions, the reign of gluttony, extravagance, and licentiousness, at once a surrendering and a celebration of self. In 1910, Coney Island claimed 20 million visitors or 22 visits for every 100 Americans, a higher proportion than even Disney theme parks could claim 70 years later.[8] Blackpool's four million at this time were 11 percent of the population of England and Wales; but a much higher proportion of its visitors stayed for several days or a week rather than a day or a few hours as in Coney Island.[9]

Coney Island and Blackpool led the field in introducing the first great permanent amusement parks in their countries, with rides generating physical excitement and appealing to fantasy and wonderment: Blackpool's Pleasure Beach, and the evocative Coney Island trio of Luna Park, Steeplechase, and Dreamland. The two seaside resorts combined popular modernity, mass consumption, and a new collective experience. At the same time, they offered settings for more traditional entertainments across a broad taste spectrum: from dioramas, firework spectacles, and music and dance halls to freak shows, animal acts, bars and pubs, sticky festive foodstuffs, games of skill and luck, girlie shows, prostitution, and much else. In differing degrees, they borrowed from the varied Victorian traditions of exhibitions and world's fairs, musical theater, circuses, fairground entertainments, and urban "museum" curiosities.

The playful crowd in the form that it emerged in late Victorian Blackpool and Coney Island seemed to take on a life of its own. The Bulgarian-born Elias Canetti's *Crowds and Power* (1960) perhaps best captured its vitality when he saw this crowd as "wanting" to grow, loving its own density, and demanding a social leveling within its boundaries. Here he echoed the comments of many contemporary journalists and social observers. Individuals joined the crowd, Canetti believed, because it offered them an opportunity to overcome their fear of being touched by others and allowed them to surrender self to the group.[10] Especially germane to our understanding of Blackpool and Coney Island crowds is Canetti's description of the feast crowd: Within the confines of the seaside resort (and later the theme park),

there is abundance in a limited space, and everyone near can partake of it. . . .
There is more of everything than everyone together can consume, and, in
order to consume it, more and more people come streaming in. . . . Nothing
and no one threatens, and there is nothing to flee from: for the time being,
life and pleasure are secure. Many prohibitions and distinctions are waived;
and unaccustomed advances are not only permitted but smiled on. . . . The
feast *is* the goal and they are there. The density is very great, but the equality
is in large part an equality simply of indulgence and pleasure.[11]

We may have some doubts about the collective agency ascribed to the crowd,
but Canetti captures much of the appeal of the crowd to the popular classes especially in 1900. The longing for a release from the "rules" of urban/industrial life in
what we call an industrial saturnalia created and sustained the playful crowds. The
crowds we describe here were dense, but quick in the pursuit of enjoyment. In this
book we recover Canetti's feast crowd from neglect; but in transforming it into the
"playful crowd" we also move it on to an understanding of popular culture through
the twentieth century.[12]

In any event, although widespread, this longing for the self-forgetfulness of the
crowd did not attract all. Many middle-class people did not want to be "touched"
even in a crowd and many feared the release of inhibition—even as many also were
fascinated by the mystery and energy of the throng. Blackpool and Coney Island
excited anxiety, disgust, superiority, patronizing amusement, and even curious admiration from middle-class and intellectual witnesses. The urban crowd had long
congregated for religious, political, or industrial purposes, in search of justice or revenge; in celebration of ritual, triumph or festivity. But toward the end of the nineteenth century as it became associated with the political and industrial demands of
the emergent working class, the popular crowd attracted the attention of the first
generation of "social scientists" like Gustave le Bon who were trying to find ways
of analyzing and controlling the potential political threat of mass urban society.[13]
Nevertheless, our playful crowds attracted less attention until the appearance of
Coney Island and the popularization of Blackpool. External observers' critiques
of these new forms of mass entertainment abounded as highbrow commentators
damned the alleged shallowness, sameness, superficiality, and commercial exploitation of these popular resorts. The playful crowd was less threatening politically
but more threatening culturally and morally. Still, celebrations of the raw energy,

agency, and even self-discipline of the crowd at play were not hard to find, often mixed in with the critical commentaries as the other side of the coin.[14]

In this context, the impresarios of Blackpool and Coney Island had to foster an air of holiday relaxation and thereby widen the boundaries of acceptable conduct in these special spaces, and yet make sure that crowd behavior would not challenge the sensibilities of potentially valuable customers or outside authorities. The critique of the playful crowd continuously threatened to take the form of intervention and restriction, even as that crowd found ways to adapt and resist, and to develop internal controls and restraints of its own. This book looks at changing ways in which playful crowds were policed or policed themselves, by whom, and with what success. And, as we shall see, there were very different impacts of this struggle in Coney Island and Blackpool.

Behind the contradiction between the snobbish rejection and wistful admiration of the playful crowd were on-going cultural dilemmas: How was it possible to create a crowd that did not threaten bourgeois privacy? How could impresarios create a form of play that was liberating but also uplifted? There were many answers to these problems (including "hardy" holiday camps or Chautauquas). Ultimately, however, the fantasy world of Disneyland (1955) and the heritage site of the Beamish Museum (1971) would provide two of the most satisfying and long-lasting responses to the challenge of industrial saturnalia.

Comparing Disneyland and the Beamish Museum may seem at first glance like comparing apples and oranges, but, in fact, they represent distinct, if not equally popular, attempts to address the problems of taming the playful crowd of Coney/ Blackpool and of balancing uplift and leisure. Neither, of course, can be seen as representative of their respective countries, but they do reveal patterns rooted deeply in the nations that gave them birth. Disney's park is universally recognized as the model of modern theme parks, a creation of the Hollywood dream machine that turns cartoon characters and movie scenes and stories into mechanical rides and fantasy spaces. Within a dozen years of its opening in 1955, more than 60 million had entered its gates and since the 1970s ten or more million visit it yearly. Its goal of creating playful, but wholesome, settings for crowds of families addressed middle-class sensibilities.[15]

Beamish, by contrast, is relatively little known outside of England, although it has many analogues and some imitators elsewhere. Located in County Durham, in the northeast of England, Beamish pulls together, on a secluded 300-acre site, a set of reconstructions of the industrial past of a region that was once famous as a center for mining and as the cradle of the steam railroad. There are farms, collieries, railways, shops, homes, cottages, and streets from about 1825, when the region was beginning to industrialize, and about 1913, the climax of the industrial era. Its founder, Frank Atkinson, conceived Beamish as a way of saving the artifacts of this period and presenting them to perpetuate a sense of regional identity. His goal was to mingle education with pleasure for crowds of locals and, as it turned out, crowds of tourists. It was an attempt to foreground learning as leisure, harking back to traditions of self-improvement that were usually hostile to commercial entertainment, and doing so under the auspices of nonprofit trustees and of local government. By 1990 it was attracting half a million visitors a year, from school parties to tourists; and although attendance has dropped, current figures have held firm at around 350,000 per year. At times unthinking commentators have referred to Beamish as "an industrial Disneyland," and Atkinson himself was always aware of the Disney phenomenon as a competitor and alternative model. In fact, Disneyland and Beamish represent two distinct ways that an emerging middle-class culture responded to the challenge of industrial saturnalia. They were products of the long debate about the playful crowd, addressing how and why that crowd seemed both threatening and reassuring.

And so we rush off the train into the teeming throng or lock the car, bundle the kids, and stroll into the ever-changing world of the playful crowd. In these distinct realms of pleasure, we will see our past and present culture in new ways, find our deepest and most superficial longings before us, and learn how the crowd has changed.

Making the Popular Resort

CONEY ISLAND AND BLACKPOOL ABOUT 1900

Coney Island and Blackpool came to define the playful crowd across the Atlantic World of 1900, creating through their innovations and diversity unique settings for industrial peoples to find release from routine and care. To explain their success, we have to ask: Why and how did these resorts break away from the ruling conventions of the Victorian seaside and embrace the exciting otherness of the popular classes at play? Simultaneously, we must question how Coney Island and Blackpool differed, leading them on sharply contrasting paths. Divergences in physical and climatic settings, land holdings, entertainment customs, political contexts, and ultimately social and cultural traditions will shape our query. What follows is a brief historical comparison of how the industrial saturnalia of the seaside emerged in all of its diversity by the 1900s.

Sites and Seasons: Origins of the Urban and Provincial Seaside Resort

Coney Island and Blackpool were shaped by their geography and climate, which led them to draw crowds in similar but still unique ways. Coney Island is a five-mile-long, oval-shaped peninsula on the southern tip of Brooklyn on the southwestern shore of Long Island. It is located nine miles east of New York City's Manhattan Island. It was little more than a flat wasteland until it was settled in 1824 when a private road covered with seashells was built over the creek that divided Coney "Island" from Long Island. Given the cost and time of carriage travel and ferryboats across the water from Manhattan, Coney's earliest visitors were mostly an adventurous handful of genteel New Yorkers and more distant travelers. Road owners opened a hotel that appealed to these pursuers of solitude and health-giving salt air. Coney attracted political and cultural notables (from leading Senators Henry Clay and John C. Calhoun to writers Herman Melville and the young Walt Whitman). Its main advantage was its south-facing east-west axis, assuring long sunny days in summer along with cool ocean breezes.

The scene became far more commercial when regular ferry service began in the mid-1840s to the western end of Coney nearest to Manhattan. In hopes of attracting the business or casual crowd from the city, two enterprising New Yorkers built a circular wooden platform upon which they placed a tent. Soon, around this "pavilion" gathered a smattering of cheap wooden bathhouses, eateries, saloons, gypsy fortunetellers, and ballad singers who attracted New York's diverse, even plebeian crowds. One visitor remembered the "barn-like bar room" with "counter boards held up with barrels."[1] By the 1860s, this western section of beach had become a notorious refuge for gamblers and crooks evading police because, though it was near the city, it was beyond the control of the authorities. The West End also drew the slumming rich and politicians seeking respite from the demands of respectable society. Later it was known as Norton's Point, named after the notorious politician Michael Norton of Tammany Hall who bought the site in 1874. The West End of Coney Island reflected the curious culture of the city with its mixture of dandies, corrupt politicians, and plebeian underworld figures.[2]

Blackpool was similarly situated close to rapidly expanding urban areas, in this case that part of the English county of Lancashire where the first Industrial Revolution got under way in the late eighteenth century and continued to gather momentum until the First World War. It was, however, further from the developing population centers than Coney Island was from New York: The nearest substantial town was 20 miles away and Manchester was more than double that distance. Its main original asset was similarly a long, open shoreline, facing westward to the Irish Sea, with generous and often boisterous tides. From at least the 1750s, Blackpool slowly built up a polite visiting season based on the provincial gentry and the middle ranks, in response to the new fashion for sea-bathing cures and seaside scenery.[3] Alongside this, and apparently antedating it, was a plebean tradition of popular sea-bathing at the August spring tides, when there was said to be "physic in the sea." Artisans and small farmers traveled on foot and by horse-drawn cart right across Lancashire to take the waters in their own way. This was an ancient custom, widespread across Europe and coinciding with the Roman Catholic festival of the Assumption of the Virgin Mary. It was eventually to be imported to the United States by Irish migrants in the form of "Cure Day," still a feature of Coney Island in the 1950s.[4] In its Lancashire guise this popular festivity involved drinking seawater by the gallon, and as well as bathing unclad in the sea and consuming spirits to "fortify the stomach." This latter custom continued to grow in popularity right up to the arrival of the railroad in 1846, which linked Blackpool to the growing industrial towns of south and east Lancashire.[5]

By this time the little town had a year-round population of perhaps 1,500, which doubled at the August peak of the holiday season. Blackpool was therefore a longer-established and more respectable place of resort than Coney Island at this stage, except when the "Padjamers," as the plebian bathers were known, arrived. Its middle-class visitors had a reputation for being plain in dress and speech; and also for a healthy appetite for food and drink.[6] By 1850, the horse racing on the beach, and the local summer fair, had both been suppressed. Uncle Tom's Cabin, on the northern cliffs, one of several public houses with dancing and other amusements, was a far cry from Norton's Point. Finally, the gypsy fortune-tellers among the sand dunes remained almost invisible. The trains brought up to 12,000 visitors from the cotton industry towns at an August weekend in the early 1850s. New local government bodies controlled bathing and licensed street vendors and donkey drivers. Some visitors dressed flashily or scruffily, swore noisily and tried to bathe naked without using the bathing-machines. But these were the only blemishes on mid-century Blackpool's respectability.[7]

Advances in road and rail transportation enabled both seaside resorts to become sites of an extraordinary range of entertainments that by 1900 appealed broadly to the popular classes. Given its location, Coney Island may have been destined to prevail over other American seaside spots. But investments in roads and rails from New York City population centers guaranteed it, especially in developing the central and eastern sections of the Island. The opening of a plank road (1850), horse tram (1862) and a steam rail link (1864) from Brooklyn to the center of the island superseded the advantage of the West End's being closer to Manhattan by sea. The land development schemes of William Engeman in the center, known as West Brighton, provided a vast range of alternatives to the notorious male-oriented West End and heralded the advent of a more hetero-social pleasure zone. The opening of two Iron Piers at the center in 1879 and 1881 made possible boat transit on a grand scale, bringing visitors from as far away as Philadelphia, Newark, and New Haven. The piers were entertainment sites in themselves, each offering a 1,000-foot platform of ballrooms, restaurants, and other activities jutting out into the sea.[8]

This was merely the beginning. Ultimately, Coney Island became the seaside counterpoint to America's greatest city when still newer railroad lines and the entertainment complexes built in conjunction with them completed the shift of commercial activities from the West End to the center and east side of Coney. In the meantime, the western section was transformed into a respectable suburban housing district called Sea Gate. Between 1867 and 1880, five railroads were constructed specifically to facilitate tourism. In 1867, what became the Brooklyn, Bath and Coney Island Railroad was extended to West Brighton, prompting the development of a diverse bathing and entertainment zone. Nearby, Andrew Culver in 1876 opened a railroad that extended from Brooklyn's Prospect Park to Culver Plaza along Surf Avenue (a commercial road parallel to the beach). Lying between the two piers, Culver Plaza became a choice area for Coney Island entertainments. These train lines opened Coney Island to the salaried employee on a day trip from Manhattan, eventually via the Brooklyn Bridge. The fare was 35 cents for a round trip ticket, cheaper than the ferry (50 cents), but still beyond the reach of most wage earners. In addition to its stately 300-foot Centennial Tower, Culver Plaza offered a telegraph office that provided current stock quotes and Paul Bauer's West Brighton Hotel for a business clientele. Nearby, Charles Feltman's Ocean Pavilion, with a dance floor for 2,000 and a restaurant that served up to 8,000, catered especially to prosperous German immigrants. In 1879, another syndicate built the Sea Beach Palace in the heart of West Brighton and linked it with a third line, the New York and Sea Beach Railroad.[9]

West Brighton became identified with what New Yorkers meant by "Coney Island." It was a classic example of a late Victorian seaside pleasure spot, but on a relatively huge scale: Purpose-built railroads fed customers into anchor hotels and pier businesses and leased concessions surrounded these featured attractions. Gradually, the crowd at West Brighton became more plebeian. In the 1890s, when these rail lines were linked via mergers that made possible direct electric trains from downtown, Manhattan wage earners could reach the Island in 45 minutes. By 1896, that trip cost only 20 cents, making Coney Island the natural destination of ordinary New Yorkers on a day trip.[10]

In response to the social mix that the new rails and private development provided, West Brighton became a curious combination of genteel pretensions and popular fascinations. The Seaside Aquarium opened in 1877 with an aviary, zoo, and aquatic tanks. These exhibits may have appealed to the more refined tastes of the middle classes. But the Aquarium also provided performing bears and ostriches, Punch and Judy shows, a music hall, and even displayed Siamese twins. The Iron Steam Boat Company stressed the scenic journey from the Battery to West Brighton in 1883, but also proudly noticed the thrills of the "flying horses, wings and velocipede machines" that could be found on Coney. A mark of sophistication was the claim that Bunnell's Brighton Museum of albinos, armless boys, and "Hindoos" was run by an "honest showman" who provided "true wonders."[11]

Even after rail travel made West Brighton a popular site, more discerning genteel visitors could still find relief from the teeming crowds. On the more secluded far eastern end of Coney Island were built two additional railroads to accommodate the more upscale customer at hotels of suitable status. Austin Corbin's New York and Manhattan Beach Railroad (completed in 1877) delivered affluent New Yorkers disembarking from Brooklyn ferryboat docks to his Manhattan and Oriental hotels on Manhattan Beach. In 1878, Brooklyn developers (including William Engeman) imitated Corbin's scheme by building the Brooklyn, Flatbush and Coney Island railroad from Brooklyn depots to the door of their Brighton Beach Hotel (located between the east end and the West Brighton center). These railroads created a relatively exclusive zone, isolated from the more plebeian center.

Despite these differences, Coney Island remained primarily a destination of the urban day tripper. The luxury hotels served mostly guests on short stays and many more visited the hotels for dining or promenading than rented rooms. Missing were the vast stands of hotels and rooming houses usually associated with seaside resorts like Blackpool or Atlantic City. The most numerous private spaces on Coney Island were bathhouses for changing into swimming suits. The proximity of the Island to New York made the crowds more ephemeral than at Blackpool. Even more significant, the increasing ease of access to the resort meant that distance and cost of transportation no longer filtered out the underclasses. Coney Island drew its visitors increasingly from the rich ethnic and cultural mix of the New York tenements, with access so cheap and easy as to pose few barriers even to the poorest so long as they confined themselves to the free entertainments of the beach and the visual pleasures of looking on. This created an extraordinary social mix that both disturbed elites and created potential social tensions on the Island.[12]

Blackpool similarly broadened, deepened, and expanded its appeal during the late nineteenth century, but with somewhat different outcomes. Its crowds grew from about 200,000 per year in the early 1860s to three million forty years later.[13] Almost all came by railroad: In addition to the line built in 1846, a second connection with industrial Lancashire was opened in 1874 and another direct line for holiday services opened in 1913.[14] The railroads were willing to provide cheap fares for day and weekend visitors and for people staying for a week. Still, the main impetus to growth came from the ability and desire of working-class people from the cotton towns to spend time and money at Blackpool. This built on the tradition of the Padjamers but extended it greatly. Of crucial importance was the growing purchasing power of working-class families from the 1870s, when basic commodity prices began a sustained fall, and where young couples and mature families in the textile towns had access to more than one income. This excluded working-class families with young dependent children and where wives were unable to work outside the home. As a result, working-class Blackpool became predominantly an adult resort, an unusual phenomenon in Victorian England. In contrast with the United States, a week's vacation was commonly available, even for factory workers. The Industrial Revolution had not extinguished the traditional Wakes' holidays of the cotton district, which at mid-century were transformed from local festivals into popular seaside holidays.[15] These were not paid holidays. They had to be budgeted during the year, but savings clubs were organized by religious bodies, the retail Co-operative societies, and even street or neighborhood committees.[16] During this period "cotton Lancashire" also gave professional soccer to the world. Music-halls, indulgence in tasty convenience foods like fish and chips, music-making (with a surprising number of piano purchases), and a cheap popular press all were part of the rise of the world's first working-class consumer society.[17] Blackpool was central to this "work hard, play hard" culture because it offered an explosive, inexpensive release from regular, monotonous work in a place that was accessible and familiar, while it also offered exciting novelty.

Here we identify a clear and enduring contrast. While Coney drew on the diversity of nearby New York City, Blackpool recruited its visitors over longer distances, but from much more closely knit, firmly established communities with a strong sense of identity and a broad familiarity with each other's occupations and ways of life. These were universally white and English-speaking, with a variety of Lancashire town and village accents; practically all Protestants but with a smattering of Catholics. Whole towns went on holiday at the same time and thus there were fewer anxieties about the anonymity and decency of the crowds than at Coney. And Blackpool kept its middle-class visitors. The central district between the two piers of the 1860s was a working-class preserve, while the North and South Shore areas were consecrated to middle-class families.[18] Even in the working-class zone, however, many stayed up to a full week, and this generated a demand for cheap rooms with breakfast, hot water, and cooking services. Whole streets of redbrick, four-story lodging-houses went up around the stations between the 1860s and the 1890s. By 1901, there were 2,642 landladies listed in the census.[19] Many of them came from the towns of Blackpool's hinterland and offered accommodation to their former workmates and neighbors. While Coney Island had a few clusters of summer bungalows for families living away from the City, they paled in comparison to the permanence and size of the Blackpool boarding houses.[20] These aspects of the local economy gave greater stability and security to Blackpool as a permanent and year-round resort settlement.

As influential as geographical location and transportation were the climate and length of the season. Coney Island's cold winters and hot summers made for a short, but very intense season. While most entertainment venues closed by mid-September and then opened only in mid-May, business was very brisk between June and August. Most seaside resorts were seasonal, but Coney Island was especially dependent upon warm Julys and Augusts, particularly on Sundays. Because very few New Yorkers had even a week's vacation time or a even a two-day weekend in 1900, businesses prayed for sunny summer Sundays that brought in tens, and later, hundreds of thousands of day trippers. A few wet and cold Sundays could make all the difference between business success and business failure.

This had a number of implications. First, the short season encouraged minimal investment in buildings and other facilities. Coney Island was noted for its shanty town look and not just in the more tawdry streets. Wood and other cheap materials were used even in the construction of hotels and music pavilions. Second, one of the main attractions of Coney was relief from the summer heat. Far more than at Blackpool, the beach was a focal point of crowds. From the 1850s, when "mixed bathing" became acceptable, Coney's long smooth sandy beach allowed thousands to wade far out into the sea before the water was deep enough to require any swimming skills. The inland amusement district, of course, drew many who never set foot on the beach, but the seaward complex of bathhouses, food stalls, and roving sellers of novelties, oysters, and steamed cob corn drew throngs. Before the coming of the public boardwalk, access to the beach was restricted. Bathhouses that leased lots above the tide allowed only patrons to use the beach. When reformers built the boardwalk in 1923, they also provided free access to the shore, bringing the center of Coney Island into line with federal law and rendering it comparable with the British conventions that kept beaches public at Blackpool.[21] As a result, by the 1930s, the beach culture at Coney Island became even more pronounced, often drawing more people than did the amusement parks, Surf Avenue, and other amusement centers.

Blackpool's beach became less central to its identity and attractiveness as the years went by. The sands between the North and Central piers could still be crowded with families in deck chairs and children making sandcastles as late as the 1960s, but they could never match the sheer spectacle of the thousands of frisky folk in bathing attire who thronged Coney's beaches over a similar period The main reason, of course, was because the weather was much less kind. Also important, bathing regulations and conventions were less permissive than at Coney: A few bathing machines were still in use until the 1930s, although most people paddled without paying for them. Nevertheless, the beach crowds increased even after the palatial municipal open-air swimming pool of 1923 provided a popular alternative. While temperatures at Blackpool very rarely reached the levels of those experienced on an August day at Coney Island, its season was longer even though few bathed outside the height of summer. It opened at Easter, was very busy for the movable Whitsuntide week holidays in May or June, and served as a center for the various regional summer Wakes holidays. From the 1870s onward, it reduced its dependence on good weather by building up an unprecedented and unparalleled array of indoor attractions in its "palaces of pleasure," solidly built of brick, stone, steel, and glass, which soon became more important than the beach in defining the town's identity. The longer season made these investments at Blackpool feasible. Thus, while Blackpool was less a beach resort, it became even more a commercial pleasure resort than did Coney. The weather then shaped the destinies of Coney Island and Blackpool in many subtle ways.[22]

Property and Power: Behind the Scenes Shaping of Coney and Blackpool

No matter how pristine or exclusive a pleasure spot may be, almost inevitably once a site begins to draw a crowd, it pulls in commerce and entertainers that challenge

1.1   A classic view of Blackpool's Central Beach and the famous Tower in about 1960, with a packed, respectably dressed and sedate crowd covering every inch of available space toward high tide. From Alfred Gregory, *Blackpool: A Celebration of the '60s* (London: Constable, 1993).

the genteel values of early visitors. Only when landed aristocrats, entrepreneurs, or public officials held large contiguous acreage of resort property (or dominated zoning and other local regulations) could they exclude the gypsy fortune tellers, push-cart merchants, target game stalls, and prostitutes who sought a piece of the market created by the beach, built-up attraction, or the crowd itself. Neither Coney Island nor Blackpool exhibited this exclusive power of elites nor were able to keep out down market diversity.[23]

By the 1880s, Coney was divided into a popular center at West Brighton and

1.2   The Bowery, that once tawdry street of bars and lower pleasures leading to Steeplechase Park, portrayed here as a promenade of respectability. *Munsey's Magazine*, Aug. 1905, 564.

an exclusive east end. While West Brighton never had the notorious reputation of Norton's Point, it too had a shanty area called the Gut, in an old creek bed between West Third and Fifth Streets that catered to criminals, jockeys, and stable boys with beer, gambling, and whores. Another center of low life emerged after 1882, when Peter Tilyou cut a planked road parallel to Surf Avenue to direct traffic to his Surf Theater. The area soon was called the Bowery because of its resemblance to New York City's rough and wild working-class entertainment district. Cabarets, featuring entertainment on raised stages or pavilions, sold drinks to the audience seated at tables. The larger places had curtained booths where the rich might be visited by women for private (sometimes nude) shows. After fires in 1899 and 1903, the Bowery became more upscale with brick buildings and music halls. Still, despite West Brighton's early respectable attractions, the area had become a dizzying assault on the senses with band music, freak shows, mechanical rides, and a "dense but good-humored crowd." When a reporter strolled down Surf Avenue on a summer weekend in 1904, he opined: "one might well image Noah's Ark to be waiting at the other end of it," so exotic were the animals and people in and around the sideshows.[24]

This diverse, often downscale entertainment in West Brighton emerged from the particular way by which land was purchased and leased, ensuring a competitive environment of cheap attractions. Gravesend, a small country township on the southeast edge of Brooklyn, held jurisdiction over Coney Island. Beginning in 1847, the township gradually took over claims to the shoreline from the dispersed descendants of the town founders, and leased the more developed western portion to showmen. From his position as town Commissioner of Common Lands in 1867, John McKane built a local empire by accumulating government offices and leasing out land at very low prices to friends who obligingly hired his construction business. In turn, leaseholders financed their projects by subleasing adjacent lots to more transient and less well-connected entrepreneurs who offered the crowds mechanical rides, food stalls, and the like. This process guaranteed the downscale character of West Brighton attractions. McKane oversaw development of the Bowery in the 1880s and tolerated prostitution and gambling on horse races and boxing matches, to the anger of Brooklyn reformers to the north. After years of defying outside authorities, McKane was finally imprisoned in 1894 for election fraud. Despite McKane's ouster and pledges of reform from new officials, the pattern of subleasing was already well-established, thus perpetuating the cheap, diverse entertainment enterprises that served the urban masses.[25]

While land in West Brighton was parceled out, much larger lots (with the aid of subterfuge) were purchased in the less developed eastern end, assuring more upscale development. William Engeman bought 200 acres of prime Brighton Beach shore land in 1868, half of which was sold to the Brooklyn, Flatbush, and Coney Island Railroad, which built the Brighton Beach Hotel in 1879. He also built the first of three racetracks that would attract the "swells" mostly to the eastern end of the island. Even more ambitious was Austin Corbin's purchase of 500 acres of Manhattan Beach to the east of Engeman's holdings, where the Manhattan and Oriental Hotels were built in deliberate isolation from the plebeians that thronged to West Brighton.[26]

Large land holding in the east assured a high social tone by the exclusion of peddlers, food stalls, freak shows, and whorehouses. Corbin even erected a high fence around his hotel to keep out peddlers and the riffraff, and hired Pinkerton detectives to weed out undesirables from his railroad in transit to the Manhattan Hotel. The beachfront was also patrolled by private police. Following an ignoble tradition started at Saratoga Springs in upstate New York, Corbin famously also banned Jews. Genteel culture prevailed in the east. The bathing house included 1,650 dressing rooms for men and 600 for women, each with running water and gas heating with an amphitheater between men's and women's wings for viewing the sea and bathers. Even if mixed bathing was allowed, participants were advised to spend no more than thirty minutes a day in the sea. Musical entertainment dominated. Military bands (especially the ensembles of Anton Seidl, J. P. Sousa, and Patrick Gilmore) were regular summertime attractions and until the mid-1890s Sundays were devoted to "sacred music." Henry Pain's fireworks spectacles also attracted this genteel crowd. This London-based showman (self-proclaimed pyrotechnist to Her Majesty the Queen) presented grand simulations of battles and natural wonders often involving hundreds of costumed actors, elaborate stage scenery, and even a man-made lagoon to display fireworks. Pain's Battle of Gettysburg, Eruption of Vesuvius, and the Fall of Pompeii were among the spectacles with elaborate scenery, special effects, and casts of hundreds staged in an amphitheater that eventually sat 12,000. His 1902 program, The Fall of Rome, included dancing "damsels gauzily clad, playing on timbrels" on the steps of the Temple of Venus, and, as Rome burned, Nero strummed his harp; fireworks dramatically ended the show.[27]

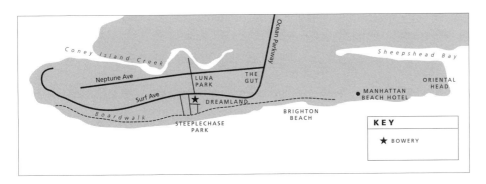

1.3   Map of Coney Island ca 1904.

The popular areas of Blackpool also had divided landownership. In 1838 the township of Layton with Warbreck, within which Blackpool developed, was found to be subdivided between 133 freehold proprietors, of whom 27 held more than 25 acres. But Bonny's Estate, a large parcel near the sea, was sold off piecemeal in 1841. Soon streets created behind the sea frontage became slums, while the front gardens that faced the sea hosted the stalls and fairground amusements that would later form the "Golden Mile." The Clifton family also sold off their estate when the railroad station opened near their property, providing another area of cheap commercial activity for working-class trippers. Thus, throughout what became central Blackpool, the competitive entertainment market prevailed without interference from ambitious developers in ways comparable to the western and central portions of Coney Island.

By contrast, the North Shore cliffs saw more up-market development, with a sea-front toll in force until 1899 to discourage working-class visitors. A land company had combined several smaller holdings together in the early 1860s to control development along the shoreline and justify the building of the Imperial Hotel. At the other end, South Shore was far enough away from the central entertainment and lodging-house district for developers to agree on middle-class family homes and superior boarding-houses.[28] The local equivalents of Brighton and Manhattan Beaches actually lay outside the Blackpool boundary, going southeastward along the estuary of the River Ribble. Lytham was a classic case where a wealthy squire preferred to develop his property in an attractive, planned way, while St Anne's, a product of a speculative land company, offered a similar controlled environment to respectable families. In such ways both the Blackpool region and Coney Island were able to be many things to many people, an essential recipe for both conflict and profit.[29]

If property-holding patterns worked to divide east and central Coney Island as well as to separate central Blackpool from its near neighbors, the economic power structures and political contexts of both resorts ultimately led to sharper contrasts. Despite the short leases and parceled land holdings that allowed small players into the game at West Brighton, big money always controlled and profited from the site. In fact, large structures dominated the vista, helping to promote and define the Island. The Iron Tower of 300 feet, which had been moved from the Philadelphia Exhibition of 1876, was the first of many such sights at Coney Island. Its innovative elevator gave visitors a special view at the top. Competing with the stately Iron Tower was the whimsical 122-feet high Elephant Hotel, a tin-covered pachyderm built of wood in 1884. The Elephant Hotel drew thousands to its gift shop and the diorama in its legs. Stairs led to thirty-two guest rooms and a public view of the shore in the howdah on top. Although it burned down in 1896, the expression "Seeing the Elephant" became a common American expression for satisfying questionable desires. More sedate was the 375-foot Beacon Tower, built in 1904 that trumped earlier towers with presumably 100,000 electric lights for night display and a beacon light shining into the sea, becoming the focal point of the Dreamland amusement park and the island itself.[30]

Blackpool also acquired landmarks that set it apart from its British competitors. Its first two piers had predated Coney's, the North Pier in 1863 catering for the "better classes" and charging a twopenny toll to make this clear, while the South Jetty, later the Central Pier, opened three years later to welcome a lower class of visitor. In 1870, it began to offer open-air dancing to an unpretentious "German band." Later, a third pier, catering to the middle class opened in the south. The 1870s saw the opening of the Raikes Hall pleasure gardens, with artificial lake, fireworks displays, dancing platform and (unofficially) prostitutes, and the Winter Gardens, a distinctive piece of pleasure architecture whose concert hall and theater soon became more important than its genteel indoor promenades.

But the outstanding landmark, the key symbol of Blackpool's opulent populist distinctiveness, was the Tower, which opened in 1894. At nearly 517 feet it presented a much stronger accent on the flat local skyline than any of Coney

Island's towers or other extravaganzas. Moreover, it was very solidly built. The Tower soon became, as it remains, the first sign of the approaching resort, an object of desire sought eagerly by children (and adults) peering through the train window as they neared Blackpool. It was constructed along the lines of the Eiffel Tower, forming yet another link between international exhibitions and leisure architecture. Below its high girders nestled a massive rectangular brick building containing a zoo, an aquarium, a circus, a theater, a spectacularly opulent ballroom, roof gardens, and a restaurant. The Tower, in fact, was a whole resort complex in its own right, accessible on payment of sixpence, a sum that could readily be afforded from the holiday savings of the Blackpool's working-class visitors. Although a speculative and probably fraudulent London company had originally promoted the project, John Bickerstaffe led a local takeover to ensure that the building was completed, to the benefit of large numbers of shareholders drawn from Blackpool residents, business people, and visitors. This kind of popular shareholder capitalism was central to the development of the pleasure palaces for which the town became famous. This element of shareholder democracy differentiated Blackpool from Coney Island, and although the men who ran the companies also played a disproportionate part in running local government, with regular scandals involving property speculation and the licensing of drink outlets, there was no Blackpool counterpart of John McKane.[31] The 1890s also saw the opening of the Alhambra, next door to the Tower and of equivalent size. Although it failed initially to pay dividends, it stayed in business for more than sixty years. Blackpool also received its Gigantic Wheel in 1896, only two years after the Ferris Wheel came to Coney Island, a second accent on the Blackpool skyline, but unusually short-lived (closing in 1928). These were substantial, lasting, indeed monumental investments, in sharp contrast to the ephemeral nature of so many of Coney Island's headline attractions.[32]

Despite the superficial grandeur of the Beacon Tower, the efforts of Coney Island entrepreneurs were seldom in any sense substantial or collective. Sharp business competition had its roots in New York City itself in the self-promotion of urban businesses attempting to attract passing crowds. Like their counterparts on the streets of New York, Coney Island entertainments and related businesses relied on ballyhoo—boisterous, dramatic, and often deceptive promotion. Its most common form was the barker, talker, or spieler (often an out-of-work actor because of the summer slump in theater-going) who used patter and exaggerated claims to "pull" crowds into freak or other shows by appealing to morbid curiosity or even the vanity of the crowd. Only different in form was the special publicity, usually with much newspaper coverage, used to promote amusement parks. George Tilyou attracted thousands to the opening of Steeplechase Park by publicizing that he had to "guard" his sister who would be wearing priceless diamonds while serving as a ticket taker. Drawing on the novelty of airplanes, Dreamland's Beacon Tower became the site of an aborted launch of a "winged aeroplane" in August 1908 that fell into the sea to the amusement of many attending. There was no effort to collectively enhance the image of Coney Island through joint advertising.[33]

Coney Island businesses advertised individually, and not much at that. In fact, much publicity for Coney Island was indirect, often in the form of postcards given away by Coney Island entrepreneurs. Beginning in 1898, the one-cent stamp allowed vacationers to send greetings to family and friends at little cost, even if they lived only a few miles away in the city. In the summer of 1907 each week the Brooklyn Post office handled one million post cards. Trade cards (advertising other products) featured the naughty side of Coney Island, as in "On the Road to Coney Island" with a humorous drawing of a man meeting a girl on the shore. Early movies such as Thomas Edison's *Cakewalk at Coney Island* (1896) cultivated this theme. Milton Bradley offered a board game, *A Wonderful Account of an Excursion to Coney Island* (1881) for adults to play on cold winter Sunday evenings. Coney Island ceaselessly called to attention to itself in the embossed ashtrays or scenic lithographs that served both as souvenirs and advertising. Still, the image of Coney Island was hardly a collective effort of its businesses.[34]

It was not until 1902 that merchants (perhaps worrying about the publicity that was focused on the new Luna Park) organized a Board of Trade. Even then, much of the publicity for the Island came from two of the great amusement parks, Luna and Dreamland, which competed for bragging rights through postcards and newspaper display ads.[35] One collective effort, however, was the mid-September "Mardi Gras" festival, first organized in 1903. It did not matter that the autumn was the wrong season for traditional Mardi Gras: the label and what it conjured up were all that mattered. The parade and various contests brought crowds back after the end of the hot summer season for a final fling. In 1904, the Surf Avenue parade featured a float fitted with a giant frankfurter or "hot dog" machine. From time to time, a dog was thrown in one end and strings of frankfurters were pulled out the other. Opening the ceremonies, Henry Pain thrilled the crowd of thousands along the beach by setting fire to a three-masted ship offshore.

In 1906, the event leaned toward self-parody when it was dubbed the Carnival of Plenty complete with Prince Plenty and Queen Prospera. A mile-long parade of floats lit in electric lights featured the theme of "the longing for luxury, [and] for a life of ease in a land beyond toil." Floats had "laughing girls perched upon huge wine glasses and mammoth bottles" and women dressed as "greenbacks" representing "Plenty of Money." The real fun began after the parade when the crowd armed with bags of noisemakers and slapsticks acted out their own celebration. Along Surf Avenue, "the soubrettes were bombarded with confetti and the orchestras were drowned by the unearthly shrieks and clang of the horn and cowbell." This bit of saturnalian disorder connected Coney's Mardi Gras to the European ancestors it invoked. But it was still the creation of Coney Island businesses, not a religious tradition. It celebrated and promoted the sublimity of technological progress (exemplified by the wonder of night-time electrical lighting) and the right of hard working Americans to enjoy a new age of prosperity provided by the entrepreneurs of pleasure. Coney's Mardi Gras was an important part of the commercial promotion of the site, but it was a comparative rarity.[36]

Blackpool's case was very different. As befitted a period in British history when urban government was enterprising, running utilities at a profit to lower local taxes and investing in parks and libraries was common.[37] But Blackpool's municipal corporation went much further. Soon after its creation in 1876, it became very active in promoting the resort as a whole. After all, representatives of the entertainment, drink, and building industries dominated it, and within three years the corporation had obtained powers from Parliament to levy a local property tax to be devoted to supporting a town band and advertising Blackpool's attractions. This was a unique privilege as rival sea resort municipalities soon found when they sought to compete. It was not until 1921 that much lesser advertising powers became generally available to other resorts.[38]

Blackpool made full use of this opportunity. It immediately set up an Advertising Committee, which issued the first in a long sequence of publicity guides to be widely distributed in libraries and other public places. In 1881 the committee launched a poster advertising campaign on railroad sites that eventually spread across the whole of urban Britain to the disadvantage of competitors. At the dawn of color lithography, these posters presented the full panorama of Blackpool's attractions. The town government also promoted fetes and special events to prolong the season at both ends. Beginning with celebrations to inaugurate the electric lighting of the promenade and a Battle of Flowers, these promotions moved on to motor racing and air displays in the early twentieth century. Culminating this trend in 1912 was the autumn Illuminations, providing a blaze of electrical color along the shore. This was entirely a municipal initiative that, while suspended because of the First World War, was revived in 1925.[39] A great deal of Blackpool's success can be ascribed to the efforts of the town government that acted as a business in competition with rival tourist towns and treated local taxpayers as shareholders.[40]

Not that the private Winter Gardens or the Tower sat idly by. They advertised directly in the press and were careful to encourage journalists to write promotional stories. William Holland, manager of the Winter Gardens from 1887 to 1896, brought London music-hall experience and a proven populist touch to the job. He jokingly invited Lancashire people to come and spit on the new hundred-guinea carpet, alluding to low media expectations of working-class behavior but conveying his understanding that folk were too civilized to do any such thing.[41] This jocular boosting mentality was common among Blackpool's entertainment bosses at a time when the "Pleasure Palaces" were locally run. It rubbed off on the local authority, whose advertising manager, Charles Noden, became a well-known figure in his own right, famous for such coups as promoting Blackpool to battlefield tourists on the site of Waterloo in Belgium by hiring a farmhouse wall to display slogans.[42]

The success of the Blackpool Corporation provides a particularly sharp contrast between Blackpool and Coney Island. To an astonishing degree, late-nineteenth and early-twentieth-century Coney Island lacked governmental regulation. As we have seen, in the two decades after the Civil War, merchants easily manipulated a leasing and land purchase system when Coney Island was ostensibly "administered" by the village of Gravesend. The machine politics of John McKane assured that moral and business laws were weakly enforced. After McKane's ouster, although the area was incorporated into Brooklyn in 1894 and into New York City in 1898 when the two cities merged, little changed except that the dominance of a few companies leasing property grew greater. At the same time as government authority became more distant from the Island, attempts of outside religious and civic reformers to improve the site had little success.[43]

1.4   Blackpool's Pleasure Beach amusement park, lit up for the autumn Illuminations in 1925: a contribution by private enterprise to a municipal spectacle promoted and mainly paid for by Blackpool Corporation. Courtesy of the Pleasure Beach, Blackpool

At Coney, government was more of a nuisance than a help to local promoters.
Regulation of its social tone was often arbitrary and certainly erratic. Police com-
missioners attempted in 1899 and again in 1909 to enforce the 1895 ban on the
Sunday sale of alcohol imposed by the City. Police found it difficult to enforce this
rule because of a loophole that allowed drinks to be served with a meal (often a small
sandwich) and immediately relaxed their standards. Police periodically cleared the
beach and streets of peddlers and even attempted to suppress *Danse du ventre* (belly
dancing) shows in 1896.[44] In June 1907, a zealous police chief prohibited barkers
on the Bowery from using megaphones to tout their shows. This only induced the
"talkers" to hang huge placards around their necks with their messages. A very

similar battle took place in 1922 when a new police inspector not only tried to drape cheesecloth over Plaster of Paris Venuses on Surf Avenue but to resurrect the old law against street shows. Neither effort lasted for more than a few days.[45]

As a freestanding municipality dominated by the tourist industry, Blackpool's local government played a much more active role. It imposed minimum building standards and street layouts and ran most utilities. Only the water supply was privately owned, but it was locally run with more concern for supplying a vital need in a health resort than for profit as such. The local authority also invested very heavily in the sea front, where a broad promenade and carriage drive was opened on top of a new sea wall in 1870. This was all freely accessible to the general public, as was the beach. This was all in direct contrast with the situation at Coney Island, where fragmentation, division, and payment for access was the norm.[46]

This is not to say that local government in Blackpool was uncontroversial. Local elections were often hard-fought, and there was sometimes fierce criticism of the business ethic that dominated the Corporation. The general legitimacy of municipal democracy in Blackpool was, however, seldom questioned, and then only from well-defined pressure groups.[47] As in Coney Island, the question of what sort of public entertainment was acceptable and of how to maintain order on the streets and beaches was particularly contentious. Opportunistic small traders were eager to clutter up streets and front yards with stalls and entertainments that some found unsightly, while uncertainty about jurisdiction over the beach between high and low tide allowed (in 1895) a proliferation of 316 stalls and shows in the popular central area of the beach. Quack doctors phrenologists, and chiropodists who cut corns in public, shooting gallery operators and ventriloquists, as well as the more commonplace vendors of fruit, ice cream, candy, oysters, and toys avoided paying local taxes. An attempt to abolish these beach businesses in 1880 had failed, and it was not until 1897 that the Corporation succeeded in getting rid of most of them and making the respectable remainder pay rent. This did not solve the problem of stalls in front of houses. Nevertheless, Blackpool appears relatively sedate when compared with Coney Island, and vice and girlie shows were kept very successfully hidden. When, in 1896, a Methodist minister and temperance reformer, angry about the running of streetcars on Sundays, complained that "Compared with Blackpool, Paris is sweet, and Sodom was a paradise," it is tempting to wonder what he would have thought of Coney.[48]

The Seaside as Magnets of Entertainment

Both Coney and Blackpool drew upon a similar pot of entertainment traditions that appealed to a transatlantic popular culture, even trading or borrowing from each other. Both shared in the legacy of traveling freak shows, acrobatic acts, menageries, and target games; they drew also upon the more recent and upscale tradition of music and dance halls, and even the uplifting attractions of exhibitions and world's fairs. Yet national differences still produced distinct mixes that made each resort unique.

Amusements associated with seaside resorts like Coney Island and Blackpool have distant roots in the trade fairs and rural hiring fairs, and in urban pleasure gardens. England and Wales had a long tradition of fairs, going back to the twelfth century, which gradually added amusements to their business functions. For example, London's Bartholomew Fair, dating from around 1133, had become by the seventeenth century a three-week venue for puppet shows, jugglers, and freaks. In the early 1830s, licenses granted for this fair included 25 menageries, 15 human freak shows, 15 displays of conjuring, rope dancing, and other physical skills, and four waxworks. London's Greenwich fair was described as, "A never to be forgotten orgy of noise, swings, dancing-booths, oil lamps, fried fish, fat women, giants, dwarfs, gingerbread nuts, unappreciated actors, jugglers and acrobats, mud, dirt, drink, gin, beer and skittles."[49] London-area fairs were suppressed during the middle decades of the nineteenth century, but elsewhere similar urban pleasure fairs survived and prospered. A great burst of innovation and investment began in the 1860s and 1870s in new fairground rides that were later borrowed by seaside entrepreneurs on both sides of the Atlantic.[50]

Another historical root was the urban commercial Pleasure Garden. It had elite origins and usually charged entrance fees, both to earn a profit and to exclude "undesirables." London's Vauxhall Gardens (opened in 1661) and the Ranelagh Gardens (1741) certainly anticipated the social tone and style of Coney Island's Manhattan Beach with their flowerbeds, elegant rotundas, and concerts. In 1774, the Marylebone Gardens also foreshadowed Henry Pain's pyrotechnic extravaganzas with its extravagant simulation of the eruption of Mt. Etna. Such attractions continued through the nineteenth century: London's Cremorne Gardens offered music, dancing, shady retreats, drink, and firework displays, as well as animal and acrobatic acts that one could also see at fairgrounds and the seaside. As the evening proceeded, respectable customers would give way to prostitutes and their clients, but the attractions of this pleasure ground outweighed its perils.[51] Such enterprises were not confined to the British metropolis: Blackpool itself had the Raikes Hall pleasure gardens, which was founded as late as 1871 and survived for thirty years.[52]

Problems of reconciling popularity with respectability weighed heavily on the impresarios of crowd pleasures in the nineteenth and twentieth centuries.[53] Mechanical rides were one solution because they offered thrills without the dangerous pleasures of commercial sex, gambling, and drink. Amusement concessions featuring hobby-horses and distorting mirrors appeared in London on St. George's Row. Gallery games, swings, and crude merry-go-rounds were attractions at commercial picnic groves serving American fraternal organizations from the early nineteenth century. Picnic groves such as Jones's Wood near New York City's East River in the 1850s offered rides, but also introduced the extravaganzas of the English Pleasure Garden with reenactments of the Battle of Magenta. Toward the turn of the twentieth century, to generate traffic on the weekends, trolley companies set up picnic places and amusement parks in landscaped settings at their suburban terminals. As with Blackpool's Raikes Hall in 1900, residential expansion brought the demise of some of these picnic groves, including Jones's Wood itself. Others, like Kennywood in suburban Pittsburgh, became major mechanized amusement parks by the end of the nineteenth century.[54]

While today we associate carousels, Ferris Wheels, and roller coasters with children, these mechanical rides did not emerge, in fact, from the child-centered culture of the late Victorian middle class. The carousel was the outgrowth of a game designed to prepare twelfth-century Arab horsemen for war. Brought to Europe by Spanish and Italian Crusaders, by the seventeenth century, it had become part of ceremonies displaying French horsemanship. In Paris at the Place du Carrousel, gentlemen speared a ring with a lance while riding a galloping horse on a circular track. This contest was mechanized in the seventeenth century with the construction of a post and spoke-like extensions at the ends of which were placed primitive wooden horses. When these extensions were rotated by servants, a mounted young equestrian could practice the art of spearing rings with a short lance. This technology was then adapted for fairground use. In England, the "dobby-horses" of the late eighteenth century were first turned by children (paid with rides), then by animals, and finally by steam in 1861. Six years later, Gustav Dentzel set up the first American carousel company in Philadelphia, and, in 1876, Charles Looff made

Coney Island's first carousel, creating the distinctive "Coney Island style" of animal carving in his own factory. Brooklyn carousel makers took things a step further when they introduced a galloping motion, using an overhead crank system. In 1893 the Englishman Frank Bostock brought home a set of gallopers to accompany his famous menagerie. Despite their modern associations with small children, these were still mainly adult rides as late as 1885.[55]

Unlike the carousel, the roller coaster had origins in thrill seeking. It appeared first as a 70-foot-high wooden incline covered in iced snow that seventeenth-century revelers in St. Petersburg, Russia descended on sleds.[56] Young adults, not children, were its patrons. In the late eighteenth century, a French entrepreneur built a track using closely spaced rollers (hence the name roller coaster). Elsewhere, however, coasters had closer ties to the railroad track. In 1870, an abandoned inclined-plane railroad for mines near Mauch Chunk, Pennsylvania was converted into a novelty ride. American inventor La Marcus Thompson adapted this device into his invention of a primitive gravity switchback coaster in 1884. While Thompson's ride required men to push the cars up an incline on both ends of the ride, steam-powered chain lifts emerged by 1885 and the track became a circuit. Thompson added exotic painted images of nature to make a "scenic railroad" (first seen at Atlantic City in 1886) that became the basic format of modern electric rail indoor "dark rides." Still, it was the thrilling sensation of vertigo that made the roller coaster appealing. In 1900, the Flip Flap coaster at Coney Island turned the rider in a complete circle in a ten-second experience that caused neck pains. Soon, improvements in the loop (by redesigning it to be more oval) made this thrill a minor success in 1902. Further developments by John A. Miller by 1910 involved under-track wheels to make higher inclines and sharper turns possible without cars jumping off the track. In the 1920s, mammoth wooden coasters were huge successes in amusement parks worldwide.[57]

While amusement rides were developing in both countries, British innovations were slower to move beyond the flourishing traveling fairground scene. While Frederick Savage of the town of King's Lynn produced the first British roller coaster in 1888,[58] large mechanical rides were slow to appear in Blackpool. Informal fairground amusements were located on the beach. This prevented anything larger than a set of swing-boats because of the need to continuously move them to cope with the tides. When a steam carousel appeared in a front yard in the mid-1880s, neighbors successfully banished it as a "nuisance." Such amusements were associated with the traveling fair, of which Blackpool was not a part. It was not until the establishment of the Pleasure Beach at the turn of the twentieth century that mechanical fairground rides became a major feature of Blackpool's attractions.[59]

The scenic spectacle was another popular amusement shared by both Americans and British. Designed for adults, like the thrill ride, it attracted an astonishingly wide range of people, including the middle classes. Originated in eighteenth-century Italy, these massive, highly realistic, and dramatic paintings of natural wonders, disasters, and battles toured nineteenth-century American and British communities. Mounted on walls or made to move in front of stationary viewer, these scenes, variously called panoramas, cycloramas, or dioramas depending on their construction, simulated a world of space and time beyond the everyday lives of viewers. In their most modern form, they were housed in circular buildings, and viewed from the center, often through foreground objects (soil, grass, trees, building models) and enhanced through projected images on the canvas paintings. In nineteenth-century Britain and the United States, dioramas became substitutes for travel, displaying Greek ruins, Swiss scenery, Niagara Falls, and the Battle of Gettysburg, for a shilling or a dime. Aided by the romantic patter of a lecturer, these scenic displays encouraged an appreciation for the sublimity of nature and historic architecture, gave a wide range of viewers a fixed image of a sacred site, and eventually encouraged tourism to these places. The American interest in the scenic spectacle was especially strong. This may be due to the self-conscious sense of distance that many Americans felt from sites of historical wonder. [60]

But the British could also be captivated by such displays and the traveling fairs helped to popularize new forms of spectacle such as the bioscope and magic lantern. The cinema itself had British origins in fairground booths at the turn of the twentieth century, although here the emphasis was on presenting large numbers of local people to themselves and their friends through moving pictures of shopping streets, sporting crowds and factory gates when people were leaving work. Although shows of this sort were presented at the popular seaside, the dioramas and their successors were less identified with Blackpool than with Coney Island.[61]

While we might well expect "uplifting" scenic spectacles to have a broad appeal across middle and working classes, the cross-class interest in exhibits of human and animal curiosities may seem more surprising in retrospect. The freak show, today associated with the tawdry, exploitative, and unrefined (despite current attempts, not least at Coney Island itself, to reclaim it), created a century ago a fascination with the extraordinary that was similar to what attracted the middle class to panoramas.[62] Freak shows crossed class and taste lines until the twentieth century. As early as the seventeenth century, dwarfs, giants, "ossified" (thin) and fat people, the gender ambivalent, and conjoined twins were displayed in traveling shows and at fairs in England. This did not mean that they appealed primarily to the popular classes. The attraction to freaks trickled down from the upper classes. Dwarfs had long been prized in royal courts, often rising to positions of power and privilege. Not only Queen Victoria, but also Charles Dickens, Mark Twain, and Abraham Lincoln found dwarfs fascinating and met with the likes of "Tom Thumb."[63] Although seventeenth- and eighteenth-century artists often portrayed freaks as grotesque, in the nineteenth century they became humanized, even cutesified. Showmen often gave dwarfs pretentious names (like General Tom Thumb) or portrayed the grossly obese as Happy Jack, Jolly Irene, or even Baby Ruth. Impresarios changed the image of giants, long pictured as enemies of children and as villains, into gentle, if sometimes sad figures. The career of Joseph Merrick, the "Elephant Man," illustrates the prevalence, and ambiguity, of such values in Victorian England.[64]

The freak was family entertainment. Despite modern disgust with the freak shows, few in 1900 distinguished them from the scientific exhibition, or simply other spectacles of the dime museums and circuses of the era.[65] These cross-cultural mixtures had a long history. In both the United States and Britain by 1810, curiosities of nature, along with personal oddities such as George Washington's shaving brush, were displayed in small commercial "scientific" museums in cities. These places offered compromises between enlightenment and entertainment, promising both to educate and to titillate. They evolved into dime museums. The most famous was P. T. Barnum's American Museum in the 1840s and 1850s, but the dime museum flourished until about 1900 in urban America. Simulations of world travel and great historical events shared a common roof with obvious humbuggery when Barnum displayed the 161-year-old nurse of George Washington and the "What is It?"—an exhibit of the "missing link" between man and monkey. Dime museums presented indifferently live musicians, hypnotists, and freaks as well as waxworks, menageries, panoramas, and other visual illusions appealing to the diverse tastes of urban audiences. Dime museums also featured chambers of horror with topical exhibits, including wax displays of the execution of criminals in the latest legal killing machine, the Electric Chair, as well as torture used in the Spanish Inquisition. Even genteel middle-class audiences attended this assortment of spectacles that later would be split into high and low culture.[66] While the middle class had begun to withdraw from freakish spectacles by the first decade of the twentieth century, the cross-cultural and cross gender appeal made the dime museum a success and model for Coney Island.

Nor was this just a matter of dime museums, as such. To give a British example, in 1892 the twentieth Earl of Shrewsbury, busily marketing his great house at Alton Towers as a tourist attraction, eagerly purchased a collection of instruments of torture on a visit to Nuremberg Castle and gained extensive press publicity when he exhibited them as part of a broader collection of eclectic curiosities.[67] *World's Fair*, the newspaper for British traveling show people, in 1913 featured advertisements seeking work from a "Human Spider," the "World's Champion Irish Fasting Lady," and "Mdlle. Flo the Tattooed Lady," while an exhibition manager at Portsmouth was in the market for "Fat Lady, Midgets, Tattooed Lady or Giants preferred on salary." Exotic animals, birds, and snakes were also available for exhibition.[68] Another cross-class entertainment was the traveling circus. Its animal and acrobat acts shared space with sideshow freaks in the mammoth circuses that toured around both countries by train from the 1850s. The Wild West show, as a genre, was also part of this complex, crossing the Atlantic through the British tours of Buffalo Bill and British imitators like Texas Bill Shufflebottom, whose enduring Wild West show toured with traveling fairs until his death in 1916 and was then perpetuated by his sons.[69]

Coney Island and Blackpool integrated the thrill ride, spectacle, and animal and freak show into their seaside pleasure sites to varying degrees before 1900, but it was the popular entertainment quarters of "World's Fairs" that created the model for the seaside amusement parks. Here the United States took the lead. While London initiated the era of the international exhibition in 1851, with eager imitators elsewhere in Europe, it was in the United States that these extravagant displays of scientific and cultural progress and national and regional pride were repeatedly built. New American cities showed off their growth and wealth in a long series of exhibitions beginning in Philadelphia in 1876, followed by Chicago (1893), Nashville (1897), Omaha (1898), Buffalo (1901), St. Louis (1904), Chicago (1933), and especially New York (1939–40).[70] Moreover, American exhibitions were especially willing to compromise with popular tastes and became more so over time.

Freaks were an essential part of these otherwise uplifting exhibitions from 1876. Even though placed in the separate Centennial City, fair goers could see the "Wild

1.5　　The freak show, preferably including an element of sexual titillation, survived as a sideshow attraction through the twentieth century on Blackpool's Golden Mile. This photograph comes from the early 1960s. From Alfred Gregory, *Blackpool: A Celebration of the '60s* (London: Constable, 1993).

Men of Borneo," "The Man Eating Feejees," and a 602-pound fat lady along with the latest compound steam engine at the main grounds of the Philadelphia Exhibition of 1876. While the 1893 Chicago Columbian Exhibition invested heavily in the stately architecture of the Court of Honor and sober displays of scientific achievement in its White City, charging 50 cents admission to keep out the wandering crowd, it also built an amusement strip, the Midway, 600 feet wide and nearly a mile long. Rather than allow a tawdry fairground to emerge spontaneously on the edge of the Exhibition, the Exhibition's Department of Ethnography managed the Midway and pretended to offer lessons in geography and world culture there. The Midway operated on a pay-as-you-go basis, thus encouraging a large and socially diverse crowd. In addition to romantic reproductions of a Square of Old Vienna and an Irish Village with a "Blarney Castle" were exotic scenes of Algerian and Tunisian Villages complete with Bedouin tents. There were African mud-dabbed huts displayed with "native warriors," a South Sea village featured supposedly cannibalistic Samoans, and the Streets of Cairo introduced crowds to "Little Egypt," the Hootchy-Kootchy dancer. These displays inevitably featured primitive and childlike, or alternatively sexual, manifestations of the "otherness" of these cultures, emphasizing the superiority of the "civilized" observers. Despite its ethnographic and educational pretensions, the Midway was actually run by Sol Bloom, a 22-year-old impresario who also introduced the Ferris Wheel, a 264-foot high steam-powered ride capable of lifting 1,440 passengers in thirty-six cars.[71]

In many ways, the world's fairs were only following a pattern established by regional fairs. As early as 1858, freak and animal shows, including learned pigs, and beer saloons congregated outside fairs in Ohio. By the 1890s, similar venues in New York featured "fakirs, freaks, and uproarious fun." "Little Egypts" appeared everywhere in the aftermath of the Chicago World's Fair. From 1894, imitators of the fair Midway also included traveling "carnivals," which combined thrill rides and side shows. By 1940, there were about American 350 carnival companies which often divided profits with local fire departments or fraternal organizations.[72] Understood in this context, Coney Island became a sort of permanent midway and carnival with only scattered signs of the world's fair's original didacticism. Isolated on the "island," Coney offered an experiential contrast to the stately look and serious business of the rising Manhattan skyscraper.[73]

Blackpool's frivolity offered a similar kind of contrast with the factory chimneys and colliery winding gear of its industrial hinterland. But its popular entertainments were firmly rooted not so much in any World's Fair or county show, but rather in the itinerant fairgrounds, local pleasure gardens, and music-halls. The British had resisted the incorporation of entertainment into the international exhibition and embraced it only in 1908 at London's White City, years after the opening of the Pleasure Beach. The great exceptions were the exhibition grounds at the Crystal Palace site in southwest London where many innovative rides and experiences were tried out in England for the first time and passed on to amusement parks.[74] Despite all these differences, both resorts from the beginning of the twentieth century became indelibly associated with the amusement park.

Amusement Parks

The amusement park, a large, enclosed area controlled by a single company regulating or directly owning various entertainments within, certainly had nineteenth-century precedents—for example, Copenhagen's Tivoli Gardens from 1843 and Blackpool's own Raikes Hall from 1871.[75] But amusement parks added new rides and experiences as well as a ceaseless quest for innovation to the traditional menu of seaside and fairground pleasure. Most distinct was their gate admission charge (though Pleasure Beach was an exception) that excluded undesirables who threatened the social tone of the park. The idea of grouping these entertainment elements into a permanent site, removing them from the helter-skelter of the temporary fair or midway, appeared in 1895 at Coney Island. Paul Boyton, famed as an ocean swimmer and inventor of the frogman suit, opened Sea Lion Park that year with a smattering of rides (the circular Flip Flap coaster, the Shoot the Chutes water slide, and the Old Mill, a scenic railroad for romantic couples) in addition to a dance hall and an arena for performing sea lions.[76]

George Tilyou, son of a Coney Island entrepreneur and a rival of McKane, followed with an enclosed amusement center in 1897 that he called Steeplechase Park. Having made a small fortune on introducing a downsized replica of the Chicago Midway's Ferris Wheel in 1894, he added a scenic railway, carousel, and a ride, the namesake of his park, which playfully imitated a steeplechase race with wooden horses on an undulating track. Like Sea Lion Park, he charged a 25-cent admission fee (but for 25 attractions), prohibited drink, and banned gamblers and whores. Located at the western end of the Bowery, this 15-acre site shared the plebeian gaiety of that street without its "moral danger." The park's motto, "The Funny Place" and trademark image of a jester's devilish face with a grin showing no fewer than 33 teeth, reinforced Tilyou's mission: "We Americans want either to be thrilled or amused, and we are ready to pay well for either sensation." Entry required more than a quarter to spare. It necessitated passing through a Barrel of Love, a 10 by 30 foot revolving drum that put visitors into each other's arms. Other novelties included an Earthquake Floor, Trick Staircase, and House Upside Down as well as a Grand Canal, Lover's Lane, and Far West Mining Camp.[77]

Even though Tilyou's park was burnt to the ground in 1907, he quickly reconstructed it (charging 10 cents entrance to see the ruins).[78] The new facility featured a Pavilion of Fun, a 2.8 acre modern building of glass and steel. It provided a rain- and sun-free array of frequently changing rides, shooting galleries, and sideshow features that was encircled by a new and improved Steeplechase ride. Though George died in 1914, Steeplechase remained in the family, first run by his young son Edward and then a second son Frank until 1964. It was the bargain of Coney Island.[79]

In 1903, Frederick Thompson and Skip Dundy bought Paul Boyton's failed Sea Lion Park north of Surf Avenue and created a 36-acre park far grander than Steeplechase. While Dundy provided financial experience, Thompson used his architectural background and experience in the "world's fairs" at Nashville and Buffalo to build an "electric Baghdad," creating not the formal classical look of the White City of Chicago's Fair, but a dense forest of spires and colonnades that he claimed "promoted release, dynamic motion, overwhelming transformation, and above all, exotic illusion." Like the temporary buildings of the world's fairs, Thompson used "staff," a mix of gypsum (used in wallboards), alumina, glycerin, and dextrin made stiff with fibers (mostly from burlap) to create a plaster-like substitute for stone. This material allowed for cheap exteriors, built over steel or wood frames that could be shaped quickly into copies of friezes, statuary, towers, domes, and colonnades from ancient European and Asian civilizations. Again, as with Steeplechase, the key was balanced contradiction: While Luna Park shared with the White City an elongated reflecting pool with monumental architecture on the sides and a 200-foot high Electric Tower at one end, this stately rectangle was disturbed by a Shoot the Chutes water slide ride at the other end.[80] Unlike the Bowery, Luna was an extravaganza of order and, at night, its 200,000 lights guaranteed decency even as they created feelings of freedom from constraint.[81]

Like Disney much later, Thompson recognized the need for a focal point, in the pool and tower, an area that also facilitated the circulation of the crowd in and out of attractions on all four sides of the rectangle. Scenic railroads and towering rides offered vistas on the whole place. Nevertheless, Luna was hardly a modern theme park. Most of the attractions were contracted out on short-term leases, producing a constantly changing hodge-podge. In its first year, near the foot of the tower, were located two circus rings for trained animals, equestrians, and clowns. To the left of the Chutes was Dr. Couney's baby incubator display and near the entrance was Thompson's own signature spectacle, the Trip to the Moon. Other attractions included the War of the Worlds (a strange miniature fantasy of the navies of the European powers attacking New York City, but saved by Admiral Dewey's Fleet) and Twenty Thousand Leagues Under the Sea, a submarine ride based on Jules Verne's famous book. Finally, in the tradition of Chicago's Midway, around the grounds were Irish, Hindu and Eskimo Villages.[82]

All of this had appeared elsewhere, but Luna Park was unique in its continuous promise of novelty and innovation. In 1904, Luna Park had four million visitors (who paid 10 cents for admission with attractions priced separately), forcing the owners to raise a second deck around the pool to accommodate the overflowing crowds. Thompson continually changed Luna Park, each year adding more and more architectural markers: "Wherever there was a chance to put up a tower or a minaret to break the line of any roof or expanse," Thompson noted in 1906, "I have stuck one on to please the eye." By 1911, Luna Park claimed 1,210 red and white painted towers, minarets, and domes.[83] In Luna's second year, Thompson purchased an additional 16 acres; there he put the Streets of Delhi, which included an Indian palace and processions of horses, costumed soldiers, and elephants. He brought La Marcus Thompson's Scenic Railroad to the park and even changed the costumes of female cashiers to Mexican hats and Bolero red jackets to create a new look. In 1905, the already dated Twenty Thousand Leagues was replaced with Dragon's Gorge, an indoor scenic railway which featured an entrance flanked by "two enormous dragons with outspread wings" and a waterfall under which cars sped. No longer a novelty, Trip to the Moon dropped its admission to ten cents. Always up-to-date, Luna Park added the Fall of Port Arthur, depicting the most dramatic event in the recent Russo-Japanese War complete with working models of the torpedo boats that had been used to sink the Russian fleet. In 1908, the Trip to the Moon was finally replaced with the Battle of the Merrimac and Monitor, followed two years later by A Trip to Mars by Aeroplane. Thompson had created a very successful formula for Luna Park that attracted 31 million admissions in its first five years.[84]

However, so much money did Thompson lavish on his ever changing park, that in April 1912, his creditors drove him out of the business when they discovered the park's debts of $665,000. However, even a financially more prudent management recognized the need for continuous innovation to draw fresh crowds every year. It added more lights and even more towers as well as new spectacles in 1914–15. Among these were the Fall of Adrianople a stage spectacle for an audience of 1,800, Vernon Castle's Summer House Dance Hall, and a village of midgets.[85]

A third amusement park, Dreamland, attempted to reproduce a permanent world's fair at Coney. Built in 1904 by William Reynolds, a former Republican State Senator and suburban housing developer, Dreamland distanced itself even further from the Bowery than did Luna. Spread out on 15 acres of choice West Brighton land extending from the old Iron Pier to Surf Avenue, Dreamland was built at a cost of $3.5 million. It promised its first visitors for the dime admission fee (attractions extra) "Avenues Wide and Imposing—No Crowding."[86] In contrast to the oriental look of Luna, Reynolds insisted on a classical appearance—all white buildings built around a stately lagoon. A 375-foot Beacon Tower modeled after that of the Giralda in Seville stood at one end, besting Luna Park Electric Tower in size and illumination. Reynolds built two Shoot the Chutes side by side opposite the Tower. Visitors arriving by night on the pier by ferry from Manhattan terminals enjoyed a magical and majestic vista of Dreamland (with a claimed one million electric lights illuminating the skyline) and had immediate access to a dance hall accommodating 25,000. The street entrance at the site of "The Creation" (brought from the St. Louis Fair of 1904) invited visitors to walk under a huge replica of a classical nude female, 150 feet wide and 75 feet high, and decorated in gold paint. The Creation took audiences on a scenic boat ride along a 1,000-foot canal encircling the interior of a domed building that showed depictions of the Biblical First Seven Days. Adding to the aura of "gentility," the young women at the cash booths wore "white college gowns and mortar boards."[87]

This White City look-alike did not, however, offer displays of scientific and cultural progress, but a combination of simulated tourism, thrill rides, and sideshow acts often veneered with grandeur and religious imagery deemed suitable for a "respectable" middling class crowd. On the East Promenade was located the Canals

1.6   The "stately" Beacon Tower at Dreamland surrounded by constantly changing attractions. Note the
       well-dressed crowd (about 1905). Library of Congress.

of Venice, a 250 by 80 feet model with gondolas carrying passengers along 54,000
square feet of painted canvas of Venetian scenes. Nearby was a scenic rail ride called
Coasting Through Switzerland with the latest refrigerated pipes to "keep this artificial 'Switzerland' as cold and as full of sweet pure air as can be found among the
picturesque Swiss mountains." But Dreamland also featured a British import, Bostock's Circus (which included a French cyclist riding on a tilted circular track above
twenty fierce lions in the Circle of Death), Ben Morris' magic show, Fighting the
Flames (reenacting a tenement fire), and the Seven Temptations of St. Anthony (a

spectacle for men with paintings of voluptuous women "tempting" the saint).[88] On the West Promenade were attractions with educational pretensions, the Destruction of Pompeii and Under and Over the Sea (a simulated submarine ride under the Atlantic), but also Lilliputia ("a city" of 300 midgets), a dog and monkey show, and the Baby Incubator exhibit (moved from Luna). And on the lower portion of the pier, Dreamland leased out stalls for shooting galleries and other Bowery fare.[89]

Like Luna Park, Dreamland underwent dramatic changes nearly every year. The Creation was so popular that Dreamland made Biblical themes a specialty, by offering thrilling encounters with the hereafter. Hell's Gate, a boat trip in a water flume to Hell done in plaster of Paris, so captured the crowd's imagination that in 1906, a new exhibit, the End of the World, replaced a staid boring scenic ride, Touring Europe. This apocalyptic fantasy featured reproductions of Doré's pictures of the dead rising from graves and the holy taking wing. The next year, "The Hereafter" stage show portrayed the destruction of the world by fire backed up by 200 singers performing melodies from the *Damnation of Faust*. Religious and classic themes at Dreamland, however, were balanced with new thrill rides, especially the Leap Frog Railroad built on a 400-foot long pier extending into the sea. In 1906, the exotic Village of Moqui Indians appeared with space taken from the Midget City and the timely display of the San Francisco Earthquake replaced Fighting the Flames. The next year, however, earthquakes were passé and this exhibit was replaced by a scenic railroad, "The Great Divide," which simulated travel across the Rockies with a mechanical volcano and pleased thrill-seekers by erupting as they passed by. Despite the high-minded rhetoric and elegant pseudo-architecture, Reynolds knew from the beginning that visitors' tastes were hardly "refined." In fact, Dreamland hired circus and sideshow showman Samuel Gumpertz to develop spectacles, promoting him to General Manager in 1909. Gumpertz featured freak shows and exotic villages along with replicas of the Siege of Richmond.

In 1911, the white paint was already peeling off the staff buildings, forcing Dreamland to undertake a major facelift, this time abandoning the purity of white for cream and firehouse red. The costly renewal was to no avail, because on May 27, 1911 a fire broke out at Hell's Gate that within three hours consumed the entire park. It was never rebuilt. Both the cost of continuous refurbishing and Dreamland's failure to find a market niche led to this decision. The site was leased out for parking and to various rides and exhibits, becoming the location of New York's Aquarium in 1957.[90]

In all their diversity, these three Coney Island amusement parks anticipated later twentieth-century theme parks, especially with their stress upon an integrated architectural fantasy. But they also called back to earlier traditions of the dime museum, circus, and fairground, which they brought together in the enclosed park, often in seeming contradiction to each other.

Blackpool had only one enduring amusement park of this kind—the Pleasure Beach. There were, of course, precedents. The town's "Golden Mile" was a central seafront strip dominated by cheap exhibitions and sideshows. The Tower and Alhambra, the great entertainment complexes of the 1890s, sat side by side on the central promenade. Fairground rides came and went as part of the menu of attractions in this area. Like the earlier fringe attractions of Uncle Tom's Cabin and Raikes Hall, the Pleasure Beach grew up at the edge of the built-up area, where land was cheaper and building expansion did not compete for space.[91] Its promoters found an ideal location, at the end of the promenade electric tramway that had opened in 1885. The combination of cheap land (though vulnerable to high tides) and accessibility proved irresistible. A partnership between Albert Ellis (a phrenologist on the Golden Mile) and J. W. Outhwaite (a Blackpool butcher with family ties to a Philadelphia carousel company) leased the 20 acres that formed the core of the new enterprise.[92]

The key figure, however, was William George Bean; and here we see an even more direct transatlantic link. Bean was a Londoner, born in 1868, but moved to the United States at 19 years of age and found his way into the Philadelphia amusement machinery industry. When he returned to England in the mid-1890s, he operated a bicycle railway, eventually locating along side Outhwaite's carousel in Blackpool. Soon the two men joined forces (as the Anglo-American syndicate) and, by 1904, had bought nearly 40 acres of unassuming sand dunes including 500 yards of sea frontage.[93] Like its Coney Island counterparts, the syndicate under Bean's leadership not only operated its own rides but also rented sites to others for stalls and mechanical rides. As the amusement park developed, Bean also negotiated with the local authority over building plans and public order issues.[94]

Attractions soon began to proliferate at what became the Pleasure Beach. In 1904, the Sir Hiram Maxim Captive Flying Machine was introduced, another piece of transatlantic technology: Maxim was an American who had introduced machine guns to Europe in 1883, and subsequently dreamed of building a steam-powered flying machine. Being unable to raise the capital for this project after a prototype

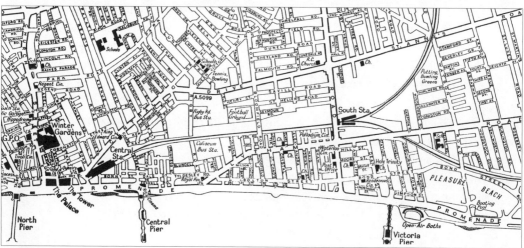

1.7   (*Above*) This view along the shore northward from the Pleasure Beach shows its peripheral location on the edge of the built-up area, with the Tower and other central amusements on the distant horizon. Courtesy of the Pleasure Beach, Blackpool. (*Below*) From the Ordnance Survey map. How central Blackpool looked in the 1930s. Notice the peripheral location of the Pleasure Beach in comparison to the Tower, the piers, and the Central Station.

crashed spectacularly, he turned to "captive flight." His flying carriages, revolving around a central pylon, proved a huge success at Blackpool after trials at Earls Court in London. Over the next few years a string of innovations followed, from River Caves (a spectacular scenic ride), the Grotto (an indoor fantasy ride), a water chute, and tobogganing tower to the Monitor and Merrimac battle show, the cake-walk, submarine switchback, oscillating staircase, and haunted cabin. The first big Roller Coaster arrived in 1907, in the form of a La Marcus Thompson Scenic Railway. Several of these were transplanted Coney Island attractions (for example the Helter Skelter of 1905, a spiral slide on the outside of a "light house" that survived until 1935). Bean, who was eager to identify with American enterprise, made annual transatlantic trips to catch up on the latest innovations. He was also keen to develop signature buildings and attractions. In 1907 appeared the Spanish Street, "themed" stalls which had hitherto been random and ramshackled, while, in 1913, the "Moorish" Casino (a word that had no gambling connotations in England) became the Pleasure Beach's defining landmark. By 1914, the Pleasure Beach had a summer staff of 600, up to 100,000 visitors on an ordinary day and 200,000 on a Bank Holiday, and £200,000 invested in its attractions.[95]

This did not match the scale at Coney Island; but there are several other significant differences between the Pleasure Beach and its Coney Island counterparts. The Pleasure Beach was built up piecemeal over several years, but it was built to last. The Sir Hiram Maxim machine is still in use, and when the original Casino was replaced in 1937 gelignite had to be used when the normal demolition methods proved insufficient. The regular devastating fires that ravaged Coney Island had no counterpart at Blackpool, where fires were unusual and did not spread. The Pleasure Beach management was even more concerned with the respectability of its image than were the Coney Island parks. For example, in 1909 Bean finally agreed to banish the gypsies who had constituted the area's original attraction. The Corporation was a hard taskmaster, because it had to deal with early opposition to the Pleasure Beach from its suburban neighbors, and because some of its leading lights (including managers and shareholders of the Tower Company) regarded the Pleasure Beach as a dangerous competitor. In 1907, in order to defend his interests, Bean found his way on to the Council. The revenue the Pleasure Beach generated for the municipal electricity works and tramways soon became a major point in its favor, creating a local-government interest in sustaining this new attraction. The owners of Coney Island's parks had no such influence in the chambers of New York City Hall.[96]

1.8   The original occupants of the Pleasure Beach site were these gypsy fortune-tellers, who had attracted
       many visitors to their exotic encampment in the sand dunes. Courtesy of the Pleasure Beach, Black-
       pool.

Even more to the point of the contrast, Blackpool's core identity at the turn
of the century was bound up less with the Pleasure Beach than with indoor entertainment in the form of the shows and dance halls at the Tower, Alhambra,
Winter Gardens, and the piers. At Coney Island the amusement parks were the
defining features, and indoor entertainment was less magnificent or distinctive.
From its beginnings Coney had its pavilions on raised platforms on the sand that
offered live music and dancing. Luna Park and Dreamland at various times offered
spectacular dance floors. But they were ephemeral like everything else at these
parks. Similarly, while many a later star started in the Bowery music halls or as
singing waiters (Eddie Cantor, Jimmy Durante, and Irving Berlin, for example),[97]

music and theater played a small part in the history of Coney Island, especially after the arrival of the amusement parks. Evidently, these entertainments were well provided for in Manhattan's theater district. Coney Island was a place for different things.

By contrast, Blackpool had a strong identity as provider of a range of indoor entertainments that were not specific to the seaside, but helped to attract people to it. Most British seaside resorts were infamously dull in the evenings and inhospitable on rainy days. But Blackpool became a regional entertainment capital in the late nineteenth century. Nor was this just downscale music-hall entertainment, although there was plenty of that. From time to time the big theaters played host to international performers like Caruso and Melba, and the Grand Theatre of 1894 would put on new plays directly after their opening run in London's West End, sometimes with the same cast. Manchester was much further from Blackpool than Manhattan was from Coney Island, and there was nothing in between to challenge Blackpool's summer status as northern entertainment capital. Here, emphatically, the playful crowd had indoor as well as outdoor incarnations.[98] The amusement park (about which more later) was important to both resorts, but, as much else, in differing degrees and ways.

Deep Differences: Cultural and Social Comparisons of Coney and Blackpool

While Coney Island and Blackpool had much in common, they represented two different cultures and societies. As we have seen, the close proximity to New York City and the short, but hot, summer season shaped Coney Island in many ways. But characteristics of 1900 American society and culture also reinforced these patterns and further framed the American seaside experience. Most important was the transient character of Coney Island. To be sure, its sidewalk and seashore novelty businesses, especially on the Bowery, were similar to those on Blackpool's Golden Mile. Both featured many businesses based on short-term leases. Such leases made it easy to open a stall or store, but because these businesses were also poorly capitalized, they came and went with equal frequency. In its American setting, however, this pattern was more extreme with the widespread use of wood and staff in buildings. Moreover, Coney Island subtenants had no incentive to build expensive brick and steel structures because their landlords refused to lengthen their leases (in anticipation of rising land prices).

Even more, in contrast to Blackpool, Coney Island's central and well-financed entertainments were equally transitory. The extraordinary Elephant Hotel was in business only fourteen years and the well-financed Dreamland with its spectacular Beacon Tower, merely seven. And even the longer surviving Steeplechase and Luna Parks changed their attractions almost annually, at least in their early years. As the *New York World* noted in 1897, "don't imagine because you were [at Coney] last year, it will bore you to go again. The frivolities at Coney are as changeable as its sands." American audiences expected novelty and the amazingly cheap construction in staff and burlap not only made change economically possible, but also a necessity. It is no wonder that these creations so often needed repair and were often easier to replace than to maintain, and, most tellingly, that they burned down so often.[99] In fact, Coney Island construction was such a fire hazard that in the 1900s insurance rates were $5.50 for $100 in insurance protection per year compared with three cents for brick and stone buildings in New York.[100] Thompson certainly reflected the common American view when he wrote in 1908 that though Blackpool was the closest thing to Coney Island in Europe, "it is a long way behind. It is stiff and solemn, and its buildings lack the other-world suggestiveness of our Coney Island erections." Coney promised fantasy and novelty above all else.[101]

This assumption that Blackpool lacked imagination stands in need of challenge, but there is no doubt that Blackpool's version of popular seaside culture was both more staid and controlled, and directed at a more solid and less ephemeral market. Blackpool drew on the stable, rooted cultures of the industrial towns of northern and midland England, not from cosmopolitan, shifting Liverpool, Britain's nearest analog to New York. Its attractions were aimed at people in regular work, often in skilled jobs, concerned to maintain their reputations among the neighbors and workmates who all went on holiday to the same place at the same time. The lines of respectability were drawn more generously on holiday, allowing for cheerful indulgence in more alcohol than usual, for chaste flirtation and holiday romance, for sexual innuendo at the music hall, and carefree excitement on mechanical rides. But these were the safety valves of the self-disciplined, in a culture that internalized repression.[102]

The two resorts also offer us sharp differences in the crowds that they attracted. While (as we will see later in greater detail) Coney Island was unable to maintain a distinct social tone and class separation on the beach, Blackpool was more successful. Whereas Coney Island was a site of a succession of socially distinct crowds, much as was true in many American urban and suburban neighborhoods, in Blackpool the class and regional composition of the crowds seemed to remain relatively unchanging throughout the decades from the 1880s to the 1930s and even beyond. Even as the catchment area extended across Britain, the overall impression was that this was more of the same, as other parts of working-class Britain adapted to the holiday culture of Northern England. Moreover, Coney Island was far less successful in maintaining the social tone of its elite eastern shore. Even in the 1890s, "genteel" Manhattan Beach did not necessarily attract small quiet gatherings of America's aristocracy of wealth and manners. Corbin expected, not hundreds, but thousands, of the smart set to take his train to the Manhattan Hotel. In the early years, 30,000 visited the Manhattan Hotel on Sundays and few were paying guests. They came for the "nice" bathing houses, dining, or even sauntering on the veranda. Corbin's railway eventually connected Manhattan Beach to the rival, but less exclusive, Brighton Beach Hotel. Even on the back stairs of the four-story Oriental Hotel, gamblers could be found; and the middle-class who could not afford to stay at the Manhattan Beach appeared at its restaurants for a special lunch. None of this marked the eastern end of Coney Island as a sanctuary of gentility.[103]

Despite claims of exclusivity, as early as 1895 the east end of Coney Island began to succumb to the mass commercialization of West Brighton. That year Manhattan Beach opened a 12,000 capacity bicycle oval and enlarged Henry Pain's arena for fireworks and drama. Even a minstrel show appeared in 1889. The building of the Brighton Beach Amusement Park in 1906 on the eastern end of the Island represented the final concession to popular taste. But, even all this was not enough to save the Manhattan, Oriental, or Brighton Hotels from decline. The claim of serenity, of course, had been compromised from the start. In 1879, William Engeman built a race track at Brighton Beach. Soon it faced competition in the more stylish Sheepshead Bay Track. A third track, an offshoot of Sheepshead, was opened in Gravesend in 1886. All three tracks drew a cross-class crowd of men from Wall Street barons and politicians to actors and professional gamblers. Court and political battles over on-track betting led in 1908 to tough restrictions and the closure of the tracks in 1910. Deprived of gambling, the Manhattan and Oriental hotels closed a few years after and the Brighton Beach succumbed quietly in the early 1920s. The rich fled to more distant elite sites and the east end became the site of suburban housing.[104]

By contrast, Blackpool did not become a one-class resort. The Corporation successfully defended the North Shore against fairground and other incursions,

partly by taking control of a key area of the land company's estate to the north of Claremont Park; and this remained a holiday area for middle-class families. Despite the arrival of the Pleasure Beach, much of South Shore remained relatively exclusive, with a large population of prosperous retired people and of business commuters to Manchester and the industrial towns of south and east Lancashire.[105]

Not only did Coney Island fail to maintain its elite zone, but also the social character of the Island's visitors was in continuous flux. While the genteel east end of Coney Island barely survived the nineteenth century, West Brighton became ever more prominent. Like the well-known phenomenon of residential succession in American cities, West Brighton over time shifted from crowds of bourgeois, to skilled workers, and finally to low wage earners.[106] For a time, the result was a uniquely mixed crowd. The mostly male entertainments were concentrated in a few areas, separate from the milling crowds. And, when gambling and brothels moved out of the Gut and the Bowery and onto Surf Avenue in the late 1880s, Coney elites drew a line and eventually drove out McKane, who had tolerated this incursion of sleaze.[107] As we have seen, for years, West Brighton catered to a cross-gender/cross-class crowd.

This diversity surely excited anxiety (as we shall see in chapter 3). Stall games like the "Kill the Coon" or "African Dodger" that involved throwing balls at black people let whites, no matter their ethnicity, displace their aggression on to blacks and made all of European descent "respectable" by excluding the African American. An unofficial color line (on beach and bathhouses) was an especially prominent feature of turn of the century Coney Island.[108] In many ways, this emerging pleasure crowd was unique. It created cultural blendings and social mixtures that were relatively uncommon in the late nineteenth century and it broke from both the code of the mostly male culture of commercial sex, boisterous drinking, and gambling that had prevailed in the West End and the genteel culture (however compromised) that had been attempted to the East.[109]

That heterogeneity, however, was not to last long. Gradually, Coney Island became a truly plebeian resort as the middle and even high-wage working class aban-

1.9   (*Previous page*) Manhattan Beach Hotel in its glory days. Despite its distance from the teeming crowds and genteel appearance, it was still a wooden structure. Courtesy of the Brooklyn Historical Society.

doned it for more distant and less crowded seaside attractions on the New Jersey shore and in less developed portions of Long Island after 1910. As we shall see, rather than preserve exclusive portions of Coney Island, the more affluent went elsewhere. They abandoned Coney to the poorer immigrants (and blacks).

Blackpool was also a plebeian resort, but not in isolation. It kept a middle-class presence throughout the period of working-class invasion, sharing a common pleasure culture, although one in which middle-class males were more at ease than respectable women of similar social standing. It lacked the sort of undisciplined or unschooled working class that still generated alarm on other parts of the British coastline, especially where the "roughs" of London's East End, Liverpool, or Glasgow appeared. When compared with Coney Island, the relative homogeneity of its visiting public is set in sharp relief. It was white, Anglo-Saxon, and Protestant (few even of Irish descent), and dominated by the disciplined, industrial (and industrious) working class who had saved for the privilege of making the journey and, importantly, the stay.

Blackpool and Coney Island in the first half of the twentieth century were the premier sites of the plebian pleasure crowd. Yet, for many reasons, Blackpool would adapt and survive for the balance of the century and beyond, while Coney Island would slide into ruin and nearly disappear. The difference says a lot about culture and class, about American commitment to novelty and mobility, and British tradition and class stability. But the contrasting results had roots in much more. Location and climate were critical: Far from London, Blackpool became the full-service entertainment capital of northern England, a destination tourist site complete with a wide range of lodging for which the sea was only a backdrop. Coney Island remained the day-tripper's seashore site for New Yorkers, as much for the cooling breezes, sandy beach, and warm waves as for its inland commercial entertainments.[110]

While Blackpool was able to extend its season and justify substantial investment, Coney Island was forever a summer weekend site and thus forever ephemeral and peripheral. Blackpool was modeled on a relatively stable entertainment tradition: piers, the lavish interiors and entertainment traditions of music halls, pubs, and fish and chip shops, and customary fairground attractions.[111] The situation at Coney Island was much less stable. In the early twentieth century it was certainly more innovative, grafting the American World's Fair experience on to older traditions to create new fantasy spaces and exciting mechanical rides and entertainments.

Within Blackpool, the Pleasure Beach worked in similar, if more conservative, ways. But Coney's ceaseless, restless pursuit of novelty made it impossible to create a viable and enduring set of traditions. At the same time, the older pleasures of the circus and dime museum that Coney Island offered were soon to be challenged by bourgeois modernizers. While Blackpool's relative distance from population centers served as a social filter that allowed it to sustain a respectable clientele of white and blue collar working people, Coney Island was progressively more accessible to the poor of New York City, unable to exclude undesirables or to maintain any sort of "social tone."

Whereas Blackpool's local government was able to promote and renew itself as a tourist destination, Coney Island was continuously at war with political forces to the north in Brooklyn and to the west in Manhattan. The Island was never able to define itself and found itself repeatedly caught between the reformers' efforts to "clean up" Coney and the pressures for commercial interests to maximize short-term profits. The key divisions within Blackpool were between the central entertainment interests (especially the Tower Company) and the Pleasure Beach, but did not disrupt the resort's success.

Despite all these differences and their long-term effects, Blackpool and Coney Island defined the pleasure crowd in industrial Britain and America. They shaped the meaning of public enjoyment for an era, becoming instantly recognizable as signifiers of a popular culture of exuberant temporary release from the daily constraints of work, neighborhood, and routine. It is to the question of why and how Britons and Americans embraced these sites for relief from the rigors of industrial life that we now turn.

Industrial Saturnalia
and the Playful Crowd

Never before had so many gathered so often in such concentrated space to play as had the crowds that thronged to Blackpool and Coney Island at the beginning of the twentieth century. Thousands had congregated in armies to fight, in factories and offices to work, in political demonstrations to make demands, at sports grounds to bet and be thrilled, and in religious rites to be saved. But at Coney and Blackpool, crowds gathered to play, spend, and forget everyday troubles and constraints in liberating frivolity. Easy, fast, and cheap access via train and tram to these Sodoms by the Sea (as contemporaries called such places) made all this possible. But there was much more, as both places drew on a plethora of established attractions—from the genteel quest for uplifting experience in sanctified time and place to the popular fascination with the freak's body and the attraction to the vertigo of thrill rides.

All this calls us to ask: what needs created the playful crowd? The intellectual's or preacher's critique of Blackpool and Coney Island may not help us much in answering this question. Middle-class observers often insisted that the urban working classes seek self-improvement through appropriate reading, contemplation, and communion with nature.[1] But the playful popular crowd sought none of that, in fact, quite the opposite. That crowd desired instead the sociable, often bibulous, sometimes violent, communal leisure activities of their rural and pre-industrial predecessors. These ancient pleasures were filtered through the veil of Victorian respectability, but they still bubbled close to the surface of industrial working-class leisure. Although Blackpool and Coney Island had different menus of entertainment, they created playful crowds that shared these atavistic desires in what we call industrial saturnalia.[2]

Before beginning our quest for understanding these appeals, we must briefly survey who made up these crowds. In the early twentieth century, visitors to Blackpool and Coney Island were structured around both community values and industrial experience.[3] Excursion trains brought crowds to Blackpool from the regional hinterland of industrial Lancashire and the West Riding of Yorkshire up to 70 miles away. About 80 percent came from these areas in 1897. Gradually other parts of England added to the range of accents and backgrounds: first mining and metalworking regions around Birmingham, then the textile and footwear towns of the East Midlands around Nottingham joined the stream. While Blackpool was moving toward national status as a popular resort, the regional core of its appeal scarcely changed.[4]

By contrast, although Coney Island had become a world-wide symbol of liberated leisure and mechanical excitement, attracting intellectuals visiting New York, few beyond the city came to Coney. And, after 1920, with the cheap subway reaching nearly every working-class corner of New York, the crowd became more down-market with proportionately far fewer middle-class visitors. Whereas Blackpool's crowd remained ethnically and culturally homogeneous, based in the upper strata of the working class, the Coney Island crowd became relatively anonymous and divided by ethnicity.[5]

From an early stage Coney Island drew in wave after successive wave of new migrants: British, Irish, Italians, Germans, Scandinavians, Greeks, Eastern Europeans, and Russians. Many of the latter, especially, were Jewish, to complicate further an ethnic and religious mix. Those from Russia and Central Europe, who had no sea-bathing traditions of their own, were drawn to Coney's rides, stalls, and beaches where they quickly learned this aspect of what it was to be American.[6]

Just as residential Brooklyn had its Italian and Jewish neighborhoods, different groups tended to gravitate to bathhouses and sections of the beach that they made their own. Novelist Joseph Heller, who grew up there in the 1930s, remembered that "McLaughlin Baths . . . drew its patrons from the Scandinavian, mainly Norwegian, and Irish populations in Bay Ridge, an area distinguished for a brawling toughness and the predictable anti-Semitism then generally common in America among groups that were not Jewish." There was sometimes mockery between ethnic groups, occasionally sparking fights. Each numbered "bay" along the shoreline had its distinctive neighborhood and ethnic character, and "visiting another bay was like visiting another country." There were also African American visitors, in small but growing numbers, already visible in the 1880s. They congregated on the beach near the Municipal Baths of 1911, were welcomed at Steeplechase (apart from the bathing pool), and were very noticeable among the entertainers.[7]

There was also a much greater variety of fast food at Coney than at Blackpool, reflecting the crowd's ethnic diversity, from knishes to salt water taffy. The straw hats, ties, and neat attire of the early frequenters of Steeplechase, Luna Park, and Dreamland gave way to the shabbier people who thronged the beach and boardwalk on the summer week-ends of the 1930s, bringing their own food and struggling to find room to spread their newspapers, blankets and bed sheets on the impossibly crowded beach. Even in the 1930s, Blackpool's visitors rented deckchairs and took their meals in the boarding-houses. The crucial differences, which undoubtedly contributed to the longevity and resilience of Blackpool's popularity, were that the crowds at the Lancashire resort, although less numerous, traveled longer distances, stayed longer, were visibly more prosperous and better-dressed, had much more in common with each other, and likely spent more.[8] With these differences in mind, let us turn back to 1900 to look at how the crowds interacted with the attractions in Blackpool and Coney.

Modernizing Saturnalia and the Playful Crowd

For centuries, the ancestors of the Blackpool and Coney Island crowds celebrated saturnalia. Like the ancient Roman festival in mid-December from which this term gets its name, the preindustrial Europeans binged in seasonal rites with unrestrained indulgence in food, drink, sex, and aggression. Traditional holidays let people break with social and psychological rules of restraint by indulging in chaotic village ball games, cockfights, or races up greased poles. The young found other amusements as well: there would be unusually large numbers of births nine months later. In addition to the winter rites, there were other annual festivals, such as Mardi Gras and May Day, during which the common people enjoyed a variety of games, plays, and songs that expressed many subtle forms of protest against the rich and powerful. Adults threw flour or even eggs or stones at one another. Roles were reversed when men wore women's clothes and women dressed as males, as at Horn Fair in Charlton, a village outside London, which also celebrated cuckoldry through the general wearing of horns.[9] Saturnalia served as a psychological release for people who daily endured the rigors of scarcity and the humiliation of authority. But if these festivals turned the "world upside down," they also took place in the confines of space and time set by tradition and, at least, were tacitly tolerated by the very authorities that they sometimes mocked. This was so because festivals released tensions and restored and affirmed community in societies that very much needed such reinforcement.[10]

The revelers at Coney Island and Blackpool inherited much from traditional saturnalia. At these sites, they found the opportunity for release and social inversion. The carnival survived despite centuries of reformers and social change. Since the sixteenth century, European religious purists had been attempting to suppress the wantonness of pre-Lenten Mardi Gras revelers. In the nineteenth century, their enlightened bourgeois successors in Britain withdrew from and eventually banned violent and unruly traditions like Derby's mass Shrove Tuesday "football" game or Stamford's bull running, and their American counterparts broke up the bands of Callithumpians in New York City who mocked the fashionable on New Year's Eve.[11] Nevertheless, "official" Victorian values of solitude, nature, and family "self-worship" hardly prevailed across society, even among the middle classes themselves, where gambling, ribald humor, and a tendency to bacchanalia remained strong throughout the nineteenth century.[12]

The uplifting and genteel leisure of quiet strolls through manicured city parks and rural cemeteries or indulging offspring around Christmas trees was insufficiently lively for many middle-class tastes, and hardly exhausted popular longings. Descendants of rowdy mummers and carnival revelers flocked to Blackpool and Coney Island, sharing much with their predecessors, but they also modified and added to their play. In place of traditional aggressive games and the mocking of authority, they sought the thrill of rides, simulated encounters with others' misfortune, and the playful ridicule of modern machines. These modern playful crowds accepted a shift from the physical encounter with one another to physical jousting with technology and an exciting, continuously changing, engagement with sights, sounds, smells, and crowds. In addition to the fearful fascination with death and divine judgment that sometimes appeared in Mardi Gras, the modern crowds were enchanted with and longed to experience "news" and distant places. And, underlying it all was their shift from longing for the symbolic world of community to the nostalgia for and wonders of childhood.

Much of both the continuity and change in the playful crowd relates to the modern experience of industrial work. The middle class often sought escape from the crowd and distractions of urban space. By contrast, workers trapped in the life-long monotony of machines or of routine office work and under the thumb of employers and landlords sought a very different sort of release in vertigo, simulated violence, and the empowering experience of "boss-less" crowds. As important, industrialism greatly accelerated change, radically extending and intensifying expectations at Coney and Blackpool. Through the creative use of new technology, these resorts produced new ways of liberating the individual from boredom and frustration in the speed and realistic immediacy of new rides and spectacles. They offered the exciting encounter with continuous novelty that could fill sometimes lonely and empty lives if only briefly. Through the mysteries of modern machines and electric lighting, fantasy could become more real and intense than it had ever been before. And, thanks to modern transport, rising incomes, shorter workdays, Saturday half-holidays and even vacations in privileged trades, the saturnalian experience could be freed from the rigid schedule of the festival calendar and enjoyed on a weekend, evening, or (especially in the British case) more extended summer holiday. Though still fixed in place and limited in time, the new playful throng was, paradoxically, an expression of modern individualism and the immediacy of "relief" increasingly possible in the industrial era.

In seeming contraction, however, the playful crowd at Coney and Blackpool was not purely a working-class phenomenon, but one of mixed, melded, and jumbled tastes and interests across classes and gender. This was unusual in modern industrial society, despite haphazard efforts to build bridges between the classes through clubs, libraries, and church-based entertainments. More successful was the social mixing of the gambling, drinking, and whoring venues of Norton's Point on western Coney Island in the 1860s and 1870s, or more generally at the racetracks and bare-knuckled boxing matches of the era; but these were for male crowds. Elsewhere in American and British society, class divisions in entertainments were still widening in the late nineteenth century, as bars became socially segregated and even the music halls divided up their audiences by price and therefore status. Coney and Blackpool created something new: not merely cross-class male pleasures, but the relaxed mingling of the "respectable" plebeian and the middle classes across gender lines.

We can see this in various photo and film collections of Blackpool[13] and Coney crowds in the early twentieth century. All this material seems to be purposively skewed toward respectability. For example, Blackpool photographs and film clips depict tranquil, orderly scenes of the North and South (Victoria) Piers outside the popular Wakes holiday season, ignoring the crowded districts between the Tower and Central Pier. Even the excellent photographs in the Pleasure Beach archive show the respectable face of the amusement park crowd: there is nothing here to shock or disturb.

While we should be able to break down these crowds by social status,[14] in our turn-of-the-century resorts working-class visitors cannot be easily distinguished from their middle-class counterparts because wage earners could afford to dress up while on holiday. Working people left their clogs, mufflers and shawls behind even though their presumption drew frequent mockery.[15] In a 1909 illustration *Daily Mirror* cartoonist W. K. Haselden sketched a pair of smart young men splashing through the rain with the legend, "These youths possess umbrellas and stout boots, but they must not use them on Bank Holiday."[16] Contemporaries thought that they could "read" the crowd, in spite of these disguises. The socialist novelist Arthur Laycock, for example, has one of his characters complaining, "That's the worst of coming to these places; one meets so many common people. It was just the same last Sunday on the North Pier. I actually saw some factory-girls walking at church parade as proud and important as anyone." The invasion of elite space was empowering, but did not deceive the knowing observer.[17] But we are not so privileged.

Blackpool's playful crowd aspired to look at least respectable, and preferably fashionable. A Yorkshire dialect comedy play of 1933 captures something enduring here through its emphasis on the importance of being "done up" properly for a trip to Blackpool: a collar and tie was essential, a muffler simply would not do, and the search for a missing collar stud almost causes the family to miss the train.[18] The Pleasure Beach photographs show very few bareheaded people (with women's headgear often very elaborate while men usually wear soft hats rather than caps). Ties worn with a suit were normal until the open-necked shirt became acceptable for some in the 1930s. The formality in dress of the Pleasure Beach crowd contrasted to the sea of cloth caps that dominated at the soccer matches of this era. Film archives show further the contrast in clothing between being "at home" and "on holiday." Scenes of street life in northern industrial towns taken on cameras attached to the front of trams show women and men dressed in workaday garb including clogs, shawls, long plain dragging skirts, mufflers rather than ties, and cloth caps or battered bowler

2.1   A formal crowd at the Pleasure Beach before the First World War. Courtesy of the Pleasure Beach, Blackpool.

hats. At Blackpool, the picture is very different: Film taken at the North Pier in 1904 show a very respectable and orderly crowd whose decorous promenading was so formal and stately as to be outside the bounds of the "playful."[19]

The look of Coney Island crowds was equally respectable. Even the "notorious" Bowery in both postcards and more objective photos showed a packed street, but of men in dark suits (even if most wore flat straw hats instead of the more formal bowler) and women in full length dresses and flowered hats. Groups of young women (in one photo three shown arm-in-arm displaying independence perhaps) defied older standards of decency, but they were clearly respectable in dress and were hardly "women of the street." Despite the size of the crowd on the beaches on a hot day in July 1902, the *New York World* could describe it as a "decorously orderly throng." Historian John Kasson's contrast between the informality displayed in the dress and body language of beach crowds at Coney and the stiff and proper look of street crowds in the business districts of Manhattan of this era made an interesting point: Coney let New Yorkers experiment with more relaxed and joyous ways of self expression. Still, this comparison did not address an equally important point—that working people who regularly dressed in work clothes that marked their status came to Coney's streets (if not its beaches) in their Sunday best.[20]

While the quest for respectability disguised the proletarian element in both Blackpool and Coney Island crowds, visual evidence sometimes did reveal the social heterogeneity of the throng. A film of 1904 shows a crowd near the entrance to Blackpool's South Pier that at first sight looks firmly middle class, but as the camera pans around contrasts appear. The display of good cloth, elaborate hats, and ornate floral dresses with expensive embroidery, elegant mustaches, cricket caps, starched shirts and ties gives way to a view of clothing that is less ornamental. Boaters replace floral hats on women and men appear in bowler hats. The overall impression is dowdier, although clean linen, that ultimate indicator of respectability, still predominates. Within a few yards again, the camera shows a portion of the crowd that appears further down-market, more masculine, older and more bewhiskered, wearing headgear no more elaborate than a basic cap.[21] All this suggests that the stories Edwardian Blackpool liked to tell about itself, that it was a socially mixed resort where the classes and genders could enjoy themselves side by side in harmony, contained a strong element of truth.

A representative piece of Blackpool publicity material, from 1928, describes it as:

> a good place for 'mixing'; by that I mean that it is a place without affectations of social dignity, of exclusiveness, of snobbery, for here you find represented every class of the community. The manual worker is there all right, and so are the clerk and the typist. So also are the tradesman, the solicitor, the parson; and so too not a few of those men and women whom the world calls gentlefolk. True, the pleasures of some may not be altogether the pleasures of others . . . it is here that one may find the heart of England presented in a scene which . . . one might go round the world to equal and fail in the attempt.[22]

Images of people in Coney postcards stressed the respectability of crowds and certainly show far fewer people than actually strolled the streets or shore on hot Sunday afternoons as seen in informal photos. And, though the poor are similarly hard to identify, cloth caps and open shirts appear mixed among the suits and straw hats. Equally, commentators saw in the Coney crowd an amazing degree of "democracy," a kind of leveling that the swimming suits and informality of the beach provided.

Clearly "mixing" and social leveling did not preclude respectability—so long as the wage earner imitated the gentility of social superiors in dress and behavior. The most basic marker of "decency," however, was whether a site was appropriate for respected females. Frederic Thompson bragged that he had the first "rowdy to have entered Luna Park soundly thrashed," telling him that "the place was not run for him, but for his mother and sister."[23] The hetero-social character of these parks placed restraints on gambling, drinking, aggression, and sexuality so characteristic of the mostly male (customer) sites like Norton's Point. To be respected, women could not be "bought" (as in renting a woman's body for intercourse or even fantasy gazing) and men had to "honor" them by not profaning them in speech and behavior.

This did not eliminate "excitement" or even sexual titillation. The seaside had become a setting for a new definition of "respectable" hetero-social interaction. From the 1870s, especially in the United States, young people had been experimenting on the beach with new, increasingly more revealing bodily display and playful gender behavior unseen elsewhere. Females "mount on men's shoulders and dive from them; they are dunked and floated and hugged by fellows of whom not infrequently they knew nothing at all and to whom they are often introduced but ten minutes before," noted a *New York Sun* reporter in 1877. "The opposite gender rush together at Coney Island and how they stay together and romp and tousle one another, and wrestle and frolic and maul each other, gray heads and youths alike, precisely as if the thing to do in the water was to behave exactly contrary to the manner of behaving anywhere else."[24]

Blackpool also provided a generally respectable setting in which relations between the sexes could be more relaxed and informal than at home. The Lancashire cotton towns, with their unusual opportunities for women in the labor market, were fabled for breeding outspoken and unpretentious women who were frequently staged in settings of courtship and flirtation portrayed as good clean fun. This was

2.2　　The Pleasures of the Human Toboggan. Note the respectable crowd of gawking guys. *Everybody's Magazine*, July 1908, 29.

revealed by dialect stories and Blackpool guides appealing to local audiences across industrial England. "A Leeds loiner's leap inta luv at Blackpool" is a suggestive title; but it was more about courtship than casual sex. This was probably even true of the couples on the sand dunes whose activities were discussed at length but in rather innocent, romantic language by "Teddy Ashton" (Allen Clarke) in a dialect guide to Blackpool, published in 1908: "Th' sandhills beyond South Shore are t'main resort o' t' sticky two-by-twos. On these sandhills an' th' cliffs up north, there's as much squeezin' goes on as at washin' day or in a steam laundry; for these rushy hillocks are full o' clippin' corners, snugglin' shades an' aw that soart o' temptation." When, thirty years later, the amateur anthropologists of Mass-Observation tried to test out

Blackpool's reputation for alfresco sex by checking out the behavior of couples on the beach, and surveying sexual activity more generally, they came up with disappointingly innocent results.[25]

The beach, and certainly the sea, played a smaller part in playful relations between the sexes at Blackpool than at Coney Island. Mixed bathing was slow to become accepted and, after the fairground on the sands lost its vitality under municipal regulation, the beach became a place for families to sit, fully and formally clothed, and children to play, and couples to cuddle, occasionally engaging in horseplay with a ball. This remained the case into the 1950s and 1960s. A rare glimpse of something more sensual and spontaneous comes on a home movie of 1929, which includes a clip of a large mixed party of young people in their late teens and early twenties, almost all bareheaded, tousle-haired and open-necked, sitting very close together and swaying as they sang to a ukulele and trombone. But there is nothing to match the vistas of exposed flesh, bathing dress as leisurewear and playful mugging to the camera that photographers captured at interwar Coney.[26]

At Coney Island subtle sex play on the sands (rather than swimming) defined the new exciting culture, offering a positive substitute to the male-dominant worlds of horse racing, boxing, burlesque, and brothel. As important, this culture drifted up onto Surf Avenue and into the amusement parks by the end of the nineteenth century. The result was a culture that from the outside seemed to threaten genteel standards of decency, but from within was still simultaneously playful and restrained. Just as in that other modern venue of hetero-social play, the dancehall, young women, who often traveled to Coney Island in groups, sometimes supplemented their relatively shallow pocketbooks by allowing male strangers who they met in the crowd to "treat" them with drinks and admission tickets in exchange for their usually brief innocent flirtations.[27]

The young writer Elmer Harris who visited Coney in the summer of 1908 well illustrates this restrained hetero-social playfulness in a story about a young working-class woman named Dora. Although she claimed "never to be afraid of a man who laughs," she was no floozy. She blissfully and quite unselfconsciously enjoyed the sensation of flying the "air ship," tried her skill at the "Human Roulette Wheel," and went with Harris to a dance hall. Through it all, she displayed an effortless self-mastery. While dancing, she gave Harris, "but the tips of her fingers, and, eyes half closed, lips parted, allowed herself to be wafted

2.3   Human Roulette Wheel (1908) at Steeplechase. A curiously posed and innocent image of this invitation to sensuality. Library of Congress.

away on the wings of the music." Then, asking him to look at something over his shoulder, she disappeared. Later Harris saw her waiting on the "L" platform for her train home, with her hands "folded on the window ledge, . . . looking at the lights of the Park in a kind of serene indifference to it, to me, and to all else about her."[28] This controlled pleasure-seeking was a seemingly common phenomenon. Rollin Hartt declared that "any well-seeming youngster may invite any girl to dance" at the seaside dance hall. A "proletarian jollity" required no "introductions," but a woman knew never to link up with "cavaliers not of her own station." Young women and men could in fact be more daring because of the "moral cleanness" of the place. It allowed them to let their guards down without fear of losing their honor.[29]

Much the same applied at Blackpool where young women enjoyed dancing, socializing, and flirtation without undue threat or stigma, despite the fears of moral reformers. Blackpool's Tower Ballroom and other pleasure palace dance floors offered opportunities both for friendship and romance in a carefully policed setting, while groups of young women could link arms and march assertively along the

2.4   The Pleasure Beach offered plenty of opportunities for friendly contact between the sexes, as in this
        example of an encounter between Australian soldiers and local women on the Witching Waves during
        World War 1. Courtesy of the Pleasure Beach, Blackpool.

promenade in line abreast, exchanging pleasantries with passing groups of young
men as they went along.[30]

Of course, as befitted this sort of liminal site, Blackpool and Coney possessed
largely undeserved reputations as centers of illicit sexual liaisons.[31] As early as 1872
the dialect writer Ben Brierley wrote a comic sketch about the reputation Blackpool had acquired for predatory women, especially widows, who tried to pick up
visiting men for lustful purposes.[32] A promotional film of 1924, offering a view of
a concert audience at the North Pier, included an inserted card with the legend,

"We offer no prizes should you recognise your husband here with somebody else's wife." This reputation was still there in the 1930s, which is why Mass-Observation thought it worth testing, and other evidence (including oral reminiscence) suggests that may have been more of it than they found, despite the concern of landladies to keep their houses respectable.[33] But neither Coney Island nor Blackpool were in fact "Sodoms by the Sea."

Both seaside settings were sites of romance and courtship, but not necessarily of sentimental family gatherings. King Vidor's silent film, *The Crowd* of 1928 opened with two male office mates picking up and treating two young women (whom they called "wrens") to an evening at Coney Island. The hero, John Simes, falls in love and marries his date. Several years after their romantic encounter at Coney Island, Vidor's story has the couple return, but this time with children in tow. The miserable and disillusioned mother has to pack and serve lunch to the kids while the dad plays the zither off by himself on the beach.[34] A more optimistic Blackpool story was Frank Tilsley's *Pleasure Beach*, whose main plot revolved around the courtship between an escapee from the Wigan coalmines to do seasonal work on the fairground, and an honest, direct, chaste local woman; but the story ends before childcare issues have the chance to cloud the relationship.[35]

Despite this, a common problem is revealed by these two stories: Although the popular resort could be both a site of respectability and hetero-social activity, the burden and expense of family dramatically reduced its appeal. In fact, Luna Park offered nursery services for "Tired Mothers" and claimed: "Babies No Longer A Bar to Pleasure." To be sure, between 1900 and 1920, children were present, but photos show them mostly at the seashore, not on the rides of Luna Park or even much on the slides and revolving discs of Steeplechase. Instead, they are found at the beach or splashing in the surf with their mothers while dad was at work.[36] The British writer E.V. Lucas, visiting Coney Island just after World War 1, was struck by "the absence of children from New York's 'safety-valve', as it was described to me. . . . It is as though once again the child's birthday gifts had been appropriated by its elders; but as a matter of fact the Parks of Steeplechase and Luna were, I imagine, designed deliberately for adults."[37]

At Blackpool, children were conspicuously few and far between on the films of piers and promenade at the turn of the century, and they were also remarkably rare in the Pleasure Beach photographs. There were more children present in the 1920s and 1930s, as Blackpool aimed to go up-market and attract young middle-class families with new parks and promenades, but their continued near absence from the Pleasure Beach remains telling. The 1928 official guide helps to explain: "For the children there is a splendid playground; equipped with miniature devices for creating health and happiness, where capable nurses watch over the youngsters. . . . Another section of this wonderful Pleasure Beach is devoted to children whose choice runs in the direction of more hilarious rides in tiny racers and mechanical contrivances."[38] This underlines the broader point that the entertainments of Coney Island and Blackpool were not particularly oriented toward family. Youth (and occasionally older couples, particularly at Blackpool) predominated. While Coney Island and the Pleasure Beach provided separate supervised amusement areas for children, the dominant objective of management was to cater to young adult males, both restrained and vitalized by interaction with respectable women.[39]

This, however, did not make Blackpool and Coney "adult" and thus serious places. In fact, this seemingly contradictory combination of playfulness and respectability went beyond offering a controlled sensuality: It gave adults permission to act like children. This stepping into boyhood and girlhood released psychological and physical tension; it largely replaced the traditional saturnalian rituals that were often violent, barely veiled attacks on social norms with playing the child. This made these crowds more individualistic and, in the end, far less threatening to elites than the old festival gatherings had been.

Luna Park's Frederic Thompson was especially aware of this dimension of the popular resort of 1900: "People are just boys and girls grown tall. Elaborated child's play is what they want on a holiday." Park amusements are "nothing more than improved cellar doors" that adults loved to swing on when they were children. The cellar door that swung into the darkness within made children shiver "for a little while there in the black—and then [they] issued forth again with a strange exultance." This quest for the simple joys of childhood suggested to Thompson that "all people are primitive in their tastes and pleasures. . . . Suspense, thrill and—grateful satisfaction—this is the body and the spirit of all amusement, high, low and middle-browed." These "grown-up children want new toys all the time," Thompson believed and thus he endeavored to provide continuous novelty.[40]

This aesthetic philosophy may have been found wanting to the genteel writers of the day, but Thompson was certainly not alone in this assessment. Edward Tilyou, son of the founder of Steeplechase Park, remarked in 1922 that because most people "look back on childhood as the happiest period of their lives . . . this is the mental attitude they like to adopt" at the amusement park. As youth increasingly became a time in life when parents indulged their offspring, adults identified the child-like with self-indulgence. Coney Island reinforced the hedonistic consumerist side of capitalism rather than its rational and productive side. As sociologist Colin Campbell notes, this modern hedonism was less about physical pleasures than the longing for the new. Playful novelty in its place was no longer merely the frivolous, suitable in male eyes only for women and children. It became a man's right too, an entitlement to pleasure, an escape from the obligations of providing, career-ladder climbing, and work.[41]

This Peter Pantheism, as Woody Register calls it, provided the rationale for times of playfulness that the adult male world of work, achievement, and responsibility denied. It offered an alternative to the seemingly mature male goal, "to elevate the spirit, instruct the mind, and purify the body." But it also released the Peter Pan from the normal constraints of economic rationality. When an adult played the child, there was no need to fulfill concerns beyond immediate delight. Again as Thompson stressed: "To keep up the carnival spirit everybody must be on the 'go.' The moment a crowd of folk. . . . catch this spirit they walk faster, they laugh, they spend money." Spending on the "child," even if it was the child "within" was becoming respectable to the middle class and it was no less attractive to working people. It was acceptable because it was consistent with female decency (unlike old cross-class male pleasures like whoring and gambling). Even more, grownup boys and girls could play without violating the still prevailing genteel standards because they were only being "children."[42]

How Coney and Blackpool Created Playful Crowds

What made the crowd playful were the sensual cues created by the seaside resort and amusement park themselves. Frederic Thompson made this point plain: "The difference between the theater and the big amusement park is the difference between the Sunday-school and the Sunday-school picnic. The people are the same; the spirit and environment are wholly different." The amusement park, he insisted, was an environment "designed to give the natural, bubbling animal spirits of the human being full play, to give people something fresh and new and unusual, to afford them respite from the dull routine of their daily lives." The "spirit of gai-

2.5   Night at Luna Park (1905) revealing the mystery of "Oriental" architecture in Frederic Thompson's whimsical tower combined with electric illumination. Detroit Publishing, Library of Congress

ety," Thompson noted "almost always . . . is manufactured." In fact, "Theatrically speaking, architecture is nothing more than scenery. . . . " setting the stage for the mood of the crowd.[43] Certainly, Walt Disney would embrace all this a half century later. Thompson's job as designer of Luna Park was to tantalize the senses with the gaudy, garish, and unexpected. But, he hardly invented this idea. A decade before his Luna Park was built, F. S. Mines described Coney Island this way: "The architecture is suggestive of a western mining camp in its palm days with a most wonderful leaning toward the Moorish. Here and there, at all turns are Alhambraic turrets and minarets, garish decorations and gilded domes utterly at variance with each other."[44]

Thompson took these dazzling displays to new heights. Not only did he use electric lights to outline his towers, domes, and minarets, giving these strange oriental shapes an even more mysterious and magical air at night, but he dared to "jumble Romanesque with l'art nouveau." Historian John Kasson dubbed this style as "Super-Saracenic or Oriental Orgasmic." Thompson even used tradition to mock itself. He festooned his Electric Tower with hearts and topped it with what looked like an upside-down-ice cream cone in parody of the pretension of the Column of Progress at the St. Louis World's Fair. Thompson proudly claimed that he presented visitors with the architecture of "Fairy Picture-Books—Toy-Lands elaborated by adult hands." Even the stately Spanish Renaissance architecture of Dreamland was interrupted with cartoon-like sculptures of modern firefighters at the Fire and Flames building. And the carousel at Steeplechase featured not the traditional horses, but chickens and ostriches to ride.[45] As art historian Michele Bogart put it, "Coney Island's lavish architectural and sculptural arrangements were designed to contribute to a riotous, carnival atmosphere. Along the way they helped to nurture indifference and even resistance to the elite values that official civic sculpture sought to transmit." This visual frivolity encouraged a playful mood in the gazing crowd, even if it also discouraged physical expressions of that playfulness.[46]

This theme was less pronounced at Blackpool. Just as the range of fantasy entertainment offered at the Pleasure Beach was less spectacular or challenging to mainstream English Protestant values than some of the Coney Island extravaganzas, so the architecture of the English resort was more prosaic than the fanciful towers of Dreamland or Luna Park. It was more difficult to sustain ephemeral frivolity in brick, steel and concrete than to throw it together in "staff." That is not to say that Blackpool's pleasure architecture was orthodox. The Tower itself has been represented as a phallic symbol, a demonstration of the hard virility of England's industrial north of manufacturing and mining against the effete south of money manipulation; but this seems a little too fanciful.[47]

Still, Oriental motifs, evoking imperial otherness, were prevalent everywhere in Blackpool's pleasure palaces in the decades either side of the turn of the century, with minarets and onion domes in glorious profusion on the North Pier pavilion, at the Pleasure Beach with its "Moorish" Casino without gambling, at the Alhambra on the central promenade, and within the Tower itself. Still, the overwhelming impression given by Blackpool's architecture was the monotony of the serried streets of stucco-fronted terraced boardinghouses to accommodate the visitors, and these were essentially oversized ordinary Lancashire redbrick homes. Luna Park's architectural fantasy was echoed only in the stage scenery of the Pleasure Beach shows, the lavish interiors of pubs and theaters, and (and especially after 1925) the autumn electrical Illuminations, which eventually stretched along four miles of promenade. In general terms, however, Blackpool's pleasure architecture was neither as flimsy nor as fanciful as the strange eclectic structures that dominated the scene at Coney Island. In fact, by the late 1930s the town's image was defined more by the smooth, swooping Art Deco styles associated with Joseph Emberton's makeover of the Pleasure Beach on clean, modern lines, and matched elsewhere by the new Woolworth store and the Derby swimming baths, than by the glorious free-for-all epitomized by the Coney amusement parks. Blackpool's architecture was less central to creating the mood than the crowd and entertainments themselves.[48]

While Luna Park's Thompson tried to create an excitement through his fantasy architecture, he knew that this release of emotions would not lead to wanton behavior as assumed by many moralists. There was no need to preach to these crowds for at the popular resort "you are dealing with a moral people," Thompson insisted, not suggestible mobs with uncontrolled libidos. That meant that there was no need to subdue or worry about overstimulating them. And it also meant that though "Coney Island is frisky. . . . It knows where to draw the line, and this knowledge is largely the result of the lessons given by the crowds themselves. . . . Innocent play is a moral antiseptic."[49] This is actually a quite radical claim, in its rejection of the traditional religious doctrine of concupiscence and recognition that the diffusion of desire across a wide array of stimulations at the amusement park in effect made crowds playful but peaceful and self-constrained.[50] Thompson understood that childlike appeals, a largely visual sensuality, and boisterousness were brakes on promiscuity and mob behavior.

All this applied equally to Blackpool in general and the Pleasure Beach in particular. James Laver emphasized the essential innocence and childishness of the pleasures offered:[51]

A Pleasure Beach is a wonderful institution, full of every kind of harmless amusement that the brain of man can devise. . . . How simple are human pleasures after all! To hurtle down a slippery slope on a doormat, to rise in the air on a flying machine firmly tethered to its central pin, to ride a horse, or a bird, or a dragon, round and round for ever to the sound of music which fatigues no musician for it is all produced by a steam-engine, to throw balls at coco-nuts, or rubber rings at brightly coloured vases, to angle for goldfish, to turn the handles of peepshows—all 'Passed by the New York Board of Censors'—to eat ice-cream and toffee-apples—does not this list contain within itself, as it were in miniature, the sum total of possible human pleasures? . . . It is the final solution of the periodical need for an orgy, a safety-valve for the high spirits of mankind.

Dangers, Intimacies, and Fantasies of Amusement Parks

Neither Coney Island nor Blackpool worried at all about overstimulating the crowd on any of their attractions, certainly not mechanical rides. This was especially evident at Steeplechase's Pavilion. Many rides there were little more than adult-sized playground equipment. The trick staircase, Earthquake Floor, and House Upside Down appealed to a childlike delight in the unexpected. The Wedding Ring was a wooden circle suspended from a center pole that functioned like a children's park swing but for seventy adults. Similar was the Scrambler, a circular dished floor, which when spun thrust oval cars on coasters outward from the center, tossing their fun-seeking inhabitants into one another. A simple novelty was a gigantic slide in the shape of a smoking pipe. Even the Steeplechase ride was, as Kasson describes it, "essentially a hobbyhorse for adults, which provided a simple but giddy sense of transport as the mechanical steeds galloped along their inclined tracks." The thrill of having one's body buffeted about recalls not only the child's "roughhousing" and the youth's physical joy at bumping into others, but the infant's experience of being bounced and tossed by an caring adult. Although these rides might evoke "anxiety as in fear of falling and seasickness," as Edwin Slosson wrote in 1904, when the "sense of equilibrium" is merely "gently excited, [it] gives a sensation of pleasure."[52]

The sensation was more than physical. The more sophisticated rides both imitated and parodied the latest mechanical contrivances, simultaneously evoking and assuaging people's fears of them. Luna Park's Tickler comically parodied modern

2.6   Blackpool's pleasure architecture was much less extravagant than that of Coney, as the utilitarian, almost industrial nature of the machinery on show here brings out. The scene is more reminiscent of a coal mine than a fairground. Courtesy of the Pleasure Beach, Blackpool.

2.7   The Loop the Loop of 1903, an independent attraction that promised an unearthly thrill, soon superseded by longer and more elaborate rides. Detroit Publishing, Library of Congress.

urban traffic when up to eight passengers seated in spinning circular cars rolled down a twisting alley, running into posts and other cars on the way. Kasson notes how the twists and undulations of the roller coaster imitated the recently constructed elevated trains, turning the daily monotony of the ride to work into a playful mockery .[53]

Another ride toyed with a common contemporary fear, the head-on train crash. On Dreamland's Leap Frog railroad two cars coming from opposite directions seemed just about to collide into one another when they passed alternatively over or under the other with the help of pairs of bent rails on the top of each car. A contemporary describes how "The passengers in breathless excitement momentarily anticipate disaster, realizing that their lives are in jeopardy, clinging to one another for safety, closing their eyes to the impending danger. . . . The cars crash into one another, 32 people are hurled over the heads of 32 others. . . . They are suddenly awakened to the realization of the fact that they have actually collided with another car and yet they find themselves safe and sound."[54] As in so many other aspects of the amusement park, the Leap Frog teased the crowd with a boundary experience. Rollin Hartt saw that "the bright face of danger, challenging the eternal juvenile within you, seems—exactly as in years gone by—to be taunting, 'Fraidycat!' . . . You utter the cry of a tiny boy, 'Scare me again! Scare me—scare me worse!'"[55]

Vertigo and simulated danger were not the only thrills. Peter Pan morphed into a childish Casanova when rides became opportunities for a snuggle or even a kiss. Arthur Laycock's dialect narrative of 1909 about two courting couples from Lancashire taking a day-trip to the Pleasure Beach, enjoying "fun an' frolic" on the various rides, illustrates this theme well. The narrator, Sally, is anxious to secure a marriage proposal from Sam, and uses the Pleasure Beach rides to advance intimacy. The young women are "donned up loike duchesses," and disposed to join in alongside the other couples who are clinging to each other during the rides, and kissing in the darkness. On the water chute: "Eh! What a scream we set up as we splashed an' dashed, an' bumped an' jumped o'er th' rowlin' waves. I were cobbed [thrown] clean on to Jimmy's knee—Jane Ann said I did it o'purpose—but Sam soon pood (pulled) me back. . . ." And then in the "Cats-an'-Clamour [Katzenjammer] Castle," Sally kisses the wrong man in the dark.[56] This is a reminder that John Urry's much quoted concept of the "tourist gaze" was only part of the story, where other senses and sensations could, indeed, thrive on temporary darkness.[57]

At Steeplechase, the Human Roulette Wheel, the Whirlpool, and the Human Pool Table were all variations on the same theme—throwing bodies in all directions and often into the flesh of a member of the opposite sex. A British visitor in 1912 reported that when he slid down Steeplechase's "long bumpy slide," "you did get awfully messed up with other people as you went down—strange girl's arms around your neck and everybody calling everybody else a silly ass." And the Human Pool Table "certainly makes you acquainted with a lot of people without being introduced to 'em." Upon exiting the Steeplechase ride, a couple had to go through a dark passage called the "dog house" on their hands and knees and then onto a brightly lit stage, at one point called the "Insanitarium." There, the woman found her dress blown up by compressed air from holes in the floor while a clown stuck her male friend's backside with an electric prod and a dwarf whacked it with a slapstick. As they made their escape, the couple had to pass along a sliding floor and a pile of barrels that seemed to be just about to fall over their heads as they scrambled for safety—all in front of a crowd who had just experienced the same thing.[58] The importance of watching other people's petty humiliations and bodily exposure, especially after undergoing them oneself, was a significant aspect of the amusement park's appeal, and photographs and films of the Joy Wheel and Helter Skelter in action at Blackpool underline how the voyeur's gaze added to the pleasure of the occasion.[59]

All of these experiences pushed shy couples into physical contact with each other, encouraging them to let down their bodily inhibitions much in the way that the horseplay on the beach did. These children of Victorian self-repression found all this liberating and even the occasion for a "safe" form of intimacy that their much regulated lives denied, all in the public and unserious setting of the amusement park. Even the whimsical embarrassment of the Insanitarium induced a playful response that doubtless led to flirtatious behavior. At the Shoot the Chutes, notes Slosson, "the apparent risk gives one a sense of personal daring very gratifying to us all, and as each boat load plunges down the chutes into the lagoon this finds expression in a cry for protection from feminine, and an answering shout of triumph from masculine, throats." Even more "a sudden clutch of his arm when the boat goes through the mill-race has often brought a young man to realize how pleasant it would be to have the right to protect and cheer the maiden by his side."[60]

Improved designs made these thrill rides ever more central to the amusement park, eclipsing the costly spectacles of Luna Park in the 1920s. The Wonder Wheel of 1920 stood 150 feet high, carrying 169 passengers. New rides like the Gyroplane and Dodgem cars appeared in the 1920s too at Coney Island. Roller coasters became the thrill ride of choice because they could become ever more "dangerous" and breath-taking, as, for example, when the giant Thunderbolt in 1925 was soon superseded by the even higher and faster Cyclone racer.[61] This child-like play at the seaside resort of 1900, and indeed 1930, was supposed to thrill and titillate. It often touched on or suggested physical danger or sexuality, but was just far enough removed from both to give release and pleasure, rather than anxiety or fear.

2.8   This promotional postcard, issued by Blackpool Pleasure Beach in 1925, illustrates
       the attractiveness and acceptability of controlled voyeurism as part of the pleasures
       of the fairground. Courtesy of the Pleasure Beach, Blackpool

All this was true of another dimension of amusement, the fantasy environments that visitors saw on the Streets of Delhi or the Canals of Venice, at the site of Fire and Flame, on the space ship Trip to the Moon, or, by boat, through Hell's Gate. Coney Island provided many replicas of exotic places, filling them with dark people dressed in "native costume." Frederic Thompson even offered the visitor the choice of riding an elephant or camel through his "Delhi." British and Americans longed for the sights, sounds, and smells of places and peoples of which they had only read about in magazines and newspapers. Though, as historian Daniel Boorstin notes, in an oft-cited critique of this pseudo tourism, these replicas were always marred with demeaning and unauthentic stereotypes that deprived crowds of discovery and true adventure, they gave otherwise immobile people a taste for a world beyond their narrow lives.[62] A popular quest for the realistic and immediate experience of dramatic events and (less often) beautiful sites prompted the attractions that replicated, in miniature, disasters like the Johnstown and Galveston floods of 1889 and 1900. The wall of water from a broken dam rushing over Johnstown Pennsylvania graphically showed the "crashing down of houses, churches, stores and mills, and piling them up in a heap of debris against the bridge." The spectacle of the Fall of Pompeii offered not only its own Roman Building, but also "new inventions" and promised that "real fire belches forth from the interior of the earth."[63]

On a life-sized scale was Dreamland's spectacle Fighting the Flames (an elaboration of a similar dramatization first seen at Luna Park). Four times a day, an audience from grandstand seats watched the burning of an artificial six-story tenement (wood on an iron frame) from across a street. Involving a reputed cast of 2,000, the show began with a fire breaking out on the ground floor. The dwellers panicked, climbing floor to floor to flee the flames, when 120 fire fighters arrived with four fire engines and hook and ladder trucks. While many people escaped the fire and smoke by jumping into nets, others fled onto the roof only to be saved by firemen from scaling ladders just before the roof caved in. The ever present fear of audience members, who themselves often dwelled in unsafe tenements, was exorcized and displaced when they watched with horror and pleasure the dangers faced by others.[64]

A very different narrative experience was Frederic Thompson's Trip to the Moon. Based on the principles of the cyclorama, this ride gave passengers the illusion of space travel. Reminiscent of Georges Méliès's silent film by the same name, the attraction combined popular views of space travel, at a time when airplanes had just been invented, with children's storybook fantasy. In a procedure familiar

2.9   "Fighting the Flames." The original caption read: "Trained fire-fighters attack sham conflagrations
       in a city block made of iron scenery. The fire-engines are real, the horses are real, the water is real."
       Munsey's Magazine, May 1907, 558

to anyone who has been to Disney World, the ride began with a mood-setting orientation from a guide presumably from the Aerial Navigation Company who explained in pseudo-scientific jargon about the secrets of "anti-gravitation and aerial flight." The crowd then filed through a narrow passage onto the "Luna," a cigar-shaped moon ship, equipped with red canvas bat-like wings and suspended by guide wires. Excitement rose when the ship made "a long undulating motion." Electric fans gave the sensation of forward movement when they blew air in the faces of passengers. And moving painted canvases and projections appearing through portholes made New York City seem to be receding, eventually becoming a cluster of blinking lights. Finally the Earth became a mere ball. Then, everything went dark when the Luna went through a storm as lightning flashed and fierce rain poured on an overhead awning. Then stars appeared along with the Man in the Moon. The ship seemed to land in a "yawning hole in the moon's side, the crater of an extinct volcano" passengers were told. Then the doors opened and the travelers were greeted by midget "Selenites," who with their "queer twitterings," offered the earthlings green cheese. The crowd was then led down a passage, this time bordered by "illuminated foliage of fantastic trees and toadstool growths," to the palace of the Man in the Moon and his Throne Room. There, surrounded by "huge jewels and masses of gold and weird vistas and abysses," they watched moon maid dancers amid lights and fountains. The naïveté of this spectacle immediately strikes the modern reader. But sophisticated visitors, including Thomas Edison and President William McKinley, were said to have enjoyed the "Trip." In fact, 400,000 people paid the hefty sum of 50 cents admission during its first year (1901) at the Buffalo exhibition. Twice that number took the Trip in its first year in Coney Island (at Steeplechase), and 4.3 million during its five-year run at Luna Park.[65] So long lasting was the concept that it was copied in Disneyland's Rocket to the Moon. The Trip to the Moon offered a curious, but also attractive combination of appeals to scientific progress and a playful, only half serious, romantic fantasy.

Darker fears were addressed in the illusions of journey into death and the afterlife. The spectacle Night and Morning had patrons enter a dark oblong room that turned out to represent a huge coffin. Through a glass ceiling, guests saw weeping willows and flowers and had the sensation that the "coffin" was sinking into a grave. A lid appeared to close over the glass ceiling and the sound of dirt above could be heard dropping on the "coffin." This dramatic anticipation of one's own funeral was followed by a tour of Hell and sites of the resurrection. On a similar adventure into the afterlife, Dreamland's Hell's Gate gave the strolling crowd a view of passengers in boats circling and dipping into a whirlpool that led to a mysterious grotto, creating a great curiosity to join in this tantalizing ride through Hell. As Rollin Hartt describes it:

> With certain highly Dantesque forebodings, you embark. Slowly grimly, your circling boat drifts nearer that atrocious abyss. . . . Then a rush, a sinking of the heart, a sound of grinding wood, and a plunge down a twisted cataract into chaos and resounding night. With your whole soul you combat fear, even transform it into joy. 'Hail, horror! Hail, infernal world!' And now you laugh. Light comes, and with it red devils amid flames, volcanoes spitting fire, gorgeous grottoes all dripping with stalactites, and—very soothing to the eschatological emotions—icebergs and polar bears. Gradually your retrace the spiral, traversing the canals built just under those of the preliminary whirlpool, and finally come out upon a little quay, rich in varied grotesqueries."[66]

The modern spirit which ignores death and denies Hell had not yet made this sort of ride sick and tasteless. But even Hell, like all the horrible and dangerous places and activities that resort goers experienced in the 1900s, was saturated with playfulness.

The Pleasure Beach at Blackpool, and even the smaller and less regulated shows of the "Golden Mile," chose not to adopt the themes of disaster, space travel and Hell. By contrast, fantasy or virtual travel, in the form of the vicarious enjoyment of versions of other lands and their spectacular environments, was entirely acceptable. The River Caves of the World, for example, arrived at the Pleasure Beach from Coney Island, via London's Earls Court, as early as 1905, and was highly successful. So was the Scenic Railway, which opened two years later. Even the Monitor and Merrimac naval battle show, despite its American theme, lasted from 1910 to 1922, although it was augmented by patriotic British content from 1914. But the disaster re-creation themes of Coney Island were entirely absent. There was a short-lived Model Colliery exhibit in 1906, but never a mine disaster: British audiences would have found that too close to home. The Trip to the Moon failed to put in an appearance. Hell was present only in the Dante's Inferno section of the Scenic Railway, and here it could be represented as primarily a literary rather than a religious concept. The only direct allusion to Bible stories came with the arrival of Noah's Ark in 1921 (essentially a "fun house"). But the Pleasure Beach preferred to concentrate on the sort of ride that put people in unexpected motion, buffeted them, challenged their equilibrium, threw them together with companions or strangers, exposed their underwear in amusing rather than threatening ways, and otherwise made a spectacle of them.[67]

British entertainment providers, usually in touch with popular tastes and preferences, were selective in what they brought in. The lack of disasters may be connected with the vulnerability of important sections of the visiting public to real disaster striking the workplace. This applied especially to coalminers.[68] On the other hand, the tenement fires, primitive Towering Infernos, offered less immediacy and empathy to an English public who lived in two- and three-story terraced houses. Probably more important was the fact that gruesome themes were capable of generating controversy, which the Pleasure Beach, vulnerable in its early years to external regulation, did not wish to court.

This applied even more clearly to the religious issue. Most of Blackpool's visitors may not have been regular churchgoers, but almost all had passed through Sunday School as children. Many had been taught in church-run day schools. There was a strong and vocal vein of Nonconformity (dissident Protestantism outside the Anglican Church) which was particularly hostile to entertainment that seemed to burlesque religious ideas. Americans (especially from the immigrant communities of New York) were awed by visions of Hell, welcoming a psychological release in a playful treatment of this theme. By contrast, in England a relative religious consensus and a widely shared sense of the seemly made Hell's Gate unacceptable. Protestant Nonconformity was a strong minority force in local politics, with its own newspaper, the *Blackpool Times*. Offering, in frivolous vein, a trip to Hell on the Pleasure Beach would have invited censure in a culture where these Protestant groups were already powerful opponents of Sunday entertainments and of public dancing.[69]

The Abiding Appeal of the Freak

In a 1904 article, Edwin Slosson claimed that the old custom of gawking at human freaks of nature was in decline: "Living skeletons, bearded ladies, five-legged calves and the like have almost disappeared. Dwarfs are still in demand, but not the ugly and misshapened kind." In an otherwise prescient study, this assessment was, at best, very premature.[70] That year, the presumably upscale and genteel Dreamland Park opened Lilliputia, a "city" of midgets, who lived in a half-sized ersatz Nuremberg of the fifteenth century, complete with red-peaked roofs. The dwarfs had their own beach, complete with small lifeguard, and even a fire department that responded hourly to a false alarm. For a time Lilliputia included the famous widow of "General" Tom Thumb, Lavinia Warren, and her second husband, whose Lilliputian Opera Company performed regularly. The site was supposed to attract children especially and provided special rides for kids on saddle ponies and in small cabs, carriages, and even toy autos. Its impresario was the showman Samuel Gumpertz who became famous for bringing 212 Bantoc tribesmen from the Philippines in 1905. In their "authentic villages," these people demonstrated the use of blow guns and made wire crafts for those curious about the "natives" of America's new colony. Gumpertz opened his Dreamland Circus Sideshow after Dreamland burned. He imported 125 Somali "warriors" who rubbed blue clay into self-inflicted wounds to still the pain. He also introduced Ubangi women whose lips were enlarged and shaped by implanted wooden disks and Burmese women with necks elongated up to a foot by stacks of brass rings. Over a 25-year period, Gumpertz claimed to have passed 3,800 exotic "natives" through immigration.

Not to be outdone Luna Park displayed in 1904 the Igarotes, the "most savage nation of our Western Island," (The Philippines). Elsewhere, O.K. White exhibited an aged member of P. T. Barnum's freak show, "What is It?," a black American, said to have been captured on the River Gambia and brought to America as the "missing link" between monkeys and man. Known also as "Zip," he had an oblong skull and a tuft of hair at the top of his "pinhead," and was often dressed in a monkey suit. He remained a cult figure at Coney Island until his death at 84 in 1926. Well-known acts preferred Coney Island to the inconvenience of traveling with the circus side show. Among Gumpertz's vaunted performers was the muscle man, Charles Atlas, the Blue Man (whose skin was tinted by the ingestion of silver nitrate that eventually killed him), Ursa, the Bear Girl, and Rob Roy, an albino.[71]

In 1916, Gumpertz bought New York's Eden Musée and relocated it next to his Coney Island freak show. Here, he displayed all the "traditional" wax museum figures from history. Writers Oliver Pilat and Jo Ranson claimed in 1941 that audiences showed little interest in the really valuable exhibits (e.g. death masks of Martin Luther, Queen Elizabeth I, and Beethoven) and "preferred heroes to be exciting rather than significant." Visitors paid to see wax reproductions of real freaks because they could stare without embarrassment. "Historical" exhibits featured

2.10   The Midget City or "Lilliputia" of Dreamland with its look of medieval Nuremburg, ca 1904. Courtesy of the Brooklyn Historical Society.

The Horrors of the Spanish Inquisition, The Whipping Post, and The Burning of the Frontier Woman, as well as The Martyred Christians. When challenged that his shows had a ghoulish appeal, Gumpertz replied: "All these scenes, I insist, are moral lessons." His exhibit featuring Chinese in scenes of opium dens, public beheadings, and torture chambers provoked a complaint by the Chinese Consul General in 1929, but Gumpertz refused to change his display, claiming that his portrayals were merely historical. His wax museum also included new displays especially a tableau dramatizing the story of Ruth Snyder and Judd Gray whose love affair in 1927 led to their murdering the woman's husband. This crime and the execution of Ruth in the Electric Chair (based on a notorious photo smuggled out of the Death House) were displayed in wax to amazed crowds.[72]

Blackpool's answer to Gumpertz was not the Pleasure Beach's W. G. Bean, who was anxious to distance himself from such degrading spectacles. It was Luke Gannon, a downscale impresario of freaks and curiosities who attracted a lot of public-

2.11   The Igarote "primitives" of Dreamland in native costume observed behind fences by curious New Yorkers. Courtesy of the Brooklyn Historical Society.

ity (and opposition from the local government). His fame culminated in the mid-1930s when he exhibited a fasting honeymoon couple, "Colonel Barker" (a woman who presented herself as a man) and "his or her bride," a show that appealed to a curiosity in the boundaries of sexual identity. Gannon also featured a defrocked Church of England Rector, who had been ejected from his living at the Norfolk village of Stiffkey for consorting with prostitutes. Presumably in order to fund a protest of his innocence, he appeared on the Golden Mile fasting in a glass case and later lying "amid the flames of an artificial hell where he was being prodded with forks." Gannon had his competitors in the same area of the central promenade: in 1933 a visitor from Liverpool complained to central government about a "most degrading exhibition" featuring a "young woman enclosed in a narrow glass coffin, supposed to be doing a 32 days fast," and alleged to be fading away. "I expect the fast is a fraud, and I hope it is so, but the effect is the same on the sightseers as if they believe it to be genuine." The show, conducted by Albert Chapman, also offered a man 7 feet, 10 inches tall, a dwarf, and a girl in a barrel. Gannon's shows, like Chapman's, were cheap, tawdry, and prurient; and the fasting theme was far from original: such shows were being advertised in the traveling showground newspaper *World's Fair* before the First World War.[73]

The "Golden Mile" on Blackpool's Central Promenade, between the main excursion station and the most popular of the piers, had a history of freak shows (two-headed giantesses and the like) going back at least to the 1880s. This area was also a center for phrenology and fortune-telling. In 1937 Mr. Ellis could be found on the promenade as he had been for 45 years offering the ancient arts of reading head shapes as well as "pathognomy, graphology, astrology, numerology and occult science." The Golden Mile also boasted two fortune tellers claiming to be the "Real Gypsy Smith." This traditional longing for knowledge of one's fate was updated with the "Telepathic Robot, the Scientific Miracle" and other fortune-telling machines in the 1930s. Representations of exotic regions and religions survived also into this decade: A spieler, introduced as "Explorer Evans," tried to pull in crowds to see the "Ashanti War Chief" whose "black face is painted in white blue lines" while a "skull hangs from his waist." And, at the south end of the Pleasure Beach, the Indian Theatre offered the exotic performances of an old fakir in "slight loin cloth" who always seemed to be praying and "Gogia Pasha" who combined acrobatics and even tap dancing with "Indian" magic tricks. Elsewhere a yogi laid on a bed of nails for fifteen hours a day doing "penance" in preparation for the next life. And, finally, Blackpool too had its wax shows, Tussaud's classic Chamber of Horrors as well as the Museum of Anatomy (featuring displays of pregnancy, child birth, and especially the physical affects of venereal diseases). While the prurient was an obvious attraction, it was clothed in the language both of science and morality. At the Museum of Anatomy under a wax head and neck of a woman distorted by venereal disease was a label warning that "The wages of sin is death." Although physically at the core of Blackpool as popular resort, the "Golden Mile," however revealing it might be, it was morally peripheral to the resort as a whole. It was more a part of Blackpool's legend than its life.[74]

To the modern western eye, the appeal of freak and wax shows seems grotesque, cruel, and primitive. But there was much more to them than the gawking at human tragedy. The appeal of the marginal certainly has had many roots: Leslie Fielder saw in adults' willingness to pay to peer at giants, dwarfs, and hermaphrodite recollections from childhood of anxious confusion about their own size or sexuality. Others argued that in viewing the freak, the audience recognized themselves as "normal" even as the freak showed audiences how really "normal" freaks were.[75]

Since the mid-nineteenth century, freaks had been far more than stereotypes. Instead, their lives were personalized in *cartes de visite* (small photos on cardboard with printed descriptions of the freaks' condition and biographies). American showmen stressed lurid details and made exaggerated and false claims: African Americans were represented as headhunters from Borneo or wild men raised by animals from Africa. Impresarios often gave dwarfs mocking names like General or Queen and forced the obese to wear dainty little girl clothes or clown suits. At the same time, many freaks were portrayed as normal people, except for the accident of their birth. Showmen in the U.S. arranged for their "marriages," displayed Bearded Ladies doing needle point on stage, and publicized their religious beliefs and personal accomplishments.[76]

Crowds found conjoined twins especially fascinating because of the stories they generated. Curiosity about their marriages and contrasting personalities appealed to audiences from the mid-nineteenth into the twentieth century. The sexually ambivalent—hermaphrodites dressed half as women and half as men—drew throngs. This interest extended to the freaks of evolution and culture. Enchantment with headhunters, wild men or "geeks" who ate chickens raw, "missing links" like "Zip," and feral children like Jo-Jo the Dog-faced Boy, presumably raised by a wolf, all reinforced the ideology of European superiority. Of course, the reassuring message of racial hierarchy was clothed in the language of science and discovery, but the fascination went much deeper than this. Sometimes the appeal of the freak was in the creature's association with the mysterious, especially oriental culture that many westerners believed was somehow more sensitive to the supernatural. This sentiment explains why Luna Park in 1904 brought a "sacred five-legged white cow" to Coney from Ceylon. Thompson hyped it as the "most revered of all Hindu idols" and claimed that "her sojourn to the New World. . . . cast an impenetrable gloom over the Hindu race."[77] Crowd wonder at the creature on the boundary of the natural world was part of a traditional religious fascination with the supernatural.

While as we shall see this sensibility was losing adherents in the middle classes, what is striking is just how wide was this appeal at the opening of the twentieth century, often curiously intertwined with science. Perhaps the best example of how this blending of the seemingly modern and uplifting with traditional fascination with the supernormal was Dr. Martin Arthur Couney's "Infant Incubators" at Coney. This Paris-trained physician, whose new technology and procedure for treating premature babies in the 1890s was resisted in European hospitals, financed his research and therapy by displaying his incubators at international exhibitions. The display of infant incubators at London's Earls Court in 1897 was reviewed favorably in *The Lancet* and was said to have attracted large numbers of interested nurses; but it did not reach the British seaside.[78]

After traveling to twenty-three fairs from Berlin, Rio, Moscow, and finally the United States at the Buffalo Exhibition in 1901, Couney took up residence at Coney. First, he was featured at Luna Park and Dreamland, but then set up his "hospital" as a separate attraction that survived until the 1940s. Despite his scientific and philanthropic purposes, the display also evoked the "magic" of folk tradition. His exhibit attracted thousands with a building that recalled a German farmhouse with a tiled roof and a basket of babies in terra cotta over the front gable. As a progressive, Dr. Couney insisted that all visitors (at 20 cents admission) hear a detailed lecture on the workings and benefits of his incubators and procedures before viewing the "premies." Admission fees paid for the costs of the two to three months of care that he provided the tiny infants (including piped-in heat and oxygen, filtered air, and professional wet nurses who were prohibited from eating any Coney junk food). Couney claimed that he saved some 7,500 of the 8,500 premies under his care during the forty years he was in business at Coney Island.

Most were children of mothers too poor to afford alternative care. His exhibit attracted mostly women who often discussed among themselves the babies' "relative merits and compared them with other babies of their acquaintance, including vivid memories of their own." The childless, especially, came week after week to check in on babies' progress. Yet, despite the philanthropic and scientific appeal, Couney's infant incubators were still a freak show, being merely a somewhat updated and more hygienic version of Meade's Midget Hall where paying visitors gawked at the wonder of tiny babies fighting for survival against nature's trickery.[79]

The playful crowds that weaved their way through the attractions of Coney Island and Blackpool were looking for both release from tensions and stimulation of the imagination and senses. They shared with their ancestors many saturnalian customs: social inversion, mockery, and a fascination with the supernatural and abnormal, but they did so with industrial means in novelty mechanical rides, fantastic exhibits, and the playful but often innocent sexuality of attractions like the Human Roulette Wheel. While they found their neighbors there, especially in Blackpool, they sought not only the traditional holiday goal of social reconciliation, but also a recovery of youthful wonder. Industrial saturnalia fit the culture of wage-earning people at the beginning of the twentieth century even as it attracted a much wider audience with its "decent" pleasures. It was playful, but still respectable, defined not by contemporary genteel or later family, child-centered values, but by an intense excitement, sensuality of sights and sounds, and a public flirtatiousness between the sexes that titillated but seldom consummated in physical expression. As the impresarios well understood, this playful crowd hardly threatened the social or cultural order. It satisfied the emotional needs of its members and made its creators money. But intellectuals and the middle class saw the plebeian pleasure crowd as a disappointment and sometimes as a threat, and looked to reform Coney Island and Blackpool and eventually to create a new kind of playful crowd.

The Crowd and its Critics

When the Russian writer Maxim Gorky visited Coney Island one summer night in 1907, he was struck with horror at the sight of the tens of thousands who flocked to the "phantom city of lights." He was appalled by the cheap artificiality of the amusement parks: "A dozen of white buildings, monstrously diverse, not one with even the suggestion of beauty. They are built of wood, and smeared over with peeling white paint which gives them the appearance of suffering from the same skin disease. . . . The glare is everywhere, and nowhere a shadow." But he was shocked even more by the individual in the plebeian crowds at Coney Island:

> The visitor is stunned; his consciousness is withered by the intense gleam; his thoughts are routed from his mind; he becomes a particle in the crowd. People wander about in the flashing, blinding fire intoxicated and devoid of will. A dull-white mist penetrates their brains, greedy expectation envelops their souls. . . . The people . . . swarm into the cages [of the Iron Pier Tower] like black flies. Children walk about, silent, with gaping mouths and dazzled eyes. They look around with such intensity, such seriousness that the sight of them feeding their little souls upon this hideousness, which they mistake for beauty, inspires a pained sense of pity.

Despite his leftist leanings, Gorky saw not a playful crowd that evoked empathy, but a confused childlike throng that "turn about in a slow dance of weary boredom" resulting from "the pressure of self-disgust" that envelops their everyday lives.[1] In 1911, the American writer William Dean Howells found Blackpool much as Gorky had found Coney Island, a site of unconscious animal-like desire: "The crowd forever writhing, forever worming, squirming, up and down at Blackpool . . . looks like some immeasurable organism, some monster of the geologic prime, never still, but creeping with one side this way and the other that. . . . It was always awful to look upon, but awfulest at high noon, when it had swollen to its hugest, and was imaginably famishing for lunch with the hunger of some consuming insect horde."[2]

Gorky's assessment of Coney Island was typical of most intellectual observers of the New York resort, whether they were American or European. Howells' perception of the Blackpool crowd, however, was not widely shared by British intellectuals. British elites were much more relaxed and tolerant of the Blackpool crowd, at least from the late nineteenth century. Its most consistently severe critics were drawn from those sectors of the organized working class where Protestant Nonconformity and romantic socialism met, expressing a strong preference for holidays involving fresh air, healthy exercise, striding out in attractive countryside or cycling along rural lanes, singing as they went in cheerful groups of like-minded holiday-makers. For such people Blackpool's commercial success was an affront, representing the false values of popular entertainment capitalism, and inducing people to tire themselves out while wasting their money on tawdry artificial amusements.[3] Elite readings of the playful crowds of Coney Island and Blackpool do not so much explain those crowds as show how the bourgeois outsider adapted to, shaped, and ultimately challenged industrial saturnalia. Differences in how British and American elites responded to the plebeian crowd of 1900 lead us directly into understanding differences in the "modernization" of the playful crowd later in the century.

Intellectuals and the Coney Island Crowd

For centuries, the so-called mob was equated with unreasonable desire—for food, revenge, or the property of others. After the American and especially the French revolutions, the literate public often believed that peasants and urban poor in crowds were immediate threats to political order, susceptible to the harangues of the agitator and professional revolutionary. The French Gustave Le Bon's influential work, *The Crowd* (1895), updated this century-old view with concerns that new democratic politics threatened stability and rationality.[4] The masses in the twentieth century, however, took on a quite different, though no less threatening, cast. New shopping and amusement sections of cities attracted crowds of people apparently uneducated, if no longer impoverished and ultimately politically less threatening. Still, the new age of mass production and cheap, fast transportation challenged the old social order by giving wage-earners access to leisure, goods, and mobility on an unprecedented scale. This generated fear and hostility among some outsiders, but more in the United States than in England.

Bourgeois observers of crowds, pouring off the train platforms at Coney Island, thought they saw desire unrestrained. The old world of suppressed longing, ritualistically liberated only during those rare saturnalian festivals that elites had sanctioned, was no more. Temporary escape from the most pressing aspects of poverty allowed these desires to be satisfied nearly anytime or anywhere. No longer was the full expression of appetites dulled by hunger, sublimated into religious fervor, work, or war; nor was it confined to the indulgence of the rich and powerful. Civilization faced a new situation that seemed to threaten vaunted traditions of self-control and edification that an educated elite was supposed to perpetuate. Uprooted from their villages and the control of clergy and rural gentry, as well as custom, gossip and neighborly surveillance, these crowds were yet unprepared to embrace the high culture of the urban elite; they seemed to be easily lured by the bright lights and promise of immediate pleasure on the street. They appeared to drown cultivated values and civility with the wash of their raucous ways and collective economic power. Elites saw mass culture as ephemeral, rooted neither in the permanence and conservatism of folk culture nor the timeless values of high culture. Instead, mass culture was superficial and its votaries were susceptible to the latest sensation. American writer Rollin Hartt made this perspective plain: "Incapable, commonly of introspection, [the Coney Island visitor] has experienced an interval of dazzling, astounding self-revelation. Out of his littleness, he rises to momentary greatness—feels himself terribly, almost especially alive."[5]

In the opening decades of the twentieth century, middle-class observers repeatedly painted this image of immigrants at Coney Island. Such a picture was perhaps mostly famously, though more generally, drawn by the Spaniard José Ortega y Gasset in his *The Revolt of the Masses* (1930). Ortega shared with most intellectuals of the period a fear that the "spoiled child," the mass of wage earners recently enfranchised with higher wages and increased leisure, was imposing "its own desires and tastes by means of material pressure" on the cultured minority.[6] Ortega's representation of the rational individual besieged by the crowd beating down the gates of civilization was shared by many who wrote about the pleasure crowd early in the twentieth century. Sigmund Freud's *Group Psychology* (1922) borrowed from Le Bon's thinking about the irrational crowd, redirecting concern about its dangers from the political to the cultural world. On the street, he argued, the masses regressed to the mental state of savages or children because of their inability to sublimate their libidinal drives.[7]

The problem of the playful crowd at Coney Island was more than its unrestrained hedonism and irrationality accelerated by affluence. It was also the dilemma of "boredom" as Gorky saw it and self-destructiveness (or, in Freud's terms, the "death instinct") that seemed to be released when workers had time free from work and other regular obligations.[8] Others saw ennui less as a natural trait of the masses than as a consequence of modern technology, work, and media. For an observer of Coney Island in 1921, Bruce Bliven, "A palate dulled with condiments must be over-stimulated before it can taste at all. A mind buffeted by the whirlwind of life in New York, assaulted by the roar of machinery, excited by the pace at which we spin along, learns to regard a shout as the normal tone, and cannot hear with comfort anything less strident." Not surprisingly, Bliven insisted, "The very architecture roars at you." The endless quest for stimulation led to an absurd attraction to danger: "A chief pleasure of battered souls, one notices at once, is battered bodies" in the joyous submission to the bounces and jars of mechanical rides.[9]

The same processes that led to overstimulation also produced passivity. Richard Edwards' 1910 evaluation of *Popular Amusements* makes the point plainly in the context of the American amusement park: "The spontaneity of playful activities, and the originality which creates them are being lulled to sleep by the *habit of being amused*. . . . The lust for profit has picked open the bud. It is no cause for wonder that youth wilts under the process." The young especially were "easy prey for exploitation, lured into immorality under the stress of unusual excitement or temptation in the glittering or unlighted portions of these parks."[10]

These writers saw danger in the Coney Island crowd, not just the desiring individual. Despite all the complaints about "passivity," most critics perceived that the masses were more than the flypaper of fads and fancies. They represented a new kind of social interaction. These crowds, intellectuals believed, did not consist of family, friends, and neighbors well known to each other; in these throngs, even traditional routines of greeting and ritualized conversation seemed to have disappeared. People in the street crowd interacted, not personally, but indirectly through the display of their clothes and the passive sharing of theater or movie images. This culture of the street seemed to suppress individuality and what was left of traditional social interaction and constraint.[11]

The apparent anonymity of the pleasure crowd especially distressed conservative observers. As Lindsay Denison lamented at Coney Island (1905): "There is scarcely any variety of human flotsam and jetsam that is not represented in its permanent population. . . . Every defaulting cashier, every eloping couple, every man or woman harboring suicidal intent . . . comes flocking to it from every part of the land." And at Coney Island, pleasure crowds meet a crowd of sellers: "a concentrated sublimation of all the mean, petty, degrading swindles which depraved ingenuity has ever devised to prey upon humanity." Bliven revealed his prejudice when he complained that "Coney is one more place from which the native Yankee stock has retreated before the fierce tide of the south European and Oriental. . . . The Coney crowd, once or twice removed from Europe, has only partially digested the Anglo-Saxon Puritanism which forms the framework of American manners."[12]

The crowd at Coney represented not only the presumed crudity of the European peasant, but also the attempt of the children of those "peasants" to escape from traditional ways in the new world of fads and Americanisms. Some may argue that the melting pot does not melt, notes Bliven. But "Helene—whose mother's name was Yashyanka—knows better. Her aunt back in Bulgaria has never seen a bathtub, cannot read or write, and sews up her children every autumn for the winter, while Helene is a cash girl at Bulger's Big Store, has seen eighty-six installments of 'The Risks of Ruth' in the movies, and buys the *Evening Journal* every night." And, says Bliven, she went to Coney Island, because it, like all the other novelties of American consumerism, liberated her from her mother's "Bulgarian" ways. More ominously, the Coney Island pleasure crowd seemed to threaten the moral stability of the family: "The home in the modern city," noted American Maurice Davie, "can no longer be the center of life in leisure hours. . . . All must go away when in search of pleasure and recreation." Street pleasures of the city separated generations by allowing the young to escape to the anonymity of the crowd.[13]

Even more, critics insisted that the crowd amplified the irrational longings of individuals. American sociologist Edward Ross saw the "crowd self" as "credulous," "ephemeral," and even "immoral." Following Le Bon, Ross lamented: "Masked by their anonymity, people feel free to give in to the expression of their feelings. . . . To be seen, one does not simply show one's self; one gesticulates." James Huneker fretted that instead of recreation that would improve body and mind, "Unreality is as greedily craved by the mob as alcohol by the dipsomaniac." Once en masse, "humanity sheds its civilisation and becomes half child, half savage."[14]

The social position of many critics explains much of this rhetoric. As inheritors of a cultivated tradition dependent upon old money or position, they were sensitive to their loss of status and felt deprived of influence over a business culture that seemed to be progressively less subservient to educated tastemakers. They saw themselves in competition with the Barnums who marketed the "easy" entertainment of circuses and sideshows, movies, and popular magazines and paid scant attention to the opinions of educated minorities. Many shared Ortega's keenly felt belief that the formerly submissive masses no longer gave respect to the elite, reflecting the growing social distance between the educated few and the crowd.[15]

These American reactions to the playful plebeian crowd went far beyond most of the British comment, and we shall see that during the first half of the twentieth century writings on the Blackpool crowds were generally much friendlier in tone. Despite the presumed democratic preferences of Americans, elites, even among the ranks of early-twentieth-century Progressivists, were more uniformly critical of that crowd than were their British counterparts. American reformers were especially concerned about the money that immigrant families spent at Coney Island. These "residual" forms of saturnalia seemed to mock the virtues of familial thrift and prudence that Progressivists saw as key to Americanization.[16] An even more forceful wedge separating American elites from immigrant crowds was moral and religious. Brooklyn's Protestant elite wanted to purge Coney of its German, Irish, and Italian Catholics who opposed their Sabbatarian and temperance projects. The *Brooklyn Union* repeatedly attacked McKane in the late 1880s, often with the support of the famous scold Anthony Comstock, for the gambling and whoring on the shore. The hostility to immigrant crowds could hardly be clearer than in these words by Dudley Herbert Cox, pastor at a prominent Brooklyn Congregational Church:

> The cosmopolitan character of New York's population has largely made Coney Island what it is. The dirt, grime and vice of Europe has been transplanted into the free and fertile soil. The vile shows are foreign to the true American spirit of truth, justice and liberty. It is objected that if we move these people, they will settle elsewhere. Let them move, let them keep moving until every neighborhood spurns them, till every recreation ground is purified of them till even the Tenderloin fails to be a resting place.[17]

Still, not all intellectuals and middle-class reformers, even in the United States, condemned the saturnalian crowd or attempted to reform it. The Victorian tradition of enjoying low life that brought elites to boxing matches, whorehouses, and gambling dens certainly survived into the early twentieth century; but there was more to it than that. Julian Ralph encouraged his bourgeois readers to go to Coney Island's Bowery for the "oom-pah bands of rusted brass." The raw energy and natural vulgarity of the crowd amused Ralph and he assured readers that the open air diluted the smell and noise of the crowd. Others like short story writer William Sydney Porter (O. Henry) were less patronizing and more sympathetic when they saw a raw honesty and vitality in the plebs. Even Huneker recognized that the thick mass of humanity he viewed at Coney's beaches on a hot August evening in 1915 really consisted of "sweethearts in pairs, families in three or four, six or seven, planted close together. . . . It was impossible for such a large body of people to be more orderly, more decent." Although 1.75 million were taken by rail to Coney on June 30, 1901, a *New York World* reporter could still claim that it was a "decorous orderly throng." The painter John Sloan delighted in the "roar of natural 'vulgar' mirth" when crowds saw "lingerie displays" as women slid down the Bamboo Slide at Luna Park. Richard Le Gallienne recognized that even modern people needed a saturnalia: "Coney Island is the Tom-Tom of America. Every nation has, and needs—and loves—its Tom-Tom. It has its needs of orgiastic escape from respectability—that is, from the world of What-we-have-to-do into the world of What-we-would-like-to-do, from the world of duty that endureth forever into the world of joy that is graciously permitted for a moment."[18]

A British observer, H. S. Ashbee, was favorably disposed to the unthreatening vigor of Coney and its crowds as early as 1882: "The people I saw reminded me strongly of those one finds at Ramsgate or Margate in the summer months with an admixture of coloured folk. . . . There appeared to be no restriction as to drinking; and yet I was agreeably struck with the fact that during the whole day I met no one the worse for liquor, heard no bad language, witnessed no disputes; everybody conducted himself in an orderly and decorous manner." Years later, another Briton, E. V. Lucas, was equally supportive of Coney Island and its crowd, comparing it with Blackpool in August: "High spirits are the rule, and impropriety is the exception. Even in the auditorium at Steeplechase Park, where the *cognoscenti* assemble to witness the discomfiture of the uninitiated, there is nothing but harmless laughter as the skirts fly up before the unsuspected blast. Such a performance in England, were

3.1   "Ah There! Coney Island." From a stereo card, five beauties of the summer of 1897 on the Coney Island beach strike a sensual, but playful, pose for its time. Library of Congress.

it permitted, would degenerate into ugliness. . . . But the essential public chastity of the Americans—I am not sure that I ought not here to write civilization of the Americans—emerges triumphant."[19]

The natural vitality of the Coney crowd was sometimes seen in the children, especially on the beach, dressed in "pretty holiday clothes . . . racing up and down the sand, taunting and defying the sea ." More typical, however, for the early twentieth century was an awareness of the naïve and natural sensuality of the adult crowd. At Coney, the painter Reginald Marsh delighted in the unassuming joy and pleasure of the crowd that contrasted so sharply with the constraint of his own genteel background. His "George C. Tilyou's Steeplechase Park" portrays a lush sensuousness in the joyous poses of women on the Human Whirlpool.[20] More typical, however, was the abstract, if ambiguous empathy of writer Robert Neal: "Bare human nature, naïve and unashamed, stands up at Coney and cries out 'Brother' and the unanimity with which human nature responds is hopeful though disconcerting."[21]

American economist Simon Patten (1852–1922) shared in this more optimistic assessment of the pleasure crowd. He argued that affluence would elevate mass desire and create a wider, more democratic culture rather than simply threaten high culture or release libidos from the constraints of scarcity. In 1915, following current economic thinking, Patten argued that, as scarcity disappeared, any new surplus could be devoted to refined recreation and the arts. For Patten, technology did not unleash chaotic desire but rather freed people from these ancient traditional compensatory reactions to scarcity (gluttony and drunkenness).[22] Patten recognized that work and traditional family and community structures would no longer satisfy social and psychological needs. Instead, the new consumer culture on the street and at the seashore would have to provide the "vital excitement" that was absent from the monotony of modern mechanical jobs. Patten also saw opportunities for uplift in the "amusements and recreations of parks, theatres, 'Coney Islands,' department stores, settlements, free lectures and socialized schoolhouses." Patten made no effort to distinguish these "grouped pleasures" into good or bad, for he found them all cultivating a common culture.[23]

Reformers often recognized the impossibility of isolating the individual from the pleasure throng. While the American James Sizer noted that "the amusement park simply charges the lonely individual 'admission' to the crowd," he also recognized that there was no alternative to popular commercial leisure. Sizer assumed that the "lower races" (blacks and the white immigrant working class) would not respond to precept and theory to raise them culturally. Instead, "Amusement is the line of least resistance. . . . [for] amusement is stronger than vice, and it alone can be depended upon to fill the vacant hours of the millions of people, who are coming into their inheritance of leisure." European-style paternalism (with subsidized summer camps, for example) would not work in "democratic" America. This, of course, was the approach of the American world's fairs with their midways that attracted far more visitors than did their enlightening and educational "White Cities." Simon Patten saw Coney Island as a site for the "pleasure economy," meaning that it and other venues of amusement could turn "stragglers of industry . . . into the steady ranks of disciplined workers." The "zest for amusement," Patten claimed, "urges [wage earners] to submit to the discipline of work, and the habits formed for the sake of gratifying their tastes make their regular life necessary in industry easier and more pleasant."[24] Modern saturnalia, Patten believed, not only was a safety value of social tensions, but also reinforced the industrial work ethic.

The Playful Crowd at Blackpool

Blackpool's plebeian throngs were treated in a generally more positive way than those of Coney Island. The consensus of contemporary observers, right through from the late nineteenth century to the 1930s, was much closer to the views of Patten or (especially) Ralph than to Cox's condemnatory tone. This was partly because by the 1880s Blackpool's working-class visitors had already modified their behavior sufficiently to disarm important aspects of the criticism of their "betters." During the transition to working-class domination, between the late 1840s and the 1870s, local criticism of the behavior of the "excursionists" who formed the original core of the playful crowd had sometimes been severe. The early cheap trippers drew the fire of a local correspondent in 1849, who complained of "railway mammon" desecrating the Sabbath by bringing in flashily-dressed "barbers' apprentices and shoeblacks," ignorant of social decencies, who bathed naked, drank heavily in the "low public houses," and defied the "bewildered" policemen. This was a regular refrain for thirty years, although by the 1870s distinctive territories were being established. On the Central Pier, according to Ben Brierley, "th' bacca reech [tobacco reek] smells stronger, an' th' women are leauder abeaut th' meauth. We know what class their return tickets are." It was in this decade that the London *Times* could still describe complaints about the scruffy dress of Blackpool excursionists, with their aggressive short clay pipes, cruelty to donkeys, spitting and swearing. The 1870s also saw the highest level of drunkenness convictions at Blackpool, but the number of prosecutions declined thereafter even as the crowds continued to grow. From the 1880s onwards the Blackpool crowd generated steadily more favorable comment from a cross-section of sources, national as well as local.[25]

Positive press comment on Blackpool's playful crowd in the late nineteenth and the early twentieth century came from some seemingly unlikely sources. As early as 1883 the *Methodist Recorder* praised the sobriety of the well-dressed holiday crowds, and commented that the spectacle of "vast masses of people" enjoying themselves rationally (a keyword of the times) at Blackpool was "one of the sublimest triumphs of modern civilization." At the turn of the century the *Daily Mail* praised the orderliness of the "amazing crowd" on the sea front, which transferred factory working hours to the seaside holiday: "By seven o'clock it is out, determined not to miss any ozone. It paddles methodically. . . . It samples one sixpenny sideshow after another with stolid perseverance. . . . Then towards one o'clock the whole of it marches off to dinner." A similar mass clearance of the streets took place at teatime, and "at half-past ten everything stops."[26]

Aspects of such commentaries might seem patronizing, but the crowd had certainly become an object of good-humored interest rather than fear. Journalists noted the working-class visitors' concern for value for money, their huge appetites, the women's unembarrassed wearing of hair curlers at mealtimes (a trait that persisted into the 1960s), and the group photographs posed in shirtsleeves, rather than drunkenness or threat. In 1897, Blackpool's own propaganda could confidently endorse this picture: "The Piers are covered with living streams of people. . . . It is possible to be carried along by the merry crowd and to be infected by the contagious joviality." Le Bon's critique of the crowd hardly fit this image of Blackpool.[27]

These views extended widely. Sam Fitton, a Lancashire dialect poet, and cartoonist for the trade union newspaper the *Cotton Factory Times*, cast a quizzical but not unsympathetic eye on the Blackpool holiday crowds.[28] Asking "Where for our holidays?" he made his own position clear: the characteristic masculine group behavior of drinking, strutting, parading and going off with young women at a big popular resort was not for him, but in his good-humored verse he eventually recognized that this was what a lot of people enjoyed, and that it was not up to him to tell them what they should prefer. The socialist Arthur Laycock went to live

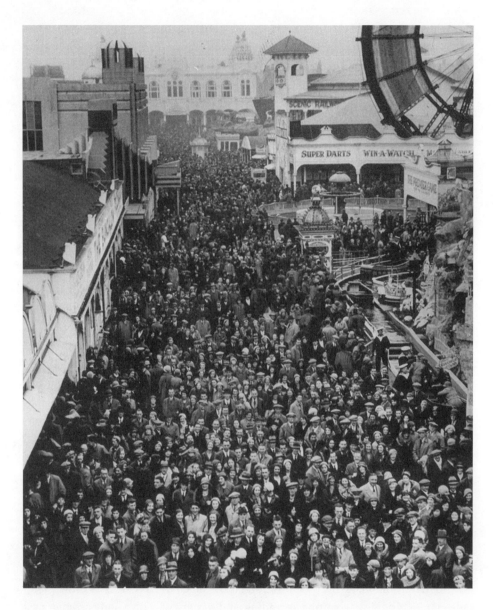

3.2   The "orderly crowd" at Blackpool's Pleasure Beach. It is made to look more disciplined because its members are aware of the camera and looking at it. Courtesy the Pleasure Beach, Blackpool.

in Blackpool and offered a much more positive view in his novel *Warren of Manchester* (1906). He gloried in the promenade with its "jostling, jovial crowds. . . . A truly wonderful, a marvellously impressive sight, these tens of thousands, all on holiday bent, all in happy holiday mood, genial, jovial, and for the most part well-conducted and orderly."[29] Laycock was joined in this frame of mind by the Bolton socialist Allen Clarke, who in 1899 had denounced the Blackpool seaside holiday as an unhealthy extension of year-round stress, but subsequently went to live in Blackpool and defended the happy holiday crowds that surrounded him, while trying to persuade them of the health-giving benefits of excursions to the surrounding countryside.[30]

Even within the ranks of Liberal Protestant Nonconformity, the *Blackpool Times* at Whitsuntide 1904 commented favorably on the crowded Promenade as an open leisure space where the classes could mix to their mutual benefit: "A common meeting ground this for all, for the merchant and the mechanic, the lady of fashion and the factory lass, for the plutocrat and the plebeian, the mightiest and the meanest. We all commingle on these spacious parades by the sea, for the time being having no castes, no precise distinctions of 'proper' and 'select' persons."[31] This at once suspends distinctions, reduces the crowd to an assemblage of unclassifiable individuals, and at the same time presents it as a healthy, homogeneous moral whole.

This was to be the predominant tone of interwar commentary on the Blackpool crowd and how Blackpool preferred to represent itself. The Official Guide of 1924 even won the endorsement of that classic Establishment figure the Bishop of Manchester: "Blackpool is rendering a really great service to the country by its ample provision of jolly and wholesome amusement."[32] These cheerful images of Blackpool epitomized what were coming to be seen as traditional English virtues of good humor, class harmony, and shared pleasures. This self-image became easier to sustain as the town invested in parks and promenades in the 1920s and 1930s. But landscape architect T. H. Mawson articulated this vision in darker social terms when he cited a Lancashire businessman: "Blackpool stands between us and revolution. May it long continue as the protector of social order." After months of disciplined labor in the industrial towns, "once a year (the workers) must either burst out or go to Blackpool; and there they go, and after a fortnight they come back, quietened down and ready for work again."[33] The reference to a fortnight was optimistic (few had more than a week of holiday), but this perception that Blackpool was a bulwark against social revolution certainly reflected the ancient view of saturnalia as a safety valve and affirmed Patten's modern notions of consumption and leisure as guarantors of industrial discipline.

This positive vision of Blackpool continued into the 1930s in the writings of journalists and novelists. In August 1934 William Holt wrote a series of profiles of Blackpool and its holidaymakers for Manchester's *Daily Dispatch*.[34] His descriptions of the crowds at Bank Holiday weekend could appear condescending when he wrote "The sands were swarming like the banks of the Ganges, multi-coloured in the intense light; and there was a confused murmur of joy everywhere." Yet, he also saw the crowd as "Something trying to express itself. Something struggling to be born out of all [the people's] powerful will for life and joy, which murmurs and becomes more highly-coloured when the sun comes out. . . . I can no longer watch individuals. I can only watch the crowd with wonder and amazement." Yet Holt also understood that crowds consisted of small groups of friends and family parties and offered sympathetic descriptions of their little extravagances in drink or gambling or visiting peepshows or the Chamber of Horrors at the waxworks on the Golden Mile, of the difficulties they faced in making their savings last through the week, and of the way the crowd still kept factory hours. Holt discussed the mysterious pleasures to be found in screaming and stimulating (or simulating) fear on the rides at the Pleasure Beach. He also enjoyed the characteristic "Lancashire singing" in the "song bazaars" where sheet music was sold along the promenade. He endorsed the picture of Blackpool as a resort that brings the classes together. Above all, writing for his populist Northern England audience, Holt was at pains to celebrate the overriding virtues of this vast and mysterious crowd:

> Blackpool breathes the very spirit of the North. The indomitable spirit of millions of factory workers and those who depend on them for their existence. Its heart beats somewhere round about Central Station where the trippers pour in. I know there are plenty of people who pretend to despise them. But I have seen such people in the course of their holidays steal down from their quiet retreats to enjoy the fun. Blackpool without its heart and Northern inspiration would be as dead as mutton with blustering sea breezes playing with its carcase.[35]

The novelist and playwright J. L. Hodson, looking back in 1937 to the Carnival of 1923, emphasized the "generous note" in holidaymakers' spending, and the eagerness with which they pursued the fleeting pleasures of the holiday: "Lancashire might be faring badly in a chaotic world, the pleasant and prosperous places in England might be a long way off, but these indomitable cotton operatives and engineers and coalminers were scraping their bits o' brass together and chancing their arms with a few days at Blackpool." Frank Tilsley, writing about "Northpool" in the 1930s found an innocent crowd, whose members assert themselves as individuals within the collectivity: "Sometimes the fellows and the girls linked arms—ten, a dozen, a score of them, all arm-in-arm, walking jauntily along and singing at the top of their voices." Tilsley's description of the crowd arriving at Northpool station sums up the position: "the crowd . . . laughed and shouted to each other, blinked at the sunshine and anxiously counted their children, and sniffed the sea air as though it was altogether different from the sort of air to which they were accustomed, as, indeed, it was." Here were pictured families, workmates, people from the same towns and neighborhoods, re-creating their societies at the seaside rather than fragmenting or dissolving them—in sharp contrast with much of the critical discourse on Coney Island. And, as D. L. Murray pointed out in another Blackpool novel, they were welcomed in a relaxed way by the locals, and the "serene and orderly throng" was controlled unobtrusively by police who were "as composed as a country constable in a village high street."[36]

Nor were these perceptions confined to journalists and novelists. Some British intellectuals challenged the negative psychological assessment of the "mass man," arguing that it was based on a "profound ignorance of common life." These were the words of C. D. Burns written in 1932 who found in new technology and rising wages a new culture that would emerge from the "energetic" crowds of youth and in "fellowship with strangers." Like Patten, Burns believed that the crowded streets of shopping districts and the promenades of seaside resorts were creating a "common feeling." These crowds were leading to a "democratic civilization" and a "freer and subtler community between all men."[37] For Burns the nostalgia for nature and "natural communities" was outdated, elitist, and isolated the bourgeois intellectual from the wider world. A greater openness to plebeian pleasures was also expressed in Ivor Brown's *The Heart of England* (1935). The English were "a cheerful people with a good notion of how to enjoy themselves" when they journeyed to Blackpool, the "capital of pleasure," and did not need "urban intellectuals" telling them the meaning and means of "true" pleasure.[38] A young intellectual from the team of "Mass-Observers" who visited Blackpool in 1938 to make an "anthropological" study of its working-class visitors wrote this about the crowd enjoying themselves at the Savoy Dance Hall:

What strikes me most about this place, its people, is the spontaneous reality and genuineness of everything. All present are working-class people—nearly all are workers in the mills and factories. To them this dance is temporary freedom from hard work and worries—'let's enjoy ourselves to-day for to-morrow we . . . ?' No class; no snobbery; no forced laughter, just reality.[39]

Across a wide range of observers, we see an extraordinarily similar message: The Blackpool experience provided the working class a well-deserved respite from labor and affirmed the good natured character of Northern wage-earners and the essential social harmony of British people. This perspective was at times self-serving and even illusory, but it made for a surprising acceptance of the commercial culture of the Blackpool crowd well into the twentieth century.

In contrast to Coney Island, critics of the Blackpool holiday crowds were drawn disproportionately from within the working class. They came from the serious-minded strata, dominated by skilled and white-collar workers, where Protestant Nonconformity met idealistic socialism in organizations like the Independent Labour Party and the Clarion socialist cycling clubs. Their publications contained eloquent denunciations of the ways in which Blackpool's artificial and commercial attractions diverted the workers away from the healthy, communal pleasures of walking and cycling in the uncommercial countryside, damaging their health and corrupting their morals in the process.

To Katherine St John Conway, writing in the *Workmen's Times* in 1893, "Black-pool was . . . hideous—a place where many men and women gather together who know not what is or what might be, who think Socialists idle dreamers, and England a glorious country so long as she keeps the cotton trade. . . . On the grey sea wall were grouped the sunshades and frocks of the lasses who learn to shriek instead of to laugh, and to parade instead of to stroll." The *Labour Leader* in 1904 denounced the waste of hard-won savings and the diversion of new-found purchasing power into sordid commercial channels: "Every where you see evidence that those who set the fashion at Blackpool look upon the British working-man as one who can be got to part with a copper on the very slightest pretext. . . . The whole town seems filled with a frenzy to imitate the worst vices of the idle class. . . . It would be a sorry result if we won elbow-room for the working man only to let him build a third-rate imitation of modern commercial conditions with rolled gold for the real article."[40] T. A. Leonard, a Congregationalist minister from the Lancashire weaving town of Colne, set up the Co-operative Holidays Association in 1893 to provide cheap-countryside holidays for those who might otherwise be drawn into the "whirligig" of Blackpool, with its "brass bands and bluster" and "shady delights" that held back the moral and intellectual progress of the working classes.[41]

Carrying on this critical tradition were the nostalgic intellectuals of the mid-1930s who lamented that the Blackpool crowd had lost some of its old spontaneity and vitality. The writer J. B. Priestley fell into this category, complaining in 1934 that, "From the few glimpses I have had of it since the war, I gather the impression that it lacks some of its old genuine gaiety. Its amusements are becoming too mechanised and Americanised. . . . It has developed a pitiful sophistication—machine-made and not really English—that is much worse than the old hearty vulgarity." He was nostalgic for the "energetic old Blackpool, crowded with vital beings who burst out of their factories for the annual spree as if the boilers had exploded and blown them out."[42] Even so, Priestley would have preferred workers to appreciate the rambling clubs.

The British writer Walter Greenwood, famous for his novels of working-class life in the Manchester and Salford of the Depression, took an even more pessimistic view of Blackpool, but one that harked back even more directly to the critiques of the early socialists: "No other county than Lancashire could have produced Blackpool. . . . It is a product of unconscious revolt, revolt of the masses against the horror of living 51 overworked weeks in hideous industrial towns. They want a holiday place in which they can give vent to their hysteria. Blackpool caters for this."[43] These views of Blackpool were certainly in a minority, and surprisingly so, in the light of the American case. But that critique of Blackpool responded to and helped to create a legacy of opposition to commercial culture and a nostalgia for "traditional" working-class life that shaped Beamish and other industrial museums later in the twentieth century.

Why Can't They Be Like Us?

Intellectuals, especially in the United States, despaired at understanding why wage-earners would be attracted to the seaside crowds. A revealing example of perplexity was American James Huneker's question: "Why after the hot, narrow, noisy, dirty streets of the city, do these same people crowd into the narrower, hotter, noisier, dirtier, wooden alleys of Coney?"[44] Huneker assumed that urban working people would seek a leisure site that reflected his own longings for escape from the city and its polymorphous crowds. They should go to the countryside or quiet seaside. This desire had a long pedigree with modern roots in the British romantic longing for villages, empty shorelines, and mountains. The "picturesque" gained a fashionable ascendancy from the mid-eighteenth century alongside the dominant vogue for taking the cure at elite healing wells and beach resorts, many of which also were or soon became social settings, like Bath, Tunbridge Wells, and Brighton. The fashion for scenic tours and the emergence of the English Lake District and the Scottish Highlands as tourist destinations were also part of this process.[45]

In the American colonies, Newport, Rhode Island served the same purpose, attracting wealthy visitors from as far away as the Carolinas. This resort's pristine isolation attracted the rich to its warm Gulf Stream waters and cooling summer breezes. Verandas and piazzas for strolling or sitting in rocking chairs allowed plenty of opportunity to see and be seen. The slow pace and ritualized activities prompted complaints of boredom. But in the nineteenth century seaside resorts like Rockaway Beach on Long Island and Long Branch on the New Jersey shore, promised distance from the hoi polloi, an opportunity to win social status and to enjoy the restful beauty of nature. In the interior, White Sulphur Springs, West Virginia and other health resorts followed the decorum of Bath—though northern resorts like Saratoga Springs were more diverse and less slavish of British models, allowing a mixed urban crowd not only to promenade and dine, but also to gamble at horse races. These retreats provided an alternative to the urban pleasure gardens, which, despite intentions of founders, could not maintain a high social tone because of their proximity to working-class neighborhoods. Of course, the east end of Coney Island with its Oriental and Manhattan hotel complexes was part of the same effort. The point of these sites was as much to be free from the plebeian crowd as it was to socialize with one's own. The genteel writer William Dean Howells complained of excursionists at New York's Rockaway Beach who made him nervous though they were an "entirely peaceable multitude." Despite differences, all of these resorts were sites of respectable gatherings, not crowds, where tradition not novelty prevailed.[46]

The genteel ideal was about more than exclusive socializing; an essential ingredient was the contemplation of nature. Vistas of green hills, mighty rivers, cascading falls or, of course, foaming surf and ocean breezes were required for genteel resorts. The site of natural beauty became part of the American Grand Tour and the See America First movement after the Civil War. While refined socializing did not easily cross class lines, middle class reformers hoped to enlist the working classes (and especially their children) into a mutually uplifting love of nature and thus to separate them from the saturnalian crowd. *The New York Times* (1866) found that "a tumble in the surf" was a "healthful and resting exercise," especially for those "forced to ply their busy tools in almost air-tight shops where the blast of furnaces consume what little air they might have." In the United States, organizations like the Fresh Air Fund (beginning in 1877) sponsored summer vacations for tenement children in the homes of suburban and rural families. The scout and summer camp movements hoped to bring children from all social ranks into a personal engagement with nature.[47] More important, perhaps, in reaching out to youth from wage-earning families were the urban playgrounds. With roots in philanthropy, the Playground Association (founded in 1907) was the voice of attempts by municipal playground staffs to organize games on city playgrounds to lure youth from the unsupervised street.[48]

British elites likewise attempted to train working class youth to appreciate nature through patronage of sports clubs, company-run summer camps, and playground centers. Notable was the interwar experiment, the Duke of York's Camp, where equal numbers of public (elite) school and working-class boys shared games and bonfires. The object was to create an uplifting but pleasurable setting where organizers encouraged self-discipline and group loyalty.[49] Beginning with a meeting of Liverpool ramblers in 1929, the Youth Hostel Association (YHA) attracted elite patronage but also offered low-cost country holidays for hikers and cyclists, promising interclass fellowship along with the beauty and serenity of nature. By 1939, half a million nights were spent in YHA facilities across Britain, an impressive statistic which nevertheless has to be compared with Blackpool's claim to seven million visitors at this time.[50]

There was also a strong independent British working-class "outdoor movement" with deep Victorian roots in footpath preservation, campaigns to protect access to open land, and working-class enthusiasm for botany and geology. This developed into the rambling (or hiking) and cycling clubs that proliferated from the 1890s and reached a peak in the 1930s. Working-class mountaineers and climbers were not always welcomed by the middle-class professionals who had been developing the sport since the 1850s and 1860s. But love of the outdoors, and especially of wild upland landscapes, was present at all levels of British society. The movement for "rational holidays" through the Co-operative Holidays Association, founded in 1891, and its offshoot the Holiday Fellowship (1913) pulled together didactic middle-class influences and working-class lovers of the open air in a movement that was directly opposed to the Blackpool style of high-pressure commercial holiday. The 1890s also saw the emergence of the Clarion movement, with its socialist ethos of returning the enjoyment of the land to the people.[51] These activities attracted only a minority, but they enjoyed a measure of respectability except when they threatened established property rights when trespassing (in the name of the "right to roam") through treasured places like Derbyshire's Kinder Scout.[52]

In contrast to the United States, where working-class love of nature more often took the form of hunting and fishing in small groups, the British tradition of proletarian social solidarity in nature offered a counter to the commercial crowd, and helped to shape the ethos that led to Beamish. Still, in neither Britain nor the United States did this kind of holiday ever come to rival the resort-based vacation with its crowds and "artificial" amusements: the excitements of the attractions and crowds of the Golden Mile of Blackpool or the Bowery of Coney Island appealed more to people whose lives were weighed down with routine and isolating work than did the tranquil contemplation of nature.[53]

The attack on the saturnalian crowd revealed a third component of the middle-class tourism aesthetic. In addition to a longing for orderly, even ritualized, social gatherings and personal encounters with nature, critics often shared a nostalgic impulse. Hostility toward the novelty and flash of Coney Island often betrayed a desire for the return to the old "picturesque features of ocean commerce" or even the old picnic parks of "noble elms and oaks and beeches." Typical were the sentiments of William Sydney Porter, who lamented the passing of beach sand and clam chowder remembered from his youth at Coney and the coming of the phony "red-flannel eruption of Mt. Vesuvius" at Dreamland in the 1900s.[54]

At the turn of the twentieth century, intellectuals longed even more for their "lost childhood" memories of rural and village life. Enthusiasm for the English countryside and "Merrie England" crossed class and political lines in Britain: In the 1920 and 1930s, it attracted the socialist George Lansbury for whom England was still a "land of hedgerows and lanes" as much as the conservative Stanley Baldwin. Even northern textile workers dreamed of traveling to the country lanes in Devon when they could afford nothing more than a few days of holiday at the nearby commercial resort of Blackpool.[55]

Accompanying this British longing for a visit to a lost past was a romantic assumption that the "real" people came from such an imagined realm, whether it was composed of simple rural craftsmen who practiced "folk" customs or courageous fishermen who had a natural bond with their shorelines and harbors. Efforts to preserve or revive customs such as Morris dancing and "folk" singing from the late nineteenth century were part of this romantic nostalgia, which was shared and propagated by intellectuals like the literary critic F. R. Leavis.[56] Cyril Joad lamented that "we are deprived of the social pleasure of those who live in a community"; instead we pass our lives "in perpetual transit from workshop and dormitory" and, while on holiday, we destroy real Dorset villages with the "all conquering car."[57]

Although Americans had only a short history, they too longed for the "lost" simplicity of the small town and rural life, and of the common people who lived in these worlds.[58] In 1929, Robert Lynd contrasted the recently departed intimacy of the small town of the 1890s with the corrosive impact of modern materialism, mass media, and the automobile on the small midwestern city of "Middletown": "In the [eighteen] nineties, we were all much more together. . . . We rolled out a strip of carpet and put cushions on the porch step to take care of the unlimited overflow of neighbors that dropped by."[59] There was an endless longing for an imagined childhood in a place where no one really lived and surrounded by people who existed only in a sanitized past or a fairy tale world.

The quest to recover this community and to restore its memory would lead to "heritage tourism." In 1891, Artur Hazelius reconstructed a Swedish village and craft life at Skansen near Stockholm. This open air "living" museum with costumed guides, dancers, and musicians became the model for heritage sites throughout Europe. Professionals and educated elites, seeking to recover a lost community of peasants and artisans free from mass production and capitalist class conflict, embraced Hazelius' vision. As early as 1876, his influence reached the United States in the tableaux of Swedish folk-life exhibited at the Philadelphia Centennial Exhibition. The living museum had even clearer roots in the conservative American movement for restoring historic houses (the Mount Vernon Ladies' Association to preserve George Washington's plantation, for example). The 1909 restoration of the John Ward House (built in 1685) by the Essex Institute of Salem, Massachusetts led to the introduction of costumed reenactors of early colonial life to lend an authenticity to the site. Urban museums also began to take interest in restoring early American crafts and furnishings and placing them in period rooms designed to evoke an emotional response to the past. Even more ambitious was Henry Ford's sponsorship of the Greenwood Village in 1929; it gathered artifacts from across the industrial northern United States and even England. This heritage site near Dearborn Michigan re-created the "common man's" world of blacksmiths and pioneer farmers of Ford's youth—the world he had helped to destroy with his Model T car. According to Mike Wallace, at Greenwood Village Ford created a "pre-capitalist Eden immune to modern ills, peopled with men and women of character."[60]

John D. Rockefeller Jr. shared Ford's vision, when in the 1930s he financed much of the early restoration of Williamsburg to its prerevolutionary status as the colonial capital of Virginia. His hope was to re-create "the complete area and free it entirely from alien or inharmonious surroundings as well as to preserve the beauty and charm of the old buildings and gardens of the city and its historic significance." More than 700 modern houses were demolished to restore the authentic look of the 1770s. Later, critics like David Lowenthal, complained that "Williamsburg has the flavor of a well-kept contemporary suburb." As places promising to make time stand still, uncorrupted by modernity, heritage sites were always fixed in time. At Plimoth Plantation, restored in 1947 close to the original site, the year was always 1627.

Outdoor history museums expanded in the 1950s (Old Sturbridge Village in Massachusetts and Old Salem in North Carolina, for example). In the 1960s and 1970s, even more emerged around restorations of regional rural and village life. The bias was toward times before industrialization, in part, because the motive of founders and staff was to "return" to a simpler time; and these living museums usually downplayed conflict and the hardships of these long past times. At Gettysburg, the site of the famous Civil War battle, visitors were supposed to feel like it was July 1863. The quest was not for historical context or understanding of the causes and meanings of the battle but for the experience of returning to the "immediacy and detail" of an imagined past.[61] British developments in this and a related vein peaked later. Still the National Trust, a voluntary preservationist organization founded in 1895 to acquire scenic and historic properties and restore historic houses, attracted substantial elite and even government support by the 1930s.[62]

A New Kind of Middle-Class Wonder

The genteel longing for sedate social rituals and escape to the serenity of nature and sites of nostalgic community explains much of the middle-class intellectual's rejection of the tawdry sites of industrial saturnalia and attempts to reform them. Yet, as we have seen, this was never the complete story. Many outsiders, especially in the British context of Blackpool, were tolerant of, even sympathetic toward, the plebeian playful crowd. Moreover, after about 1900, genteel standards were under attack, not only by commercial popular culture, but also from within the middle classes themselves, some of whose members had long been drawn to the disreputable pleasures of drink, gambling, and sexual indulgence. Even more important, the very people who used the genteel code to define themselves against wage earners began to accept a fun morality that challenged the ideals of ritual, serenity, uplift, and contemplation. This occurred even as the "official" middle class aesthetic continued to rebuff the Saturnalian crowd and most that it entailed.

The first thing to note is that none of the key elements of genteel tourism survived the nineteenth century entirely intact. As American historian Jon Sterngass shows, resort entrepreneurs were regularly torn between stressing exclusivity and trying to increase access (and thus paying customers). This led to the decline of genteel locations like Saratoga and the east end of Coney Island. The appeal of the sublimity of natural sites like Niagara Falls suffered a similar fate. Though by the late 1830s Niagara Falls was an essential venue for genteel contemplation of God's natural world, it also quickly became commercialized in ways that appealed to the plebeian crowd. Moreover, the romantic vistas of the rapids, falls, and whirlpool could not hold the attention of even the middle-class visitor who paid to see the still more exciting diversions of daredevil tightrope walkers, showmen spinning tales of accidents and rescues at the Falls, souvenir shops, and dime museums. While purist landscape architect Frederick Olmsted objected strongly to the commercialization of "sacred places" like Niagara, this did not stop Barnum and others from popularizing the Falls in museum dioramas. The nostalgia for pristine sites of ancient villages, restored founding settlements, and heritage battlefields inevitably drew cheap and often tawdry hangers-on.[63]

In Britain, commercial holiday camps run by Billy Butlin and others from the mid-1930s copied elements from nature-loving trade union or cooperative camping grounds, but they added chalet accommodations, cheap bars, dancing, playful competitions and opportunities for heterosexual encounter, as well as child care for established families. The customers for places like this were drawn from white-collar workers as well as the skilled working class, and the effect was to subvert the "back to nature" ethos by turning it into a mirror of the popular resort.[64]

The middle classes made significant compromises with the fun morality. This is a long and complex story. But signs of it appeared across many venues. English elites in the 1910s and 1920s were hostile to American popular phonograph and movie entertainment, to the point of regulating the number of American films that could be shown in British cinemas and prohibiting Sunday exhibitions.[65] By the thirties, however, populist intellectuals were beginning to defend film as harmless entertainment, and general Sunday opening of cinemas was allowed in 1932. In the early 1930s, popular pressure from citizens and competition from commercial stations reaching from Europe into Britain forced the BBC into offering more popular musical and educational formats.[66]

The accommodation to fun went much further in the United States. Advocates of gentility tried valiantly to maintain cultural distant and uplift—from liberal arts higher education and ad-free classical music on the radio to the massive commercial effort to disseminate the "Five-Foot Shelf of Books," selected by Charles Eliot, President of Harvard, to provide the adult reader with the essentials of a classical liberal arts education.[67] However, subtle changes in middle-class values weakened the legitimacy and appeal of genteel authority. In the decades after 1920, the broad middle class abandoned the expectation that it was really necessary to embrace genteel values to rise in social status.[68] Middlebrow magazines introduced the idea that ordinary people had "ready-made capacity for independent judgment," making culture a matter of personal choice, no longer a bulwark against the barbarian mass culture. Instead, by mid-century, an individual lifestyle free from the "elitism" of imposed standards became the accepted norm.[69]

This was, of course, not a capitulation to plebeian crowd pleasure and the industrial saturnalia. The middle classes and their intellectuals continued to reject them, in America at least, but found an alternative to the genteel gathering in a new kind of social setting and new pleasures. They redefined the playful crowd by reducing as much as possible the presumed negative elements of the plebeian pleasure crowd—the physical crush of people, the disorder and dirt, the competing appeals of barkers, and unpredictability of the throng. The new middle-class idea of the playful crowd was no longer an amalgam of strangers, but rather semi-autonomous clusters of individual families and friends. Because, as we have seen, middle-class anxiety about the proletarian crowd was less extreme in Britain, this theme was much less evident at Blackpool. Increasingly, as the middle-class version of the playful crowd emerged, those clusters would be focused on children and child-like fantasies. And, although the new playful crowd shared with the old a longing for sensual envelopment, the content of those sensations changed dramatically.

The critical addition of the child to the playful crowd occurred slowly. Youngsters came with mothers and even fathers to Coney's beach and to Blackpool in the nineteenth century, but children remained a distinct minority. As we have seen, the Bowery and Golden Mile were very unfriendly to minors and even the amusement parks appealed to adult sensibilities with the playful sexuality of Steeplechase, the orientalism of Luna Park, and the religious fantasy of Dreamland. Even the mechanical rides and circus shows attracted adults in 1910. Grown-ups may have acted like children, but they seldom burdened themselves with kids when they went to the parks. Most important, the thrills and adventures that excited them—the dance halls, the freak shows and even dioramas—had little to attract innocent children's wonder.

Gradually, this begins to change. In 1920, Steeplechase introduced Babyland at one corner of the Pavilion of Fun, featuring two child-sized slides, hobbyhorses, and a kiddie carousel. In the summer of 1925, the National Association of Amusement Parks promoted new children's rides at member parks.[70]

Beginning in 1906, an annual baby show was held at Coney Island, complete with a carriage parade of the 1,200 participants and a contest judging the most beautiful, fattest, smallest, and most strenuous baby. Done in obvious fun, the contest became an integral part of the Mardi Gras celebrations. In the 1920s, as the final days of the revelry drew rowdy throngs of 500,000 requiring extra police to handle the drunken brawls, the baby parade became a way of civilizing the crowd. Under the auspices of Laura Riegelman, sister-in-law of the Brooklyn Borough President and Chairman of the Bureau of Child Hygiene, Mardi Gras was quickly tamed with this parade designed to attract a "family crowd." The appeal to the cute babies on parade was not pure maudlin. Some mothers dressed their infants and toddlers mockingly as marginal adults: First prize in the 1923 parade went to a three-year old dressed "in full harem regalia as Fatima." In later years, mothers costumed their toddlers as the boxer Jack Dempsey, as "Eve and the Forbidden Fruit," or as the mayor Jimmy Walker (festooned with a tilted derby). Others, however, adopted a more "sweet" look when they dressed their children as popular dolls (Baby Bunting) or cupid.[71] The appeal to the "cute" child, a concept new to the twentieth century,[72] had become part of the crowd culture of Coney Island itself, a "fun" alternative to the racy playfulness of the traditional Mardi Gras. Carnival had become cutesified in a way that met the needs of Coney Island. At Blackpool,

3.3   The Ponies at Coney Island (1904). An early image of indulging childhood fantasy. Library of Congress

there were no baby parades. This was not only because the British crowd evoked less anxiety but also because the "wondrous" child was a less needed substitute for earlier forms of delight.

Still, the real innovation came not from these historically plebeian pleasure sites, but from new American amusement parks that catered to a new crowd—the fun-seeking middle-class family with children. The opening of Rye Beach's Playland in 1928 signaled a major break from the old idea of the amusement park. At a cost of $5 million, this seaside resort, built on the lower end of Long Island sound, was a clear alternative to Coney Island's plebeian commercialism. Playland was owned by the Westchester County Park Commission and built over the demolished Paradise Park, a standard turn-of-the-century commercial amusement park. Fulfilling the dreams of middle-class reformers, Playland featured flowerbeds bordering walks around a small lake, a boardwalk and "fireproof bath house" on the beach, and a 1,200-foot mall ending in a 100-foot high music tower—a "natural" version of Dreamland. Significantly, it was approachable only by car (with parking for 12,000), excluding the tenement crowd. Its popularity was immediate. While Coney Island attracted about 600,000 on the Fourth of July in 1928, the Rye Beach resort drew an impressive 325,000. Despite its middle-class appeal, Playland was hardly the epitome of gentility. On the mall, it offered thrill rides (a whirl ball and tumble bug as well as a carrousel and Noah's ark) and even excursions on the still new and exciting airplane. Also, unlike the old genteel resort (but like Coney Island), Playland introduced a "Kiddyland" with miniature roller coasters and other rides. This was still a long way from Disneyland for Kiddyland also offered a child-care service with the motto "Park'em and forget'em," allowing parents to enjoy a romantic stroll or the thrills of the roller coaster free from small children. Instead of the fairy tale fantasies much less thrill rides, Kiddyland featured sandboxes and seesaws. Still, Playland's familial ethic was a step along the way to a new form of the happy crowd.[73]

Even earlier, Blackpool's Pleasure Beach began accommodating this new focus on the young when it opened a Children's Playground in 1924. Like Playland's Kiddyland, it included no thrill rides, but featured a sand pit, paddling pool, and teeter-totters. From 1934, a baby crèche with appropriately dressed "nurses" provided care for babies and toddlers (it would survive until 1960). By 1927, this rather ordinary park playground was made more fantasyful with a collection of "Bingle and Bob" rides, miniature carousels, railroads, airplane swings, Ferris Wheel, and even Kiddie Kars (imported from Coney Island–area manufacturers). Like its American counterpart, the Pleasure Beach gradually began to accommodate crowds that included young families. Even so, the park remained primarily for adults—the Children's Playground was a place to deposit children, not for adults to play with them. This would come much later.[74]

Although children slowly became part of the new playful crowd, even more important to this transformation were new ways to express wonder. A new middle-class ideal of fun abandoned some traditional delights and found new ones. The absence of the freak show at Playland is very instructive of this change. While human curiosities prevailed on the Coney Island Bowery and even Dreamland, the most "respectable" of Coney Island's major amusement parks, middle-class sensibilities had already begun to turn against this traditional expression of wonder by

3.4   The children's playground at the Blackpool Pleasure Beach in the late 1920s where offspring were left while parents played in the amusement park on their own. Courtesy the Pleasure Beach, Blackpool.

1900. Although the boundaries between entertainment and science had often been blurred in the dime museums of nineteenth-century America, legitimate scientific display retreated to the publicly supported and professionally credentialed museum in the first decade of the twentieth century. Scientific understanding of the medical origins of freaks made giants and dwarfs less amazing than pitiful. Discoveries in genetics turned physical anomalies into intelligible accidents of nature and fostered a eugenic movement calling for the elimination of future "deformed" genes through sterilization of "abnormal" adults. A *Scientific American* article of 1908 fully revealed the new attitude: "Most of these humble and unfortunate individuals, whose sole means of livelihood is the exhibition of their physical infirmities to a gaping and unsympathetic crowd, are pathological rarities. . . . A more refined and a more humane popular taste now frown upon such exhibitions." Fascination with the "elastic skin man" declined when his condition was reduced to "generalized dermatolysis" and the "wild men of Borneo" were revealed to be merely examples of "microcephalous idiocy." In the 1920s and 1930s, popular magazines explained how standard freak types (giants, dwarfs etc) were really victims of glandular malfunctions. Sideshow barkers' claims that they displayed a member of a "lost tribe" of pygmies or "natives" with tails lost credibility when global exploration demystified distant places and peoples.[75]

The freak show that had been integral to the old "dime museums" of the nineteenth century largely disappeared from the cities in the first decade of the twentieth century. By 1915 even the waxworks of the Eden Musée in New York City had closed. With the exception of one traditional dime museum in Harlem, the survivors relocated to Coney Island, becoming exclusively freak shows, no longer part of the traditional dime museum's wider cultural appeal with its diorama, camera obscura, and even stage shows. Following a pattern identified by historian Lawrence Levine, the city became a center for more upscale and "progressive" exhibits in scientific natural history museums and middle-class inspired movie palaces while the freak was confined to a few blocks in the seediest streets of Coney Island.[76] The freak show had lost its wonder, at least to the urban middle classes.

Even at Coney Island, the freak show became discredited. While in the 1900s newspapers had reported the latest additions to the freak shows in a tone similar to announcements of the newest Broadway show, by the late 1920s, Bertram Reinitz wrote approvingly in the New York Times that the sideshows were growing "more conservative," not only because of the "growing scarcity of dog-faced men, mermaids, and many legged live stock," but also because of the "marked slump in the credulousness of metropolitan throngs." The "broad and dignified boardwalk" at Coney Island along with the "tall shoulder-to-shoulder apartment houses and retail enterprises . . . reminiscent not of the erstwhile leading honky-tonk center of the nation, but rather of [upscale Brooklyn neighborhoods like] Washington Heights and Williamsburg" were finally closing in on the old freak shows and catch penny amusements. Another pair of writers in 1928 took pride that only the freshly landed immigrant or the "holiday maker from Harlem" still gawked at the horror of the wax museum and was convinced that civility had finally come even to the working class: "A few hundred years have so developed our sense of decency that what was customary with the gentlemen of [the past] . . . would now be scandalous to the most proly of the proletariat."[77]

Critical comment on Blackpool's remaining freak shows of the 1930s, which were confined to the stalls of the "Golden Mile," was much more muted, largely because there were so few of them and the crowds reacted with increasing knowingness to the impostures. Starving honeymoon couples and transgressors against the accepted moral order were more in evidence than alleged physical freaks in any case, alongside horrific "educational" exhibitions (at the waxworks) of the consequences of venereal disease, and Blackpool's relative overall respectability and elite tolerance of plebeian taste was demonstrated by the absence of critical focus on freak shows.[78]

By 1950, American sideshow impresarios were finding it more difficult to find suitable human attractions due to early medical intervention preventing glandular disorders and the institutionalization of individuals with "freak" deformities.[79] But, by then, the freak show was also rapidly losing its audience even while amusement parks and circuses that surrounded them were still flourishing. Even though the freak show was resurrected in Coney Island in the 1980s, its self-display of sexual and cultural difference that tried to "combine flamboyant campiness with bawdy sexual humor" contrasted with the traditional serious, almost religious appeal of freak shows.[80]

This story of the decline of the freak did not mean the victory of the severely rational and humanistic goals of reformers. Wonder may have shifted away from the liminal and bizarre, but the longing for fantasy and excitement hardly vanished. Like the carnival itself, the freak was cutesified and passed on to children. It is no accident that the 1920s children's ride, the Pleasure Beach Express in Blackpool, used dwarfs as conductors. Even earlier, photos show parents taking their children to visit dwarf shows at Dreamland. Over time, "little people" were taken from the world of the bizarre to the realm of the innocent. Snow White had her cute seven dwarfs in Disney's first feature length cartoon of 1937. All sorts of gnomish figures found their way on to and in children's amusement park rides. If, as we shall see in chapter 5, Disney perfected this trend in his cartoon animals with their neotenic or childlike features, he was only conforming to a shift in adult sensibilities—abandoning the fascination with the boundary of nature for an obsession with nostalgia for a fantasy-based innocence.

The new middle-class sensibilities that were to provide the market opportunity for Disney were much more evident in the United States than in Britain. The British playful crowd, in its Blackpool incarnation and at other popular resorts, had become acceptable to mainstream middle-class opinion by the 1930s. At the same time, the British tendency to sentimentalize the virtuous working-class crowd led to the opening out of alternative routes to respectable communal pleasures after 1945, culminating in the rise of the "heritage industry" and the celebration of a variety of popular pasts, whether rural or industrial. These were alternatives ultimately to Blackpool, but also to Disneyland.

The elite critique of industrial saturnalia "won" with the triumph of middle-class values by the 1950s in the United States and, with more ambiguity, much later in Britain. Elements of the genteel aesthetic were sloughed off. There was a decline of the formality and ritual of class codes in both nations, but in Britain, the longing to affirm heritage in various guises ("natural," rural, aristocratic, industrial) would be important to postwar democratic innovations like the Beamish Museum as well as to more established, upscale institutions like the National Trust. Significantly, this impulse derived in distinctive ways from the descendents of the romantic socialists and improving trade unionists as well as from the nostalgic aristocracy and genteel bourgeoisie. At Beamish, as at such popular National Trust venues as Tatton Park or "stately homes" like Chatsworth, the noise, novelty, and artificiality of the saturnalian crowd was banished while the encounter with the beautiful natural setting and the recollection of a lost heritage, whether aristocratic, populist or a blend, was to be shared between adults and children.[81]

In the United States, the flight from gentility was more extreme, even as the critique of the plebeian crowd was sharper. Affluent Americans rejected the late Victorian plebeian crowd, but not all of their fun in the rides, bright lights, and frivolous fantasy of the amusement park. These middle-class Americans found this pleasure acceptable when enfolded in genteel codes that celebrated nature, order, and progress (as at Playland) and when expressed as the playfully childish. Middle-class children and youth embraced the thrills and fantasy of the plebeian pleasure crowd, thus allowing excitement to be embraced by middle-class adults. If carnival was defanged with the decline of freak shows and bowdlerized with the sentimentality of fairy tales, a new kind of wonder appeared in the nostalgic and childish fantasy of Disney.

In this chapter, we have seen that the middle-class reaction to the plebeian playful crowd took distinct forms in Britain and the United States. In the long run, this contrast would lead to the radically divergent creations of Disneyland and the Beamish Open Air Museum. In the short run, it would also help to shape the very different fates of Blackpool and Coney Island in the decades following World War I. This will be the topic of our next chapter.

Decline and Reinvention

CONEY ISLAND AND BLACKPOOL

By 1900, Blackpool and Coney Island had become emblematic sites of the playful crowd and industrial saturnalia. In the late 1920s, however, their career paths began to diverge sharply. Especially after the Second World War, the differences became more pronounced, revealing the cumulative effects of economic, political, and geographic divergences as well as contrasting tendencies within the crowds themselves. In many ways, both sites went through a similar cycle: from "discovery" and initial commercial exploitation, to the dominance of the artificial over the "natural," threatened loss of distinctiveness and desirability, and incipient decline. From that point onward, however, Coney Island went into an accelerating slide from which it never recovered, while Blackpool was able to reinvent itself in a succession of new guises, appealing to new constituencies and thus keeping the resort alive and dynamic.[1] Blackpool has not gone as far as Las Vegas in a "tradition of invention,"[2] but it has been resilient to threats on a variety of fronts, using the myths and legends of its past, as well as the surviving buildings and practices, to good effect.

Coney Island's problems can be traced back to the 1930s and even the superficially prosperous 1920s, when despite ever-growing crowds on Coney's beaches at summer weekends the increasingly proletarian visitors spent less while affluent New Yorkers abandoned the Island and took their cars along the new parkways to the more respectable environs of Jones Beach and Rockaway Beach. While Prohibition damaged the drinking culture of Coney Island in the 1920s, Robert Moses, as New York City's parks commissioner, launched a personal crusade against the raunchy frivolities of Coney in the 1930s. Coney's problems intensified in the postwar decades, coming to a head in the mid-1960s with the closure of Steeplechase, the last of the great amusement parks, together with the spread of redevelopment blight and the emergence of gang violence and racial tensions. This was part of a wider pattern of decline among blue-collar northeastern resorts in the United States as the more seductive climates of Florida and California became increasingly accessible. It was also the fate of a resort plagued by continual conflict between middle-class reformers and the plebeian crowd of Coney.[3]

Blackpool, by contrast, reinvented itself at the urban margins and drove itself up-market during the 1920s and 1930s with municipal promotion of parks, promenade extensions, and planning schemes, while keeping the older attractions of its popular core. The relative lack of antagonism between the old plebeian crowd and elite reformers explains much of this success. After World War I, it benefited from the extension of holidays with pay and improved material living standards to new sectors of the British population. It was not until the 1960s that the wider spread of a new car-based leisure culture, and developing competition from the sunny southwest of England and then from the Mediterranean, began to challenge Blackpool's dominance. Even when these changes really started to bite, the main sufferers were smaller northern resorts. But since the 1970s Blackpool has been on an accelerating treadmill, struggling to keep pace with changing trends in a political environment where local commerce has shifted toward international conglomerates.[4] This chapter addresses questions surrounding the contrasting fortunes of Blackpool and Coney Island since the original heyday of industrial saturnalia. We begin by comparing attempts to "civilize" the crowd in both places, especially in the interwar years.

Coney Island: Caught Between Down Markets and Inept Reform

Reformers never gave up hope that the plebeian crowd would embrace the sedate family group, develop a preference for tamed and controlled versions of nature, and even identify with a romantic past in settings that, as the urbanist Rem Koolhaas notes, could serve as a "remedy against the spontaneous urbanism of the masses." This was true on both sides of the anglophone Atlantic, but in the twentieth century this agenda was pursued with greater intensity and didactic intent at Coney Island than at Blackpool. New York reformers tried repeatedly to replace the dance halls and amusement park novelties with parks, improved beaches, and even enlightened entertainment (like the aquarium that was eventually erected in 1957). Following the annexation of Brooklyn (and therefore of Coney Island) by New York City in 1898, and the burning of part of the amusement area in one of Coney Island's regular fires, Bird S. Coler, the New York City Controller, made a gallant, if perhaps naïve, attempt to convince the city to purchase and transform the entirety of the West Brighton amusement zone into a public park in 1899.

Coler thought he saw an opportunity to transfer the idea of Olmsted's Central Park in Manhattan to Coney and to imitate the success of the green spaces created along Chicago's Lake Michigan shore. His plan called for a series of concrete esplanades, lawns, fountains, and flowerbeds. It won the support of the Methodist clergy of New York and others in letters to the *New York Times*. One enlightened citizen argued that public control alone would prevent those "objectionable features" that were inevitable under the system of private ownership and allow "natural attractions" to be "developed to the maximum." Another writer insisted that a rehabilitated Coney Island alone could create in city dwellers that idealism "roused by some nearness to nature, to the woods and fields, and most of all, to the ocean." Despite popular support, City officials voted nine to five against Coler's proposal, concerned about its estimated $15 million cost. Coney Island had been subsumed under New York City's budget planning (as opposed to being an independent municipality representing primarily the tourist industry as in Blackpool). This guaranteed that a costly proposal for building a public park in Coney Island could not compete with politically popular spending on streets, sewers and police across metropolitan New York City. Nevertheless, while this attempt to gentrify Coney Island failed, middle-class efforts to "clean up" the Island dominated the politics of the area, contributing ironically to an eventual decline of the pleasure district by the 1950s.[5]

The more modest goal of constructing a boardwalk to rouse the "idealism" of New Yorkers and restore their access to the shore gained support in the early 1910s. For decades public access to the beach had been cut off by commercial bathing concessions, which posted guards to prevent anyone from approaching the beach except through their gates. Hotels had their own boardwalks, but they were accessible only to paying guests. As a democratic gesture, the city built the Municipal Bathhouse in 1911, which competed successfully with the private operators. In the same year a civic group called the West End Improvement League proposed a public boardwalk to make access to the shore a public right. The group's plan required a state court to affirm public ownership of the beach from high to low tide zones. Tension heightened as discussion continued during the war years, when the private bathhouses dramatically raised their entrance fees. Many tenement dwellers sought cheaper alternatives (for example, by changing clothes in grubby side street houses for a dime). Bathhouse owners tried to enforce licensing requirements and prohibitions against appearing on the street in bathing clothes, but popular pressures for cheap access to the sea grew.[6]

Popular and elite demands combined to bring the public boardwalk to fruition. But it took eight years of lawsuits and debate before a plan could be forged, after which the work moved ahead rapidly. The new public promenade was two miles long and 80 feet wide and included tons of sand to deepen the beach. When the new boardwalk opened in May 1923 five days of celebrations included a baby show, a perambulator parade, fashion shows, a fancy dress parade, and a bathing beauty contest. For the time, these appeals to the charms of childhood and dignified female beauty were markers of respectability, antidotes to the plebeian mockery and garishness of Mardi Gras celebrations each September on Surf Avenue. Photos of opening day show throngs of men in dark suits and ties on the boardwalk, even under personal cabanas on the beach. Women were equally formal with fur collars on long coats and flowered hats. At the spring reopening of the boardwalk the next year, a gigantic "birthday" cake was cut and distributed to children. The boardwalk was expected to raise the social tone of Coney. The promenade offered opportunities for healthy family exercise and sociable communion with nature in the form of beach and sea, at a safe distance from the bars, stalls, sideshows, and rides of the old Bowery and amusement parks. When the scars of development healed, new buildings, fringing the boardwalk were built, with attractive features in granite and terracotta, as befitted an area that had been pulled up market by careful municipal investment.[7]

On a summer 1924 visit the French Prime Minister, Edouard Herriot, commented that "To understand the crowd, one must go to Coney Island." In his enthusiasm for the new boardwalk, Herriot compared it with the elite French Riviera resort of Nice by describing Coney's boardwalk as a "'Promenade des Anglais' for the proletariat. Here there is no noise . . . a haven of relaxation and rest." This was especially true on spring and even winter weekends, as the boardwalk filled up with quiet strolling couples and families while the stalls and entertainments remained in hibernation. The free beach and its boardwalk seemed to promise an opportunity for universal uplift or, at least, democratization of access.[8]

4.1   Coney's new Boardwalk in 1923 advertised as "wide enough to accommodate the multitude of people who flock there to enjoy the cool breezes." Courtesy of the Brooklyn Historical Society.

But the users of the boardwalk and its amenities did not always share the values of the city's governors. Proletarian beach goers continued to break the rules. Many arrived via subway with swimming suits under their clothes or changed in the bungalows of locals for a small fee, avoiding the pricier bathhouses. They hid peddlers from police during periodic crackdowns (preferring the peddlers' convenient services to the distant and expensive cafes and licensed vendors on the streets). While in 1900 exceptionally hot days attracted only 100,000 beachgoers, on a hot July Sunday in 1925, 750,000 beachgoers found that the 150,000-person capacity of the bathhouses was entirely insufficient. The shoreline was packed with humanity, utterly defeating the genteel dreams of reformers. Their efforts coincided with a massive increase in the popularity and accessibility of Coney Island. The mid-1920s appearance of five massive roller coasters lining the back of the boardwalk appealed to a youthful crowd that was looking for thrills and had little in common with the gentlefolk riding on roller chairs on the boardwalk.[9]

Despite the disapproving glances of the respectable when bathers changed in public on the beach or "dripped" on the subway ride home still dressed in swimming suits, they broke decorum and enjoyed themselves practically for free. Still, the City happily protected this site of democratic play for poor New York citizens. Municipal officials repeatedly extended and improved the boardwalk, provided competent life guarding, and eventually built sewage treatment plants on Coney Island Creek to reduce shoreline pollution. Here New York City, with all its limitations, was a long way ahead of Blackpool, where raw sewage poured directly into the sea from long outfalls along the bathing beaches. All this reflected a prevailing assumption within the New York elite that boardwalk and beach were places where mass play, social uplift, and the pursuit of health could coincide.[10]

The boardwalk development had made the beaches and sea freely accessible without mounting a direct challenge to the resort's amusement parks and catchpenny shows. In the short run this improvement encouraged investment in sumptuous new theaters, a boxing ring, and the impressive, if ultimately ill-fated, Half Moon Hotel, as big business came into the resort. After about 1910, there was a rapid growth in bungalow vacation rentals. This trend reinforced the stable middle-class element even though, because these families provided their own meals, it also reduced demand for restaurants at Coney.

Nevertheless, the dreams of uplift and a democratized gentility at Coney Island were not to be. Even while the "natural" was promoted alongside the commercial at Coney, the automobile made alternatives to the crowded Island increasingly accessible in the 1920s for those who could afford it. Those seeking nature's solitude, or at least a more select and less outrageously crowded pleasure environment, took to the wheel on Sunday drives to beaches out of reach to the nickel subway crowd. Thousands of cars journeyed further, as New York families visited the "Jersey Shore" (Long Branch, Bradley Beach, as well as the popular Atlantic City and Asbury Park). On one warm May day in 1926, while 450,000 were said to have visited Coney, 200,000 went to the middle-class beach at Rockaway.[11] To accommodate the growing demand for automobile touring, the Long Island State Park Commission began in 1924 an ambitious project of reclaiming coastal land and beaches for a chain of 14 parks accessible via new state highways. The largest of these public parks, Jones Beach, became the main rival of Coney Island, a popular rendezvous for the millions, sited an hour from the city by road. But these "millions" did not include families without cars. The overpasses above the new highways were deliberately made (it was said) too low for buses to pass under, and requests for railroad connections, with their democratic implications, were firmly denied.[12]

Even more frustrating to this dream of uplifting Coney Island was the persistence of the "Nickel Empire" and the decline of the middle-class family atmosphere at Coney Island amusements. Dreamland, with its genteel presumptions had never been rebuilt, while the Coney Island amusement district shifted subtly to a more youth-focused and down-market crowd. A boom in amusement technology, beginning with the Wonder Wheel of 1920 and following on with five big new roller coasters during the decade, brought a shift toward the thrill ride over the old dioramas, sideshow, and other performance attractions. The tension between the "Nickel Empire" of plebeian crowds dependent upon the subway ride and hot dogs (each costing five cents) and the attempts of reformers to uplift and refurbish the Island constituted a formula for disaster.[13]

Doubtless the Depression accelerated the downward trend. Even the ending of Prohibition in 1933, which brought beer out of the speakeasies and back to the bars and restaurants of Coney, failed to work its magic in the difficult decade before World War II. The economic insecurity of the masses who poured out of the subway made it more difficult to turn a profit, however crowded the streets and boardwalk might be. Prices for rides were halved and halved again, but this did little good. The subway crowds continued to evade the bathhouses, brought their own food, and went to the beach rather than the amusements. The shows themselves shrank in scale and ambition, and in 1933 Luna Park went bankrupt and had to open in receivership. The famous Feltman's restaurant reduced its staff by two-thirds, as it resisted the pressure to lower prices. Five cent hot dogs and three cent sodas cut profit margins to the bone as did Steeplechase's 25 cent combination ticket for 25 attractions. Sam Wagner, the freak show impresario had once attracted 20,000 customers on a good Sunday, but by 1939 he had to be content with 8,000, while only one tattoo artist now survived out of the nine or ten who had plied their trade at Coney's peak. The resort had become a cheap playground for the impoverished masses, with disproportionately cheap, garish, and freakish attractions. The playful crowd had become a swirling, congested mass, seeking what enjoyment it could in the noisy streets, careening along the boardwalk and carving out tiny individual and family spaces amid the astonishing overcrowding of the freely accessible popular beach. In some people's eyes the results of this took away any residual hint of populist magic: "A million people, treading gingerly among broken glass and filth that seemed never to be cleaned up, jammed the beach so full on a Sunday that they could hardly see the sand."[14]

Coney Island still had magic enough to feature prominently in the popular entertainment of these years, as in films like "Manhattan Melodrama" and "The Devil and Miss Jones," or songs by Rodgers and Hart ("Manhattan," and "The Lady is a Tramp") and Cole Porter ("You're the Top"). It is also remembered as a safe place to live, with strong neighborhoods, a high level of mutual trust, and stable local businesses to cater for the resident population.[15] But the writing was on the wall.

Meanwhile, Robert Moses came into the frame. His rise to a dominant position in the city planning of Long Island and Greater New York after 1924 brought sustained pressure on the old amusement zone without successfully transforming Coney Island into a modern genteel resort. From 1924 as President of the Long Island State Park Commission and chair of the State Council of Parks, he opened new beaches with "parkway" road access along the Long Island shore. His failure to provide public transportation facilities to any beaches other than Coney Island, however, drew this comment from a critical biographer: "[Coney Island was] the lone bathing beach reachable by public transportation, and therefore the one to which, because of Moses' class-separating policies, the city's poor were herded." The municipality had off-street parking for 3,000 cars in 1932, half of it on the old Dreamland site, but it also charged 50 cents for parking there at weekends. When in 1934 the Board of Aldermen countermanded Moses by halving the charge, one member commented that most of these car owners at Coney were "poor people" who could not afford to pay 50 cents.[16]

Moses' dislike of Coney Island's crowds and amusement area was already no secret. He blamed itinerant candy and refreshment salesmen for the high levels of litter generated by what he saw as an essentially undisciplined, rather than, playful crowd. In a single June day in 1934, no fewer than 350 peddlers were arrested. His powers were extended to cover the boardwalk and beaches in 1938 and he was able to intensify his campaigns against the hundreds of fast food, souvenir retail, and cheap amusement businesses that still dominated the Coney Island scene. He

4.2   World War II saw some of the largest beach crowds at Coney Island (1942?). Library of Congress

banned advertising, human pyramids and gymnastics, speechmaking, and phono-
graphs and loudspeakers near the beach. Moses also attempted to curb the "ballyhoo" of "barkers" for the shows and posted ostentatious signs listing rules and
regulations. As the *New York Times* noted, some changes were cosmetic: "Beach
attendants now wear sailor suits instead of drab khaki. Chair-pushers are garbed in
special uniforms, too. A few of the millions visiting the beach have been fined $5
for sitting on newspapers on the sand. Others have paid small fines for undressing
beneath the boardwalk, playing poker on the beach, walking on the Boardwalk in
bathing suits."[17]

But Moses' longer-term agenda had already been laid out in a letter to the Mayor in 1937, which made clear his intention to squeeze out "catch penny" devices and mechanical amusements and replace them with parks, play areas and more extensive beaches. He also encouraged a transition from amusements to residential uses: "There is no use bemoaning the end of the old Coney Island fabled in song and story," he noted. "The important thing is not to proceed in the mistaken belief that it can be revived. There must be a new and very different resort established in its place. . . . There must be more land in public ownership, less over-crowding, stricter enforcement of ordinances and rules, better transportation and traffic arrangement, less mechanical noise-making and amusement devices and side-shows, and a more orderly growth of year-round residents." In effect, Moses declared war on the old Coney Island. And New York's Mayor La Guardia endorsed this goal in 1939: "I feel that the present Coney Island layout is an anachronism. The best proof of this is that it is difficult for present holders of property and operators to make their investments pay under the old type method of resort amusement." A chronic lack of investment in new rides and other facilities was becoming apparent, but Moses' interventions were also accelerating an already apparent economic decline in the amusement business.[18]

To be fair, Moses was most concerned about the crowding on the beach: In a 1939 report, he complained that the 16 square feet per person available on many Sundays were about the "same as required for a coffin." In his plans for pulling back the boardwalk and adding huge quantities of white sand to the extended beach, he insisted that a "civilized" community "might do a little more by way of recreation for its citizens between the tight places of the cradle and the grave." In the grand genteel tradition, Moses demanded that New York not perpetuate "out of doors the over-crowding of our tenements." His improvements at Coney, completed in 1941, pulled the boardwalk inland and added mountains of white sand to the beach, but also caused significant demolitions in the amusement zone. The two worlds of Coney Island, the boardwalk and the Nickel Empire, could never make peace or find a compromise.[19]

The Playful Crowd and Planning in Blackpool, 1920–1940

There was no hint of any similar crisis in Blackpool's entertainment industry between the wars. The town's situation contrasted sharply with that of Coney Island.

As we have seen, its local government was master of its own municipal destiny, rather than being a remote outlier of a metropolis. Its rulers collaborated with local business interests rather than conflicted with them, and understood that continuing growth, especially of the middle-class housing of commuters and retirees, would require more planned development, but without posing any threat to the established amusement sector. Within a year of the passing of the national Housing and Town Planning Act of 1919, Ernest Lawson, a local politician and the manager of the Queen's Hydro hotel at South Shore, had won popular support for the first systematic local government plan for a British resort town. Blackpool had more need of this than upscale resorts like Eastbourne, Llandudno, or neighboring St Anne's, Lytham, and Southport. The town's rulers embraced Lawson's new thinking with enthusiasm. They hired the eminent landscape architect T. H. Mawson to plan a new park and extensions to the promenade. The 256 acres of Stanley Park, on an inland site that had been an area of wasteland and shanty towns, opened to the public in 1926, contrasting sharply with the inability of New Yorkers to do the same at Coney. Soon, the new park was surrounded by detached houses in spacious, tree-lined suburban roads. Meanwhile, the promenade extension south of the Pleasure Beach was carefully arranged so that attractive houses with neat front gardens would face the railroad, enhancing Blackpool's image to visitors arriving by train.[20] While Coney Island floundered in finding a use for the abandoned Dreamland, Blackpool built a huge municipal open-air swimming pool near the Pleasure Beach at South Shore in 1923. This initiative also reflected another contrast with Coney Island: the declining use of Blackpool's beach for bathing, as opposed to sitting on hired deckchairs while fully clothed. "Drippers" were not a Blackpool issue, nor was "mackintosh bathing," wearing bathing dress under a raincoat and disrobing on the beach. That infamous eighteenth-century British institution, the bathing machine, was already in terminal decline at Blackpool by the 1920s.[21]

On the eve of World War II, Blackpool's ambitions were running even higher. The Corporation was planning a central redevelopment scheme, which would sweep away the slum housing behind the "Golden Mile" and set back the Central Station to make way for boulevards and flowerbeds on the City Beautiful model; but this was overtaken by events. This civic determination to transform the resort's image and environment stopped short at treating the town's sewer system; but otherwise it provided a spacious and civilized setting for crowds whose behavior was expected to improve in step with this investment, and helped to ensure the town a

good press in this period, as its Carnivals and (after 1925) autumn electrical Illuminations successfully extended the season and attracted the middle classes.

Where Coney Island lost the newly mobile middle and upper working visiting
publics to new, more salubrious beach resorts in the 1920s and 1930s, Blackpool
successfully attracted them with an environment designed to appeal at least in part
to genteel values. The upscale north and south shores survived and were even
extended in Blackpool after World War I while a similar affluent zone in Coney
Island faded after the abolition of horserace betting in 1910, although Sea Gate and
other residential areas remained. The planning policies of Blackpool Corporation
between the wars not only averted the flight of the middle class, but also actively
encouraged upscale new settlement, especially in the area around the new Stanley
Park. At the same time, the continued domination of rail transport for all social
classes in Britain through the interwar years meant that an older pattern of tourism survived at Blackpool. Here, different social strata congregated within walking
distance of the train stations, sharing some amenities near the center even while
lodging in distinct zones. Bus services expanded rapidly but also brought their
passengers to a central coach station. While a large segment of the British middle
class did not embrace the private car until the 1950s, it had become the norm in
the middle strata of American families as early as the 1920s. This contrast explains
the delayed impact at Blackpool of the new forms of holidaymaking that were associated with car ownership, although the town built its first multi-story car park in
1939. But the continuing, and indeed expanding, importance of the middle classes
at Blackpool marked a widening contrast with Coney Island, and the general com-
patibility between the classes at Blackpool helped to assure the respectability of
Blackpool's playful crowd. [22]

The logic of Blackpool's abortive 1939 central redevelopment plan ran parallel
with Moses' efforts to "reform" Coney Island, but with very different implications.
The buildings of the "Golden Mile" that were threatened by the redevelopment
scheme included both the greatest concentration of freak shows, waxworks, games
of chance and stalls that existed in the resort, along with some of the earliest and
most disreputable housing at the back. Removal of this "Whitechapel of Blackpool"
(a common allusion to an infamous district of London's East End that was associated with Jack the Ripper) was accepted as a desirable byproduct of the redevelopment; but in the meantime the local police and councilors were quite relaxed about
the area and those who frequented it. When occasional complaints were made to

central government about particularly controversial exhibits such as allegedly fasting young women, the Corporation reassured the Home Office in London that local officials found these women to be in good health, with local homes to go to at the end of the working day. Not only was the Corporation not too worried about the petty deceptions practiced on customers, it made only a half-hearted attempt to regulate such shows. There was certainly no local equivalent of Robert Moses to drive forward the forces of control.[23] In the end, the Second World War, and the succeeding period of austerity in Britain, put the great redevelopment scheme on hold for over thirty years.

Again in contrast to Coney, there were numerous efforts at modernization in the Depression decade including the introduction of streamlined trams, a new Opera House at the Winter Gardens, the Derby Baths indoor swimming pool on the North Promenade, and the "world's greatest Woolworth's" opposite Central Station. The Pleasure Beach especially saw extensive upgrading in the 1930s in striking contrast with the lack of innovation at Coney Island. Here the impetus for change came from within, as Leonard Thompson, who had taken over the reins from his father-in-law, W. G. Bean, after his untimely death in 1929, aimed at confirming the respectability of the amusement park. In this he was following Bean, who had hired T. H. Mawson to remodel the Pleasure Beach in 1926. While Mawson's plan never was realized, Thompson proceeded to make the Pleasure Beach look less industrial. It had lacked the fantasy architecture of Luna Park, and some of its rides bore an uncanny resemblance to the winding gear of coalmines. In 1933, Thompson hired the modernist architect Joseph Emberton to give the park a new, clean, tidy, modern look. The park had already introduced enduring attractions like the Whip, Noah's Ark, the Virginia Reel, and the Big Dipper in the early 1920s at the same time as had Coney. But, unlike the New York resort, this continued after 1930 with the Ghost Train, Pleasure Beach Express miniature railroad, Fun House, Grand National roller coaster, Tumble Bug, Eli Wheel and Octopus.[24]

Thompson had been able to take advantage of the cheapness of materials and labor during the Depression. But even more important was the creation, starting in 1934, of a completely revamped Pleasure Beach environment. After years of conflict, the Blackpool Improvement Act of 1932 obliged the Pleasure Beach's boundaries to be clearly and attractively defined. Thompson brought in an American designer to provide new frontages and begin the redevelopment of the park's interior. But the key appointment was that of Emberton, who imposed a distinc-

4.3   These two pictures (*from 1925, above, and the late 1930s, below*) illustrate the transformation wrought on the Pleasure Beach by Joseph Emberton and other modernist architects and designers during the mid to late 1930s, from an almost industrial aesthetic to a streamlined Art Deco look. Courtesy of the Pleasure Beach, Blackpool.

tive flowing modernity on the whole site. Thompson took pains to distinguish the clean healthy fun of the Pleasure Beach from the enclave of freaks and occultism on the "Golden Mile." In 1932, he issued a lofty dismissal of the defrocked Rector of Stiffkey's request to move from the Golden Mile and exhibit himself on the Pleasure Beach. In 1936, Thompson invited eminent scientists conventioneering at Blackpool to try the rides and won endorsement from psychologists for their therapeutic value. By 1938, *The Scotsman* could even suggest that the Americans were now coming to Blackpool to look for new ideas about amusement parks. The Pleasure Beach's success was firmly founded on an increasingly positive relationship with local authorities and on a determined drive for artistic and even intellectual respectability. It would be hard to imagine a sharper contrast with Moses' relationship with Coney Island, and the pattern of development there.[25]

After the War

The decades after 1945 confirmed earlier trends. Still the collapse of Coney certainly was not inevitable. During the late 1930s and through the 1940s Coney Island showed some symptoms of recovery from the Depression. While Frank Tilyou hoped to get "a sizeable share of . . . the bonanza" from the New York World's Fair of 1939, by attracting out-of-towners with money in their pockets rather than the usual crowd who "come for the bathing dressed in their bathing suits and don't spend a red penny,"[26] the World's Fair proved disappointing. Even so, when it closed, Coney's two amusement parks were able refresh their tired menus by taking new attractions from it. The Parachute Jump was a particularly striking landmark, installed at Steeplechase in 1941 on the site of a recent fire. To one local observer it was "The most exciting ride ever to hit the Island."[27] Otherwise, Steeplechase stuck to its tried and trusted menu and prices. Luna Park, which had endured a second bankruptcy in 1938, purchased 15 rides from the World's Fair. For Joseph Heller and his circle of local friends, who had plenty of opportunities to judge, Luna Park was always more enticing than Steeplechase.[28]

It was, however, Luna Park that ceased operation first. On August 12, 1944 yet another of Coney Island's fires, this time starting with an electrical fault in the washroom of the recently refurbished Dragon's Gorge ride, destroyed half the park. Following another Coney Island tradition, a crowd estimated at 750,000 watched 62 fire companies try to restrain the flames. Also characteristic was the

4.4   The sensual fun of old Coney survived in the 1940s. Here five young women seem to enjoy the fact that their skirts were blown up by concealed air blasts. Library of Congress.

prompt reopening of the remains of the park, which carried on until the season's end in mid-September.[29] But this was the end of the line. The syndicate that owned Luna Park sold the site back to the Prudence Bonds Corporation, which had taken it over during a previous bankruptcy. The company decided not to reconstruct. Instead, when they found in 1946 that "Reconstruction of the buildings and the elaborate network of rides would entail a heavy expenditure under high post-war construction costs," they opted to sell. As the company's president put it, Luna Park on choice land just north of Surf Avenue was destined for "a new and higher purpose," that of housing 625 war veterans and their families in high-rise apartments.[30] As we shall see, this development was entirely in line with Robert Moses' vision of Coney Island's respectable residential future.[31]

Meanwhile, despite the war and demolition of Luna Park, Coney's beach was attracting unprecedented crowds. On summer Sundays in the 1940s up to a million people would throng its beaches and streets, and 400,000 was an average figure for an ordinary warm weekend. Coney Island was an inevitable calling point for servicemen on leave during the war years, while gasoline rationing made it more difficult to reach the more distant beaches. In 1943, Coney attracted 46 million, the best year since 1925. In 1946 Coney Island accommodated up to 4,800 bathers per acre, "an allowance of nine square feet per person," far worse than the 16 square feet that Moses had found so uncivilized several years earlier. Photographs show astonishing expanses of people, most of them in swim suits and happy to play to the camera, stretching into the distance across sand made invisible by the sheer crush of tightly packed bodies. Holiday crowds on this scale were unique to Coney Island. Blackpool, with its seven or eight million visitors per year and up to half a million in the town on its busiest weekends, was far behind in the numbers game. The biggest crowd of all at Coney gathered two years after the war to watch a military air show and fireworks display. Otherwise, the Fourth of July 1955 took the prize with, it was said, well over 1.5 million.[32] After the war, too, the surviving amusements received a long overdue coat of paint. At the start of the 1953 season the streets were full as well as the beaches, with crowds seven deep on the sidewalks and cars parked three abreast in the busiest streets.[33]

But most of the crowd still provided disappointing patronage for amusement businesses. Steeplechase Park continued to take pride in its manicured lawns and gardens, uniformed employees dressed in white shirts and ties who ousted gangs of youth without parental supervision, and reasonably clean facilities. It dominated the entertainment section with its 11 acres of rides (including the new Parachute Jump, pool, ballroom, and pavilion). Yet while annual visitor numbers to Coney were said to be running at 40 million and beyond, as it entered its fifty-first season in 1947, Steeplechase welcomed six-year-old Patricia Lyons as only its 20 millionth visitor. Relatively little had changed in the 1930s and 1940s. Little investment was made, and although the down-market crowd seemed not to demand it, this certainly did not bode well for the future. While freak shows were in sharp decline in middle-class resorts, an August 1945 spread in *Life* Magazine about Coney, featured an Elephant Girl (with an unusually long nose), along with a headless girl, and a wax re-enactment of the death of the gangster John Dillinger. In the public eye, Coney represented a now fading carnival world.[34]

In 1953 a concessionaire at Coney commented that there was, "Not much dough there. You can't do much clipping any more. You clip a guy today and they call it grand larceny. See these barkers. They're mostly guys with bum tickers. The old-style grifters they gave up. What's the use? These people nowadays, they want their money's worth."[35] Such defeatist sentiments, expressed by one of the petty exploiters of the crowd, would have gladdened the heart of Robert Moses.

Part of Moses' motive for pulling back the boardwalk in 1941 was undoubtedly to undermine the old entertainment economy.[36] And, while he certainly improved the beach, the project also displaced many amusement businesses. As the *New York Times* noted, "veterans of the island concede that the carnival is ended." Many property owners saw the writing on the wall, and they were unwilling to invest and improve with the prospect of additional condemnations for redevelopment.[37]

The pressure for change gained additional force in the 1950s when Moses dominated the New York City Housing Authority, enabling him to pursue his general agenda of "slum clearance" and of replacing most of the entertainment district with residential development. As the first new high-rise housing schemes got under way in the early 1950s, Moses secured the rezoning of most of Coney Island from commercial to mixed business and residential use, hoping to foster the building of apartment buildings near the seaside. The City Planning Commission assumed that Steeplechase and other "large amusement arenas" would "continue to thrive indefinitely at Coney," but that rezoning would encourage the gradual disappearance of the more tawdry areas. Meanwhile, following an earlier proposal from the Coney Island Chamber of Commerce in February 1940, he moved the New York Aquarium, an uplifting recreation entirely compatible with his vision of a new Coney, to the former Dreamland site. Completed in 1957, this project required the demolition of amusement property on Surf Avenue, along with additional land for a parking lot. City plans also included beach and park development in the Manhattan Beach area. However, not only did local residents block parts of this plan, but also the Coney Island Chamber of Commerce opposed these attacks on petty amusement businesses. In 1953, a local businessman argued that, "It would be criminal to tear down the Bowery and Surf Avenue. . . . Where would the poor people go—to the Riviera?" The unresolved conflicts between the Nickel Empire and heavy-handed gentility of Moses could not be resolved.[38]

Who won? In many ways, of course, "reformers" did; they destroyed the seedy side of Coney, but without creating an uplifting residential or natural setting.

Moses' maneuvers of the 1940s and early 1950s cleared the way for some of the urban renewal he sought. High-rise redevelopment began in earnest in the late 1950s, hemming in the shrinking amusement district. Renewal also generated speculative rack-renting in the time period between proposed and actual demolition, precipitating the departure of established residents who could not afford the new rents in the new high rises. Jewish and Italian neighborhoods were broken up, and the 1960s saw a migration of black and Hispanic welfare tenants to western Coney Island, paving the way for wholesale demolition in this "slum" district. In 1967, the West End of Coney was declared a Poverty Zone and slated for what became very spotty renewal.[39]

Three years earlier Steeplechase, the last great amusement park, closed for what turned out to be the last time at the end of the 1964 season, after the patriarch Frank Tilyou died and his elderly sister Marie chose to close rather than to try to bring her feuding family together on a plan. Critics have suggested also that underlying this decision was an unwillingness to adapt to the changing ethnic and racial character of Coney Island crowds. Although James Onorato, son of the long-time manager of Steeplechase, insisted that the park had welcomed blacks since the 1930s, the "whites-only mentality" of patrons of Steeplechase's mammoth pool led to an informal exclusion of racial minorities. In 1964, complaints about this policy in the context of racial conflicts at Coney that summer, plus costs of a required water filtration system, led to the closure of the pool, an important money-maker at Steeplechase and thus a contributing factor in closing the park. In 1965, Marie Tilyou described her park as a "gorgeous rosebud in a garbage can," complained about the "horrible types one sees in the summer," and worried about even more change with "urban renewal."[40]

After various attempts to salvage Steeplechase as a going concern, the developer Fred Trump, already active in the area, bought the park for a housing development and demolished it. Failing to gain legal permits, he abandoned the project, selling it to the city, which left the site a vacant eyesore. In sharp contrast with 1939, Coney was left out of the planning for the 1964 World's Fair in New York, whose president was Robert Moses. The beginning of the 1968 season saw a frightening riot on a hot April Sunday when there were 600,000 people at Coney, and the violent scenes attracted extensive media coverage. Coney Island had finally lost the reputation for security of person and property that was essential to its success.[41]

The 1970s were disastrous. The loss of Steeplechase had eliminated one of the keystones of Coney's appeal to families. Further destructive and disruptive redevelop-

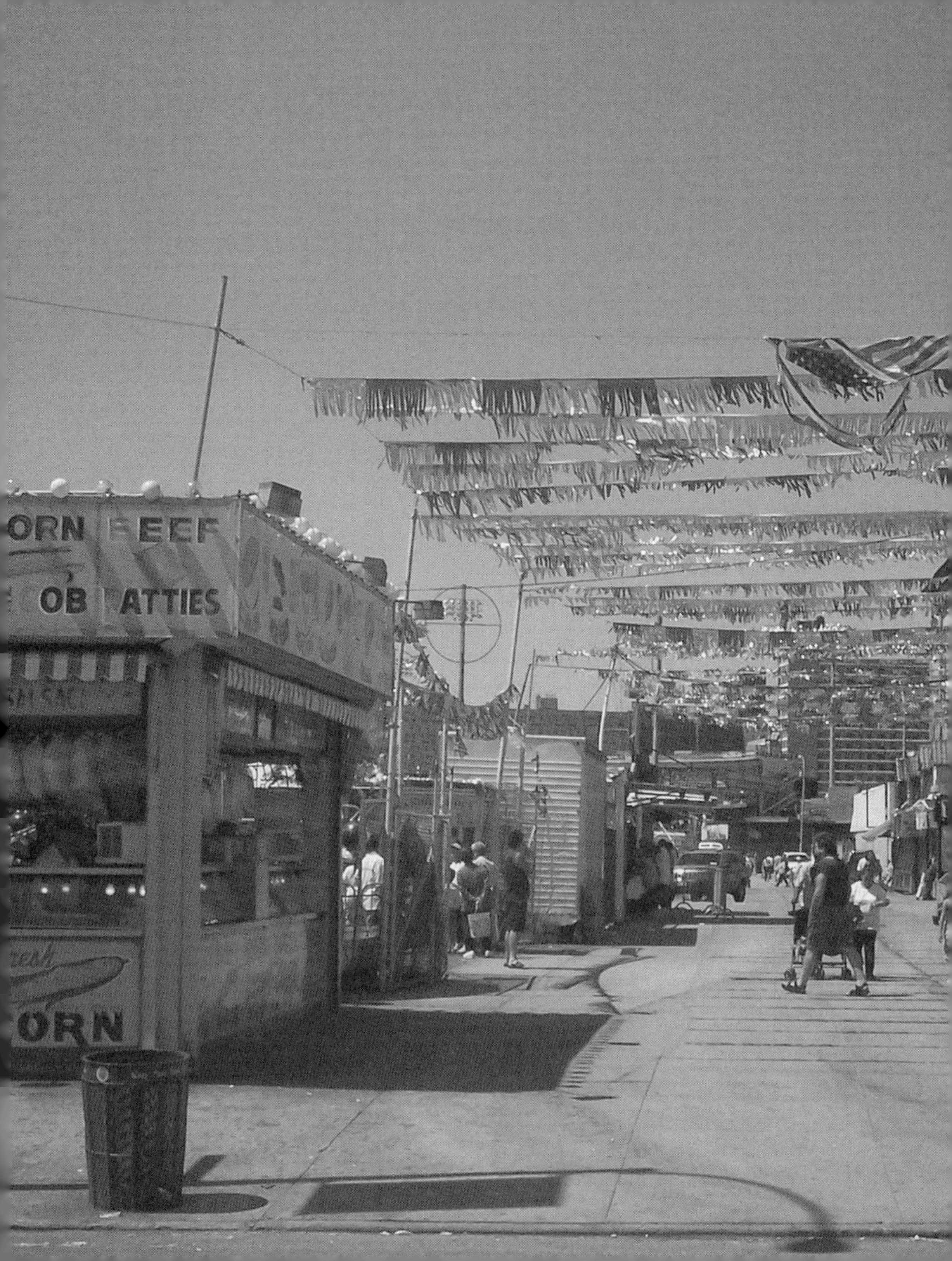
ORN BEEF
OB PATTIES
ORN

ment accompanied an epidemic of arson and the loss of ride after ride and building after building. The John Lindsay administration tried to move Harlem residents into the West End, many of whom ended up in the old bungalows that lacked adequate heating for winter use. Muggings drove away revelers and shop owners complained that police would not patrol after 2 a.m. Drug addicts stole even the copper wire on the boardwalk. A shrunken entertainment zone remained, while Nathan's Famous Hotdogs survived proudly amid the ruins and a new amusement park, Astroland, had developed from 1963 onwards. The Cyclone roller coaster survived a series of demolition threats, not least from the New York Aquarium, but these were isolated landmarks among the rubble and vacant lots. Gangs ran riot and Coney became unsafe for the elderly to visit the remaining shops. Proud cinemas were given over to pornography. In 1976, one resident of Coney commented of his neighborhood: "It is a great dumping ground."[42]

Persistent efforts have been made to revive Coney, including a flirtation with the idea of casino gambling in 1979 (opposed by the Trumps with their holdings in Atlantic City and by others fearful of additional crime in the area). An effort beginning in 1985 by black entrepreneur Horace Bullard to buy out remaining commercial lots secretly in order to build a massive theme park failed when his scheme was discovered by remaining owners in 1991. "Nothing gets off the ground," complained a resident in 1986. Rivalries (some based on old ethnic and family disputes) stood in the way of corporate-led renewal. What remained of the old Bowery was mostly closed in 1998, by which time all but one roller coaster and Ferris wheel had disappeared. In 1985 Coney Island USA revived the freak show tradition and opened a museum and in the late 1990s a minor league baseball park was built on part of the old Steeplechase vacant land. But Coney Island in the new century had become a shadow of its former self.[43]

By contrast, Blackpool's popular vitality would be sustained in the postwar generation. At Blackpool, as in Britain generally, the crowd's spending power was further increased by the belated general introduction of holidays with pay after 1945. The rationing and short supply of consumer goods, which persisted into the

4.5   (*Previous page*) In 2004, the Bowery was a pale shadow of its former self, with neither the excitement nor notoriety of the past, but instead features makeshift amusements. This view looks toward what was once Steeplechase Park (to the west). By G. Cross.

early 1950s, also left more in the budget for leisure and holidays; and the 1950s and 1960s brought full employment and a consumer boom. The domestic seaside holiday continued to dominate, and competition from cheap flights to Spain and Mediterranean resorts did not yet present a challenge. Blackpool was especially fortunate immediately after the war. As Paul Axel Lund remarked, "Blackpool was one of the few seaside places which wasn't mined and barbed-wired, so it was packed with holiday-makers all having their pockets stuffed with money and not enough to spend it on."[44] Under these conditions, Blackpool's playful crowd became more cheerful and more affluent than ever. The Ward Lock guide to the town in the mid-1950s expressed the conventional sentiments: "Blackpool is an astonishing place . . . tourists from all over the world have come—and continue to come in ever-growing numbers—to see what it is all about. . . . Blackpool romps through the superlatives . . . the happy faces and ready friendships of the holiday multitude are a fine 'mixture as before' . . . Blackpool is no longer an all-wakes resort. Far from it. The catholicity of its appeal is one of its chief attractions. It is one of the most cosmopolitan towns in the world, and every taste is provided for."[45] However excessive this rhetoric may have been, postwar Blackpool was certainly a national resort with an international leavening and a regional core, and at ease with itself in this guise.

In retrospect, however, clouds can could be found on the horizon. Novel attractions in the postwar generation were almost confined to the Pleasure Beach; and even here very little happened during the decade of austerity, given the building materials shortages that followed the war. A sudden spurt of new rides began in the late 1950s with the Hurricane, Wild Mouse, and Derby Racer, continuing steadily through the 1960s with an average of one significant innovation per year, with the Monorail (1966) and Log Flume (1967) standing out for their novelty value.[46]

Elsewhere the great burst of creative investment in the late 1930s was not resumed after the war. The Tower Company did replace its sumptuous Ballroom in all its late Victorian glory after a fire in 1956, but this expressed confidence in the enduring continuity of popular taste rather than any quest for innovation. In 1961, indeed, the adjoining Palace, originally the Alhambra, gave way to a department store, providing a strong marker of changing tastes and priorities.[47] The Corporation's autumn electrical Illuminations returned in 1949, a powerful symbol of the transition from postwar austerity, and later even introduced Disney characters. Blackpool's pleasure palaces were still able to pull in guest appearances from international stars like

4.6   Coney Island from the pier. While the beach and boardwalk have never been cleaner and more pleasant on this Sunday in August 2004, the high-rise apartments have long encroached on the amusement section with little left but two small amusement parks in the center and the aquarium to the right where Dreamland stood a century before. By G. Cross.

Frank Sinatra in the early 1950s.[48] But Harold Tunstall, an "artist" for the Blackpool Tower Company, was correct when he lamented in 1961 that, "I'm afraid at present the Town . . .tend[s] to live in the reflected glory of the great ideas of the past."[49] Tunstall's attitude was probably shaped by the fact that he was seeking work on a "Themeland" project that was investigating the possibility of building a Blackpool version of Disneyland that ultimately failed to materialize (see chapter 6). This was not the only failed proposal for an integrated corporate entertainment zone. A few years later municipal proposals for a central redevelopment, to include "a casino, elevated walkways and skyscraper hotels," fell foul of the skeptical fears of elements of the established entertainment industry, and had to be shelved.[50]

Despite these failures, Blackpool was able to thrive without major innovation. The expectations of its visitors in the 1950s and even 1960s had changed relatively little from those a generation earlier. They spent their increased wages and longer holidays on the things that their less wealthy parents had enjoyed. By contrast, the children of those who thronged Coney Island in the 1920s and 1930s not only expected innovation, but some of them abandoned Coney for Disney.

While Blackpool prospered without renovation, it still had to face the first stirrings of an assertive new youth culture that threatened to divide the generations in potentially disruptive ways. The advent and influence of the Teddy Boys, with their sideburns, "quiffs," and distinctive dress, is visible in photographs from the late 1950s and early 1960s, as groups of roving adolescents and young men adopted aggressive postures at the Pleasure Beach, roamed the central promenade, and petted ostentatiously with young women on the beach and in the streets. Still, Alfred Gregory's photographs put this challenge into perspective by showing adolescents in multigenerational family groups as well as hunting in packs and revealing a persistent formality in dress (with sweaters replacing suits among younger men, while most women continued to wear skirts rather than jeans). Children were more in evidence than previously, too, as improved living standards meant that even working-class families with youngsters could afford a Blackpool holiday. Far from becoming a hangout of gangs and youthful rebellion, Blackpool had actually become more of a family place.[51]

Gregory's published photographs are slanted toward the more downscale parts of town, the crowded central beach and adjoining "Golden Mile." Still, despite the incipient changes, the persisting respectability of the crowd on the beach is captured convincingly in Gregory's own description: "They sunbathed fully dressed;

4.7   The first stirrings of a new youth culture on the Pleasure Beach in about 1960 showing tough-looking
       teenagers. Courtesy the Pleasure Beach, Blackpool.

collars and ties were seldom removed. Early in the decade [1960s] not many people
wore swim suits and when the bikini made an appearance here it was only for the
young and daring. Most kept on their dresses and suits and only went into the
water to paddle. . . . Often I would see a gentleman, conservatively-dressed with
cap, waistcoat and gold watch chain dangling on his chest, roll up his trouser bot-
toms, take off his socks and shoes and quietly walk into the shallows. . . . Women
still wore stockings and fashionable young teenagers, hair rollers covered by a scarf,
would frolic together playing with a ball, full skirts swaying over frilly petticoats,
their stockinged feet pounding the sand."[52]

The journalist Graham Turner underlined Blackpool's enduring stability and
respectability in 1967: "Blackpool is also, for all its gigantic paraphernalia of fun,
an extraordinarily staid and puritan town. The hatches, one feels, are battened
down very tightly to scotch any possible impropriety. . . . One result of the conservatism of both the town and the majority of its visitors is that teenagers have made

relatively little impact on its character. . . . The town seems to be run by and for the over-forties and the under-fourteens. . . . It is there to entertain the millions without causing offence, to feed them efficiently, to jolly them up a bit, whiz them round a couple of times, blow their frocks over their heads and send them down the dual carriageway towards Preston and the night shift."[53]

In the mid-1960s, then, Blackpool was still prospering, and its "traditional" playful crowd was still recognizable. More of them now arrived by road than rail, and the town's Central Station, the great hub of tourist arrivals as recently as the early 1950s, closed in 1964, reflecting the rising importance of the bus as well as the private car. A growing proportion of the crowd was probably drawn from the working class, and perhaps from the "unskilled," while many erstwhile middle-class visitors were seeking quieter or sunnier climes in southwest England or on the European Continent. But Blackpool's heart was still beating strongly, despite the central entertainment companies' failure to innovate and a general dependence on habit and tradition. This enduring culture of the English North survived despite greater affluence and generational change. The Blackpool experience in the 1950s and 1960s points out that the American cycle of innovation and decline need not be the only way that the playful crowd coped with change.

Explaining Coney Island's Decline and Blackpool's Reinventions

As early as 1939 Henry R. Lieberman identified "at least four factors" that explained why "Coney Island's star has been growing dimmer gradually for more than a decade."[54] Its customers' spending power had declined, a trend recognized by concessionaires whose prizes took the form of "hams and cans of coffee" rather than "kewpie dolls and crockery." Secondly, it had been damaged by changes in public taste, as the rides now had to compete for thrills with "the automobile and the airplane," the exhibitions "pale by comparison with actual newsreel shots and newspaper photographs," and even the children had become skeptical about what they had formerly accepted with wonder. Thirdly, the visitors now came for the bathing rather than the amusements, undermining the commercial foundation of Coney Island. Finally, there were the campaigns for regulation and "improvement" undertaken by those whom Lieberman called the "M-Men," Robert Moses and the New York City License Commissioner, Paul Moss, with their ever-tightening restrictions on ballyhoo, advertising signs and games of chance.

During and after the war the balance between these adverse influences shifted, and others came more strongly into the frame. Continuing technological advances, especially TV made the exhibitions less novel and sophisticated. Far more than Blackpool, Coney had flourished on novelty and caught between the jaws of corporate disinterest and down-market crowds, it could no longer deliver innovation. Instead, the "new" appeared elsewhere along the parkways of Long Island and the Jersey Shore, and, with air travel more distant sites like Las Vegas and Disney World promised not only sparkling novelty, but a warm respite from New York winters as well. The continuing push toward residential development and rational recreation on the Jones Beach model, with the beach as a strictly regulated public park, did most to undermine the distinctive character of Coney Island. Since the 1840s, Coney had combined, often in tension, commercial entertainment with natural beauty and recreation. As Coney's commerce moved down-market and was burdened with racial and social conflicts, Coney's natural beauty was compromised and the beach became more ordinary in a world where fun-seekers had far more choices. The readiness to abandon threatened or outdated assets, and to leave them to decay if alternative uses were not forthcoming, was a damaging aspect of American business culture in this and other resort settings. The capacity of amusement parks to sustain wonder was destroyed by the vacant lots, torched buildings, and mundane new high-rise apartment blocks that literally put the roller coasters in the shade. Moses certainly did not want this, but his policies were partially responsible for what occurred. After the closure of Steeplechase, whose land then laid fallow and derelict, followed by the riots of 1968, there was no hope of returning to old glories. The brave rhetoric of a new Coney Island for the new century, founded on a new baseball stadium and some revived amenities, has yet to find fulfilment.[55]

Not that Blackpool had an easy ride during the final third of the twentieth century, despite the continuing commitment of its local authority to the entertainment industry and an easier transition from trains to cars, planes, and buses. But it was not until the very end of the century that a sense of serious crisis began to pervade the British resort. Even then, the symptoms of decline were far less advanced than those exhibited by Coney Island or Atlantic City in the late 1960s. In the early twenty-first century local government was returning to its traditions of enterprise and innovation, in partnership with business, to try to turn the ship round. The contrasts with Coney are revealing.

By the late 1960s Blackpool was encountering troublesome changes to its visitor base and entertainment industry. The decline of its core visitor catchment area in the industrial North of England was beginning to accelerate, and the traditional "Wakes" holidays of the cotton manufacturing towns were disappearing. The spread of working-class car ownership made new areas of the country more accessible, and the better-off Blackpool visitors were being drawn to smaller resorts in the sunnier climes of the south and west. The rising generation was particularly susceptible, and some were already being drawn to package holidays on the Mediterranean coast and elsewhere in Europe, although many of these people also continued to take short breaks in Blackpool, especially during the Illuminations.

By the 1970s, the fuller development of a separate youth culture made it more difficult to recruit a rising generation for whom family traditions held less appeal. This was hardly unique to Blackpool (in fact, something very similar occurred at Disney). Still, the lack of investment in new attractions during the 1950s and 1960s, apart from the Pleasure Beach, gave the town's pleasure menu an increasingly tired air. At the same time, control over the central entertainment businesses passed from local to national firms and Blackpool's ability to recruit national and international star entertainers was increasingly compromised by the higher payments demanded in the television age. It was difficult to meet rising expectations about accommodation quality in Victorian boarding houses which lacked in-room bathing facilities.[56]

These were all long-term problems, but by the end of the 1960s Blackpool was facing an immediate traffic crisis. While the Corporation's Traffic and Transport Plan of 1969 assumed that more than 8 million people still visited Blackpool every year, crowd patterns had drastically changed. The railroads' share of the traffic had fallen from 3.2 million in 1937 to 630,000 in 1966 and the traffic load was shifting from the summer to the Illuminations season in September and October. Continuing growth in motor traffic had resulted in increasing congestion on the Promenade, which already "seriously detracts from the environment of the sea front and presents hazards and frustrations to both drivers and pedestrians. . . . The people who visit and holiday in Blackpool enjoy a crowded atmosphere. . . . The presence of motor vehicles, however, detracts from the enjoyment of the crowded holiday atmosphere."[57]

The Blackpool Corporation faced a daunting problem: How to preserve in the era of the car a crowd culture based on what was now an obsolete urban layout centered on railroad depots? In the late 1960s and early 1970s, proposals included extensive central demolitions to make way for an elevated inner relief road. High costs and local opposition led to this scheme being abandoned, and a new route into the town center followed the line of the old railway to the demolished Central Station, where the old carriage sidings offered ample space for parking lots. [58] This willingness to retreat from the planners' excess stood in sharp contrast to the inconsistent, but bureaucratic response to Coney Island's problems.

In the late 1960s and 1970s Blackpool Corporation also promoted the innovations that too long had been neglected. It sought, and obtained, permission from Parliament for a long list of initiatives, including a zoo, a golf course, roller-skating rinks, various entertainments in the municipal parks, and a hoverport to provide a high-speed water transport link to other coastal towns in northwest England and North Wales, although this particular futuristic scheme never came to pass.[59]

Nothing of this kind could happen in Coney Island. The Aquarium had been imposed externally and took more than a generation to become popular on its new site, while Blackpool's Zoo occupied an accessible vacant site on the urban fringe that met the needs of its intended clientele. Blackpool's eventual redevelopment of the "Golden Mile" area, though controversial, was also less damaging than the changes that New York's City Hall forced on Coney Island. The main period of demolition and replacement, removing some of Blackpool's oldest housing from the 1830s and 1840s, took nearly ten years, and the new seafront architecture was corporate and concrete, with a large parking lot and a police station, in the "brutalist" style that was currently in favor, lurking behind the entertainments. Comment in the local press was critical, but the new "Golden Mile" still drew in the crowds.[60] Meanwhile, a spokesman for EMI, the big conglomerate that now ran much of Blackpool's established entertainment industry, concurred with those who condemned local planners for wanting "neat well behaved buildings that had nothing to discriminate one from the other," when the essence of the area's attractiveness should be "haphazardness" and the capacity to surprise. Even so, he concluded that "the showmanship is still there" and "it is still a fun place."[61] There were elements here of the critiques that had been directed at Moses, but in practice the "Golden Mile" had been updated rather than abolished, as the "Horror Crypt," "Devil's Den" and other new delights made clear.[62] This kind of entertainment remained entirely acceptable as part of the Blackpool scene.

The changes on the "Golden Mile" prompted a measure of nostalgic comment, as old landmarks disappeared and some critics lamented a perceived "Americanization" of the new attractions, including displays of space technology and references to science fiction cartoons. It was even possible to look back wistfully at the innocence of the 1920s and 1930s, when the "tough cigar-smoking liquor lads" who ran the "starving bride" shows took care to hide their intrinsic kindness behind a brusque exterior. "But all the razzmatazz is as dead as a dodo, and nothing can revive it. Nowadays it is all pubs, clubs and cabaret and what's on telly." Blackpool no longer "rode the crest of the entertainment wave," and one commentator asked, "Is it just nostalgia that makes one wonder why people don't enjoy themselves in the same way as they did in the past, when there was plenty of horseplay, but no mugging, drugging, stabbing and senseless violence?"[63]

This was a very dangerous kind of talk to surface in a popular resort, although in practice Blackpool remained a relatively safe environment for vacationers at this time, especially when compared to Coney Island. By the early 1970s, however, the Corporation was becoming sufficiently worried about its future to commission its first professional visitor survey. Its social profile of the visitors found only 4 percent from professional and managerial occupations, and 13 percent from white-collar and supervisory workers, while five-sixths came from skilled (predominantly) and unskilled manual workers and state pensioners. The visitor profile was also significantly more elderly than the national pattern, provoking worries that Blackpool was sliding down the social scale and failing to recruit a new generation. In what sense, if any, could a crowd of British pensioners be "playful"? This might have marked the beginning of a crisis to match those experienced in the 1960s by Coney Island and Atlantic City.[64]

Remarkably, this proved not yet to be the case. At the very point where competition from the Mediterranean package holiday began to damage British resort economies, especially in the North, Blackpool's holiday season revived. A regional plan written in 1987 treated Blackpool as an asset, stressing the Victorian themes of its new Hounds Hill Shopping Centre and other sites along with the new Sandcastle pool complex as important tourist attractions.[65] Further Corporation surveys at the end of the 1980s found that visitor numbers had actually increased since 1972 (although the average stay was only three or four nights) and that the relatively lucrative middle-class, white-collar and supervisory cohorts now accounted for one-third of the visitors. This move upscale was assisted by a growing gay presence, as local entrepreneur Basil Newby began to cater to this lucrative market whose delight in kitsch and tackiness made Blackpool an unexpectedly attractive venue. There were already 150 small gay or gay-friendly hotels by 1991, and growth continued as Newby expanded his own entertainment network and its success drew others into the field. Blackpool also became a "big night out" destination for weekend clubbers and stag and hen parties, generating occasional tensions where assertively gay and straight cultures collided. More troublesome for the authorities was the danger of alienating the family and retiree market when the daytime culture of the elderly and family collided with the "evening" culture of gays and clubbers. As the new crowds became more numerous and notorious, the more "respectable" ones faded. From the mid-1990s especially, Blackpool's future became increasingly problematic and a matter for debate. The tone of outsiders' comments on the Blackpool crowd in general shifted from (at worst) condescension and amused tolerance to outrage and disgust: Paul Theroux and Bill Bryson were among those who found Blackpool's *mainstream* visitors to be flabby, vulgar, ill-dressed, ill-mannered, and even threatening. By 2000, the town's reputation as a safe visitor venue was compromised, and the long-postponed crisis seemed finally to have arrived.[66]

Several related sets of problems were coming to a head. Despite the reassuring visitor statistics of the late 1980s, parts of central Blackpool close to the Promenade were beginning to experience the sort of serious poverty and unemployment, with associated violence and drug abuse that had undermined Coney Island in the previous generation. Small hotels competing on price rather than amenity for what remained of the old working-class market found it easier to take in welfare tenants, often from outside the town, at guaranteed year-round rents. Inevitably, this practice brought disruption and disturbance to the surrounding area. Blackpool consistently had the highest rate of unemployment in Lancashire, a county of many seriously deprived areas. To make matters worse, the town's identity as a seaside resort was challenged by growing awareness of the polluted state of the sea, although this began to be addressed in the late 1990s. Expenditure on the Illuminations became controversial as the holiday industry carried declining weight in the town's politics. Rumors of municipal corruption became a stronger theme in the 1970s and 1980s, and, in 1991, the Labour Party took over control of the Town Hall from the Conservatives for the first time in Blackpool's history. The Corporation's failure to develop the airport after taking it over in 1961, or to provide a new conference center like its competitors, began to look increasingly damaging, and the crisis of confidence outlasted the change of ruling party.[67]

The Corporation struggled to spearhead innovation through a plan to capitalize on the proposed liberalization of the casino gambling laws, using gambling revenues to drive a Masterplan for resort renewal. Blackpool seemed to be taking a leaf from the experience of Atlantic City, which had used casinos as a route to recovery from a desperate situation, with mixed results, from 1976.[68] Fittingly, the plan itself envisaged new green spaces, a conference center, covered walkways, a revolutionary new approach to the Illuminations borrowing from techniques used in Las Vegas, a new Aquarium, and the rehabilitation of many Victorian guesthouses (in hopes of maintaining Blackpool's distinctiveness) alongside enormous new casino hotels. This showed that the spirit of enterprise was not dead and that the tradition of public/private collaboration could be revived. It all depended not only on getting special casino concessions from the central government, but also on the attractiveness to outsiders of the proposed mix of "heritage" and innovation.[69] Blackpool's problems were undeniable, but so was an underlying vitality that made it well worth investing in and turning around. And it was clearly in a much better situation than Atlantic City had been when the casinos arrived in the late 1970s.[70]

The local government's sustained, if recently checkered, support for Blackpool's popular holiday industry played a large part in the town's success in catering to a changing playful crowd. Perhaps the most important single influence, however, remained the Pleasure Beach, the most popular free-entry attraction in Britain, with a sustained record of innovation that was unchallenged elsewhere in the town. It was edgier, more excessive, more threatening, and there was more litter and untidiness than Leonard Thompson or Joseph Emberton would have liked to see. Some of its participants were also experiencing it as post-tourists, savoring the ironies of its artificiality in knowing ways while enjoying the sense of nostalgia and kitsch that some were associating with the whole Blackpool experience. The British seaside in general, and Blackpool in particular, was beginning to live partly on the recycling of versions of its past for consumption in the present; and this helped to preserve the distinctiveness of place identity that might otherwise be under threat from globalizing redevelopment.[71] This was very different from the industrial saturnalia that emerged at the end of the nineteenth century. Contemporary Blackpool also stands in sharp contrast to other alternatives to the playful crowds of the old Blackpool and Coney—the late-twentieth-century fantasy associated with Disney and other theme parks and the pleasurable didacticism of the open-air museum at Beamish. We shall explore these alternatives in the next two chapters.

We conclude this chapter, however, with a very recent perception of the Pleasure Beach itself. Paul Flynn, writing with relatively youthful nostalgia in 2004,
summed up its new but also continuing appeals:

> Blackpool looked like Sodom and Gomorrah to the teenagers of the north
> west. And there, winking salaciously at you from the seafront like some
> buxom hooker who's going to rob your wallet, your innocence and your dig-
> nity, is the Pleasure Beach. This, we all nodded, is what heaven will look
> like. . . . To the uninitiated, the Pleasure Beach can come on with the menace
> of a school bully. Crop-haired boys with stud earrings and pristine Reeboks
> snarl malevolently. . . . But the democratising effect of a rollercoaster turns
> the most ardent tyke into a pussycat. Once on the rides, the wind-in-the-
> air, arms aloft sense of pure, unfettered joy makes everyone equal. . . . Every
> year it gets more outlandish, each monolithic structure more spectacularly
> terrifying. Yet the battered old rust-buckets they leave behind—the Grand
> National, the Cat and Mouse, the Big Dipper—are bequeathed nothing but
> charm in their wake."

The playful crowd at the British seaside may look very different at the beginning
of the twenty-first century, but the democratic vigor and sense of release of the
past remains.[72]

FIRE ENGINE

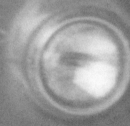
HAMPTON

The Disney Challenge

Disneyland was a radically new site for the playful crowd when it opened in July 1955. Shaped by its Southern California setting with its culture of optimistic Midwestern migrants, the film industry, and automobile and suburban society, this 160-acre site on former orange groves in the sleepy town of Anaheim promised much. Walt Disney insisted that he had created a new kind of pleasure park, free from the dirt and danger of the carnival world of freaks, barkers, and thrill rides. It was designed for baby boomers and their parents from middle America, offering entirely new forms of entertainment. And, although Walt Disney died in 1966, his vision of the playful crowd remained for decades thereafter in his company's careful cultivation of Disneyland and, after 1971, Walt Disney World in Florida. For some, Disney's transformation was a blessing, substituting clean, orderly, and family-oriented fun for the grimy disorder and working-class and minority crowds of America's declining urban amusement parks and seaside resorts.

At the same time, others found Disneyland an example of the culture of the "midcult," the aesthetic of a lower-middle-class corruption of gentility, the sentimentality and false optimism of the *Saturday Evening Post* and *Readers' Digest*, and the uprooted culture of the suburbs, torn from both highbrow European traditions and earthy and vital immigrant and rural cultures. Disneyland was a particularly powerful, even emblematic example of commercialized tourism in the twentieth century, a "pseudo-event" (Daniel Boorstin), or a "simulation" (Jean Baudrillard), a "hyperreality" (Umberto Eco), or an example of "hypermodernity" in its obsessive concern with efficiency, predictability, calculability and control.[1]

Again and again, critics claimed that the passively received image from Hollywood had replaced local and organic visions of life. Disney, too, has been seen as central to a deplored trend of cultural "globalization," running parallel to "McDonaldization" and synthesized with it as "McDisneyfication." George Ritzer identifies it as part of the rise of a bland culture of international corporate placelessness.[2] Ritzer has argued that in simulating enchantment, Disney and similar organizations actually disenchant at a deeper level, by stripping out the magic and layers of meaning that go with complexity and disorder.[3] Disneyland sought to control and tidy nature and history, or indeed to invent its own version of them, not mock, bend, or parody them as did Coney. Disney's obsessive control of the "fun" required that the company treat the audience as children. Even when it seemed to celebrate the playfulness and delight of the child in its the architecture, Disney did not foster the play of children.[4]

Disney's intellectual defenders have repeatedly denounced these critiques as elitist and ascetic. Typical is the response of science fiction writer Ray Bradbury, who in 1958 insisted that Disney critic Julian Halvey "truly loved Disneyland but is not man enough, or child enough, to admit it. I feel sorry for him. He will never travel in space, he will never touch the stars." Intellectuals like Halvey "steadfastly refuse to let go and enjoy themselves."[5] While critics have consistently dismissed Disney crowds as manipulated or self-satisfied, defenders of Disney have too often denied the need to ask the serious question, what makes so many consumers identify Disneyland as the "happiest place on earth" as claimed by Disney publicity. More important still, what changes have occurred in contemporary sensibilities to make the Disney experience a central attraction of the playful crowd in the second half of the twentieth century?

The Disneyland phenomenon cannot be simply encapsulated in the familiar cultural debate between defenders of a populist commercialism and the jeremiads against consumerist modernity. We need a longer view. Walt Disney challenged, but also borrowed, quite explicitly, the industrial saturnalian values and practices of 1900s Coney Island. He visited Coney in its decline, and reacted sharply against its "tawdry rides and hostile employees," its dirt and lack of planning, and its uncultivated patrons. It was East Coast, metropolitan, and working class; and its customers did not spend enough. It was an "other" against which Disneyland could be defined by contrast, like a photographic negative.[6] But Walt Disney also borrowed from Coney Island. His object was cultural inversion, a counter-world to everyday experience—just as was Coney's, even if Disney's carnival corresponded to a culture very different from the urban working-class immigrant of 1900. Disney's saturnalia was expressed not in the childlike play of young adults breaking from work and family constraints but in the child-centered play of families seeking temporary escape from a world of suburban consumerism while encountering it again in a different form.

Disney deliberately departed from Coney's self-abandon in thrill rides and fascination with the boundary worlds of the freak and afterlife. Yet Disney offered movie-themed rides that had a lot in common with Coney's scenic railroads. Disneyland's Tomorrow- and Adventurelands (and later Disney World's Epcot and Animal Kingdom) presented fantasies that were, in important senses, modernized versions of Coney's Trip to the Moon and exotic villages. Disney embraced more scientific understandings of space travel and rather less overtly racist views of "primitive" tribesmen, but there remained continuity.

Disney believed that his park revolutionized the old fairgrounds and amusement parks by eliminating the "maze of criss-crossing streets and sidewalks." Again, this was not as new as he thought, for the three parks at Coney Island attempted to use their colonnaded lagoons and well-policed pavilions to eliminate the noise and confusion of the Bowery and Surf Avenue. The key difference with Disneyland was that it was far more systematically organized into "scenes" like in a movie that created visual coherence. Its central architectural principle was separate "lands" or themed areas that radiated from a Plaza marked by Sleeping Beauty's castle.[7] But this design was made possible by the fact that Disney had far more space to spread out and had more control over his attractions (unlike the Coney Island parks that leased out space to independent showmen).

The resulting experience was not merely manipulated, sentimentalized, or sanitized. Rather, Disneyland expressed a playfulness that attracted a mass audience as much as had Coney fifty years before, but responding to the desires of an expanded and transformed American middle class. Disney offered a consumerist saturnalia, both expressing and in interesting ways protesting a new commercial culture, driven by the evocation of childhood wonder and the nostalgic longings of the "child within" and expressed through a playful reenactment of Disney's cinematic creativity. In the following analysis of Disneyland and (to a less extent Walt Disney World), we will try to show how the Disney enterprise has come to define an important form of the playful crowd that emerged in the mid-twentieth century.

Situating Disney's Innovations

Although scholars dispute just when Disney first thought of building his park, by the mid-1940s, he was surely exploring other ways of expressing his imagination than in his recent movies (e.g. the cartoon feature *Fantasia* in 1940 which had been a commercial failure).[8] According to art historian Karal Ann Marling, he wanted to "build something tangible and true, something perfect, a place where nothing could ever go wrong," unlike his own studio, which was ridden with labor strife. He certainly was not thinking of the conventional amusement park full of the mechanical rides and sideshow attractions that had survived from the late 1890s. Despite the advice of amusement park owners consulted by touring Disney staff in 1954 that "if you don't put up a roller coaster and a Ferris wheel, you'll go broke," Walt had other ideas. In his oft-quoted words, he wanted "some kind of family park" not like those "dirty, phony places run by tough-looking people." Disney recalled: "It started with my taking my two kids around to zoos and parks. While they were on the merry-go-round riding 40 times or something, I'd be sitting there trying to figure out what you could do that would be more imaginative."[9]

Despite Disney's claims of originality, he drew on a vast reservoir of architectural fantasy and commercial amusement to create the aesthetic of his themed environment. Most proximately, he owed a debt to the international exhibitions of San Francisco and San Diego and amusement parks at Long Beach and Santa Monica. He borrowed also from the whimsical architecture used to attract customers to southern California restaurants, gas stations, and bakeries. Southern Californians were accustomed to buying bread in a store masquerading as a storybook "Dutch" windmill.[10] The same playful architecture had been exhibited seventy years earlier in Coney Island's Elephant Hotel. Marling traces Disney's landscape design and many architectural themes to his fascination with shadow box miniatures that led him to commission playful reproductions of frontier and small town American buildings in Disneyland.[11] His nostalgia for late-nineteenth-century trains (manifested in his own building of a miniature hobby train at his home) and his attraction to the Chicago Railroad Fair of 1948 with its models of scenes of historic Americana deeply influenced his decision to build a scaled-down train around his fantasy scenes in Disneyland.[12]

Disney clearly reflected the sensibilities of middle-class America in the 1950s, certainly not genteel in the tradition of Coney's Manhattan or Oriental Hotels, but also not the aesthetic of West Brighton of 1900. While even the "upscale" Dreamland park of 1903 freely mixed Bible-inspired scenic railroad rides with side show attractions, Disneyland rejected the entire tradition of freaks, fortune tellers, and even shooting gallery stalls and stayed away from now controversial themes of death and the afterlife. There were not even trained animal acts, clowns, or other standard circus entertainments (beyond an unpopular Mickey Mouse Club Circus that lasted only one season in 1956). In the early years, even the tradition of the roller coaster and other thrill rides was absent. Disney rejected the carnival or fairground ambience and the personnel who went with it. As one reporter noted, there were "no shouting nasal carnies" and "no Little Egypt girlie shows" at Disneyland.[13] Middle-class discomfort at the sight of gypsies, Egyptian Fakirs, Indian snake charmers, and other "exotic" show people finally had won the day. No longer would these visitors have to endure the shouting and outrageous lies of barkers and the intrusive huckstering of sellers of food, drink, and trinkets of dubious quality and cleanliness. No longer would there be the irritating confusion of competing demands on their coins. Long Island's "Playland" in the 1920s had surely anticipated all this change, but Disney not only rejected the old (now working-class) carnival tradition, but also systematically replaced the culture of the sideshow and show people. He went much further than the tamed amusement park mixed with genteel elements of promenade, gardens, picnic grounds, and tower by which Playland distinguished itself from Coney Island.

Rather, he created a new complex of commercialized entertainment. Instead of the exotic and oriental, he offered the cute and cartoonish; in place of the noisy and cheesy competition of the stalls, he offered integrated themed attractions with much more subtle appeals to spend (for example, licensed merchandise in shops disguised as part of the ride or show). Employees, from security staff to ride operators, were people like the visitors—clean cut, "normal," and middle class, not members of a mysterious subculture of the "carnival" immortalized in Rodgers and Hammerstein's musical "Carousel" (1945). By reaffirming middle-class values through numerous clues (order, cleanliness, but no longer religion), Disney made people comfortable, even in crowds of thousands.

Disney's appeal to middle-class sensibilities was not purely negative or bowdlerized. He blended the emotional "release" of fantasy and abandon with claims of uplift. Genteel codes of self-improvement, what the English Victorians had called "rational recreation," made Disneyland acceptable to suburban consumers in an era of seedy amusement parks, but that code had been adapted to a new "play morality" in middle-class families, first identified in the 1950s by anthropologist Martha Wolfenstein.[14] Publicity claimed that Disneyland was "a place for people to find happiness and knowledge," both a "city of Arabian Nights" and "a metropolis of the future." As we shall see, Disney claimed the mantle of the popular educator of history and science, but he also made clear that this learning was to be a family experience. A plaque in Disney's Town Square expressed what would be learned and by whom: "Here age relives fond memories of the past and here youth may savor the challenge and promise of the future."[15] Disney was a place for the old to tell stories inspired by Disney nostalgia and for the young to learn of their future and how they were to surpass their elders in a playful, childlike way.

Disney modeled his park on the international exhibition. In doing so, he followed a long historic trend away from the uplifting programs of art, history, and science so prominent in Chicago's White City pavilions of 1893. Instead Disney celebrated middle-class American self-understandings through appealing references to scientific progress and a virtuous past. As cultural historian Neil Harris notes, Disney succeeded by co-opting the genteel culture of the exhibition without engaging in "its heavy didacticism," wrapping Victorian ideals of progress, world adventure, and distinct American myths about pioneer virtues in "childhood nostalgia," thus giving the educational and uplifting goals of Disney a playful quality, making them part of a cross- generational act of story telling.[16]

Disneyland was an artifice, created out of featureless orchard land, miles from the ocean, mountains, and even desert. It surely had nothing to do with the sacred places, those majestic creations of nature or history that had inspired feelings of the sublime in nineteenth-century American tourists. Still, Disney re-created in steel, concrete, and fiberglass cues to those feelings in most of his "lands." Most think of the cartoonish world of Fantasyland when they think of Disneyland, but that took up only a quarter of the park. In Adventureland Disney evoked genteel ideals of sublime vistas of faraway places and, even more, he promoted late-Victorian bourgeois values—the white European's superiority and duty to explore the world. In Frontierland, Disney featured America's imagined history, with its rugged images of the American West. And in Tomorrowland, Disney promoted the power of progress.[17]

Yet, Disney never intended that any of these places be simply outdoor museums or to imitate the "official" and didactic qualities that characterized natural or historical museums for most of the twentieth century. Disney saw his uplifting mission from the perspective of a boy, a middle-class boy, perhaps a reader of early-twentieth-century magazines like *Youth's Companion* or *St. Nicholas* where boys (and even some girls) of 10 or 12 read about exciting places far away and the promise of new technologies. That same "boy" might have also read Zane Grey westerns. Disney assumed the mantle of this boy's culture in his TV program, "Disneyland," which premiered in 1954. Repeatedly, Disney publicity evoked the middle-class child's imagination. Frontierland was supposed to inspire the "pioneer spirit of our forefathers," not only in civilizing the American West by subduing nature and the Indians, but also in the testing of the individual's moral fiber in the face of adversity. The past was to teach a patriotic and moral lesson just as fifth grade social studies classes were intended to do. But Disney's "history" had other objectives like attempting to re-create a socially binding emotion: Frontierland was to "give you the feeling of having lived even for a short while, during our country's pioneer days" so that "all of us, whether 10th generation or naturalized Americans, have cause to be proud of our country's history, shaped by the pioneering spirit of our forefathers." Most of all, despite claims that "our country's past is accurately reproduced in Frontierland," Tom Sawyer's Island there promised to be "a playland out of a youngster's dream" where "everything an adventurous boy could want" was to be found, including "Injun Joe's Cave and the Tree House." Frontierland was to be a storybook version of history. The Golden Horseshoe Saloon featured, of course, the "tallest glass of soda pop" and the show girls did a wholesome version of the Can Can. Adventureland taught the boyish pleasures of "traveling to mysterious far-off places," offering a romantic travelogue which evoked memories of reading Hardy Boys and Tom Swift adventures or accounts of distant places in *St. Nicholas* or *National Geographic* magazines.[18]

Tomorrowland was where visitors "step into the future atomic age" and the "challenges of outer space and the hope for a peaceful and united world." It was an extension of the adventure and frontier theme with its appeals to courage and challenge, but with a Rotarian undercurrent of one-worldism and Victorian progress. A 1959 press release expressed this bourgeois optimism in full voice: "Science and technology have already given us the tools we need to build the world of the future . . . we will prove with the new Tomorrowland that today is the future." The future is not a fantasy, but "is here if we use our tool right now." There one could find a Home of the Future and Hall of Chemistry, where visitors could see "how innovative uses of plastics could shape our homes of tomorrow." Somewhat more exciting, but equally didactic in conception, was the Rocket to the Moon (designed with the assistance of Werner von Braun of NASA and space authority Willy Ley.) TV screens (rather than dioramas) showed "passengers" their travel path. Unlike Coney Island's Trip to the Moon, there were no moon fairies or moon cheese. Once again, the didacticism was tempered with childish romance and science fiction. The first version of Tomorrowland included the "20,000 Leagues Under the Sea," based on Disney's recently released adventure movie and Jules Verne's turn-of-the-century fantasy of deep-sea travel. The most popular attraction in Tomorrowland was Autopia, where little children could drive their own cars (and adults could pretend to compete with them) at 11 miles per hour.[19]

These "lands" were not ultimately to be sites of learning, or even entertaining erudition. Disney's simulations of the Rivers of America and Tom Sawyer's island, his Jungle Cruise, and even the Rocket to the Moon appealed to a storybook imagining of places where the lines between fiction and fact were blurred. Of course, they intensified, romanticized, bowdlerized, and otherwise adapted schoolroom versions of history, nature, and technology. They also reduced the world's geography to a "simulacrum," in David Harvey's language, while presenting a dominant narrative of American pseudo-history, helping to create a hegemonic "common sense" about the past, the world, and America's place in it.[20] But in doing so, they were copying in three dimensions the tradition of the child's storybook. With the child in the lead, these "Lands" were to be accessible to all members of the family, despite conflicting interests and differing attention spans.

In fact, what made Disney an especially middle-class cultural experience were his efforts to make his park a place of positive family interaction, in "happiness" as well as "knowledge." The problem for him was not that amusement parks did not appeal to adults, but that they excluded parents from a playful time unless they first excluded their children. His objective was not to let adults become kids without the burdens of children (as was the case in Coney Island and even the early Playland), but to create a setting "where parents and children could have fun together."[21]

This playful crowd became acceptable to the middle classes because it was visibly composed of many independent family units presumably sharing time together. Adults became parents relating both to the delights of their children and to their own "inner child." In turn, the young enjoyed parents and other grown-ups who temporarily abandoned their authoritative and serious roles as adults to glory in the childlike and children. These families were supposed to be interacting not with the "mass," but with each other around the shared goal of childhood wonder. Disney was often quoted as saying: "we don't aim at children. . . . Everything we do . . . we do at the family level. We try not to insult any age level. We try to get the right balance. Adults far outnumber kids at Disneyland and I call them honest adults, not afraid to shed a tear of nostalgia and romance."[22] Disney created neither a park just for kids or for regressing adults. It was a place that not only reached the sensibilities of every age group, but also claimed to bring all to a common experience of delight, free of the obsession, refinement, pedantry, and other forms of life's advance beyond the holy wonder of the child.

All this fastidious concern with negative middle-class feelings about amusement parks, the childlike version of uplift, and the family-focused play may strike the reader as merely confirmation of the typical critique of Disneyland as bowdlerized carnival. But this would reduce it to the pallid and saccharine. Disney's "happiest place in the world" created a new positive and vital form of wonder, middle-class perhaps, but also in tune with the broader consumer culture of the second half of the twentieth century. Disneyland codified new forms of "happiness" around three essential ideas: 1) putting the visitor into a cinematic fantasy; 2) creating real excitement around the child and the childlike (taking the essential attraction of the freak and circus show and transforming it into the cute, encapsulated in cartoon characters and their stories); and 3) partially replacing the quest for novelty with the appeal of nostalgia (reliving the "inner child").

From the beginning, Disneyland rejected the old cluster of mechanical rides and circus sideshows for carefully reproduced and mechanized sets from his movies. While for New Yorkers of the 1900s, appealing scenes came from mental images of Renaissance Venice, ancient Rome, the mythical Baghdad of the Arabian Nights or even popular understandings of hell and heaven, for Americans of the 1950s, such scenes originated mostly from movies and television and were already visually familiar to visitors. Characters and dramatic scenes from *Snow White and the Seven Dwarfs* (1937), *Dumbo* (1941), *Adventures of Ichabod and Mr Toad* (1949), *Alice in Wonderland* (1951), *Peter Pan* (1953), *20,000 Leagues under the Sea* (1954), and *Third Man on the Mountain* (1959) were made into rides. The thrill of Disney came neither from the physical sensation of the roller coaster nor the sensual/sexual tease of the Human Whirlpool, but from realizing the "dream" of a fantasy place. In fact, the object was not primarily to transport the visitors to a historical site or even to evoke the sense of being in such a place, but to propel them into a story, peopled with familiar characters from a Disney movie.[23]

Movie-based rides encouraged patrons to identify emotionally with a familiar "scene" and to feel fulfillment by transforming the memory and passive viewing of a movie like *Peter Pan* into the multisensory experience of flying in Peter's pixie-dusted ship over London as he triumphantly returns the Darling children home to their nursery. Similarly, Mr Toad's Wild Ride simulated the most exciting action scene in the movie, giving riders the sensation of being chased through London by police and crashing through walls. Moreover, the visitor is greeted with "inside" jokes which they understand because of their familiarity with Disney culture.[24]

In ways, all this was simply a new version of the religious pilgrimage where a three-dimensional site (a ride instead of a church or holy city) gave physical depth and reality to a set of stories and symbols (based on movies instead of scripture) and allowed the faithful to walk in the steps of the divine (or in this case to ride through a fantasy space of Snow White or Tom Sawyer). Pleasure, if not renewed faith, came from seeing the familiar cartoon figure in "life." In this way, Disney creations had much in common with the scenic railroads and dioramas of old Luna Park's Trip to the Moon and Dreamland's Fighting the Flames. The references in Luna Park or Dreamland attractions to current events, faraway places, or even Bible stories shared much with Disney's efforts to place visitors into a story. But Disney's references to movies and cartoons were far more effective commercially than were the scenic railroads and fantasy attractions of Coney. Instead of relying on a common folk or religious culture or access to news, Disney created his reference points through his own successful commercial fantasies. Disney could build on the profitability of "tie-in" marketing, selling Mickey first as a cartoon and then as toy, comic book, and eventually a theme park. His references could be controlled and coordinated because he owned them. While interest in the Johnstown Flood of 1889 waned soon after the opening of the diorama, references to Dumbo or Peter Pan remained powerfully attractive for decades thanks to the enduring ability of Disney to reintroduce the company's movies and characters to new generations of viewers without loss of appeal or novelty. The "cartoon sensibility" of Disney's architecture, its whimsical colors and playful decorations, reminds us of the child-like and whimsical facade of Dreamland's Lilliputia (the "city" of dwarfs) and the oriental excesses of Frederic Thompson's Luna Park. However, even when Dreamland subverted the pretension of the White City with a Shoot the Chutes that dropped revelers into the lagoon of a mock majestic plaza, it still had a tower as the focal point modeled after a stately European monument. By contrast, Disneyland's focal point was Sleeping Beauty Castle, inspired more immediately by a cartoon than by the architectural fantasies of King Ludwig of Bavaria. The difference was subtle, but Disney's park created the "liberating sense of the limitless malleability of pictorial space" (notes Beth Dunlop), and a child-like playfulness compromised at Coney Island with its associations with classical columns, rectangular pools, and towers (especially at Dreamland).[25]

This leads us to the second theme that constituted Disney's idea of wonder, the appeal to "timeless" childlike delight and the "cute." Disney took pains not to overwhelm his visitors, but rather to delight them with toy-like buildings that would attract children. As often noted, this effect was achieved by such devices as constructing the train that circles Disneyland to 5/8 scale and the use of "forced perspective" that made buildings appear taller than they were by making higher portions of buildings successively smaller, reducing the physical intimidation of Sleeping Beauty's Castle, for example, while making it look real. Disney buildings evoke the feeling of a toy, and, as Walt Disney noted, "the imagination can play more freely with a toy."[26] At the same time, the Disney scene is not mere order and kitsch. Because the overall impression is reassuring, elements of topsy-turvy can run through the design of Disney parks. In all this the buildings appealed to the delight of children.

The fact that most Disney stories and buildings took the perspective of a child allowed a cross-generational bonding insofar as grandparent, mother, father, teenager, and child were expected to enter into a shared "innocent" fantasy. Absent from Disneyland was any encounter with the fears and fascinations of adult life, disasters, death, and the hereafter. Such themes had become taboo for children, while adults preferred to shift their gaze toward the fresh imaginings of young life. This was more than "taming" the imagination, defanging the old world of the carnival. Disney exploited the growing appeal of a relatively new source of wonder, expressed through the aesthetic of the cute child. Pictured in comic strips, dolls, child movie stars, magazine illustrations, and ads from the 1900s, the cute child had the look of wonder, often with a slight tinge of impishness. The cute was a celebration of the seemingly untethered delight of innocence. Although this "wondrous innocence" could be evoked by the child's discovery of nature, in the twentieth century it was sparked also by commercialized fantasy and novelty.[27]

Part of Disney's achievement was his success in inducing adults to encourage children to "act out" the cute in wide-eyed enchantment with Disney cues. Disney once bragged that his greatest creation was "the smile on a child's face." Many have noted how Disney cutesified nature, history, and even artistic styles by making the mysterious, dangerous, and even mundane full of childlike wonder. Instead of earlier adult responses to the young, Disney believed that nothing should awe or frighten the child and all stimuli should cause delight.[28]

The result was the culture of the cute, which emerged not simply because of the family's need for a lowest common denominator of culture (set at the child's level) nor even because of adults regressing into play in order to escape from the terrors or tedium of modernity. Instead, the cult of the cute was more the result of a need to replace the magical charm of belief in the supernatural and fascination with disaster with the child's belief that "dreams can actually come true."[29]

The play and imagination of the small, dependent child, which was shaped by modern parental expectations and modern commercial entertainment, defined Disney's appeal to the cute. The story of the emergence of cute is a complex one, but it can be illustrated in recalling the transformation of Mickey Mouse. Mickey first appeared on the screen in 1928, not as a figure of childhood innocence but as a rascally rodent, having more in common with the rebellious and violent tradition of working class and adult-oriented slapstick comedy, the roguish behavior of comic strip characters (like Ignatz Mouse from the "Krazy Kat" strip or the Katzenjammer Kids), or even the threatening posturing of masked mummers and Mardi Gras paraders. Within a few years, however, Disney had made Mickey "small, soft, infantile, mammalian, round, without bodily orifices, and nonsexual," a perfect example of "neoteny." He had become a classic form of the cute, following in the pattern of the Teddy Bear (1906) and the Kewpie doll (1912). The neotenic transformation not only evoked protective feelings in adults, but also made Disney's animal characters appear innocent and thereby less threatening in their desires and behavior. Moreover, this Disney look replaced the natural, sometimes dangerous animals at the circus or in animal acts at old Coney Island. The middle-class embrace of the innocent allowed Disney to transform the freak show and circus into his menagerie of loveable mice, dogs, and ducks. The dangerous elephant electrocuted by Frederic Thompson in 1903 had become the childlike Dumbo with big floppy ears that allowed him to fly while children and their parents could ride on his back in Fantasyland. Disney still provided pleasure and wonder in the inversion of social standards (as in earlier forms of saturnalia). Disney's cartoon animals were often feisty, sometimes rebellious (as in Donald Duck's nephews), or even silly (like Goofy), but they were now "naughty but nice" like small "innocent" children. That was essential to the appeal of the cute and is often missed by critics.

Disney rides played on the presumed child's fantasy with over- and under-sized objects, making it possible for families to ride in The Mad Hatter's tea cups. The Small World ride (1966) offered a classic Disney look of the cute. On this boat journey, we see big eyed, big headed mechanical children of different shades of skin and dressed in all the stereotyped costumes of the world of nations, who despite cultural differences are really the same delightful young, making the world "small" with their incessant dancing to, playing, and singing a catchy tune ending with words, "Though the mountains divide and the oceans are wide, it's a small world after all."[30]

For decades, Disney ads featured not textual appeals but pictures of the cute: People sized Mickey, Minnie, and Goofy delighting small children, or granddads and toddlers laughing together riding Dumbo. Like the Coney Island of Steeplechase and Luna, Disney encouraged adults to play the child, riding mechanical toys, but they also put on the cute by wearing Mickey Mouse ears. At Disneyland, brags Disney publicity, we find "the dancing eyes of a grandfather wearing an orange-billed Donald Duck hat." The idea was more than to feel like a kid, but to put on the mummers' mask of the cute, even reversing roles, not across classes as in the old Mardi Gras tradition, but across ages.[31]

The cute was as different from the genteel appeal of the majestic and sublime as it was from the carnivalesque world of the plebeian playful crowd. It was not the only replacement for the late Victorian dyad of the genteel and plebeian (as we shall see in the next chapter), nor the only modern form of the child-focused family. The cute was also different from the pleasure complex of the "cool" youth, older than the cute kid, and freed from adult supervision and imagination, who was attracted to the anti-cute. The dark and violent images of science fiction, gangster stories and monster movies as well as the exhilaration of pinball games and roller coasters were associated with youth and the cool by the 1930s. In the same decade, Disney had his first successes with commercializing the cute. But Disney specialized and had nothing to do with the emerging culture of the cool. Even haunted houses would only come much later to Disney and they would be systematically cutesified. It was not until the late 1970s, a decade after Walt's death, that his company made compromises with the cool.[32]

Playing the movie and glorifying the cute redefined the playful crowd for Disney's middle America in the 1950s, but he brought still one more element of change. Not only did Disney rally the family around the child's imagination and even invite the old to regress to their own inner child, but he also encouraged them to "recall" the worlds of their own childhoods. For Disney that meant the time of his own youth, a magical era of childhood wonder, 1900s America, expressed in his romantic reconstruction of Main Street U.S.A.

Disney's hubris succeeded because his idea of the romantic past coincided with the emergence of modern commercialized nostalgia. In the 1950s, fantasy was no longer just or even particularly for the young, but for the old waxing nostalgic about the worlds of their youth. For Disney, "helping" adults return to the place of their childhoods was, at least, as important as appealing to children—even more so. It was only in 1993 that Toontown opened for kids to play in their cartoon world, but the iconic Main Street U.S.A. was the most essential construction of Disney's original 1955 park. It became a time and fantasy "tunnel" through which all must pass to get to the happy "Lands" of fantasy, adventure, the American frontier, and even of tomorrow. In his widely distributed park guides published in the 1960s, Disney himself noted "Many of us fondly remember our 'small home town' and its friendly way of life at the turn of the century." The year 1900 was perhaps a time for discovery and rapid technological and social change, but for Disney it was also a time where the intimacies of the strolling town were still happily spared from the dangers and speeds of the soon-to-emerge car culture. Only a quaint 1905 horseless carriage "that pops and sputters down Main Street" was allowed to pollute the gentle world of the horse tram and pedestrian. Corporate and chain stores had not yet driven out of business those little shops that Disney so lovingly reproduced, the Candy Palace, Penny Arcade, Swift Market House, and Hills Brothers Coffee House. This nostalgia for small towns was repeatedly reinforced in the movies (think of the Andy Hardy series of the late 1930s or *It's a Wonderful Life* of 1946). The postwar flight to the suburbs made Main Street U.S.A. powerful nostalgia. Disney, at this time in his late fifties, could lecture his customers: "When you visit the apothecary, . . . we hope you'll visualize, as I often do, your own home town Main Street, or the one your parents and grandparents have told you about."[33] Disney envisioned that this aspect of the park would promote conversation across the generations that would continue as families entered the storybook "lands."[34]

Main Street recalled a youth that was foreign to most young visitors, and, over the years, it was alien even to parents and grandparents as fewer were raised in small towns. However, Disney's fantasy of his youth, because it was made delightful, became the nostalgia of subsequent generations. This was possible in part because American nostalgia was not about returning to an ancestral village. After all one family in four moved every year in the 1950s, and mobility and marriages across ethnic and neighborhood groups meant that there was often no obvious home to return to. Migrants from across the Atlantic were even further from their "roots." Going home in such a setting, meant "returning" to a romantic idea, one easily blended and idealized in an all-white, all-American Main Street U.S.A., a 1950s romance about the beginning of the twentieth century that still continues to represent nostalgia.[35]

But this nostalgia was much more than a retreat into an idealized American past. Disney's dream of Main Street represents a kind of protest against both suburban sprawl and the dirt and alienation of big city centers, two lasting consequences of modern consumer capitalism. Rather than either harking back to the Renaissance European Square (attractive to turn-of-the-century immigrants and culturally aspiring Americans at Coney Island) or attempting to dazzle visitors with novelty lights and neon (as were Americans in 1900 New York at both Times Square and Coney Island), Disney offered an idealized past of small towns and frontier life. European grandeur and the image of ever changing spectacle that appealed to immigrant visitors of Luna Park and Dreamland in the 1900s had long faded.[36] Main Street U.S.A. was both a protest against the contemporary city, "unpleasant places for parents to live with their children," as noted Walt,[37] and the suburb where many sought sociability, but often found status seeking and a car culture that impeded the neighborliness that presumably prevailed in the small towns of the past.[38] Since the 1920s, Robert Moses and many other planners had been finding solutions to the disorder and grime of the city and its paired site of Coney Island through the promotion of sanitized, geometrical modernity in the form of suburbs, parkways, state park picnic grounds. By contrast, Disney returned to the idealized urban setting, the walking city. And he safeguarded this by obliging grateful City Councils of Anaheim over many years to block the construction of any buildings that defiled this vista of Disney magic.[39] As a form of commercial saturnalia, Main Street U.S.A. was an alternative and protest against the contemporary reality of progress and innovation.

In 1955, Disney made it clear that "Disneyland will never be completed" and planned to add and change attractions to make "each return visit . . . a new experience for our guests."[40] Yet, for at least twenty years, Disneyland remained faithful to Walt's nostalgia for the 1900s, building merely modernized versions of early-twentieth-century dioramas and other middle-class attractions. Early changes were adjustments, such as replacing the slightly didactic Canal Boats of the World for the more playful Storybook Land Canal Boats (with scenes from Disney movies) that worked better with toddlers in Fantasyland. Disney infantilized the old scenic canal boats of Luna Park as families rode through an entrance shaped like the mouth of Monstro (the whale that swallowed Disney's Pinocchio). The appeal of Disneyland to the small fry led to new Fantasyland rides in 1958 (the Mad Tea Party, a spinning ride in tea cups, and an Upside Down Room from Alice in Wonderland). The 1959 construction of the Matterhorn, a track ride on make-believe bobsleds up, through, and around a replica of the Swiss mountain, which ended in a "glacier lake," represents a slight break with the Disney vision. Although really a very mild roller coaster, it still has as much in common with Coney Island's scenic railroads as it does with a modern thrill ride.[41]

Tomorrowland was a site of frequent change because of its unfinished state in 1955 and because the theme of "tomorrow" continually needed to be updated as tomorrow became yesterday. Walt Disney built America's first Monorail in 1959, presumably the wave of the future, and opened Monsanto's House of the Future in 1957 with promises of the wonders of plastic.[42] Still, even the new Tomorrowland harked back to an earlier era. The rather crude 20,000 Leagues under the Sea disappeared, but it was replaced with the Submarine Voyage where patrons looked out of portholes to see the submerged lost continent of Atlantis as well as the polar icecap, a curious mix of fantasy and celebration of technology that shared much with the Trip to the Moon of the 1900s. Also in 1959, Disney updated another nineteenth-century tradition, the diorama, when he built models of the Grand Canyon along the route of the Disney train (showing the canyon at dawn, dusk, and in a lightning storm probably drawing on the pop classic, *The Grand Canyon Suite* of Ferde Grofé). Again, appealing to the child's imagination was a new diorama along the same rail route in 1967—Primeval World with dinosaur models. Disney revived and improved the nineteenth-century tradition of the panorama and cyclorama in the America the Beautiful film (1959) shown on a 360-degree screen in Tomorrowland. The next year, Frontierland offered another version of the old scenic railroad, Nature's Wonderland, a series of scenes of waterfalls, deserts, and even a Graveyard of Dinosaurs, Rainbow Cavern, and an Old Unfaithful Geyser, simulating, in a short ride, the excitement of the Old West. While the Matterhorn may have been a concession to thrills, Nature's Wonderland promised awe and inspiration through the innovative artifice of its scenery, a traditional bourgeois tourist's gaze, not the more modern pleasure-seeker's vertigo. Long after Disney's death, Disneyland planners conformed to his nostalgic vision. [43]

Disney's development of Audio-Animatronics, a magnetic tape–driven system that coordinated sound with movements of mechanical characters and objects, was central to much of the innovation in the 1960s. Still, Disney stuck to the appeal of the cute and Victorian fascination with mechanical ingenuity. The Enchanted Tiki Room (1963), a sentimental musical production featuring four talking birds (representing stereotypical Irish, German, French, and Spanish personalities) was the first use of audio-animatronics. Soon appeared the patriotic Great Moments with Mr. Lincoln, featuring the speaking and moving figure of the President (1965), It's a Small World (1966), the Pirates of the Caribbean, a whimsical boat ride through scenes of a brigand attack on a hapless sea port (1967), the Haunted Mansion, "a delightfully dreary adventure suitable for every age" (1969), and the Country Bear Jamboree, using the same format as the Tiki Room but in a wild west setting of cute bears, moose, and raccoons (1972).[44] Some were technically more sophisticated versions of old amusement park "dark rides;" others were little more than updates of the automata that had fascinated nineteenth-century Americans and Europeans. All remained within the world of the nineteenth-century dime museum and middle-class attractions at Luna Park and Dreamland.

The Disney company was relentless in pursuing Walt's didactic themes after his death, not only with uplifting messages from Lincoln but also with an updated Flight to the Moon (1967) with far more accurate simulations of contemporary space travel (including the sensation of a rocket thrust). The moon show was appropriately replaced in 1975 (after the 1969 Lunar landing made this attraction "history") with the next American space adventure, "Mission to Mars." The 1967 renovation of Tomorrowland brought also the Adventure Through Inner Space (a tour of the atom) as well as a more prosaic audio-animatronic lesson in General Electric's Carousel of Progress (showing the impact of electricity on homes since the 1890s).[45] Until the late 1970s, at least, Disney continued to provide a link to the uplifting goals of late Victorian middle class culture (while affirming corporate American's inheritance of those values).

Even more important, innovation was less a theme in Disney than Coney Island, despite regular upgrading. In part, this was because Disney used steel, reinforced concrete, plastic, and fiberglass instead of wood and "staff" to construct his fantasy world, making it almost as durable as Blackpool's brick and iron pleasure palaces. After a season, Luna Park's artificial turrets and Dreamland's felt and canvas flames and devils in Hell's Gate looked tawdry; and their owners were obliged to engage in a ruinously rapid turnover of attractions. By contrast, quality, long-lasting construction made possible slower, more deliberate transformations at Disneyland, enhancing rather than compromising its "trademark" look. Even more important here was the profitability of Disney, based as it was on a far more affluent crowd than visited Coney. There were no nickel rides or 25 attractions for 25 cents as at Steeplechase Park, or even the inflation-adjusted equivalent. Instead, Disney was able to lavish its park with details of which Frederic Thompson could only have dreamed and thus made return visits interesting. There was always more to see, even if little changed.

Most important, Disney's advantage was that his park was less about novelty for its own sake than something more complex. The company solved a problem that had plagued Coney's amusement parks, whose novelty-based thrills brought crowds in, but could not keep them coming back because the new, once experienced, was no longer new. Crowds returned again and again to the beach, but the amusement parks had to produce novelty year by year, and this they could not afford to do. Disney instead emphasized the past (nostalgia), the future (technological optimism), and "timeless" fantasy, not the present new. Indeed, the present and thus immediate change, was to be escaped at Disneyland. Novelty was thus secondary. The Disney package worked especially well for evoking the imagined "past" and "timelessness," but less so for the future, as witnessed by the need to renovate Tomorrowland numerous times and then to increasingly stress science fiction fantasy rather than future technology.

The core reason for Disney's success may be in the bonding of nostalgia and "timeless" cuteness across the generations. Rides and other attractions did not get "old" because oldsters expected to return to their pasts at Disneyland and adults picked up visual cues throughout the park that they should feel romantic about that past. At the same time, adults "passed" on to the next generation these same sites and experiences, which, for the very young, were truly new. Their "newness" was supposed to be enjoyed, not simply as novelty, but as "timeless" wonder, that same look and presumably feel of delight shown on the five-year old's face in 2000 as had been on the face of her parent 25 years before. This many explain why core attractions in Fantasyland remained for decades: Peter Pan's Flight, Mr. Toad's Wild Ride, Dumbo The Flying Elephant, and the Mad Tea Party, staples from the mid-1950s, remained into the twenty-first century. And the nostalgic appeal of Tom Sawyer's Island, the Rivers of America and the Mark Twain steamer remained iconic to Frontierland a half century after their construction. Even the now campy (and racist) cannibals seen on Adventureland's Jungle Cruise have survived. Although hardly an attraction for contemporary teens, these "frontier" and "adventure" rides continue to create wonder in the young and evoke nostalgia in the old. This self-referential nostalgia for the invented traditions of Disney itself is an impressive illustration of the durability of his ideas.

Sustaining the Disney Crowd

By 1967, a dozen years after the opening of Disneyland, 60 million had visited the site and had made Anaheim into a major entertainment town.[46] Yet, despite the congestion of cars and crowds in and around Disney's California site that led the company to colonize the open spaces of the central Florida marshland for its new venture in the mid 1960s, Disneyland made every effort to reduce the anxiety about crowds that seemed to obsess middle-class visitors. And, it has survived for a longer period than most of Coney's amusement parks, whose down-market crowds eventually helped to drive away the middle classes.

Disney tried to filter out the "dangerous classes" by an informal policy of exclusion (prohibiting "hippies" in the 1960s, for example), and by discouraging the poor through high-priced attractions (the all inclusive one-day ticket by 2003 cost $37 for children under the age of 10 and $47 for "adults.")[47] This not only eliminated the "freeloading" poor who paid little and took up space in their wandering through the crowd, but also relieved anxious middle-class family groups from concern about their presence. After all, many middle-class families had moved to the suburbs to be far from these people and had carefully avoided buses and trains to avoid physical contact with the "Coney Crowd." Disney invested heavily in keeping his grounds squeaky clean and well-landscaped, a policy that not only reassured crowds and made the crush seem more bearable, but also had the effect of encouraging visitors to use ubiquitous waste baskets instead of littering. Disney's landscape director, Bill Evans, claimed that Walt Disney, inspired by his visit to Tivoli Gardens in Denmark, made sure his landscaping was "so beautiful that no one would dare toss a candy wrapper or trample the grass." The clean and orderly look of the place, noted one journalist in 1965, "sort of restores one's faith in humanity. Some of it rubs off on every visitor." As John Hench, one of the important early designers for Disney insisted, "Walt's thing was reassurance. The message is you're going to be O.K."[48]

The famous Disney look and demeanor of the staff (or "cast members" as Disney insisted on calling them), clean cut but cheerful, polite but friendly, reinforced the social tone of an orderly but playful experience. Disney training materials (from the 1980s) gave the cast explicit instructions on grooming for a "neat trim appearance" with no extremes to distract from the show. Women, for example, were not to wear more than two combs in their hair; they could use mascara, but not eye liner; and were expected to wear black shoes with a plain toe and defined heel. Depending on their "roles" and "costumes," their skirts should be from three inches above the knee to three inches from the floor. In the mid 1980s, management still held to Walt's ideal of 1955 when he said, "I don't want anybody hired who has anything to do with an amusement park." For years, the company combated contemporary fashion, prohibiting, for example, in 1958 the beehive and ducktail hairdos on young staff. By 1965, regulations on men's hair were relaxed slightly, allowing side burns to drop from "the corner of the eye to mid ear." Across the years, cast members, when they were "on stage" in the sight of "guests," had to present themselves as perpetually cheerful. This meant that they had to "present a positive image at all times," "sit erect and look attentive" never look "too tired to be bothered" or cross arms giving guests a "do not disturb" signal. Staff were to anticipate the needs of guests, solve any problems quickly, and end any encounter with guests on a positive note. Cast leader training even involved study of life-style and attitude differences across age (based on the curious principle that most people's values were determined by events and the culture they experienced by the time they were ten years of age). By reaffirming middle-class values through numerous clues, the Disney Company tried to make its customers comfortable, even in crowds of thousands.[49]

Disney designers became famous for moving crowds efficiently. Lines of people waiting for an attraction snaked back and forth and were treated to eye-catching and mood-shaping sights and sounds to allay boredom and anger. Even Disneyland policing maintained a low-key image. Walt Disney quickly dropped his contract with Burns Security in 1956 and hired instead moonlighting teachers and others accustomed to working with youth to police his crowds. Dressed in blazers and without weapons, Disney security relied on psychology to prevent flare-ups between guests. Costumed staff, Disney officials claimed to the press, "make people feel as if they're at a party" of a sedate and respectable kind, and thus less prone to argue or fight even when unhappy.[50]

Disney had perfected these techniques, but he had by no means invented them. Coney Island amusement parks, especially Luna and Dreamland, featured controlled admissions (expelling undesirables and using entrance tickets). The difference was in the fact that Disney has been able to maintain the social tone for almost 50 years. One of the key differences was that Disney eliminated much of the "intervitality" of the crowd. First, the family nature of the attractions and their relatively high cost discouraged groups of young people on the prowl for the opposite sex. Second, nothing promoted the formation of autonomous throngs as appeared on the streets of Coney Island and Blackpool in the interwar years. The street parade traditions of the European Carnivals and Easter processions and the Coney Island "Mardi Gras" were co-opted by Disney performers who made the crowd into spectators rather than actors. It was the animatronic characters at the Enchanted Tiki Room and later the Country Bear Jamboree that swapped wisecracks, not the crowd itself. It was costumed Disney characters, not autonomous Krewes as in New Orleans Mardi Gras or cheerfully inebriated throngs as in Blackpool, who acted "goofy."

Key to Disney's success at maintaining a middle-class social tone was its almost "trademark" commitment to treating the crowd as friend and family units. While commentators note that adult visitors far outnumbered children (citing ratios of 4 to 1 or greater), these figures are suspect in part because Disneyland charged older children (today from ten years of age) adult prices. A rare Disney survey of 1958 suggests more subtle statistics: only 61 percent were over 17 years old, while 11.5 percent were between 12 and 17 and 27.5 percent under 12 years of age. Disney publicity touted the 4 to 1 figure in 1971 but did so in the context of attempting to overcome a reputation as a kids' destination and probably to reach out to new markets, especially elders, to compensate for the decline in the birth rate.[51] The surprising number of adults (whether or not one accepts the 4 to 1 ratio) reflects, in part, the fact that groups of parents, aunts, uncles, and grandparents had shared the Disney experience with a smaller number of young children.

What worked in 1955 during the first year of Disneyland still worked 45 years later, despite much social and economic change. In a visit to Walt Disney World's Magic Kingdom in Florida in 2000, Gary Cross noticed how dads in their forties appeared to regress to their youthful years of parenting while 16-year old sons obligingly reverted back to six-year olds. Visual and audio cues encourage this intergenerational exchange by almost hypnotic suggestion, sending these fathers and sons back to that time when they first shared "Toy Story" or "Dumbo." Contemporary ads continuously stress the magic of childhood across the generations, often showing kids playing the tour guide to their elders or in shock at the childlike and playful regression of their parents. These were the mini-stories that continue to charm twenty-first century adults, just as did similar humorous exchanges illustrated by Norman Rockwell over half a century earlier.

Disney's lasting appeal also encompassed the nostalgia of older adults for their youth and for a mythical time of intergenerational harmony and respect, which seemed particularly poignant with the rise of assertively independent youth cultures. In addition to the sentimental anchor of Main Street, new nostalgic themes appeared with new cohorts of older visitors. As early as 1957, Disney tried to increase night-time audiences by appealing to adult tastes. In 1960, Disneyland first offered Dixieland concerts and antique car shows on Main Street U.S.A. in order to attract older visitors. Vaudeville '67 featured the Mills Brothers and Rudy Vallee for a graying crowd. By 1965, Disneyland was featuring swing bands (Tommy Dorsey, Duke Ellington, the Glen Miller Band, etc.) appealing to memories of the youth of couples in their forties and fifties at the time. In the 1970s discounts were offered during May on "Senior Citizen Days." In 1974, Disneyland presented the easy listening sound of Lawrence Welk's big band, familiar to millions of Middle Americans from his weekly TV variety show. While Dixieland and Swing remained staples into the 1990s, programmers responded to a new group of nostalgic adults with vintage rock music, as in the "Blast to the Past" festival in 1988 that featured late 1950s rock and car shows.[52]

The appeal to an older audience went beyond nostalgic music and commercial artifacts. Especially from the mid-1960s to early 1970s, Disney attracted mature audiences with the promise of a clean show, free of rebellious unkempt youth. In a letter to Disneyland in 1969, an older guest thanked the company in this age of "hippies and delinquents . . . for hiring such fine and outstanding types of youth. It restores an elder's faith." Disney exploited this longing in the image of wholesomeness projected in its female tour guides who dressed modestly in red kilts and jackets and were selected based on their "natural charm and a happy personality." Each year, one of them became a "Disneyland Ambassador," to represent the park across the nation and beyond, like a Miss America beauty queen.[53]

Underlying all this was a somewhat faltering faith in the universality of the suburban and small-town culture from which many of Disneyland's visitors came. The company's efficient publicity machine received an endless stream of free advertising on the feature pages of provincial newspapers. Disney was also extremely adept at appropriating symbols of a bygone era of American rural and small town life and exploiting suburbanite nostalgia for long lost community centers. This was most evident in Main Street U.S.A., but was reinforced by the building of the New Orleans Square in 1966 (Walt Disney bragged that it was far more clean than the original) and the rustic village of Bear Country in 1972. The Disney marching band recalled fading traditions of small-town America. Moreover, Disney planners co-opted town traditions like the annual lighting of the Christmas tree and "Candle-light Caroling Ceremonies" as well as Independence Day parades and State Fair festivals (in the fall). Beginning in 1972, Disney even improved on this celebratory culture by offering daily summer performances of the Main Street Electric Parade with elaborately lit floats and costumed Disney characters. Any summer night that a visitor came to Disneyland was the night of the big parade.

Even if the voluntary organizations of middle America were no longer up to the task of organizing American Bicentennial celebrations, Disney stepped up to the plate with 15 months of daily parades offering colorful mobile musical stages that presented Disney's version of American greatness (complete with the first Thanksgiving and Betsy Ross's first flag) led, of course, by Mickey, Donald, and Goofy. Lest the audience not see the connection to the older tradition of town parades, high school bands would compete for the chance for guest appearances. While Disney appealed to this "general" white middle-class audience, gradually the company recognized the persistence of ethnic identity. Beginning in 1969, Disneyland celebrated Irish culture on St. Patrick's Day and Mexican customs on Cinco de Mayo.[54]

Disneyland also appealed to youth, obviously not teens in rambunctious groups, much less protesters or minorities, but young people suitably fitting the Disney image. As early as 1961, just when the company was reaching out to oldsters, Disneyland presented "Grad Nite," an alternative all-night party for graduating high school kids. This annual event was both well-supervised (one adult chaperon for every 20 grads) and alcohol-, violence-, and sex-free. High schools throughout the west sent 8,000 dressed-up kids to this 11 p.m. to 5 a.m. event. By 1968, 100,000 participated in multiple Grad Nites. As early as 1957, Disney had experimented with Date Nite on weekends, offering rides and tame youth music in the summers, and an alcohol-free New Year's Eve Party that attracted clean-cut (not the counter-cultural) youth of Los Angeles and Orange County.[55]

Change in Disney's Land: Attractions and Crowds Since 1977

These largely conservative appeals served the park well throughout the 1960s and 1970s (as attendance rose from 5.9 million in 1960 to 10.8 in 1979, with particularly sharp increases in the troubled late 1960s, increasing from 6.7 million in 1966 to 10.3 million in 1970). The 1970s and especially 1980s, however, proved to be disappointing for Disneyland with declining attendance between 1981 and 1984. Only special promotions, including car giveaways, could raise attendance to 11.9 million in 1985. Of course, a rocky economy was partially to blame and for years Disneyland was hampered by the diversion of funds and energy to Disney's Florida enterprises. The limited land holdings in Anaheim also blocked diversification. Still, in the early 1980s, the old Disney formula was no longer working anywhere.[56]

The company faced a problem far more daunting than the hippies and protesters of the 1960s and early 1970s—the decline of the cute and the rise of the cool. The decrease in births in the 1970s translated into smaller numbers of young families in the 1980s. Probably more important, the child's, especially boys' attraction, to the mystic of the frontier, global adventure, and science upon which Disney built three of his "lands" was in decline. The "Star Wars" trilogy and its licensed products (1977–83), along with a more cynical popular culture that "bled" into children's culture, challenged these older ideals. Part of that change was the downward push of the cool when children abandoned the "cute" culture imposed by their parents at younger ages. The striking manifestation of this was the youth's attraction to the thrill rides that their parents and grandparents had rejected decades before in the old amusement parks.[57]

Company officials began to recognize the need to adapt to the demands for a more thrill-seeking audience with new more daring rides designed to appeal to teens and "tweens" (10- to 12-year-olds). Despite attempts to appeal to a cross-generational audience as well as distinct age groups at different times and seasons, Disneyland was obliged to adjust to the independent, older child, especially in the context of increased competition from other amusement parks in the region. From the late 1970s, Six Flags Magic Mountain of Valencia California catered to teens with thrill rides like Free Fall (a 55 mph drop in two seconds) and a series of roller coasters (especially Revolution, featuring a scary loop and the Colossus noted for its height). By 2003, Magic Mountain offered 16 roller coasters. Even the once staid Knotts' Berry Farm adapted to change by opening the Wild Water Wilderness complex in 1987 and a teen night club and restaurants serving adults alcohol in the mid 1990s. Sea World of San Diego offered an alternative to Disneyland, a clean and more modern image of childhood wonder around a theme of nature and ecology that appealed to "soccer moms" (and recently this park too has introduced thrill rides).[58]

As early as 1977, Disneyland began to adapt, premiering the first of a series of more thrilling rides with Space Mountain. Though advertised as an educational ride in a space capsule followed with displays of future uses of electronics on the exit ramp, Space Mountain was really an indoor roller coaster, a gut-wrenching experience of "twisting and banking" as the rider "plunges into swirling galaxies, past shooting stars, and meteoric showers." In 1979, the sedate Mine Train through Nature's Wonderland was replaced by the embellished roller coaster, the Big Thunder Railroad. Although featured as a re-creation of the Bryce Canyon in the era of the 1850s, youth were attracted to it as an energetic thrill ride through caverns, waterfalls, the "dangers" of an avalanche, and the scary scene of a "dinosaur gulch." While hardly as fast or as heart-pounding as the new roller coasters elsewhere, it was a compromise with an amusement park tradition that Disney had purposively shunned in 1955.[59]

Instructive is the list of attractions that did not survive to 1985, the thirtieth anniversary of Disneyland: the Carousel of Progress, Monsanto's Hall of Chemistry, the Story of Aluminum, Frontierland's Indian Village, Hobbyland (an exhibition of model planes), the Mickey Mouse Club Circus, and the sedate Flying Saucers ride. Disney did not entirely abandon the didactic tradition of presenting science and "history." The Tomorrowland of 2003 still featured "Innoventions," an interactive display of new technology and an exhibit commemorating the history of NASA, even though few line up for admittance to these concessions to tradition.[60]

Most of the new rides thus appealed to the "cool" rather than the cute, nostalgic, or the genteel values of progress and patriotic history. Disney staff recognized the marketing power of George Lucas and his Star Wars trilogy and accommodated changing youth taste by hiring the film-maker to produce several space fantasies for Disneyland. Although Tomorrowland had always had its science fictional quality, never was it so brazen as in the Lucas projects. In 1985, Lucas presented Captain Eo, a 12-minute three-dimensional film and light show fantasy starring singer Michael Jackson who struggles against horrible aliens to save a "music starved planet." Another Lucas project was the 1987 simulated space ride, Star Tours, an early example of the use of film coordinated with moving seats to give a small theater audience the sensation of a thrilling journey into the world of the Star Wars movies. Not even a shadow of pretense of real science was offered as Star Tours replaced the semi-educational attraction of the Adventures Through Inner Space.[61]

Of course, Disneyland had hardly capitulated to the demand for "white knuckle" rides among teens and young adults of the period. In fact, it reinforced its old commitment to the "cute" by refurbishing Fantasyland in 1983 when it added "old world" facades on existing rides. More important, however, was Disney's careful compromise of the cute with the cool. The opening of Mickey's Toontown in 1993 was an important update of classic Disney cute. This new "land" finally offered children and their parents a chance to see where Mickey and other Disney characters "lived." But this was far different from a walk through a storybook land of miniature sets. Toontown was sardonically suggestive of Hollywood in the 1930s (complete with a Toontown sign on the side of a hill similar to the icon of Hollywood). Despite the tone of safety and sweetness (for example in the Gadgets Go Coaster and the Jolly Trolley), a frenetic and even slightly cynical quality saturated Goofy's Wiseacre Farm. Roger Rabbit Car Toon Spin, a dark ride featuring strobe lights, menacing bad guys, and hard mechanical images, was softened only by cartoonish whimsy. All this is a far cry from the sweet romance of the old Fantasyland.[62]

In 1994, Disneyland increased its commitment to meet the needs of the cool child with the 3-D movie Honey, I Shrunk the Audience. Drawing on a 1989 Disney movie, Honey, I Shrunk the Kids, that featured a bumbling scientist who clumsily reduced his children to the size of bugs with his new invention, Disneyland's new attraction centered on the illusion that the audience is shrunk by the scientist on the stage screen. In addition to the 3-D effects of a snake and other objects popping out at the audience, air, water, and moving seats are used to give the audience the sensation of mice scurrying under them, a giant dog sneezing on them, and giant people shaking the auditorium. Even more in the 1995 Indiana Jones Adventure, thrills prevail over wonder, memory, or uplift. "White-hot oozing lava, careening boulders, vicious vermin and snakes" are encountered on this ride that "hurtles you helplessly through the cursed Temple of the Forbidden Eye!" The delight in the future, the distant, or timeless past are replaced with background stories of technology run amok or of a world out of control. [63]

By the summer of 2003, Tomorrowland was no longer touted as a place to discover the future in the technological breakthroughs of today. It was simply a "place of imagination and beyond," as proclaimed a continuously running TV ad (seen at local hotels). The ad featured thrill rides to promote Tomorrowland as well as the other "lands." The old images of the delighted child, the romancing couple, and the nostalgic elders remained, of course. But a new crowd of autonomous youth could no longer be ignored or opposed by Disney. The culture of the cute had to make room for the culture of the cool.

Disneyland had to adapt to the social change that surrounded it. In the late 1980s and 1990s, it relied increasingly on local crowds. Despite ongoing publicity about how Disneyland attracted notables throughout the world, it was predominantly a California attraction (53 percent of visitors came from California and 76 percent of that group from the southern half in 1958). Later statistics showed little change. As population increased in Orange and Los Angeles Counties, Disneyland became the amusement site of a densely populated area, not unlike Coney Island of the early twentieth century. And with this, Disneyland became a magnet attracting youth, but no longer necessarily the clean-cut teens of white suburbia. Instead these areas were becoming more mixed ethnically, with Hispanic and Asian newcomers. A 1987 survey of customers found that 60 percent of local 18 to 24 year olds had been to Disneyland in the past year as compared to only 29 percent of over 55 year olds. Disney continued to try to filter out the "trouble making" youth, for example, by ejecting teens with spiky black and teased hair in 1985 and withdrawing the annual pass of teens caught swearing loudly in 1992. However, company staff found themselves confronted with a problem: They depended on local, youthful crowds, and thus periodically offered off-season discounts to Orange County residents and bargain season passes. Yet, with the rise of two-income families, it was tempting for parents to drop their offspring off at Disneyland during school vacations and on weekends, in effect making Disneyland "baby sitters." Moreover, these changes created a youthful "gang" society within the park. Press reports of increased crime discouraged some families from visiting. The tendency of local youth, increasingly of minority racial and ethnic origins, to "hog" benches and congregate in large groups, only accelerated this trend.[64]

By 2003, the old Disney "magic" certainly remained for many who still brought their children or grandchildren to Anaheim for that joy of innocent wonder; and many came to remember their first time at Disneyland as children or when their children were still young. Yet the park was no longer as clean, the paint as fresh, the staff as polite and cheery (or middle-class white) as oldsters remembered.

Disney Beyond Disneyland

Walt Disney's vision of the playful crowd survived long after his death in December 1966. His company transported his formula to Orlando, Florida with the opening of Walt Disney World's Magic Kingdom in 1971. Although Disney never saw his "World," his fingerprints were everywhere on it. As often noted, Disney had wanted a property so large and unimpeded by outsiders that his company could completely control the environs and keep staff busy designing new projects for the "next 25 years."[65] There was to be no jungle of cheap motels nearby, nor any roadblocks to indefinite expansion. Disney had bought land in central Florida with the acreage of Manhattan and gained legal control over utilities and zoning regulations Walt Disney World could thus become the perfect expression of the Disney vision, uncompromised and unfettered. At the same time, Disney World emerged and developed when the Disney vision was being challenged and had to adjust to social and cultural change, accommodating the "cool" in children and new demands for age-segmented play in adults. A brief review of the story of Walt Disney World will serve as a summary of the persistence and adaptation of the Disney version of the playful crowd.

Disney World became much more than an amusement park. From the beginning, it was conceived as a cluster of resorts that distant visitors would make a destination. Disney World, thanks in large part to air travel that had only recently become feasible for middle-class family vacations, became a national, indeed international destination. It became very popular with a British tourist public in the late twentieth century. Located far from major cities, and from the ocean and the beaches that made Florida famous, Disney World was able to attract 28.4 million visitors by 1990, easily the biggest tourist draw in the US with out-of-town visitors spending an average of nearly a week at the site. In 1997, Walt Disney World attracted almost twice as many visitors as had traveled to Britain from the United States (38 million to 19.2) and more than 25 times the number who had visited the White House (1.5 million).[66] While its first project in 1971, the Magic Kingdom, was basically a replica of Disneyland, plans were soon underway for a second park. Before his death, Disney had planned to use part of his vast Florida real estate to create a model urban utopia, the Experimental Prototype Community of Tomorrow (Epcot). The cost and complications of this dream proved too much for Walt's successors, who, in 1982, opened instead a permanent world's fair under the same name. They divided it into a cluster of futuristic exhibits (Future World), sponsored by major corporations, together with international exhibits (World Showcase), a semicircle of idealized replicas of tourist sites.[67]

The company drew upon Disney's earlier successes at the New York World's Fair of 1964, building a classic icon to the future in a gigantic geodesic dome (Spaceship Earth). Within it was placed a leisurely ride that passed a series of audio-animatronic tableaux sprinkled liberally with gags that told the story of human communications. Nearby are the pavilions of Future World promising to teach the wonders of the imagination (sponsored by Kodak), motion (GE), energy (Exxon), and land (Kraft at first, and from 1992 Nestlé) with entertaining stories of the history and future of technology. All this was classic, if Disneyfied, World's Fair fare with no fast rides, and seemingly little to appeal to thrill-seeking kids. The equally important World Showcase, a semicircular area across an artificial lake from Future World, was a distant relative of the World's Fair villages depicting African, South Sea, or even European life. Instead of phony natives, however, Disney was careful to recruit on six-month stints pleasant young English-speaking college-age nationals from each country in the Showcase. A miniature replica of the Eiffel Tower is featured in the French site and a detailed reproduction of St Mark's Square identifies the Italian pavilion, while a lookalike of Beijing's Temple of Heaven and an eighth-century pagoda mark the Chinese and Japanese exhibits. Instead of mysterious (or tacky) replicas of the villages of "darkest Africa," Epcot visitors received a classic world (especially European) tour of the middle-class traveler, seeing the high points without any of the travails of travel.[68]

In 1989, Disney World opened a third park, Disney-MGM Studios. The concept was borrowed from Universal Studios' park built near Hollywood in 1964, which combined movie-based rides with tours of stage sets and real movie and TV productions. By 1989, no longer was it possible to base a theme park primarily on Disney's appeal to children's imagination or the nostalgia of grandparents for the early twentieth century. By that time, Disney's magic in producing children's programs had declined and most of those grandparents were gone. Nostalgia had moved up a generation to a group with fond memories of 1930s and 1940s Hollywood and the classical movies of that period. Instead of the nostalgia for small-town America, Disney MGM romanticized the Golden Age of movies with a "charming" scaled-down reproduction of 1930s Hollywood Boulevard, ending at a replica of Grauman's Chinese Theater. This classic theater was the home of the park's flagship attraction, the Great Movie Ride, with exciting video clippings from famous movies and stars seen from cars shaped like sound stage vehicles. The Backstage Tour allows visitors to stroll through TV and movie sets. For the small fry, Disney bought the rights to Jim Henson's "Muppets," a collection of puppets that were familiar to all American children (and most adults) through more than 20 years of TV and movie appearances. Jim Henson's MuppetVision 3-D was the first of a new wave of three-dimensional movies with in-theater special effects.[69]

Yet, Disney's Florida complex went far beyond a collection of rides and uplifting exhibits. From the beginning, company executives devoted considerable energy to building a series of hotels, golf courses, campgrounds, and water parks making Disney World an enveloping experience of destination tourism that the small California site never could be. In 1971, Disney opened not only the Magic Kingdom but also Fort Wilderness (a camping compound) as well as two hotels, the Polynesian Resort and Contemporary Resort. Golf courses appeared in 1973; an open-air aviary (Discovery Island) and Lake Buena Vista Village and Community (a themed shopping center with a cluster of hotels and a golf course) emerged between 1971 and 1975; and a water park, River Country, opened in 1976.[70]

All of this certainly would have pleased Walt. The essential themes of the cute, nostalgia, and playful gentility, remained. However, just as Disneyland had to adapt to change, so did Walt Disney World. Despite the success of Epcot in its first full year in 1982, the company faced a major downturn in revenue in the early 1980s, especially from its movie business. Only in 1984, with the succession of Michael Eisner, a successful movie producer, to the helm of the company, did the company's fortunes begin to turn. Eisner's revamped company began subtly to change the old Disney formula by accommodating the youth culture of the cool and creating age-segmented entertainment in response to the decline in the ideal of intergenerational play. The former shift parallels changes in Disneyland; the latter is more evident in Florida where space and other resources allowed for its expression, but is also reflected in changes in the Anaheim site in 2001. A few examples from the 1980s and 1990s will illustrate these points.[71]

While Epcot was certainly a boastful continuation of the genteel tradition of uplift in science and world travel, by the 1980s it could no longer evade the demand for "excitement." The park got the message when it added to its program of entertaining education a ride called Body Wars, a simulation of going through the blood stream in pursuit of bacteria (1989). Using a format similar to Lucas's Star Tours, this "ride" was almost purely an emotional rush.[72] In 1998, Epcot found a better way of illustrating General Motors' "World of Motion" display than amusing audio-animatronics. Disney engineers built "an incredibly cool ride" called Test Track presumably based on a behind-the-scenes-look at automobile development, that consisted of riders participating in a series of car endurance tests on a mile-long track, complete with 50 degree hairpin turns, careening through a series of pylons, and being subject to arctic cold and desert heat before the vehicle was crash tested. Developers promised riders a "big adrenaline payoff."[73]

Soon after the opening of Disney MGM Studios, the company was preparing to accommodate the increasing demand for thrill rides for the youth who had no nostalgia for old MGM movies. Disney introduced a relatively tame, but imaginative, theme ride, the Twilight Zone Tower of Terror in 1994. Instead of joining a long line in front of a mechanical device, customers enter a decrepit hotel and wind their way through its lobby and into its basement where eventually they are led into an elevator. A mood of dreadful anticipation is created, even though few recall the not-so-successful horror story about an old Hollywood hotel and its ghastly elevator upon which the ride is based. The ride itself is a trip to the top of the elevator shaft and then a 157 foot drop in two seconds followed by repeated rides up and down. It is really a very elaborate version of a common vertical lift and drop ride found in many amusement parks, but wrapped in the dramatic foreboding created by Disney artists and architects.[74] Appealing to the ever increasing demands of the "tweens" and teens for "cool" rides, Disney followed the Tower of Terror with the Indiana Jones Adventure that appeared both in Disneyland and MGM Studios

(1995) and an indoor Rock 'n' Roller Coaster in 1999 that catapults riders from zero to 60 miles per hour in three seconds, and winds and twists them through a thrillpacked course with "multiple complete inversions," while 1950s rock music blares from speakers in each car.[75]

Other indications of a shift toward the thrill ride can be seen in the evolution of Disney water parks. The first, River Country (1976), located in the rustic setting of Fort Wilderness with its western appeal (campground, Fort Apache Playground, and horseshoe courts), is an attempt to recover the "Ol' Swimmin' Hole," with rope swings, barrel bridge, and a water slide. Nothing could be more of a contrast than Typhoon Lagoon (1989) with its 95-foot artificial mountain, nine water slides, snorkeling pool, rain forest, and especially its wave-making machines that overwhelm fun seekers with waves of up to seven feet in a gigantic pool. No longer was there any attempt to make a cross-generational appeal combining adult nostalgia and children's freedom. The third water park, Blizzard Beach (1995), is both more exciting and more fantastic than the other two. Built on a "story" about a freak snowstorm in Florida that led some overenthusiastic entrepreneurs to construct a ski resort, the park looks like an Alpine resort with the snow "melted" into a tropical lagoon. It features a 120-foot high Mt. Gushmore with a number of exciting water slides. The nostalgia and cross-generational play of River Country was abandoned for the sardonic and for fast-paced thrills.[76]

At the same time, Disney World shifted its appeal toward a more adult audience. It built on earlier adult resorts at Buena Vista, but increasingly with adult fantasy themes: The Grand Floridian Beach Resort (1986) was designed to evoke "memory" of the days of the gilded age when the rich discovered the south Florida beach. Soon the somewhat less lavish Swan and Dolphin hotel resorts were built near Epcot. Beginning in 1988 with the Caribbean Beach Resort, Disney erected other themed hotels around simulated travel to exotic places and times (with Port Orleans, 1991 and Coronado Springs, 1997). In 1994, Disney also opened a string of inexpensive family hotels themed around movies, music, and sports and featuring gigantic icons (cartoon characters, guitars, and sports equipment). These were designed for young families, presumably with parents still willing to defer to children's fantasies. But the main trend was accommodating adults. In 1989, the company opened Pleasure Island, a 16-acre complex of restaurants and night clubs (most of which serve alcohol) as well as a teen dance center and roller rink disco for the evening entertainment of visitors who have had enough of family fun and seek to be with their own age group. In 1996, Pleasure Island became part of an expanded Downtown Disney complex. That year appeared Disney BoardWalk modeled after the Atlantic City of the prewar era with a luxury Inn and numerous shops and nightclubs. Disney World even opened a Sports Complex in 1997 with facilities for amateur and professional sports of all kinds.[77]

By the end of the 1990s, Disney World had invested fully in the idea of entertainment for every stage across the life course. By 1995, a Wedding Chapel was offered to couples willing to buy one of Disney's wedding packages. The chapel included many Disney touches: a glass-enclosed pavilion on its own island located on the Seven Seas Lagoon with a backdrop of Magic Kingdom's Castle. The World also appealed to thousands as a honeymoon site.[78] In 1996, the Disney Institute opened to offer exciting short recreational education courses in animation, orchestra conducting, golf, gardening, and sixty other "if onlys," activities that adults always wished they had learned when younger. The appeal to childhood memory remained, but the Institute was primarily to be a chance for adults to "learn" alone without the children. It even provided seminars on "quality services strategies" for business groups (under the title of "Service, Disney Style"). Activities were provided for children of various ages as well, allowing family members to separate and to discover what interested them personally. With "courses" on animation and tours of Disney architecture and design, the Disney Institute provided the "backstage" view of Disney theatrics, adding a new dimension for admiring "intellectual" patrons. The Institute grounds were notable for the lack of the usual Disney merchandising, including only a small gift shop.[79]

In 1998, Disney World took the concept of age-segmented, life-stage entertainment a step further with the launching of Disney Magic Cruise Line that brought families to a special "deserted Island," the Castaway Cay. While the ship included a Mickey Mouse shaped pool, it also featured a pool for adults where Disney music was never played. Staff kept children amused at the Oceaneer's Club (featuring story telling and Captain Hook décor) while teens and adults joined separate clubs for age-appropriate group activities. On the island, a beach designated for families with small children was separated from other beaches for teenagers and adults, all in an effort to accommodate the desire of older children to be free of parents and younger siblings and to allow adults who were not into "the family thing" to enjoy themselves.[80]

The clearest example of how Disney accommodated the social and cultural changes of the 1980s and 1990s was the opening of the fourth theme park at Disney World, Animal Kingdom, in 1998. Eisner called it "a celebration of animals that ever or never existed." This marriage of theme park and zoo was hardly original: Sea World and Busch Gardens had long featured live animals and highlighted threats to wildlife in exhibits and shows. But Disney, responding to a slump in business in the early 1990s, decided to re-create an African Savanna and Asian Jungle on a 500-acre site (nearly seven times the size of Disneyland's amusement area). The central focal point of the wildlife park is a 145-foot concrete Tree of Life with an ancient, rugged look of nature. The close observer will see friezes of 325 animal sculptures. The Tree became a hub for the "lands" of Africa, Rafiki's Planet Watch (a themed nature and ecology center), Asia, DinoLand, U.S.A. and Camp Minnie Mouse (animated animals). Like other Disneylands, the Animal Kingdom made animals into cute characters, even props of story lines for the rides and attractions. The success of the feature-length cartoon, *Lion King*, set the tone and advertised the Animal Kingdom with its cutesified animals learning to live in harmony. Its happy time live show, "The Festival of the Lion King," encourages audience participation while dazzling the child within with song, tumblers, and stilt walkers performing in the frenetic style of modern circuses.[81]

Still, Disney made direct appeals to a new middle-class obsession, no longer with technological progress as in the original Tomorrowland or Epcot, but with a stress on "authenticity" and conservation. The African and Asian buildings have purposively weathered walls with cracked and faded paint. Boats and trucks are dented and painted in rust. Even potholes were built into the safari road. And, in the quest for authenticity, Indonesians from the island of Bali worked for three years carving animal figures on buildings and Zulus from South Africa built thatched roofs for the themed village of Harambe. The Animal Kingdom's Killmanjaro Safari copied modern zoo design by creating ecosystems rather than simply displaying animals in cages, but took the idea to its ultimate extreme. Not only did Disney place the gazelles, elands, ostriches, zebras, and many other animals close to visitors (though behind hidden trenches), but Disney turned the traditional viewing of animals into a ride and story during which guests travel in "authentic" African safari trucks on a 20-minute voyage chasing would be "poachers" while snapping pictures of the animals in their natural habitats.[82]

This new gentility again was not enough, nor was even the old tried and true

Disney formula of the cute animal. The appeal of the thrill ride and anarchic, even slightly "rascally," adult-defying world of the cool could not be ignored. At the very center of Animal Kingdom, within the Tree of Life, was placed a trend-setting attraction: It's Tough to Be a Bug!, a 3-D film with special in-theater effects similar to those seen at the Honey, I Shrunk the Audience attraction in Tomorrowland. Inspired as usual by characters from a Disney film, this spectacle features plenty of special effects to spook squeamish parents and grandparents (including the Termite-ator, who blows his nose on the audience with water jets).[83]

On the West Coast, in 2001 the company followed the same pattern in a new theme park, Disney's California Adventure to complement the 45-year-old Disneyland. Though the new park imitated Disney-MGM Studios with the Hollywood Pictures Backlot and continued its travel simulations with rides like Soarin' over California in the Golden State attractions, Disney finally broke from its old hostility to the Coney Island tradition by including a replica of the old seashore amusement park, Paradise Pier, a land in California Adventure. Though Disneyfied, the Pier features "iron rides," including the faux wooden roller coaster, California Screamin,' and the Ferris (Sun) Wheel. The now familiar age-segmented scheme guided the decision to offer sophisticated fare like tapas at its restaurants and drinks at a new nightlife zone called Downtown Disney (modeled after a similar Orlando project). The earlier Disney message of childhood nostalgia had not disappeared, but, by the 1990s, it was not the only message.[84]

In many ways, Disneyland represented the triumph of the genteel over the plebeian crowd. Disney certainly would have agreed with the critics of the massed throngs of revelers at Coney (and Blackpool). His goal was neither to titillate nor to promote vertigo in his shows and rides, but to inspire, uplift, and to make people "happy." He copied the tradition of orderly and clean promenades of the Victorian park and did everything possible to reduce the feeling of congestion and anonymity that so distressed genteel visitors to Coney Island. And like the reformers of the first half of the twentieth century, he tried to defuse the threat of the alien crowd by focusing play not on the young adult or working class seeking an escape in the impersonal throng, but on the face of the very personal "innocent" child. This targeting of child-like wonder freed Disney from the formal, status seeking, and didactic qualities of 1900 gentility. Disney was and is "fun." The formula worked for many years, and continues still, because "happiness" built around cinematic fantasy, childhood delight, and nostalgia continues to meet the needs of middle-class America.

Gradually, however, even Disney has had to adjust to changing taste as the culture of the cute and nostalgic has been overtaken by new trends and expectations. In the 1980s and 1990s, Disney was obliged to accommodate the "cool" and adapt to the segmentation of entertainment preferences across the life-cycle. The company has even reached out toward a playful form of adult education at the Disney Institute, a new longing for environmental "authenticity" at Animal Kingdom, and a wide range of simulated places and times at Disney's many themed resorts. Although basic themes remain, Disney's Lands have changed, in fact, to become many things to many people. In the process, they have become attractive to many British long-haul holidaymakers, especially families with young children. But neither Britain in general, nor Blackpool in particular, has ever created anything quite like Disneyland. There are British theme parks, but nothing to approach the scale or nature of the Disney enterprise. What the British created and why and how it differed from America's Disney will be the topic of our next chapter.

"Enrichment through Enjoyment"

THE BEAMISH MUSEUM IN A THEME PARK AGE

The Disney-style theme park was not the only postwar approach to assembling the playful crowd. The second half of the twentieth century also saw an alternative approach—the open-air museum of industrial and social history. Its range of artifacts and reconstructions laid claim to nostalgia grounded in historical authenticity in contrast to the fantasy offerings of commercial theme parks. While this phenomenon was not unique to any single country, a significant British pioneer in this field was the open-air museum at Beamish in County Durham, in the old industrial northeast of England. Seeking to represent a relatively recent industrial past, Beamish rode the wave of interest in industrial archaeology that grew out the work of L.T.C. Rolt and Charles Hadfield in the 1950s and 1960s and the subsequent development of academic social history.[1] A close look at Beamish will let us see that Disney was only one route from the industrial saturnalia of 1900 to the playful crowd of today.

Since 1971 the North of England Open Air Museum at Beamish has displayed working relics of the industrial, agricultural, and urban past of northeastern England over the last two centuries. Established by a consortium of local government bodies within the region, it was conceived as, and remains, a public service rather than a commercial organization. It is ultimately answerable to local taxpayers despite the increasing reliance on other kinds of funding and is dedicated to showing how things worked in the past to an audience that has lost touch with that past. Beamish tries to promote a kind of popular, accessible "living history" that is firmly grounded in research, but also encourages local pride, interactive enjoyment, curiosity, and the sharing of experiences between the generations. Its founder, the entrepreneurial museum curator Frank Atkinson, was a very effective publicist, defending its principles against a many-sided opposition.

As we saw in chapter 3, the antecedents for open-air museums were Scandinavian. Atkinson's inspiration for Beamish certainly came from Skansen, and especially its Norwegian counterpart at Lillehammer.[2] In his autobiography Atkinson describes a moment in 1952 when "leaning on the handrail of a little wooden bridge at Lillehammer museum" he decided that "we *must* have such a museum in England: otherwise so much would be lost along with the equally important chance to tell everyone about their own past."[3]

Despite roots in a quest for preserving a world threatened by rapid technological and cultural change, Atkinson's Beamish also responded to the play-seeking culture of the late twentieth century. Beamish appeared fifteen years after Disneyland and was never isolated from the theme park tradition that Disney created. Beamish was inevitably propelled into the forefront of debate about the proper role of the museum and the relationship between the educational and the commercial. It became the focal point of tensions between history and nostalgia, between the museum and theme park.[4] Beamish stood between the edifying tradition of the nineteenth-century museum and the "fun morality" of the twentieth-century theme park. As a public supported institution, in contrast to Disney, it had to accommodate various special interests and make compromises. In this context, outsiders often misunderstood Beamish's objectives and impact on visitors. In order to appreciate how Beamish fit into the new world of the playful crowd, we need to situate it within the broad range of tourist sites that Britain produced (and failed to produce) in the second half of the twentieth century.

Disney and Its British Alternatives

There has never been a Disneyland or Disney World in Britain. British families have made their pilgrimages to Florida (especially) in growing numbers with the advent of transatlantic package tourism in the late twentieth century, and Disney characters and films have been as influential in Britain as anywhere. Still the Disney version of the playful crowd in Europe was built in France, not Britain.[5]

This is not for lack of trying, however. The most determined attempt to establish a British Disneyland took place at Blackpool in 1961, under the auspices of a syndicate headed by the circus proprietor Billy Smart; it included other luminaries of the British entertainment world such as Cecil and Sidney Bernstein of Granada Television, Billy Butlin the holiday camp magnate, Lord Thomson the media mogul, and Sir Leslie Joseph the proprietor of the Coney Beach amusement park at the popular seaside resort of Porthcawl, in South Wales.[6] The promoters used the word "Disneyland" in early publicity to convey an idea of their intentions; but, despite their standing in the entertainment industry, efforts to involve Disney, or to obtain the company's assent to the use of the name, fell on stony ground. In April 1961 a Disney representative rejected any use of the Disneyland trademark in the Blackpool project.[7] Reluctantly, the planners were forced to rename their project, "Themeland."[8]

There never was a plan to slavishly copy Disney. The proposed content of the site bears out the irreducible Britishness of the syndicate's vision. Elements under consideration included "Peace Square," which was a possible center for the park, with United Nations Avenue leading to it; Piccadilly Circus with "Memory Lane" crossing it at right angles; a landscaped area with a lake, a castle, Lilliput, and "Colly Wobble Valley"; a heliport, planetarium, "Halls of Knowledge, Achievements, etc., History of Mankind etc. etc." Alternative plans included Botanical and Tivoli Gardens (in allusion to a northern European model drawn from Denmark), a Big Top Boulevard leading to "Marine Studios and Circus," a Living History Area adjoining "Fairy Tale Land," and a Commonwealth Exhibition. A "Historical Cavalcade of Britain" was also under consideration.[9] Even if the Disney Company had wanted a presence in rainy, northern England, this was much too didactic, with its European and British patriotic themes, and remained too closely linked to older popular entertainment forms (as befitted a project proposed by a circus proprietor) for Disney to be attracted to it.[10]

Still, the syndicate was very anxious to learn from American practice and experience, and a subcommittee planned a tour of American theme parks including Disneyland.[11] In the end, Billy Smart concluded "that the only Themepark that was paying its way was one in an area where the climate was so good it remained open all 52 weeks of the year." This was almost certainly Disneyland itself, and contrasted with Blackpool where even a six-month season, with two million visitors, was thought unduly optimistic in some informed quarters.[12]

Blackpool Corporation was hospitable to the Themeland idea, and had arranged to use Disney motifs for the autumn Illuminations for several years. It is doubtful, however, whether Blackpool, with its powerful existing entertainment companies to look after, could ever have been as accommodating as Anaheim.[13] This proposal was the nearest approximation to a full-scale Disneyland that Britain experienced, and it is significant that nothing came of it. Obviously, without Disney's support and access to the stories and characters that gave Disney's theme parks their power to attract a middle-class family crowd, Themeland would have had difficulties. The hodgepodge character of the preliminary plans reveals little understanding of what made Disney work.

This is not to say that the British were incapable of creating new forms of playfulness. Perhaps the nearest British parallel to Disney can be found in the distinctive chains of commercial holiday camps that were established on British coastlines from the 1930s, reaching their peak in the 1950s and 1960s. The Butlin and Pontin camps, and others like them, offered informal chalet lodging at an all-included rate, with food, bars, and communal entertainments provided on sites that excluded outsiders unless they bought day admission tickets. The isolation of the camp crowd allowed for a very different kind of experience than occurred on the Blackpool Promenade or at Coney Island amusement parks. The Butlin staff (Redcoats) organized children's games and slightly surreal contests of all kinds (knobbly knees, glamorous grandmother). Like Disney staff, the Redcoats had to meet imposed conservative standards of public behavior and appearance. But also like Disney, they brought out the spontaneity of camp participants and created playful solidarities among people who did not know each other. At the same time, the camp's cleanliness and structure, as well as the fact that most visitors shared a common (middle) income level, created a playful crowd of people who felt comfortable with each other. The Butlin motto, "Our true intent is all for your delight," entailed the provision of bars and entertainment areas with tropical or exotic island themes, featuring an extravagant version of the ultra-modern décor preferred for home redecoration in the 1950s and 1960s. Without the movie-set experience of Disneyland, Butlin offered fantasy escapes that still met middle-class or "respectable" working-class standards of decency.[14]

These camps were, in a sense, theme parks, but cheap construction made their myths more difficult to sustain than those of Disney. While great public emphasis was placed on respectability, popular legend soon spoke otherwise and they moved down market over time. In a way they fell between Disney and Coney Island, not least because, echoing the culture of Blackpool's Golden Mile and the seaside comic postcard, they came to celebrate innuendo rather than innocence, know-ingness rather than wonderment.[15] Still the Disney Company ultimately imitated Butlin (even if not directly) as seen in Disney's 1998 attempt at creating a playful crowd on its "Magic Cruise Line" with Disney's own camp environment on "Cast-away Cay."

Variations on a Theme Park

The fact that Britain produced imperfect parallels with Disney in the holiday camps points to a wider fact—the sheer variety of theme parks and other invented pleasure places on both sides of the Atlantic. By the early 1960s, they offered vary-ing combinations of learning, uplift, thrills, and fantasy. Many were "placeless" on the Disney model, taking over and dominating existing landscapes and more concerned about crowd accessibility than with any connection to the region or its history.[16] The Blackpool "Themeland" would have followed this model. Others, however, sought to derive some distinctiveness, commercial advantage, and claim to authenticity by appealing to one or more aspects of the "power of the real," as delineated by Kevin Moore: real things, real places, and real people. The theme park and museum could never be completely reconciled, but neither were they polar opposites.[17]

Toward the Disney end of this spectrum were theme parks that incorporated real places with distinctive histories of their own. A British example is Alton Tow-ers, in the rural Churnet Valley of England's North Staffordshire. As Steve Mills remarks, "though Alton Towers now at last calls itself a theme park it still retains its historic setting, its gardens and its castle, quite unlike any Disney theme park with its deliberate placelessness."[18] Its historian describes it thus: "Reputed to have been the largest privately-owned house in Europe, Alton Towers now (1999) serves as the picturesque backdrop to one of Europe's most popular tourist attractions; a significant slice of England's architectural and social history set in the midst of 'white-knuckle' rides and a fantasy-world."[19]

Alton Towers belonged to the Earls of Shrewsbury, who gave the house and gar-dens a Gothic fantasy makeover in the second quarter of the nineteenth century. As early as 1849, when a railroad was built nearby, it became accessible to working-class excursionists from the nearby "Potteries" industrial towns. In response to this op-portunity, in the 1890s the twentieth Earl of Shrewsbury promoted his property as a tourist attraction, with fetes, illuminations and firework displays, balloon ascents, lions, and a torture chamber imported from Nuremberg. In 1924 Alton Towers was sold to a syndicate of local businessmen who concentrated on cafes and popular entertainment for the "hordes of visitors" who came to see the gardens. New owners in the mid-1970s saw more possibilities in the buildings and their heritage, as did the Tussauds Group who took over in 1980; and, as in American theme parks at that time, the focus has increasingly been a regularly updated menu of thrill rides. Alton Towers is a historical site whose past has become less relevant although the distinctiveness of the surroundings remains an asset. This is an unusual example where heritage and amusement park are united, but it serves also as a variation on a recent growth in the "heritage industry."[20]

Alton Towers was not the only place that incorporated local historical relics into a theme park environment. The Knott's Berry Farm in southern California (originally a fruit farm and site of a very successful chicken restaurant in the 1930s) drew crowds with its "authentic Old West Ghost Town" with "REAL buildings transported from mining towns throughout the West." According to a 1959 leaflet, Walter Knott's objective was "to faithfully bring back this boisterous mining camp as it was in the early 1880s." Like Alton Towers, Knott's Berry Farm gradually became a modern amusement park with six themed areas, which included roller coasters, a log ride, and what was (falsely) claimed to be the world's last narrow-gauge steam train, with authentic locomotives and rolling stock from Colorado. This is a hybrid theme park with an unusually strong sense of historical authenticity (however "staged"), anticipating in ways the work of places like Beamish.[21]

Toward the other end of the spectrum we find museums that rejected thrill rides for greater historical authenticity but also accepted commercial practices to gather crowds. Here we find the "stately homes" and preserved railroads. Beside Alton Towers, Warwick Castle was the only other aristocratic site that catered to popular tourism as early as the nineteenth century.[22] It was not until after World War II, when the financial crisis of the landed aristocracy combined with the emergence of a car-induced demand for rural pleasures, that the "stately home" industry really gathered momentum. The National Trust expanded its collection of historic country houses and opened them more regularly to a widening public. It exhibited changing patterns of aristocratic taste in architecture, decoration, furniture, and park and garden design to curious and admiring audiences drawn mainly from the expanding car-owning public. The volunteer-based, membership-funded National

Trust's activities were imitated for profit by many aristocratic families who had been struggling to keep up their great houses. Still, not all of the private families shared the same vision of history and heritage as the National Trust, and museum-like authenticity was often violated by entrepreneurial aristocrats who turned their landscaped grounds into leisure parks, with exotic animals, motor museums, and even fairground rides. The National Trust itself was not above adopting the new country house decorative styles associated with the firm of Colefax and Fowler and *Home and Garden*. After 1970, these trends accelerated with the explosive growth in National Trust membership to more than one million in 1980 and two million by 1990. Here was a very conservative, (self)-disciplined crowd, at leisure rather than play. They followed the direction signs, prevented their children from transgressing boundaries as they filed through the homes and gardens of the British aristocracy, and picked up tips for enhancing the surroundings of their own homes and gardens, as well as buying the National Trust's carefully crafted souvenirs, linked to television dramas or series celebrating country house lives and artifacts.[23] From the 1970s onward the servants, who numbered among the ancestors of many of the expanding visiting public, were increasingly celebrated alongside the landed families. Visitors to Erddig, in North Wales, were brought through the servants' hall, and the National Trust began to acquire humbler properties such as Miss Toward's Glasgow tenement house. This was part of a wider democratization of the agenda of this nostalgic crowd, whose members were increasingly in search of empathy with people across the chasm of time.[24]

Following the boom in stately homes by about a decade was the interest in preserved steam railways, which fed off nostalgia for stability, eccentricity, craftsmanship, tradition, and even Empire. The origins of steam railway preservation in Britain can be dated from as early as 1922, when the Ravenglass and Eskdale Railway was rebuilt and reopened as a miniature line for tourists after its closure as a mineral railway. Its position on the edge of the scenic Lake District was helpful here, as were the Welsh mountain locations of the narrow-gauge railways that were the focus of the preservation movement immediately following World War II.[25]

The hard-won success of this dedicated band of enthusiasts owed much to British literary celebrations and whimsical mockery of the ancient country branch line with its eccentric Victorian rolling stock, quaint station names, and idyllic countryside. The parodies of patched-up and distorted locomotives, displayed in the cartoons of Heath Robinson and Rowland Emett and represented improbably in the Emett railway at London's Festival of Britain exhibition in 1951 (otherwise a celebration of functional postwar modernity), helped to define this frame of mind. All this created affection for idiosyncratic, old-fashioned, inefficient railways among a wider public.[26] The Rev. Wilber Awdry's Thomas the Tank Engine children's books, first produced in 1945 and featuring cute little engines on an imaginary island railroad system, took matters in a Disney direction. In the late twentieth century, spinoff merchandising for Thomas the Tank Engine was adapted for the American market; but there was no Thomas the Tank Engine theme park.[27] Instead, these impulses of cute quaintness and engineering nostalgia were focused on the steam locomotives themselves. Associated at first with young teenage boys, an obsession with "trainspotting" (identifying and accumulating locomotive numbers) masked a wider appreciation of the workings and even the aesthetics of the steam railway.[28]

As the nationalized British Railways embraced a version of modernity that had no room for the steam locomotive, and began to close rural branch lines, the stage was set for the emergence of the restored steam railway that tried to re-create the sights, sounds, and smells of a recently vanished past. Depending on voluntary labor, and beginning with the evocatively named Bluebell Railway in 1958, this expanded railway preservation movement rescued hundreds of locomotives and other rolling stock from scrap yards and put them to work on reopened branch lines. By the end of the twentieth century there were 63 such standard-gauge lines in Britain and 65 narrow-gauge or miniature ones, each attracting visitors with meticulous attention to period detail—alongside a willingness to accept necessary anachronism and to use the "Thomas the Tank Engine" week-end as a valuable marketing ploy.[29] Like Beamish later, these railways drew on the hobbyist's enthusiasm, as well as scholarly precision, the pursuit of authenticity, and the acceptance of the need to relax standards where necessary in pursuit of enjoyment and commercial viability.[30] The crowd here, as at the stately home, disciplined its playfulness, not least in the interests of safety; and it had to learn long-forgotten rules about rail travel, including keeping to timetables and platforms. This is another mixed experience, but this time closer to the museum than the theme park.[31]

Alongside these very widespread developments, other hybrids between the museum and the theme park began to appear in Britain during the 1970s and 1980s. They ranged from displays of historic sites (either at their original locations or artifacts brought to a convenient and appealing site such as Beamish) to reenactments

6.1   The departure of a restored British Railways steam train from the 1950s operated by the North Yorkshire Moors Railway at Grosmont, May 2004. By G. Cross

of important and exciting events in British history. The second of these genres was much closer to Disney than to Alton Towers, and perhaps the most spectacular example, Littlecote, has been described as "bricolage at its most extreme." It offered a Roman villa, medieval combat, waxworks depicting the British Civil War, a "Red Indian" siege of a British colonial fort, and a steam railway. It was "little more than a series of representations of sets" from time-traveling TV programs; but it blazed across the British tourist firmament like a meteor, winning the British Tourist Authority prize for best commercial attraction in 1987 but closing three years later to make way for alternative activities with higher profits.[32] This was the kind of outcome that was satirized by Julian Barnes in his novel *England, England*, which imagined the Isle of Wight turned into a huge theme park based on popular myths about British history and identity.[33]

Perhaps the most extreme form of co-opting authenticity for commercial purposes was the creation of museums sponsored by manufacturers of consumer products to romanticize their own history. Cadbury World, for example, which opened in Birmingham, England in 1990, provided "an idealised image of the Cadbury factory and Bournville village in bygone days," with great emphasis on the Quaker paternalism of the firm's founders and their benevolence in setting up a model settlement for the factory workers. The displays present the history of chocolate and Cadbury, demonstrate chocolate making in the 1930s, show nostalgic TV commercials for the firm's products, and finally lead visitors into a gift shop. Michael Rawlinson comments that, "The management of Cadbury World has never sought the advice of academic historians. The core themes for Cadbury World were first set out by a team of leisure consultants." According to the company the site is designed for "chocoholics" rather than "historical culture vultures," and nearly half of its visitors are under sixteen, many of them presumably on educational outings. This is a purely commercial venture, with no public money or charitable status, and it attracted more than 5 million visitors in its first ten years. This practice of inventing and representing an idealized, easily digested version of the past, which conveniently ignores such issues as the use of slave labor on cocoa plantations, may well be a legitimate target for critics of the "heritage industry." It is hardly fair, however, to tar the open-air museums in the public sector with the same brush.[34]

Similar were the Bass brewery museum at Burton-on-Trent and, in the United States, Hershey's Chocolate World in central Pennsylvania and the World of Coca-Cola in Atlanta. At Hershey, the historical content is overwhelmed by the nearby amusement park, and the ride through a simulation of chocolate making concentrates on easily grasped information on technology and packaging, ignoring the story of Hershey's model workers' settlement and extraordinarily well-endowed orphanage on the doorstep.[35] The World of Coca Cola has been identified as "just another inauthentic theme park, where the prevalence of a corporate logo symbolises the privatisation of memory and indifference, if not downright hostility, to historical dialogue." Such places may meet the expectations of their consumers, but have little to do with historical re-creation. At this point the industrial museum meets up with McDisneyfication, and the latter wins out.[36]

Beamish and Its Critics

The tension between the goals of authenticity and commercialized fun ran through all of these variations on the "theme park." Beamish shared that tension, but it found its own solution that distinguished it from Disneyland. Beamish has become the standard-bearer of the industrial open-air museum movement in Britain, attracting a great deal more critical attention in the academic literature than its near-contemporaries at Ironbridge Gorge in Shropshire and Dudley in Worcestershire.[37]

Cultural critics drawn from various shades of opinion have treated it harshly. The relevant debates are also present in the United States; they seem, however, more virulent in Britain, where they are enmeshed in a long-running argument about the "Wiener thesis," the claim that the dominant British culture has always been hostile to industry and enterprise, and has preferred to take refuge in bucolic nostalgia for an imagined rural past founded in a hierarchical, traditional vision of landed society.[38]

Critics of the open-air industrial museum like Robert Hewison have embraced this thesis, arguing that Beamish and similar sites are merely sanitized views of the past that blend industry into countryside and privilege continuity over sudden change, social tranquility over conflict, and the masculine over the feminine. Beamish supposedly minimizes past hardships and injustices and justifies the social order of the past, inducing a tranquilizing nostalgia in its visitors.[39] Hewison, in his attack on the "heritage industry"[40] identified the rise of the industrial museum with the decline of traditional mining and manufacturing industry. He saw it as sentimentalizing an industrial past which had never been fully embraced by English high culture, while purporting to replace "real" jobs in productive industries with poorly paid, often part-time work in tourism. As part of his critique, he damned the industrial museum by association with the theme park.

Beyond this, Beamish was central to important debates on how best to communicate an understanding of the past, especially to what extent museum educators should be "in character" by wearing historical costumes and adopting historical speech, and even showing no awareness of historical changes since the period they represent.[41] Finally, the central expectation of historical authenticity has led much criticism of Beamish for its artificiality in grouping together artifacts and buildings from all over the region away from where they were actually used and lived in.[42]

Although Ironbridge Gorge at least had its industrial ruins on their original site, Hewison complains that Beamish "has [an] ironic relationship to the region whose life it memorialises" because until 1970 the site's only connection with industry was its National Coal Board ownership (even though he admits that there was a small coalmine there). Hewison objected to the importation of buildings from elsewhere to a green field site, and to the costumed attendants: "The paradox of Beamish is not that it is false, the exhibits are as genuine as they could possibly be, but that it is more real than the reality it seeks to recall. The town street evokes an indistinct period of between the two wars, at just that distance in time where memory softens and sweetens. But there is no need for personal nostalgia. Here, the buildings do it for you."[43]

Kevin Walsh, writing five years after Hewison, finds no difference between Beamish and the theme park.[44] He begins by conflating Disneyland with open-air museums as places producing "representations of life-styles that are devoid of conflict and anti-social behaviour, and exist within a calming rural landscape." There is insufficient representation of squalor, adversity, danger, industrial conflict, unemployment, poverty, or sudden change; and the visitors, unaided, have insufficient cultural capital to "understand or appreciate" the site in the ways Walsh would prefer. They are unable to transcend a kind of passive nostalgia that only gets worse over time: "before long, a generation will exist whose heritage lies with the heritage industry." Beamish thus becomes damned as a "fantasy island," only "perhaps" less disconcerting even than Littlecote.[45] Walsh's position deprives Beamish's visitors of agency and fails to see how they might experience Beamish differently than a theme park.

Tony Bennett's less strident critique comes from a similar perspective. He argues that the introductory tape-slide show he saw privileged an authoritative middle-class voice above that of the "miner" who narrated the regional industrial history, and that the museum systematically excludes or marginalizes labor movements or women's suffrage campaigns, and fails to explain the ideals of the British Co-operative movement. Beamish does celebrate the collective genius of a region's people, but, for Bennett, it does so through creating a vision of a timeless, unchanging past that turns history into (and here he quotes Michel Foucault) "a place of rest, certainty, reconciliation, a place of tranquillised sleep."[46]

None of these critics seems to have talked to anyone involved in the running of Beamish in order to find out what they were trying to achieve and how they justified the museum's approach. Another more sympathetic critic, Kevin Moore, emphasizes the strength and depth of the regional collections that back up Beamish's presentations, and praises it as a place he has enjoyed particularly, alongside a range of other experiences that include Plimoth Plantation and, strikingly, the "Luxor" re-creation of Tutankhamun's tomb in Las Vegas. "What they share is a sense of 'real things in a real place', . . . They successfully *recreate* a sense of real things in a real place, if they do not sufficiently possess this in the first place."[47]

As a museum professional, Moore may have more of a practical sense of what it is possible for museums to achieve than Hewison, Walsh, or Bennett. It is, as he points out, almost impossible to find "real things, real place, and real person" all together on one site; but this does not mean that there is no difference between an open-air or "living" museum and a theme park. The problems involved in meeting the critics' expectations can be illustrated from an example of an open-air museum on an authentic site. It is the Luostarinmaki Handicrafts Museum in Turku, Finland.[48] The Museum is a small, planned, artisan housing estate of the late eighteenth and early nineteenth century which, under public auspices, became the Handicrafts Museum in 1940. The houses were gradually repopulated with craft workshops, under the guidance of retired craft workers, many of whom "continued to work in the museum for as long as they lived." Still historical authenticity was an elusive goal: While most of the houses have been carefully restored to their early-nineteenth-century condition, most of the crafts were not practiced in the houses where they are now located. Only in a couple of cases are allusions made to the political struggles of the past. The rooms are probably cleaner and tidier than when they were in everyday use, and there is certainly no authentic squalor. Most of the museum is frozen at a particular point in time, but that was necessary to convey a meaningful and intelligible experience. Would even this effort satisfy Hewison, Walsh, and Bennett? If not, what would?

Pursuing this example in this way helps us to get a more appropriate perspective on places like Beamish. We need also to understand how such places come to be. Inevitably, what is offered to and expected of the visiting crowd is the product of the museum's own history. The critics of Beamish have never seen any need to understand this fact. Even in the case of Beamish, where there was a strong curator and a clear vision, the need to satisfy a shifting group of local authorities, whose political complexion might—and did—change from election to election, proved particularly problematic. And yet, despite these pressures and the lack of the financial resources of a Disneyland, Beamish managed to find its way between the goals of a museum and theme park. What follows is an explanation of the growth of Beamish, the development of the philosophy that lies behind it, and the impact of this on the Beamish variant of the playful crowd.

Beamish Origins

Beamish was the brainchild of Frank Atkinson. As he wrote in his autobiography, "There is little point in being unduly coy or modest about it: I made Beamish happen and kept on making it get better, until I retired in 1987." Atkinson was a Yorkshireman with a scientific and industrial background, who moved into museum work with a job at Halifax's Shibden Hall museum. In 1958 he became curator of the Bowes Museum, an extraordinary set of collections, housed in a decaying Victorian French chateau in County Durham.[49] Immediately after his appointment he won support of and land from the County Council for setting up a museum "about the everyday recent past way of life of the County itself." Here was the germ of what was to become Beamish; but it was not until 1965, when he began to encounter serious obstacles in Durham, that Atkinson decided on a regional as opposed to a county museum. As initially conceived, the museum was not intended as a mass tourist attraction. Atkinson's purpose was "to rescue a representative collection of objects illustrating a way of life in the region which was rapidly disappearing; to present this in an exciting and relatively novel way which would enthuse visitors; and therefore to help encourage the people of the North-East to appreciate that the history of their forbears and their past way of life were worth remembering and something to be proud of." Atkinson was an early defender of the local past against the global present, but also he was willing to preserve the playful in the crowds he wished to enlighten.[50]

Atkinson was no isolated idealist: he was a political animal, and appreciated the importance of allies among the councilors of Durham. His first major challenge came in 1965 when the county, facing a fiscal crisis, withdrew financial support from his project. By this time he had already amassed extensive collections, using the local press to publicize his activities and touring women's institutes and village halls in search of donations. But the financial crisis enabled Atkinson's leading opponent, the Deputy Director of Education, to win political support for the abandonment of the museum. In this adversary, Atkinson faced an attitude that dogged him for years. According to Atkinson, this opponent "particularly despised my concern for the industrial past of the county, believing that the 'old black image' should be destroyed." This desire to abandon a dark industrial past for a clean, modern, rational version of postwar modernity was common at the time.[51] These views prevailed among those Labour Party activists who wanted to move on from a past they saw as bound up with the economic exploitation and degradation of the coal mining era and who also identified with a modernizing vision of the new housing estates and clean light industries.[52]

Atkinson's response was to mobilize support for his project on a wider scale. A barrage of letters went out to local allies from the Labour Party, but also to aristocrats with local interests. While Atkinson wanted to reverse the decision against the Durham project, he also proposed to establish the industrial museum on a new site with funds drawn across the region.[53] By winning support from the local media, he preserved exhibits like the Seaham Harbour coal drop, the last North Eastern Railway J-21 class steam locomotive, and the region's last hand-charged coke ovens.[54]

The struggles of 1965–66 had not yet been resolved. A crisis followed the Conservative Party victories in the local municipal elections of June 1967 and soon support seemed on the verge of collapse throughout the region. However, Atkinson enlisted the support of the local press and lobbied Newcastle's Conservative "boss," Arthur Gray, to bring that important city government (along with most of the region) back into the fold by the end of the year.[55]

The next goal was to decide upon a site, itself a political question, as it had to be acceptable to all the local authorities that subscribed to the project. Beamish had been on Atkinson's agenda since 1966. While the site did indeed have Beamish Hall, a potential "stately home" with its own ghost story and other connections to regional myth and legend,[56] Atkinson was most attracted by the site's relative ease of automobile access from all parts of the region, although it was isolated from the rail network.[57] Above all, he prized the self-contained nature of the site, in a bowl surrounded by wooded hills, with no hint of the contemporary world to damage the museum illusion. In this concern to control his surroundings he was at one with Disney; and the museum management later protected this visual seclusion by securing the purchase of additional land on the higher ground.[58] The choice of site, however, had nothing to do with the promotion of a rural idyll or an old hierarchical society, as the critics suggested. Sites that much better fit that purpose (such as the countryside near the remote and picturesque estate village of Blanchland), were rejected as too far from population centers or unsuitable on other grounds.[59]

By early 1969, as promoters sought permission to go ahead from local and then national government, a vocal opposition movement once again emerged, this time, within Beamish village and the surrounding area. The Beamish Park Preservation Society objected to the despoliation, as they saw it, of attractive countryside by ugly industrial eyesores, the loss of farmland and agricultural jobs, the potential burden on local taxation, and of course the anticipated drop in property values. They argued that such a museum should be built in one of the Durham villages that had lost its economic viability when its coalmines closed and was slated for demolition. In February 1969, the objectors wrote a letter of protest direct to the Prime Minister and gained a sympathetic hearing from the London *Guardian* and the *Daily Mail*, unusual bedfellows, whose reports referred to the museum as an "industrial Disneyland," a lazy confusion that was to be repeated.[60] It is significant that the museum's opponents in these formative years saw it as damaging a rural idyll rather than enshrining one.

Local opposition, however, proved to be weak. When the proposals went up to the Minister of Housing for final approval in April 1969, only about twenty local objectors came forward, and the museum was accepted without fuss.[61] Still, criticism dogged Beamish for years. As preparations began for opening in late 1969, opposition reemerged from both the left and right; and the loss of the financial support of any local authority continually threatened to derail Beamish. Sunderland's Conservative municipal majority refused its financial support during 1969 on cost grounds. One member of the Labour Party group in July 1969 wanted to spend the money on alleviating local unemployment, and commented, "It is about the past, but I don't like looking back. I like looking forward." Alderman R. B. Spain attacked the educational argument on the grounds that children should be concentrating on the "3 Rs" rather than "experiments and fads." There were justified complaints about the difficulty in reaching Beamish by public transport, which mattered politically because it was supposed to be democratically accessible to all local taxpayers.[62] Unlike the corporate development of Disney World taking place at the same time, Beamish faced continuous political obstacles.

In addition, outsiders continued to read into Beamish their own prejudices and misunderstandings. The *Morning Advertiser*, the newspaper of the drink trade, could report on the proposed re-creation of a "traditional" English working-class pub in this way: "A quaint carousal is in store for drinkers in Durham who like museums. A pub-of-the-past is to be rebuilt, and staffed on special occasions by barmaids in period costume. The life-like Tussauds with a liquor licence is planned at Beamish Park. . . . [It] is to be a Disneyland of yesterday's things, as I understand it."[63]

By contrast the traditionalist Michael Wharton, "Peter Simple" of the London *Daily Telegraph* (March 1969), showed a much more empathetic (though satirical) understanding of Beamish's problems associated with "authenticity."[64] While declaring Beamish to be "excellent as far as it goes," Wharton quipped:

> But there should also be shawled women, miners with their whippets squatting on their heels by the wall, public houses crammed with shouting drunkards, their carbuncular faces lit by flares, watching in wonder as men compete in swallowing pies and hard-boiled eggs or biting rats' heads off. There should be illicit trade unionists, too, meeting at night in defiance of the combination laws, converging on the mill where the hated mill-owner has barricaded himself in with shot-gun and ferocious dogs; and close to hand, a company of yeomanry to make sure that Mr Atkinson's paraphernalia are never completely demolished.

Wharton has his history wrong, imagining the early nineteenth century rather than the early twentieth and West Yorkshire rather than the Northeast, but he points to the need for, but implicitly the impossibility of, depicting the historical reality of disreputable behavior and social and political conflict.[65] Perhaps ironically, the cultural right seemed to read Beamish better than the left despite Atkinson's efforts to depict the everyday life of the industrial working class. Beamish was able to attract support from cultural conservatives like Wharton, who put tradition before economy and preferred quaint, archaic inefficiency to calculative rationality. The *Evening Chronicle* gave strong support to Beamish and the preservation of the Victorian past, partly as an antidote to the present "diet of pop and permissiveness," while the Bishop of Durham was very supportive, urging church-goers to become Friends of the Northern Regional Open-Air Museum.[66] This organization, founded in January 1968 and chaired by Professor G.H.J. Daysh, a regional geographer and planner at Newcastle University, included a large number of people with expertise in engineering and practical restoration.[67]

Here Atkinson's skill at harnessing enthusiasm, generating good publicity, and manipulating the media was essential. He openly predicted an attendance of more than a million people per year.[68] The regional press was almost always supportive, emphasizing the museum's contribution to a sense of regional identity and its potential to attract international tourists: "In a world of all-consuming sameness in everything Beamish will stand as a living reminder of the way it used to be, a place where the visitor can stop the world, step back and savour an earlier moment in time and draw his own conclusions."[69]

Without Atkinson's success in mobilizing volunteers, assembling the collection and moving it to Beamish would have been much more costly.[70] Above all, though, it was their collecting activities that provided good copy for the local press with stories about dismantling and re-erecting traditional chemists' shops or miners' cottages. Many people responded enthusiastically to requests to provide a new life for discarded items from their lofts, cellars, or garages.[71] Despite all the outside criticism and local in-fighting, Beamish became a reality in 1971.

Through all of these local political and financial struggles and amidst the external debates about the Disneyfication of heritage and the problems of authenticity, Atkinson remained steadfast in his vision for Beamish. He made that vision clear in 1966, when he wrote: "An open air museum serves to illustrate vividly, the way of life, the institutions, customs and material equipment of the ordinary people. It is an attempt to make the history of a region live, by showing typical features of that history as accurately as possible. If it is to be valid history these examples must be carefully chosen and as carefully presented, so as not to distort the truth. Happy and unhappy aspects of the history of the region should be shown in their proper proportion."[72] This was, of course, a world away from Disneyland.

Finding Its Way: Beamish in the 1970s and 1980s

Lofty goals hardly produced impressive results at the beginning. The "Museum in the Making" display at Beamish in 1971 attracted about 50,000 visitors in a few amateurish summer weekends.[73] After full opening in 1972, admissions grew steadily for most of the decade to reach around 200,000. These crowds strained the facilities to the breaking point but still fell significantly short of the original projections. This modest success owed more to the attractiveness of the concept, the level of free publicity, and the cheap admission prices than to the professionalism of the presentation.[74] Still, despite entrance fees of only 20 pence per adult and 5 pence for children, only 4,718 tickets were sold on the Spring Bank Holiday Monday in

1973. The car park was still a grass field; there were no public toilets on site; the Tea Room only held 45 people; and there were long queues for the exhibitions. A confidential report complained that, "This new museum began with too small a staff and too limited a revenue and capital programme." At this point, in fact, the chair of the Friends suggested bringing in industrial investment and running the museum on a commercial basis.[75]

Atkinson certainly recognized these and other problems even as he adhered to his original vision of Beamish. At a speech in 1975 he addressed the challenges of rising expectations about presentation and interactivity, and the lower thresholds of boredom, that resulted from television and, of course, competition from amusement parks and shopping centers. Museum curators had to respond or join the dinosaurs:[76]

> This is the point at which you have to make up your minds. Do you wish to be serious institutions with little interest in the public and its needs—collating and cataloguing and preserving your collections? Or do you wish to communicate with the untutored—but very experienced—public and interpret your collections for its greater enjoyment? I offer you the phrase, 'enrichment through enjoyment.' Not only leisure for learning and learning for leisure, but learning *through pleasure*! This will not be easy. There will be many terrible chasms which we shall have to cross... balanced on tightropes. On one side of our first tightrope lies Disneyland and the amusement arcade. Pleasurable for some, but hardly meriting public expenditure. On the other side of our tightrope may be said to lie more formalised instruction which may be acceptable in school or college, but is hardly so to the average man in the street looking for a little enjoyment. We therefore have to tread this tightrope and . . . if we do not, others will.

Atkinson recognized the need to adapt to the age of the theme park even as he adhered to the idea of the museum.

In that spirit, Atkinson emphasized the need for museums to employ communicators and use interpretive centers. He considered the role of the "museum shop," which entailed walking another tightrope between consumerism and the communication of ideas and experiences. He emphasized the need to relate displays to people's lives to promote "environmental awareness" and, heretically in some eyes, he promoted the value of using replicas to show how machinery worked, thereby prolonging the life of the original artifacts, which might be displayed elsewhere. But this was a far cry from theme-park fantasy:

> Any funfair can provide "pretend" equipment and Disneyland is probably the most elaborate example of this. But a museum is built on the principle that only the real object can, in the end, be guaranteed accurate and correct. The philosophy of truth which lies behind our education is seen here, and it is the antithesis of Orwell's "Newspeak" of *Nineteen Eighty Four*.[77]

Replicas may be acceptable for practical and pragmatic reasons, but only if they are backed up by the real article and knowledge of its correct use. By the same token, Atkinson resisted suggestions for a Site Manager, arguing that, "Such a post might . . . tend towards emphasising 'visitor-popular' activities at the risk of historically accurate presentation. One has to maintain a happy balance between 'academic aridity' on the one hand and 'disneyland' on the other." The educational emphasis remained strong: nearly 50 percent of the visitors were children, with their parents or with school parties, and an Education Officer would be a more important appointment than a Site Manager because Beamish was expected to provide a gateway experience for opening out new perspectives and interpretations for the rest of the region.[78]

In the 1970s, the museum was beginning to attract external funding from the English Tourist Board and Manpower Services Commission that made it less dependent on local authority support. By 1979–80 the local authorities' revenue contribution to Beamish had fallen to 42.3 percent from 84.6 percent in 1971–72. This may have reduced dependence on the whims of local politicians, but a sudden drop of 20 percent in visitor numbers during 1980 was disturbing, and forced a reappraisal and an inevitable tilt toward commercial solutions.[79]

Atkinson was quick to call in a consultant from the private museum sector, Kenneth Robinson, who ran Beaulieu Motor Museum. Robinson emphasized the overriding need simply to increase visitor numbers, and he observed that the site had no single dominant attraction. He was especially struck by the very high average size of visiting groups, at 5.75. This may have been distorted by school parties, but it was still evident that Beamish was a "family day out experience." It was also dominated by locals: "The [average] distance travelled by visitors to Beamish of 23 miles for day visitors and 25 miles for tourists is very low for a feature as significant as Beamish." The social composition was also unusually down-market in comparison with other heritage sites. Robinson advocated building a new audience, more diverse and less regional. And to attract repeat visitors (already 42 percent of the gate), Beamish needed more regular innovations and special programs. Moreover, "far too little" was being spent on publicity. The advertising budget should be doubled, the expected catchment area for day visitors extended to a hundred-mile radius, and coach operators and hoteliers should be targeted. Atkinson responded positively to this push toward a more commercial approach and to attracting a more diverse and more fun-seeking crowd. He even admitted the need for commercially realistic pricing. Despite these concessions, Atkinson was hardly turning Beamish into a theme park. He still worried about how much the Beamish "product" should be designed for the "customer's" interests and insisted that " 'regional heritage' and 'nostalgia' is a necessity and is indeed the full justification for Beamish."[80]

One very concrete way Beamish walked the tightrope between theme park and museum was the decision after about 1982 to shift emphasis from the history of technology to social and popular cultural history. With this move, Beamish proved able to reach wider audiences by appealing to nostalgia and imagination. In 1982–83, Beamish attracted 212,824 visitors; by 1987–88, the year of Atkinson's retirement, the total had reached 373,916; and the following year visitor numbers topped the half million mark, as they did again in 1990–91. This could not be sustained, and the next decade saw a decline before admissions stabilized at about 320,000 by 2000. Beamish was unable to come close to Disneyland or Blackpool in terms of sheer numerical popularity, and even after thirty years, seventy percent of visitors still came from northeastern England. But these would not be fair comparisons, given their different target audiences. Beamish succeeded in creating a different a site for "enrichment through enjoyment" and ultimately a different kind of playful crowd.[81]

The Beamish Experience Since 1990

So what was a visit to Beamish like, as it extended its displays through the 1970s and 1980s? As we have seen, Beamish (unlike Disney) lacked the financial resources and freedom to present a "completed" architectural statement at its opening. Still, over many years of accumulation, it formed an identity and coherence in exhibits connected with historic transportation, coal mining, steam technology, and historically authentic domestic and commercial buildings.

By the early 1990s, two particular foci of interest had fully emerged: the reproduction of village and work life of 1913, set at the high point of the development and relative prosperity of the industrial Northeast; and a reconstruction of farm and industrial life in the region in 1825, at the beginning of industrialization and the year when the steam railroad first appeared. The choice of high points of economic activity, which were also quiet interludes between periods of industrial and political struggle on the coalfield, attracted criticism that conflicts were marginalized by an unduly rosy and nostalgic picture of regional life. Why not choose 1842, the climax of the Chartist campaign for manhood suffrage and a year of economic severity, or 1926, the year of the British General Strike?[82]

Although Beamish did not try to use buildings and landscaping to lead the visitor through a story in the way that Disney did, Beamish did immerse the visitor in the lifeworlds of 1825 and 1913. As we would expect, instead of bulldozing the area and creating a totally artificial world in the manner of Disney, the museum's offerings were built around what was already on the site, and expanded by bringing in buildings and artifacts from all over Northeast England. Beamish Hall itself was not presented as a "stately home," in the tradition of the National Trust, but used as gateway, space for shopping and orientation, and administration center. Pockerley Manor, a substantial farmhouse that proved to contain medieval remains, was presented as a yeoman farmhouse of 1825, with gardens and local Cleveland Bay horses. The old drift mine on the site formed the nucleus for the re-creation of a colliery village as it might have been in 1913 (including steam winder, engine shed, and chaudron wagons for transporting coal). The miners' houses that were brought in from Hetton-le-Hole were arranged internally to show change over time in living conditions, decoration, and amenities. The reconstructed colliery village included a school and a Methodist chapel. A further resource already on site was the Home Farm, which was also part of the 1913 re-creation, using additional farm machinery brought in from other parts of the region and also housing rare breeds of farm animals. The webpage brochure makes the appeal plainly: "Now visitors can discover how the farm was worked in the early years of last century and how the farmer's wife spent her busy day in the large farmhouse kitchen." Additions to the 1825 area included the Pockerley Waggonway, a short steam railroad and engine shed representing the earliest days of the railroad. Its replicas of early locomotives,

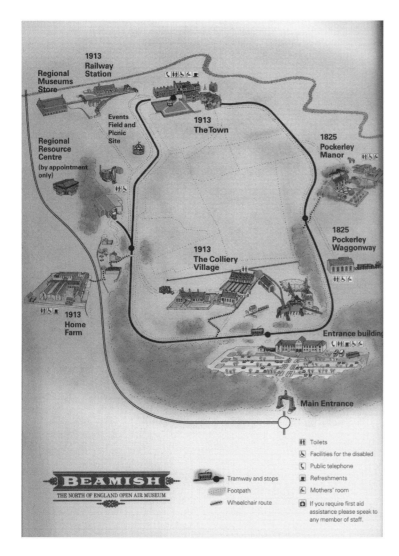

Regional Museums Store

1913 Railway Station

Events Field and Picnic Site

1913 The Town

1825 Pockerley Manor

Regional Resource Centre (by appointment only)

1825 Pockerley Waggonway

1913 The Colliery Village

1913 Home Farm

Entrance building

Main Entrance

BEAMISH
THE NORTH OF ENGLAND OPEN AIR MUSEUM

Tramway and stops
Footpath
Wheelchair route

Toilets
Facilities for the disabled
Public telephone
Refreshments
Mothers' room
If you require first aid assistance please speak to any member of staff.

6.2   Map of Beamish. Note the open space between the exhibits at Beamish that diminished any crowd feeling. Courtesy of Beamish, The North of England Open Air Museum.

6.3   The Pockerley Waggonway with the replica locomotive of 1825. Courtest of Beamish, The North of
       England Open Air Museum.

one of which had been "lost" in the 1840s, were reconstructed from engineers'
drawings. For safety's sake stronger modern materials and techniques were used
in sensitive parts of the reconstructions, but this necessary compromise was un-
obtrusive.[83]

Additions covering the "1913" section included the railroad depot, the main
buildings of which were transferred from an abandoned station at Rowley in
the Durham hills, with additions from wherever good quality material could be
rescued, and the "J-21" steam locomotive, preferred by Atkinson because of its
ordinariness as the last survivor of a large class of standard freight locomotives
that had been familiar all over the region. Publicity tried to lure visitors with the
promise of riding "in replica 1825 carriages behind The Steam Elephant or the

Museum's replica of 'Locomotion No.1' built by George Stephenson in 1825," recalling the locomotive that "headed the first public, passenger-carrying, steam train in the world."[84]

Most attractive (and most artificial) of all, perhaps, was the market town street of 1913, with a cooperative store painstakingly dismantled and reconstructed from nearby Annfield Plain, a candy factory (not a usual feature of such a town, but obviously marketable), an automobile and cycle works, a livery stable, a bank, a public park with bandstand, a row of lower-middle-class houses that doubled as working premises for a music teacher, solicitor, and dentist, and of course the Sun Inn, the reconstructed pub.

Here, above all, Beamish might be criticized for pulling together an adventitious and unrepresentative cluster of buildings to provide a fake urban environment, without the long featureless streets of workers' cottages that were characteristic of the region's villages and small towns. Outsiders who had visited Disneyland might find it reminiscent of Main Street U.S.A. But here too, each individual building was genuine and rooted within the region. There could be none of the tricks of perspective and height that Disney adopted to increase the appeal of his streetscapes. The ensemble was artificial, and perhaps understandably calculated to attract, but the components, as Hewison admitted, were absolutely genuine. The same applied to the vehicles of the electric tramway that took visitors round the extensive grounds, and the other archaic means of transport that were available alongside it.[85] Backing up what visitors could see and experience were enormous collections of artifacts, including large numbers of common household objects, and featuring a huge collection of Trade Union banners and other memorabilia of the region's working-class organizations. The research potential of this material, including oral history tapes, is now beginning to be exploited.[86]

Beamish developed distinctive ways of presenting its material to a visiting crowd who were supposed to be educated through enjoyment, at a variety of levels from simply being exposed to something "new" and different, to developing a systematic program of interactive learning. Building on Scandinavian practices, it made extensive use of "interpreters" and "demonstrators," using staff in period costume ("in character" but not playing a specific role) who were given very detailed briefings about the sites and artifacts they were explaining. Each site within the museum was eventually supported by a "Handbook for Demonstrators," following a policy that

6.4   The reproduction of a Northern English market town of 1913. It is romanticized but a close ob-
servation of its authenticity will lead no one to mistake it for Disney's Main Street U.S.A. By G.
Cross.

was introduced in the early 1980s. The Pockerley Manor handbook, for example,
was rigorously didactic. It provided demonstrators with

> information on Pockerley Manor, its furnishings and fittings, and the uses
> to which the various rooms were put. . . . Pockerley has been carefully re-
> searched and a wealth of information has been built up from local records.
> Information, however, has been kept deliberately general, enabling you to
> answer most of the visitors' questions. If more specific information is needed,

it will be provided in the Book of Days for Pockerley. . . . If you do not know the answer to a question, do not invent one. . . . If you are in doubt, refer to your Interpreter."

Accuracy was more important than the theatrics of staying in a role; and detailed support was provided. The plants in the gardens, for example, were supplied on the basis of the contents of the catalogs of a contemporary Gateshead nurseryman, and information was available about the subject matter of all the prints on the walls. Many of the demonstrators worked seasonally and part-time, and theirs was a demanding job with every effort made to ensure historical accuracy in their communication with visitors.[87]

The staff training manual for interpreters, a step further up the hierarchy, emphasized another aspect of the presentation: "Involving the visitor is a crucial aspect of the presentation. Both interpreters and visitors benefit when visitors participate in a presentation." A form of role-play was sanctioned, involving the interpreter getting into character and even inviting others to do so, but this "requires the ability to assume the thoughts, feelings and emotions of an historical personage, and an in-depth knowledge of history." The implication is that most staff could not be expected to sustain this, and the training of interpreters involved both basic teaching skills and learning complex historical information. It required a great deal of commitment and enthusiasm from staff whose primary motivations were interest in the job rather than levels of pay or other conventional rewards. As Rosy Allan, who has worked at Beamish since its origins, has pointed out, "Staff who work in the interpretation department are proud to work at Beamish, and if and when they leave they normally go on to work in other museums and would probably not consider working in a theme park." This "official" view accords with the enthusiasm and commitment shown by such staff when encountered informally on an unannounced site visit by the authors.[88]

Beamish thus adopted a compromise position, rejecting reenactment or placing interpreters fully in character to act the parts of specific historical persons, but embracing costumed interaction with the passing crowd, assembled into manageable groups almost on a seminar model.[89] Visitors were, of course, free to choose whether to respond and listen to interpretation or to pass on and ignore it, enjoying the site in their own way. Many visitors to Beamish were at least as attracted to the picnic and fairgrounds, shopping, gazing at perceived quaintness, or indulging in soft-focus nostalgia as they were interested in historical knowledge. But, as the museum's management is well aware, that does not mean that no messages get through.

In contrast to Disney, crowd management at Beamish has been more a matter of trying to keep queues to a minimum on busy days than of structuring the visitor experience. The early troubles with school parties, discussed in the Introduction, were overcome, and the main concerns have been to predict demand, manage internal transport, and entertain the queues that do develop by providing someone "in character" to demonstrate crafts and related activities.[90] As there are no additional charges for the various experiences, there are no pressures, and people can be left to follow their inclinations. This is, then, a family-based crowd, policed by parents or teachers, and internally structured accordingly. It is a respectable crowd, because of the reputation of the destination, the need to make a special effort to arrive there, and the absence of the sort of pleasures that might attract the crowds that haunted Coney's Bowery or a modern thrill-ride amusement park.

In comparison to the Disneylands, the most striking character of Beamish is its evocation of the pace and relative simplicity of the past rather than the sensual intensity of the present, especially as expressed in modern amusement parks. The Beamish site is large (300 acres as compared to the 160 acres of Disneyland, much of which was devoted to parking lots), and within this vast green space are six exhibits, widely separated from one another in a rough square. In the middle of that square are open fields; there is no central tower or other focal point. The point is to give visitors a feel for a time when music was not continuously blaring, when the eyes were not continuously assaulted with color, shape, and movement. Although there is a playground with swings, fun house, and even a vintage carousel, these are set in a picnic grounds. Beamish made no compromise with the contemporary thrill culture of the cool. The relative emptiness of the site encourages family conversation as groups walk from attraction to attraction over relatively long distances. Unlike Disneyland, Beamish does not overpower relationships with sight and sound. Even on a busy day, like the Bank Holiday of May 31, 2004, family groups, not an anonymous crowd, dominated the scene.

Even the special events, designed to attract return visitors, complemented rather than challenged this mood. In April 2004, Beamish offered "The History of Meccano" for enthusiasts of this very "1913ish" construction toy: "Meet the makers and see fascinating models and historical items tracing more than a century of development of one of the world's best-loved hobbies." Other events scheduled for

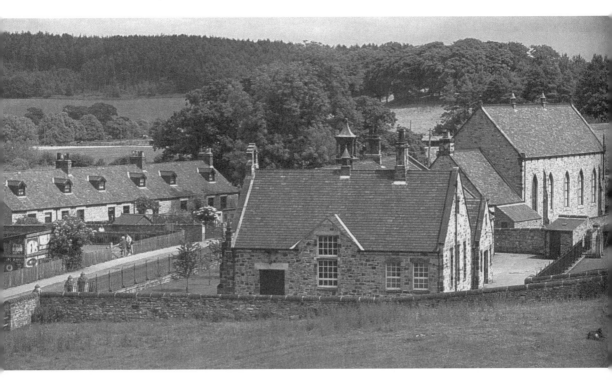

6.5   The Beamish Colliery Village in a rural setting of 1913. Courtesy of Beamish, The North of England
       Open Air Museum.

that year included Maypole and Morris dancing at the Colliery Village, exhibits
of vintage motorcycles, bicycles, and horse-drawn vehicles, demonstrations in the
art of corn doll making and leek and flower gardening, as well as competitions in
traditional plowing and reenactments of a British imperial celebration (at the end
of the Boer War) complete with colorful bunting and brass bands, a 1913 military
encampment, and an 1825 Fair at Pockerley Manor. In 2004, as at the beginning,
Beamish remained a center of regional culture and memory.

Of course, there are still genuine problems surrounding what the museum can
and cannot show. In the name of historical accuracy, Beamish could not depict men
baking bread in the miners' cottages. Because this is a region in which women's
paid labor outside the home was very limited, and there was no equivalent of the

Lancashire working-class women's suffrage movement, Beamish could not stress women's wage work or political roles, even if this seemed to some to be neglecting the historical legacy of women.[91] While Atkinson himself was less sensitive than he might have been on gender issues, he reflected the culture of his time and place. More to the point, a museum committed to accuracy would be wrong to misrepresent the past for ideological purposes.[92]

Senior museum staff, meanwhile, are well aware of the problems raised by confronting visitors with stomach-turning renditions of "how it really was," with tubercular miners coughing blood, peeling wallpaper, and disgusting renderings of unsanitary conditions. Evidence from the Wigan Pier heritage center, where visitors rejected a role-play exhibition of death in a cottage, refusing to touch the coffin as requested, suggests that shocking visitors is counter-productive. It is also difficult to represent past conflicts, and the number of people required to stage a strike or demonstration would be impossible to assemble on an everyday basis. Even chapel services are a problem: are they to be respected as acts of worship, or divorced from their ostensible content and regarded as instructive entertainment? Where does that leave believers? Even more problematic is that fact that increasingly the culture of Protestant Nonconformity and the traditional labor movement are no longer part of the memory or understanding of most of the visitors. Intergenerational conversations about the past with family elders passing on recollections of their youth become increasingly rare with each passing year. While nostalgia at Disneyland can be renewed with each generation because it is based on a fantasy fed by reissued Disney movies and adult recollections of visiting Disneyland as children, a grounded nostalgia for the world of 1913 is impossible for people born in the second half of the twentieth century. Because recent popular culture is increasingly national and even global, the regional identities that Beamish at first wanted to nurture may today be lost to many visitors in the twenty-first century. Underlying all this is the persistent problem of presenting authentic material without being overly or intrusively didactic. Beamish's contribution to the history of regional culture, the labor movement, and religion may prove to lie in providing the raw materials for "academic" pursuits or in accommodating specialized audiences for special events, leaving the museum itself mostly to do what it does best.[93]

The critics of Beamish seem not to have taken any of these issues into account. Nor have they considered the political tensions inherent in representing (for example) class conflict through a museum whose governing body has representatives

6.6   A family crowd gathers at Beamish's park to hear a traditional brass band on a busy Bank Holiday in May 2004. By G. Cross.

from a broad and shifting spectrum of political opinions and has to accommodate them all. The relocation and opening of the Annfield Plain Co-operative store is a case in point. At a meeting of the Joint Committee in April 1976 one member described the acquisition as "the most absurd proposal I've ever heard," and a local resident wrote in protest to the *Durham County Advertiser* at the "sheer waste of public money on such a ridiculous scheme, on a building built since 1900, which is I am sure of little interest to the community." Atkinson and Professor Conzen of Newcastle University had to defend the importance of the store as an essential part of the fabric of every Northeastern town of the period. All this illustrates the necessity for running an obstacle course of political and ideological objections before one of the most popular items in the Beamish repertoire could be put in place.[94] The museum was a product of what was physically, politically and, economically possible.

Beamish and the other open-air museums offer a distinctive variant of the playful crowd, seeking fresh air, nostalgia and entertainment in varying measures, but all within a framework balancing edification and fun. This is a world away from Disney and the theme park. This is, dare one suggest, a very British crowd, in a very different sense from the other Britishnesses of, for example, the soccer crowd or the Blackpool week-end crowd. It remains a viable, if less popular, path from the world of both industrial saturnalia and the gentility of 1900, constituting its own distinctive version of the playful crowd.

The Crowd Transformed?

On both sides of the North Atlantic around 1900, entertainment entrepreneurs discovered a wage-earning people with free time, money, and mobility. These enterprisers turned this realization into profit by providing a plethora of pleasures, which reflected the diverse and often localized taste and experience of the crowd. Their methods were diverse—offering everything from the latest music and dance hall entertainment and mechanical spectacles and thrill rides to the seemingly archaic attractions of the trained animal and freak show—and thus appealed to taste that was simultaneously modern and saturnalian. By 2000, the nature of the crowd at play had changed dramatically, becoming more affluent and in many ways less diverse in its taste in entertainment as it shed many of its plebeian and traditional characteristics. Powerful entertainment corporations had learned how to package pleasure internationally, efficiently transporting and managing crowds while creating and responding to a shared vocabulary of increasingly globalized desires.

To many these changes constituted improvement: Not only were the pleasure seekers of 2000 more reliably profitable, but they were less threatening to the social order. The family-oriented fun of Disney and the controlled and potentially "improving" experience of a heritage open-air museum like Beamish seemed to measure cultural progress over the bizarre stalls and freak shows along Coney Island's Bowery and Blackpool's Golden Mile. But is it enough to simply say that entrepreneurs had learned to create and sell pleasure crowds more efficiently? Is it sufficient to claim that the crowd itself became more "civilized?"[1]

Crowds and Attractions: Explaining Difference

As we have seen, such understandings of a century of consuming crowds fail to confront subtle continuities and deeper contrasts between the two ends of the century. Without acknowledgement, Disney borrowed much from Coney Island's four amusement parks, and recently has even sought to capitalize on nostalgia for the seaside resort in the company's California Adventure feature, Paradise Pier. Meanwhile, British seaside resorts have marketed their own pasts as "heritage" attractions. Open-air museums of life in the recent past feature the Edwardian fun-fair with its carousels and steam fairground organ. Images of uncomplicated transatlantic "progress" are also clouded by the contrasting experiences of the decline at Coney Island and continuing reinvention and vivacity at Blackpool—a fact that may lead us to reevaluate common claims of American adaptability and presumptions of British cultural conservatism. This uneven history of progress with different paths to the contemporary aesthetic of pleasure crowds has been central to our story.

In some ways, it is not surprising that Blackpool survived for decades after Coney Island became an urban/industrial ruin. Blackpool was a regional entertainment center, a northern Piccadilly Circus. By contrast, Coney Island was a summer seaside sideshow to America's most important urban entertainment center, never providing an alternative to Broadway or Times Square because they were so close by. The beach lured the earliest crowds of the 1830s and a century later the seashore prevailed over artificial entertainment. Blackpool was a vacation destination in the days of trains, while Coney Island soon became merely a day trip for the subway crowd. Blackpool's majestic buildings—the Tower and Winter Gardens—were permanent vessels that floated on the ongoing stream of British popular culture. Even the Pleasure Beach took on this quality in the 1930s with the construction of Joseph Emberton's Casino and other modernist structures that have survived to this day.

In every way, Coney Island was transient: Physically and architecturally, it was much more like an extensive circus or fair grounds than a Times Square. In 1900, the Island certainly was more innovative than Blackpool—creating the enclosed, but out-of-doors, themed amusement park with novel rides and spectacles. But, built as they were, Coney Island was perpetually threatened with shabbiness and tackiness. Even more, Coney Island's amusement parks, by making novelty as well as entertainment central to their appeal, eventually made themselves obsolete. While in 1900 Blackpool had lodging houses and hotels that perpetuated an established holiday tradition, Coney Island had bath houses that many saw as a barrier to a free beach and "hotels" that served mostly as restaurants. Eventually both became superfluous and disappeared. The very short summer season at Coney partially explains the tacky structures there. And, the famous American predilection for building for the short run (revealed in everything from industrial machinery to housing construction) was certainly reflected in the "staff" castles of Luna Park. Dreamland's Beacon Tower never played the iconic role of the Blackpool Tower. Unlike Blackpool, Coney could never have a real "tradition," because its tradition was novelty itself. Of course, Blackpool also had its freak shows, mechanical rides, and dramatic spectacles, but it had disproportionately more stable entertainment forms—stage shows, fish and chip shops, and pier entertainment.

Another sharp contrast was the far more rapid impact of the car culture on Coney than on Blackpool. In Britain, where until the 1960s the automobile remained accessible only to the relatively well-to-do, most travelers to Blackpool took the train until that decade of transition. Even when the motor car became dominant, Blackpool adapted, eventually replacing the Central [train] Station and its approaches, with a sequence of large car parking lots. At Coney Island, the automobile was an earlier and much greater challenge: Already in the 1920s, the automobile allowed the more affluent elements of its crowd to go elsewhere. Parking places were insufficient to accommodate potential demand, and by the 1930s, because of the car, Coney became a far more proletarian place—the destination of youth and families too poor to own cars. Increased racial tension was inevitable as poor whites and blacks clashed after World War II.

As we have seen, Blackpool was a site for the playful crowd longer because it had much more effective political support. Impresarios were well connected with government at all relevant levels, but especially at the local council, more effectively promoting the site in competition with rival seaside resorts and complementing private seaside entertainments with public works to improve the beach and promenade and build green parks. On the edge of the city and dependent upon it, Coney Island lacked urban sponsors. First, the resort was the political plaything of the village of Gravesend. Then, after it was annexed by Brooklyn and then becoming part of New York City, Coney Island was perpetually caught between the interests of reformers who tried to make the site into a Central Park by the Sea and developers looking for more profitable land uses (like housing and commerce). No political or even corporate interest promoted the modernization of the entertainment purpose of Coney.

All of these physical, economic, and political factors were decisive (suggesting a contrast that cannot be explained by something as simple as differences in the rates of "modernization"). In addition, there was a more subtle divergence that helps explain the contrasting fates of Blackpool and Coney—the playful crowds themselves. For decades Blackpool's throngs were created around a simple repetitive, even nostalgic theme—coming back year after year. This repetition was more than a continuation of the ancient annual trek to the village or regional fair—part of a seasonal cycle, running from festival to festival. Instead, it was a key element in the modern life cycle, a habit of youth renewed annually as part of an on-going culture of memory fed upon renewal. Blackpool was the gathering place for a cross-generational and relatively stable working-class culture. Blackpool and its largely Victorian culture of memory and renewal reflected the stability and relative homogeneity of the northern English working class.

By contrast, the American crowd at Coney was in a continuous state of change, of migration. In the 1930s, forty or sixty year olds who had visited Coney Island at the age of twenty felt little need or desire to return. This may have been because Coney Island had become as early as 1900 a site of teens and young adults on a day's adventure. It already depended on a generationally defined crowd that eventually was no longer able to recruit a new generation. In comparison to Blackpool, Coney Island was not a place that people aged with. This pattern of the perpetually changing youth crowd became even more pronounced by the 1920s with the shift from the dioramas and scenic railroads that had once appealed to adults with cultural roots in the dime museum to the raw excitement of the giant roller coasters that attracted a daring crowd of youth. This phenomenon is hardly unique to Coney or even the seaside resort; it happened to many amusement parks built around 1900 as well as to roller skating rinks and dance halls at different points in twentieth-century America.

Reinforcing these generational cycles in the U.S. was the fact of social mobility across class and space. By the 1920s and 1930s, older, now more *affluent* Italian Americans, for example, had no desire to return to the loud, fast-paced, and to their altered eyes, cheap and tawdry site of their *impoverished* youth in 1900. The fate of Coney Island crowds was the same as that of the America of immigrants who moved from the city into the suburb. The people and especially their children forgot the old playground of Coney Island just as they forgot the old neighborhood in Brooklyn or the Lower East Side. Immigrants followed the WASPs out of Coney Island just as they imitated the residential movement of the rich and middle-class native-born from the city outward to the suburb. Coney was not a life-long annual pilgrimage, but a place one grew out of and moved up from. By contrast, for much of the twentieth century, Blackpool was a life-long tourist destination because it never took on the reputation of an exclusive site of youth and, even more, because Britain saw a much slower migration out of the working classes.

Two Routes to Middle-Class Modernity

Beyond these differences between the attractions and crowds, these two sites point to still another perhaps even more important contrast. The broad middle class in Britain and the United States responded in dramatically different ways to the culture of the plebeian crowd. This becomes even clearer when we think also about the successors of Coney/Blackpool—Disney/Beamish. Although we are suggesting neither that Disney represents American culture nor that Beamish is the "essence" of Britain, the contrast between the two pleasure sites reveals distinct patterns that are embedded in American and British culture.

At first, we need to recall that the critique of that crowd that emerged from the literati of both countries was different: While American intellectuals and reformers decried the seeming anonymity and suggestibility of the crowd, their British counterparts often found a tolerable good-natured vulgarity with mostly a minority of working-class and leftist intellectuals sharing the American (and European) perspective. Of course, members of the respectable classes in both countries found parallel ways of escaping from the industrial saturnalia at the beginning of the twentieth century. Some of the "better classes" retreated to resorts that featured fashionable self-display, perpetuating an older tradition of "aristocratic" socializing well illustrated at both the American Newport and the British Torquay. One difference remained: At Coney Island, the respectable classes abandoned their genteel Manhattan Beach hotels, while at Blackpool they remained on the North and South Shore. Still, in both countries the apostles of "moral improvement" and "rational recreation" preferred fresh air and the simple life, hiking and holiday camps, mountains, "Nature and Nature's God," and the different freedoms offered by the bicycle and later (with more moral ambiguity) the automobile. These groups were offended by the perceived disorder and moral anarchy of pleasure crowds at Coney /Blackpool, and some consciously tried to organize alternatives to it. In many ways, these critiques and contrasting visions of the proper holiday illustrate ongoing culture wars. Shaped by ethnic and class prejudice and the pursuit of "high culture" as well as romantic notions of nature, these attitudes survive in the perceived contrast between the praiseworthy "traveler," seeking new experiences in informed and adventurous ways, and the sheep-like, exploited (mass) "tourist."[2]

Nevertheless, over the long run, more effective challenges to industrial saturnalia neither defended status nor nature in either country. These alternatives have been obscured by the tenacity of the original taste wars. Ultimately, what divided the consuming crowds of 1900 from those of a century later was less the refinement or pacification of the masses than the emergence of a new holiday aesthetic constructed around middle-class values, although versions of them appeared in the "respectable" working class. The vacation destination of the late twentieth century came to reflect a new society that no longer sought relief from and meaning in industrial work. Rather, holiday-makers in 2000 endeavored to find wonder experienced through two separate but overlapping appeals: child-like innocence captured in a commercialized fantasy world that culminated in Disney and nostalgia for imagined older versions of community grounded in craft and manual skill, technologies using steam and water, and the visible proximity of nature as seen at Beamish. Although these ideals shared much with the several forms of genteel culture of around 1900, they were adapted to the longings and concerns of a consumer culture that would not fully emerge until the 1950s. While this new sensibility, of course, drew on Victorian notions of status and pure experience and, even more, sought alternatives to the psychological oppression of the crowd, it also broke new ground. New technology (especially the mass-produced automobile and affordable air travel) radically changed the possibilities of the tourist experience, both dispersing and widening the potential range of the crowd.

Even more important for our purposes, middle-class sensibilities were divided in the twentieth century much as they were in late Victorian times. In the 1950s, Americans separated from prevailing British sensibilities by offering an alternative to the plebeian pleasure crowd in a fantastic nostalgia, rather than the grounded version that emerged more strongly (though certainly not exclusively) in Britain, and constructing it around the culture of the child as cute rather than the child as inheritor of tradition. We have represented the former with Disney and the latter with Beamish. Now is the time to stand back and try to explain this difference.

At both Disneyland and Beamish, nostalgia was a dominant appeal and both attracted mostly a respectable, even middle-class, crowd of child-centered families. Yet these similarities were the beginning of the difference. Disney created nostalgia by blending a fantasy of America in 1900 (turned into a playground) with the transformation of a real 1900-era playground at Coney Island into a form acceptable in 1955 America. The secret to the success of Disney was not in the capture of kitsch and the creation of a safe, saccharine sentimentality or even the perpetuation of a sanitized memory of small-town life. It was in making a "memory" of the past into a playground, not by re-creating the past, but by fashioning a dream world of nostalgia through the power of emotional associations.[3] Main Street U.S.A. was more like the memory of a child's play set than the actual small-town center that some visitors may have experienced. Disney also transformed the industrial saturnalia of Coney into forms acceptable to a newly affluent middle class of the mid-twentieth century. Disney preserved much of the playfulness of Coney without its reliance on "outdated" wonder—"unnatural" freaks and exotics and the supernatural or afterlife—the public display of which middle-class Americans had rejected by 1950. The carnival culture of freaks and circus took cartoon forms in Disney that appealed to the old need for "turning the world upside down," but were liberated from premodern sensibilities by the creation of wondrous innocence. At Disney, nostalgia was about a fantasy of the past and a symbolic world of "timeless" and childlike images of Mickey Mouse and pixie dust rather than the bizarre mysteries of Lilliputia or Hell's Gate.

All this was not simply the product of Disney's "genius," but a reflection of some rather distinct American patterns and trends that emerged gradually in the half century before Disneyland. Walt Disney drew upon the circulation of characters and stories with which Americans identified and which ultimately became substitutes for traditional and religious images and narratives. Historians of American consumer culture have long noted the central element of imaginative narrative and graphic fantasy in the seemingly endless expansion of consumer needs.[4] This was hardly unique to the United States, but Americans learned especially well how to associate emotions and satisfactions with the stories and characters into which advertisers placed their products, making their purchase part of the happy ending. From the late 1890s, the American entertainment media developed an exceptionally icon-rich culture—especially in serial form that ranged from comic strips and storybooks to movies and radio/TV programs. Many of these icons appeared also as trademark characters on the labels and boxes of new consumer goods (sometimes, like the childlike images of Skippy, Buster Brown, Kewpie, and Shirley Temple, appearing in several media). Disney's success grew out of and flourished in this hothouse—first when he created his own menagerie of fantastic characters for cartoons, movies, and comic books and then when he placed them in his human-sized play sets with which the crowd was to interact at Disneyland.[5]

Disney and his apologists have long insisted that this formulation of the playful crowd is unique and revolutionary. Yet, in taking a long view, Disney adopted elements of the freak show, carnival, circus, amusement park, and diorama of 1900, transforming them for the consumer age and bringing them to the children and grandchildren of the Coney crowd of 1900. Disney's attractions and crowds were different from old Coney's (and we have emphasized how in chapter 5), but they also shared an aesthetic of playfulness quite foreign to the genteel and improving cultural heritage of the late Victorian bourgeoisie. This points to an obvious fact—the cultural distance between the Coney Island immigrant crowd of 1900 and the scrubbed WASP-ish Disneyland crowd of 1955 was not so great as most suppose. This cultural and social connection between the two can be explained by the fact that Disney replaced the genteel sublime in American middle-class culture that had largely died by the 1920s, with a more playful, but still respectable, aesthetic. The key was that Disney (and American popular commercialism in general) learned how to make middle-class culture fun by selectively imitating Coney. This was possible because the "original" Coney Island of 1900–1910 had, in fact, been a cross-class cultural mix, drawing on middle-class playfulness (as, for example, exemplified in Frederic Thompson) as well as the sensibilities of the wage-earner.

Only after 1920 did Coney go thoroughly down-market. This suggests once again that there was less a break between the eras of the "original" Coney and mid-century Disney than often thought, and, even more, that the continuities between the two were part of an American "mass" culture. As seen in the success of American films and much else, what distinguished American popular commercial culture from Britain and elsewhere in 1900 as well as 1955 was the cross-class appeal, drawing on icons and stories that stretched across the "mass" of Americans. Middle-class observers of Blackpool in the first half of the twentieth century may have tolerated, even encouraged, the playful crowd there, but they stood outside and seldom embraced popular taste in entertainment beyond a shared presence at music-hall and cinema programs. For the generation of 1900 (but not beyond), Coney was a "mass" culture in the sense that it reached both (respectable) working- and middle-class audiences, as did Disney in the 1950s and long thereafter.

It is significant that there are many parallels between Coney and Disney, but fewer between Blackpool and Beamish. At base, this British contrast can be explained by the fact that nostalgia and middle-class sensibilities took on very different forms than they did in the United States. Beamish, like Disney, romanticized early-twentieth-century social life, albeit on a basis of careful reconstruction and research, and invited crowds to pretend to "return to the past." But Beamish was painstakingly protective of its ideal of a time-warped community, re-creating, for example, the commercial small-town street and colliery village (stressing the collectivist/voluntarist character of the cooperative store rather than the romanticized "origins" of contemporary corporations as did Disney's Main Street U.S.A.). Even more, Beamish gave much space and attention to the re-creation of the hard world of the coalmine and the serious business of the school.

Beamish is not "real," but neither is it a deliberate fantasy, a play set in the manner of Disneyland. The model for Beamish was not a fantasyland or even an entertainment district like Edwardian Blackpool. No one had to re-create "old Blackpool" as Disney created Main Street and more recently "Paradise Pier." Old Blackpool is still there! The model instead was the outdoor museum of Skansen in Sweden, a site that was supposed to recall the lost crafts and culture of Europe's preindustrial past. Of course, Americans had their own versions of this quest to recover the "real" past (Colonial Williamsburg and Old World Wisconsin, for example). But the British did not create anything like Disney.

Beamish was supposed to evoke a nostalgia that brought crowds back to simpler and even "tougher" times and induced elders to teach the young both the pride of crafts and the struggles of the past. Although Beamish had continually to compromise with this rigorous vision of time travel to appeal to fun-seeking crowds, the end product remained a grounded, not fantastic, nostalgia. And, its rationale and point of pride was that it displayed exhibits from the real world, accurate (if relocated and rearranged) re-creations of places of work and everyday living, not a playground. Even if Blackpool no longer existed, there is little doubt that no one in England would have re-created it as a site of nostalgic fantasy in the way that

Disney did (only half aware) in imitating Coney. In fact, Beamish is as much an anti-Blackpool of today *and* 1900 as it is an anti-Disneyland.

All this points to a very different sensibility that spanned significant elements of the "respectable" British middle and working class (especially in the professions, the trade unions, and Protestant Nonconformity—i.e., non-Anglican Protestants). The playful crowd of Coney, updated in Disneyland, was not possible in Britain, where the important aspects of "respectable" culture remained far more distinct from the culture of hedonistic consumerism than in the United States. Although the British middle class visited twentieth-century Blackpool it made no effort to transform it; it kept itself apart on the northern and southern shores and chose to enjoy selected central pleasures on its own terms. Blackpool could not be "Disneyfied" as a blend of class tastes. The plebeian crowd dominated Blackpool for generations, hardly a threat to civilization much less to themselves, but serving as a continuous target of the high-minded scold as a symbol of the manipulated leisure of the working class. This attitude passed on to the creators of Beamish. There was no possibility of even an unacknowledged borrowing from Blackpool at Beamish as there was from Coney at Disneyland. As an anti-Blackpool, Beamish was starkly anti-commercial and anti-tacky, but also anti-play in the saturnalian sense of the word. If bourgeois British indulgence of plebeian Blackpool assured its survival, British social and cultural divisions help explain Beamish.

By contrast, Disneyland was a commercial saturnalia—both an affirmation of consumer culture and an escape from its daily form. It rejected the barkers and the cheap huckstering of the old Coney, but its unrelenting merchandizing was as "catch penny" or should we say "catch dollar" as anything that Coney or Blackpool ever tolerated. Still, by its celebration of wonder, especially childhood wonder, Disneyland was an answer to the banality and boredom of suburban consumer society, recalling in playful delight an era of coherent and human-scale space before the contemporary era of the freeway, the mall, and the sidewalkless suburban residential street. Even more, Disneyland returned the jaded affluent adult to the wonder of first pleasures as the child within, or the child accompanying the adult, grinned with delight at the sight of Sleeping Beauty's Castle.

The enchanted child renewed the sated consumer. Wonder was no longer the genteel sublimity of nature or the awe and terror at encountering the "super" natural, or even the vertigo of the thrill ride. Those old quests for excitement gradually gave way to the pleasures of awakening consumer desires in children while recovering a childlike excitement of consumption in adults. Wonder became the timeless, childlike amazement in Disney's world. It was best expressed in Disney's movie set playground that stimulated fantasies of both bygone childhoods and contemporary children's dream-worlds. Disney created a saturnalia for the age of suburban consumption. The vacation was no longer mostly a release from the routines of workplace and neighborhood. It had become a recovery of the purity of the pleasure of consumption, long lost to the modern middle-class adult in boredom and obsession, through the wondrous response of the child (or nostalgic adult). Disney's consumerist saturnalia was as appropriate for his time as that of Frederic Thompson's industrial fantasies at Luna Park in 1910. These in turn liberated audiences from industrial and consumerist cultures, while also confirming their central realities.

There was continuity between Coney and Disney in the appeal to the child, but with very important differences: Steeplechase and Luna Parks let the adult "return" to the carefree adventure of childhood without the burden of real children, while Disney invited adults to make that trip back to innocence through the inspiration of the child in attendance. In the process, the idea of the child changed: the associations conveyed by the idea of the child no longer meant "freedom" from the rules of the everyday adult life of work and responsibility; they were now an affirmation of delight. The child served a very different purpose at Disney than at Coney: The "child" no longer meant separation from adults in a boisterous youthful crowd (the attraction and ultimate curse of Old Coney); Rather, with Disney, the "child" created a crowd acceptable to middle-class American sensibilities—"playfully" engaged in the childlike, but consisting of intimate family groups, not a "mob." Thus, some of the old excitement in the teeming crowd was transformed and refocused when the family unit toured together.

These Disney rituals were adapted from a half century of middle-class experimentation with "wondrous innocence" as adults learned to take children to seaside resorts and to offer them ice cream cones, teddy bears, and kiddy rides. This transition began in the late Victorian middle class where increasing affluence led to more tolerant child rearing practices and a fantasy world presumably derived from childhood sensibilities. Think, for example, of the popularity of *Peter Pan* among adults as well as children when it premiered in 1903.[6] This was a long process. Whereas Coney Island/Blackpool visitors rarely brought children in 1900, as much for reasons of cost as purpose, by 2000, many parents could now afford family vacations and happily made the Disney trip an affirmation of love for children. This child-centeredness, as it spread among the working class, began to break up the older crowd culture, imposing on the industrial saturnalia new standards of decency, order, and cleanliness of the kind long identified with bourgeois respectability. But the wondrous child also introduced a new rationale for pleasure acceptable to the middle class, enabling that new playful crowd to transcend class boundaries through a shared culture of wonderment.

By contrast, in Britain this role of the child was slower to develop. Many British have long enjoyed Disneyland, Disney World, and Disneyland Paris, but they did not build their own. British cinema embraced the marketing ploys of Walt's brother Roy Disney in the 1930s and offered Saturday morning cartoon programs in the form of "Mickey Mouse Clubs." Blackpool Illuminations in the late 1930s featured Disney-like themes of grottos and dwarfs. Even the Pleasure Beach built a "Bingle and Bob" kiddie park in 1927; in 1960, in flattery of the American innovations in theming, they installed a complex of children's rides called Candy Land and in 1992, Bradley Beaver Creek.[7] Still, these were imitations and never as central to the park or as successful as what Disney had created. The iconic figure, Bradley Beaver, was no Mickey Mouse. He lacked a popular "background story" promoted in cartoons and films, and the imaginative oversized representations of Gulliver, a pirate, bull dog "Bobbie," frog, totem pole, space rocket, and clowns lacked thematic coherence, no matter their charm. By the 1970s, the Pleasure Beach conceded "ownership" of the Disney formula to the Americans, and revitalized the amusement park with new thrill rides to attract a teen and young adult crowd. Not only did the Pleasure Beach lack the means or money to "theme" their facilities around the characters and stories of iconic Hollywood films or cartoons as did Disney, Universal Studios and other American amusement parks, but, it was apparently simply too wed to the ways of the old Blackpool, and too aware of their enduring popularity among its visitors, to Americanize itself.

Beamish did not even try. Its view of the child was as radically different from Disney's as was its conception of nostalgia. And, here the contrasting sensibility comes out in full relief. Whereas the child in Disney served to evoke wonder and to make the playful crowd acceptably intimate, the child at Beamish was to be the recipient of heritage, elevating the crowd to an educational purpose.

Of course, the contrast between the two was never stark. Walt Disney hoped that his Main Street U.S.A. would help grandparents draw the grandchildren into their reveries on their small-town upbringings (or imaginations of such childhoods) just as elders visiting Beamish were expected to recall to their presumably curious offspring the rituals of home baking, the coal fire, the washing of clothes with mangle and dolly tub, and the distinctive experience of shopping at the Co-op. Yet, in the Beamish case the objective was always to use enjoyment as a means to education, an attempt to provide children with an alternative to the commercialized, alienated, even overly comfortable and artificially stimulating world of their contemporary experience—not in a fantastic, but grounded nostalgia. Beamish drew on a well-established strand of middle-class culture, that of recreation as self-improving and educational, with its hands-on experience to re-create past environments and promote their understanding. Beamish rejected fantasy and the rushed excitement of the amusement park. Based upon accurate re-creations of past realities, it tried to pull back the child and adult alike from their fragmented, uprooted, hedonistic, and overexcited lives in contemporary consumer culture to an appreciation of a close-knit, natural world of honest work and local traditions. The child was not supposed to reflect wonder back on the adult as in Disney, but to guarantee the survival of a valued way of life or at least an "appreciation" of it.

The child at Beamish was supposed to experience and emotionally embrace an everyday life that adults had, in some cases, only recently abandoned. Even more, by implication, at least, they were expected to adopt the critique of modernity that their parents (or the Beamish leadership in any case) embraced. This was a romantic vision of the past, but still was rooted in the original rejection of the "escapism" of the plebeian pleasure crowd. While some miners, textile machine operators escaped their work-a-day lives by embracing the industrial saturnalia of Blackpool, their descendents at Beamish were fascinated by representations of their ancestor's working lives in the mine or on the farm. The alternative to the potentially dangerous pleasures of the hedonistic crowd was the thoughtful, though enjoyable, engagement of the crowd that learns— especially, if at its center, is found the *enlightened* (not the *wondrous*) child. Beamish did not adapt the plebeian crowd of Blackpool to a middle-class sensibility, as had Disney, but instead combined the self-improving culture of Victorian "rational recreation" with the family-oriented popular pleasures of contemporary Europe.

Who Won and Why?

These contrasting resolutions to the "challenge" of industrial saturnalia naturally lead us to the question: Which modern concept of the playful crowd has prevailed? The obvious answer, of course, is Disney's, even though not without ambiguity. His ideas and practices in park design, crowd control, thematic entertainment and commerce, and much else won global acceptance in the half century after the opening of Disneyland. The Disney formula was sold to a group of Japanese investors whose Disney Tokyo has attracted growing crowds since its opening in 1983. EuroDisney (1992) near Paris was, at first, a failure, but with lowered prices and more thrill rides (along with a name change in 1995 to Disneyland Paris) it has become a financial success. The foreign versions differed. For example, the Paris entrance featured an elegant Center Court presumed to be expected by Europeans, and Main Street was supposed to be less a nostalgia of the American past (which few Europeans could relate to) than a collection of images of shops recalling 1900 America—a candy shop à la Atlantic City and a Gibson Girl ice cream parlor.[8] Tokyo Disney understandably did not copy Main Street U.S.A. but instead build a World Bazaar shopping center at the entrance and added Meet the World, a Japanese perspective on progress in the context of this island nation's encounter with the West.[9] Still, the basic format remained: a single entry point, a central hub in the form of a castle with "lands" radiating from it, and a surrounding berm that separates the entertainment complex from the "outside" world. The continuing and global success of this formula raises questions beyond the scope of this book. But the fact that a plan designed for the baby boom families of the 1950s has survived is an expression of the persistence and adaptability of the fantasy and family themes of that era. That it translated with few changes to Japan and Europe shows not only the appeal of American popular culture, but also the transnational character of this middle-class fantasy world.[10]

Disney's influence went well beyond the company's theme parks and products. The word "Disneyfication" has come into common use and has been applied to a wide assortment of settings—from amusement and theme parks to malls, museums, and even heritage sites. Not long after the success of Disneyland, numerous amusement parks appeared in suburban American locations copying Disney's basic themes. After years of stagnation, the number of amusement parks increased from 400 in 1954 to 786 by 1967. Especially important were the corporate sponsored sites: Six Flags (Dallas, 1961), Busch Gardens (Tampa, 1975), Marriott's Great America (Chicago and elsewhere beginning in 1976), Harcourt Brace and Jovanovich's Sea World (San Diego, 1977), MCA Universal Studios (1964 in Hollywood and 1990 in Orlando), just to name the best known. Legoland, the theme park of the Danish manufacturer of colorful construction blocks and figure sets, opened in Billund, Denmark in 1968, expanding to Windsor, England in 1996, and opening near San Diego in 1998. Older, privately owned amusement parks, including Southern California's Knott's Berry Farm (1940) and Cedar Point (west of Cleveland, Ohio in 1897) also adapted Disney themes.[11]

Disney's impact was obvious. Six Flags was divided into themed zones designated by the six flags (and cultures) under which Texans had lived. It too relied on the suburban family crowd (with freeway access). These parks tended to displace the carnivals and fairground amusement grounds of the past by interlinking TV, movies, toys, rides, and other themed amusements and organizing the park design to facilitate the crowd's flow through movie-like sets and scenes in the manner of Disney.[12]

The impact of Disneyland extends even to places that seem to be its opposite—like Las Vegas hotel and casino complexes. That influence is obvious in the immaculate, but carnival-like setting of the casino Circus Circus, in the Luxor and the Venetian that echo the architecture of Epcot's World Showcase with their replicas of Egyptian and Italian icons, and in the family-coded fun of MGM Grand (with its indoor amusement park).[13] Las Vegas and the Disney sites share much as artificial tourist sites that offer well-orchestrated and intense play environments with little of the "travail" of traditional travel. Unlike Coney Island or Blackpool, Disney and Las Vegas sites offer no natural or historic beauty. Instead, their totally artificial movie-set-like attractions can be constructed *ex nihilo* like the towers and turrets of Luna Park, but out of sterner stuff than staff and without the distraction of a wonderful beach. Moreover, Disney (in Florida, at least) and the "Strip" in Las Vegas can easily expand to accommodate increased crowds without the limits of the sea and urban housing.

Even staid museums of natural history, science, and history were seduced by the crowd appeals of Disney. In 1991, John Terrell wrote that the once lowly museum educator was on the verge of taking exhibitions in American museums away from the curators with the support of Museum Boards determined to increase attendance. These "educators" sacrificed learning and authenticity for entertainment.[14]

Paul Reddy, one of many who designed animated exhibitions for Disney, has spread his expertise and perspective to the museum: "Rather than looking through a glass case at something and reading about it," he explained in 1985, "we want people to be able to participate in some way. We want to create excitement. The education gets through, but you don't realize it so much." The goal of sugar coating the bitter pill of learning is today commonly shared by museum administrators. J. Rounds of the Museum of Science and Industry at Los Angeles' Exposition Park insisted museums must help visitors overcome their fears of subjects that seem "forbidding, unapproachable and threatening." He oversaw the development of eighteen "interactive" exhibits in 1984. Rounds admitted that such exhibits have limited educational value: "In the few hours most people spend at the museum, we can't expect to convey a great deal of factual knowledge, but we can get them over their fear of the subject."[15]

In the 1990s, public aquariums tried to expand their audiences, spending millions to theme their facilities in order to give visitors with little knowledge of aquatic wildlife a sense of immersion in the habitat. Pressure to revitalize old tourist areas led to a proposal for a $30 million history museum at San Francisco's Fisherman's Wharf that was originally planned to include a fog machine, a simulated earthquake, and even a ride through a diorama of the 1960s hippie neighborhood of Haight-Ashbury aboard imitation Volkswagen convertibles. These schemes failed, but many cheered Disney's efforts to revitalize Times Square in the mid-1990s by staging studio musicals like *Lion King* and refurbishing the New Amsterdam Theater, driving out the tawdry sex shows.[16] When Disney became the language of the wondrous child as it has in so many ways today, anyone wishing to tap into that sentiment, be it a museum eager to draw young families to its exhibits, commercial caterers of kids' birthday parties, or even Las Vegas casinos must talk and look Disney.[17]

Those sites that cannot or will not adapt the Disney style risk losing crowds. Certainly, in the United States the edifying and rooted nostalgia of Colonial Williamsburg has recently faced the threat of dwindling crowds (dropping to the lowest level in four decades in 2003) and the prospect of compromising its tradition as a living museum of American heritage, with its careful restoration of the eighteenth-century capital of the state of Virginia and reenactments of colonial political, craft, and social life. While this site of heritage tourism has entertained more than 100 million people since it was created in 1934, the private Williamsburg Foundation laid off 400 of its 3,200 staff and cut programming by 20 percent in 2004 in the face of a deficit of $30 million on an operating budget of $200 million. Williamsburg is still a place that families think they *should* visit, rather than *want* to visit. The pace is just too slow especially when just down the road are the Busch Gardens, a themed amusement park in the Disney tradition, and Water Country USA with plenty of thrills. Like Beamish, Colonial Williamsburg also faces criticism from advocates of authenticity and opponents of commercialism. Despite efforts in recent years to emphasize the role of slavery, some visitors see it as a "sort of three-dimensional *Better Homes and Gardens.*" In fact, in 2002 about 4,000 licensed products based on Williamsburg's colonial themes ranging from furniture and linens to toys and baseball caps brought in $40 million compared with merely $27 million from visitors. While some argue for more fun and emotion at Williamsburg, it probably will not be able to build a thrill ride through the American Revolution without alienating that "cultured" base of support. Williamsburg, like so many other heritage sites, is caught between its appeal to historical authenticity and a public that measures meaning and enjoyment with a Disney yardstick.[18]

But Disneyfication has hardly gone unchallenged. We have seen that the company has had to adapt to changes in family and childhood in the 1980s and 1990s. Universal Studios and other amusement parks picked up on the appeal of the age-specific fad and the teenager's rejection of the intergenerationality of Disney.[19] Universal Studios draws on a strategy that had roots in 1900-era Coney Island itself, that of peer-gathering icons that separated the young from both their childhoods and from authoritative adults. Disney's strategy of the cute was an answer to the middle-class fear of the plebeian crowd, but it never satisfied the needs of a large part of that crowd—youth—and the often cross-class appeal of the cool.[20] Universal, especially with the opening in 1999 of its second theme park, Islands of Adventure, took the movie theme into a more "cool" direction with blood-pumping roller coasters themed around Marvel Comic characters.[21] In a 2004 TV ad, Universal had only to say, "If fairy tales and Pixie Dust aren't your thing," then come to Universal Studios. This dig at Disney appealed to an age and style group that could not be ignored. By the 1980s even Disney went after the cool crowd in the attempt to inject thrills and sarcasm into their rides and shows. TV ads in the winter of 2003–4 featured preteens coolly introducing their petrified parents to Disney's terrifying rides.

Finally, critiques of the Disney solution to the problem of industrial saturnalia have hardly disappeared. Disneyfication has met with much resistance. Not only was the Disney-like museum on Fisherman's Wharf scrapped but also a much larger scheme to build an actual Disney amusement park near Washington D.C. was defeated in the early 1990s. "Disney's America," was to be a "new" and more entertaining way of learning American history than provided at the "boring" museums in Washington D.C., including a ride through a nineteenth-century steel mill and cotton plantation. The demand for a state subsidy of $150 million for road and other improvements, as well as the fact that that "Disney's America" would have desecrated the Civil War battlefields at Bull Run, doomed the project. Even though Disney hired prominent American historians for advice and legitimacy, Disney's candy-coated history sparked strong objections across the political spectrum.[22]

In fact, Disney provokes continual hostility. By 2001 there was a Society of Disney Haters on line (www.sodh.org) giving vent to people "forced" to go to the Disneylands with spouses, in-laws, or kids. One such correspondent complained that his relatives "like having everything laid out before them, with no thinking involved. . . . I found [Disney World] to be the most crass, dehumanizing, cheesy, smarmy pap I've ever seen. I simply cannot comprehend how so many people are willing to shell that kind of money for such an inauthentic experience."[23] Though it is impossible to know for sure, this view still is in the minority and its espousers almost seem to glory in their status as "outsiders." Though Disneyfication meets resistance, it still seems to call the shots in America, at least. Britain has remained much more resistant, as attendances at the successful industrial museums, stately homes, and preserved railways (for example) continue to hold up well, and highly popular theme parks like Alton Towers as well as the Blackpool Pleasure Beach continue to prioritize thrill rides rather than cute fantasy.

How have Americans and British changed what they desire when free from work and obligation? This history of variations on the theme of twentieth-century tourism addresses this highly meaningful, but seldom raised question. We have emphasized how the changing taste of the consuming crowd reflects less the refinement or manipulation of the masses, than the triumph of particular strands of middle class and "respectable" popular culture. This culture finds answers to the dilemmas of the crowd and consumption in the child-centered family and the celebration of a preconsumerist community. But the working out of this triumph has taken various forms, on a continuum from commercially generated fantasy of the cute to the careful re-creation and recreational re-presentation of historical pasts. These changes, in all their complexity, go to the heart of what makes the contemporary Western world distinct from that world a century before.

Notes

Introduction

1. "Bad Elephant Killed," *The Commercial Advertiser*, January 5, 1903; "Coney Elephant Killed," *New York Times*, January 5, 1903.

2. *Blackpool Carnival: Official Souvenir Programme, June 9th to 16th (inclusive) 1923*, British Library 103609.47, 30–31.

3. J. K. Walton, "Popular Entertainment and Public Order: The Blackpool Carnivals of 1923–4," *Northern History* 34 (1998): 170–88.

4. "Main Street Electric Parade," *News from Disneyland*, 1972, Anaheim Public Library Disneyland Collection; "Main Street Electric Parade: Grand Return—May 28, 1999 Last Show April 1, 2001"http://allearsnet.com/tp/mk/msep.htm, © R.Y.I. Enterprises, LLC. Accessed Jan 4, 2004.

5. F. Atkinson, *The Man Who Made Beamish: An Autobiography* (Gateshead: Northern Books, 1999), 133.

6. Beamish Museum Archives, Newspaper Cuttings, Boxes 1971–5 and 1978–9.

7. Neither had a direct challenger or counterpart within its own country: in the United States, Atlantic City would come later and would provide a less spectacular and variegated outdoor popular entertainment experience, while Blackpool overshadowed regional competitors like Morecambe and New Brighton, and surpassed popular resorts in London's orbit, such as Southend and Margate. M. Immerso, *Coney Island: The People's Playground* (Piscataway, NJ: Rutgers University Press, 2002); J. K. Walton, *Blackpool* (Edinburgh: Edinburgh University Press, 1998); Nelson Johnson, *Boardwalk Empire: The Birth, High Times and Corruption of Atlantic City* (Medford, NJ: Plexus, 2002); Bryant Simon, *Boardwalk of Dreams: Atlantic City and the Fate of Urban America* (New York: Oxford University Press, 2004).

8. In 1989, Disney's resorts attracted 44.5 million but only 18 visits for every 100 Americans). David Nasaw, *Going Out: The Rise and Fall of Public Amusements* (New York: Basic Books, 1993), 95

9. J. K. Walton, "The Social Development of Blackpool 1788–1914," Ph.D. dissertation, Lancaster University, 1974, 263.

10. Elias Canetti, *Crowds and Power* (translation by Carol Stewart, London: Penguin, 1973), 15–20, 32–34, 40–41.

11. Ibid. 71–72.

12. Canetti's feast crowd has not attracted much attention from subsequent commentators. They have followed earlier interpretations, especially those of Gustave le Bon and José Ortega y Gasset, who have been more concerned with political crowds and the perils arising from domination by a charismatic leader, or from the collective unconsciousness of a crowd that functions as an organism with shared instincts that subordinate its members to a common purpose. J. S. McClelland, *The Crowd and the Mob: From Plato to Canetti* (London: Unwin Hyman, 1989), 293–310; Carl F. Graumann and Serge Moscovici, *Changing Conceptions of Crowd Mind and Behavior* (New York: Springer-Verlag, 1986); Howard N. Tuttle, *The Crowd Is Untruth* (New York: Peter Lang, 1996); and from a literary/cultural studies perspective Mary Esteve, *The Aesthetics and Politics of the Crowd in American Literature* (Cambridge: Cambridge University Press, 2003).

13. Gustave Le Bon, *The Crowd: A Study of the Popular Mind* (London: Penguin, 1977; first published in French in 1895 and in English in 1960); W. M. Conway, *The Crowd in Peace and War* (London, 1915); John Lionel Taylor, *Social Life and the Crowd* (London: Leonard Parsons, 1923).

14. See, for example, D. L. LeMahieu, *A Culture for Democracy* (Oxford: Oxford University Press, 1988).

15. Walt Disney Productions, *Project Florida: A Whole New Disney World* (Burbank, Ca, 1967), 4; "Booming Amusement Parks: The Theme is Extreme," *Newsweek*, March 30, 1998, 12.

1. Making the Popular Resort: Coney Island and Blackpool about 1900

1. Brooklyn, Flatbush and Coney Island Railroad, *Coney Island, An Illustrated Guide to the Sea with Official Time Tables, Season of 1883* (Brooklyn: Truax and Co, 1883), 10; Stephen Weinstein, "The Nickel Empire: Coney Island and the Creation of Urban Seaside Resorts in the United States," Ph.D. dissertation, Columbia University, 1984, 38–40.

2. Julian Ralph, "Coney Island," *Scribner's Magazine* 20 (July 1896): 9; Robert Snow and David Wright, "Coney Island: A Case Study in Popular Culture and Technological Change," *Journal of Popular Culture* 9 (Spring 1976): 960–75.

3. Alain Corbin, *The Lure of the Sea* (Cambridge: Polity, 1994).

4. Michael Immerso: *Coney Island: The People's Playground* (Piscataway, NJ: Rutgers University Press, 2002), 157.

5. J. K. Walton, "The Social Development of Blackpool 1788–1914," Ph.D. dissertation, Lancaster University, 1974, 234–38.

6. A. B. Granville, *The Spas of England, and Principal Sea-Bathing Places* (Bath: Adams and Dart, 1971, reprint of 1841 edn.), 1: 349–51.

7. John Walton, *Blackpool* (Edinburgh: Edinburgh University Press, 1998), ch. 3.

8. Weinstein, "Nickel Empire," 94; Henry Stiles, ed., *Civil, Political, Professional and Ecclesiastical History, and Commercial and Industrial Record of the County of Kings and the City of Brooklyn New York from 1683 to 1984* (New York: Munsell, 1884), 195; *Coney Island and the Jews: A History of the Development and Success of this Famous Seaside Resort* (New York: C.W. Carleton, 1879), 13–15; Jon Sterngass, *First Resorts: Pursuing Pleasure at Saratoga Springs, Newport and Coney Island* (Baltimore: Johns Hopkins University Press, 2001), 82.

9. Brian Cudahy, *How We Got to Coney Island: The Development of Mass Transportation in Brooklyn and Kings County* (New York: Fordham University Press, 2002), chs. 5 and 6; Stiles, *Record of the County of Kings and the City of Brooklyn*, 199–200; Eugene Armbruster, *Coney Island* (New York: Self-published, 1924), 12–13; Sterngass, *First Resorts*, ch. 3; Kathy Peiss, *Cheap Amusements* (Philadelphia: Temple University Press, 1986), 121–22; Gary Kyriazi, *The Great American Amusement Parks* (Secaucus, NJ: Citadel Press, 1976), 26–30.

10. Cudahy, *How We Got to Coney Island* , ch. 6.

11. Sterngass, *First Resorts*, 104–5; Immerso, *Coney*, 30–32; José Marti, *The America of José Marti* (New York: Noonday, 1953), 103–7; Iron Steam Boat Co., *Coney Island* (New York: Iron Steam Boat, 1883), 10–14, 16; and Brooklyn Railroad, *Illustrated Guide*, 55–56.

12. Edo McCullough, *Good Old Coney Island* (New York: Scribner's, 1957), 39. Weinstein, "Nickel Empire," 95–98; Sterngass, *First Resorts*, 83–92, 95; Kathy Peiss, *Cheap Amusements*, 121–22.

13. Walton, "Social Development of Blackpool," 263.

14. Ibid., 240–58.

15. Robert Poole, *The Lancashire Wakes Holidays* (Preston: Lancashire County Books, 1994).

16. J. K. Walton, "The Demand for Working-Class Seaside Holidays in Victorian England," *Economic History Review* 34 (1981): 249–65; Patrick Joyce, *Visions of the People* (Cambridge: Cambridge University Press, 1991); Trevor Griffiths, *The Lancashire Working Classes, 1880–1930* (Oxford: Clarendon Press, 2001).

17. J. K. Walton, *Lancashire: A Social History 1558–1939* (Manchester: Manchester University Press, 1987), ch. 13; Walton, "Regions, Lifestyles and Consumption Patterns: Lancashire and the Basque Country of Northern Spain," in H. Siegrist and M. Schramm, eds., *Regionalisierung europäischer Konsumkulturen im 20. Jahrhundert* (Leipzig: Leipziger Universitatsverlag, 2003), 35–52; A. Fowler, *Lancashire Cotton Operatives and Work, 1900–1950* (Aldershot: Ashgate, 2003), ch. 3.

18. See, for example, *Seaside Watering Places* (London: L. Upcott Gill, 1885), 262.

19. J. K. Walton, "The Blackpool Landlady Revisited," *Manchester Region History Review* 8 (1994): 27.

20. Joseph Heller, *Now and Then* (London: Simon and Schuster, 1998), 40–41; Charles Denson, *Coney Island: Lost and Found* (Berkeley: Ten Speed Press, 2002), 145.

21. Immerso: *Coney Island*, ch. 2; *New York World*, July 20, 1902, Sp. Section, 2.

22. J. K. Walton, "Consuming the Beach: Seaside Resorts and Cultures of Tourism in England and Spain from the 1840s to the 1930s," in E. Furlough and S. Baranowski, eds., *Being Elsewhere: Tourism, Consumer Culture and Identity in Modern Europe and North America* (Ann Arbor: University of Michigan Press, 2001), 272–98.

23. This was not an infallible rule for all resorts, but holds true in our examples. Harold Perkin, "The 'Social Tone' of Victorian Seaside Resorts in the North-West," *Northern History* 12 (1976): 181–94; David Cannadine, *Lords and Landlords: The Aristocracy and the Towns* (Leicester: Leicester University Press, 1980); J. K. Walton, *The English Seaside Resort: A Social History 1750–1914* (Leicester: Leicester University Press, 1983), ch. 3.

24. Peiss, *Cheap Amusements*, 124; Brooklyn Railroad, *Coney Island, An Illustrated Guide*, 12; Immerso, *Coney Island*, 113; *New York World* July 17, 1904, 11E.

25. Weinstein, "Nickel Empire,"117–118, Stiles, *Record of the County of Kings and the City of Brooklyn*, 195–97; Sterngass, *First Resorts*, 82–83, 193–223.

26. Weinstein, "Nickel Empire,"55–60; Immerso, *Coney Island*, 27–29.

27. *New York World*, July 29, 1906, 23; Photo of the Fall of Pompeii, Brooklyn Historical Society, v1974.22.6.50 (1903); *Story of Manhattan Beach* (New York: Francis Hart, 1874), 36; Weinstein, "Nickel Empire," 62–65; *Coney Island and the Jews*, 20–30; Sterngass, *First Resorts*, 88–95; Immerso, *Coney Island*, 34; *New York World*, July 20, 1902, Spec. Sect 1.

28. Walton, "Social Development of Blackpool," ch. 1; J. K. Walton, "Residential Amenity, Respectable Morality and the Rise of the Entertainment Industry: The Case of Blackpool, 1860–1914," *Literature and History* 1 (1975): 62–78.

29. G. Rogers, "Social and Economic Change on Lancashire Landed Estates during the Nineteenth Century, with special reference to the Clifton Estate, 1832–1916," Ph.D. dissertation, Lancaster University, 1981.

30. William Mangels, *The Outdoor Amusement Industry from Earliest Times to the Present* (New York: Vantage, 1952), 147–48; Kyriazi, *American Amusement Parks*, 30; McCullough, *Good Old Coney Island*, 55; "The Colossal Elephant of Coney Island," *Scientific American* 53 (11 July 1885): 1–21; *History of Coney Island: List and Photographs of Main Attractions* (New York: Boroughs, 1904), 9–10.

31. J. K. Walton, "Municipal Government and the Holiday Industry in Blackpool, 1876–1914," in J. K. Walton and James Walvin eds., *Leisure in Britain 1780–1939* (Manchester University Press, 1983).

32. Walton, "Social Development of Blackpool," chs 6 and 9; Walton, *Blackpool*, 47–49, 87–96.

33. "How the New Yorker Meets All Creation on Surf Avenue," *New York World*, July 14, 1904, P11E; Dana Gatlin, "Amusing America's Millions," *World's Work* 26 (July

1913): 327 McCullough, *Good Old Coney Island*, 251–53; and *New York Times* (hereafter cited as NYT), August 24, 1908, 7.

34. Weinstein, "Nickel Empire," 233. Scenes from *Cakewalk*, a film featuring Coney Island, were reproduced in Ric Burns and Buddy Squires; *Coney Island: A Documentary Film* (Santa Monica, 1991); Sterngass, *First Resorts*, 243–44; and Richard Snow, *Coney Island: A Postcard Journey* (New York: Bright Waters Press, 1984), 20.

35. Immerso, *Coney* Island, 39–41. See Coney Island ads in the *New York Evening Journal*, May 16, 1903; and *New York Sun*, April, May and June 1904, especially May 6, 1904 for Luna Park with claims of being "Twice as large as any amusement resort in the World. More illumination than any spot on Earth. Greater even than St. Louis World's Fair. The Regenerator of Coney Island."

36. Weinstein, "Nickel Empire," 356–59; NYT, September 26, 1903, 8; September 23, 1904, 9; and September 22, 1905, 8; *Brooklyn Daily Eagle*, September 6, 1906, 7; September 19, 1906, 7; and Frederic Thompson, "Amusing People," *Metropolitan Magazine* (July 1906), 601.

37. Martin Daunton, ed., *The Cambridge Urban History of Britain*, Vol. 3 (Cambridge: Cambridge University Press, 2000), part II, chs. 9–13.

38. For full documentation of this theme see Walton, "Social Development of Blackpool," ch. 7; S. V. Ward, "Promoting Holiday Resorts: A Review of Early History to 1921," *Planning History* 10, no. 2 (1991): 7.

39. Peter Marsden, *Lighting the Waves: A Pictorial Social History of Blackpool Illuminations* (Blackpool: Blackpool Corporation, 2004).

40. N. Morgan and A. Pritchard, *Power and Politics at the Seaside* (Exeter: University of Exeter Press, 1999).

41. Walton, "Social Development of Blackpool," 318.

42. Ibid., 356, for Charles Noden's career.

43. Weinstein, "Nickel Empire," 217–23.

44. NYT, May 29, 1899, 2; June 18, 1899, 12; August 21, 1899, 10; April 22, 1909, 10; and May 18, 1909, 18; Immerso, *Coney Island* , 112; and *New York Tribune*, June 30, 1896, 12.

45. NYT, June 24, 1907; June 2 and 19, 1922, 8.

46. Where Blackpool's local authority drew the line, at this stage, was investment in parks and libraries: the beach was regarded as the only public park that was needed, while the library of 1880 was neglected after it proved not to be important in attracting tourists. Walton, "Social Development of Blackpool," ch. 4; Walton, "Municipal Government."

47. Walton, "Social Development of Blackpool," 457–61.

48. J. S. Balmer, *Blackpool, Paris and Sodom* (Blackpool, 1896); Walton, "Social Development of Blackpool," ch. 8.

49. Mark Judd, "Popular Culture and the London Fairs, 1800–1860," in Walton and Walvin, eds., *Leisure in Britain*, 18–20; R. Storch, ed., *Popular Culture and Custom in Nineteenth-Century Britain* (London: Croom Helm, 1982).

50. National Fairground Archive, University of Sheffield, essays by Vanessa Toulmin on the history of British pleasure fairs: www.shef.ac.uk/uni/projects/nfa (accessed December 31, 2003).

51. Lynda Nead, *Victorian Babylon* (New Haven: Yale University Press, 2000).

52. Walton, "Social Development of Blackpool," 314–15.

53. Mangels, *Outdoor Amusement Industry*, 8.

54. Ibid., 10, 17.

55. Frederick Fried, *A Pictorial History of the Carousel* (New York: Barnes, 1964); Mangels, *Outdoor Amusement*, 50–54, 85–88; Judith Adams, *The American Amusement Park Industry: A History of Technology and Thrills* (Boston: Twayne, 1991), 7–18; Immerso, *Coney Island*, 88–89; Vanessa Toulmin's history of fairground technology, National Fairground Archive website, www.shef.ac.uk/uni/projects/nfa

56. In Spain it is still known as a Russian Mountain.

57. Mangels, *Outdoor Amusement*, 37–50, 137, 163. Todd Throgmorton, *Roller Coasters: United States and Canada* (Jefferson, NC: McFarlane, 2000), 1–18, Weinstein, "Nickel Empire," 236. See *Scientific American* pieces: "Looping the Double Loop" 90 (July 8, 1905): 493; "Leap-Frog Railway" 93 (July 8, 1905): 29–30 and especially "Mechanical Joys of Coney Island" 99 (August 15, 1908): 101; and "Mechanical Side of Coney Island" 103 (August 6, 1911): 104–5, 112–13.

58. Vanessa Toulmin, at www.shef.ac.uk/uni/projects/nfa cited above.

59. Walton, "Social Development of Blackpool," 315, 397–400.

60. Laurent Mannoni, *The Great Art of Light and Shadow: Archaelology of the Cinema*, translated and edited by Richard Crangle (Exeter: University of Exeter Press, 2000), 176–190; Mangels, *Outdoor Amusement*, 166

61. Vanessa Toulmin, *Pleasurelands* (Sheffield: National Fairground Archive, 2003); Simon Popple and Vanessa Toulmin, eds., *Visual Delights: Essays on the Popular and Projected Image in the Nineteenth Century* (Trowbridge: Flicks Books, 2000); Vanessa Toulmin, Simon Popple and Patrick Russell (eds.), *The Lost World of Mitchell and Kenyon: Edwardian Britain on Film* (London: British Film Institute, 2004); Mannoni, *The Great Art of Light and Shadow*, 115–35, 268.

62. Rachel Adams, *Sideshow U.S.A.: Freaks and the American Cultural Imagination* (Chicago: University of Chicago Press, 2001), 212–17.

63. Leslie Fiedler, *Freaks: Myths and Images of the Secret Self* (New York: Simon and Schuster, 1978), 53–54.

64. Martin Howard, *Victorian Grotesque* (London: Jupiter Books, 1977); Michael Howell and Peter Ford, *The True History of the Elephant Man* (London: Allison and Busby, 1983).

65. Robert Bogdan, *Freak Show: Presenting Human Oddities for Amusement and Profit* (Chicago: University of Chicago Press, 1988), 44–45, 129, ch. 3, 5.

66. Andrea Dennett, *Weird and Wonderful: The Dime Museum in America* (New York:

New York University Press, 1997), 7, 40 44, 48, ch. 2. See also Benjamin Reiss, *The Showman and the Slave: Race, Death, and Memory in Barnum's America* (Cambridge: Harvard University Press, 2001) and James Cook, *The Arts of Deception: Playing with Fraud in the Age of Barnum* (Cambridge: Harvard University Press, 2001), 73–162.

67. Michael J. Fidler, *Alton Towers: A Gothic Wonderland* (Stafford: M. J. Fisher, 1999), 160.

68. *World's Fair*, July 12–26, 1913.

69. Bogdan, *Freak Show*, 40, 44, 48; C.J.S. Thompson, *History and Lore of Freaks* (London, Senate, 1976 [1930]), 32, 70; Helen Stoddart, *Rings of Desire: Circus History and Representation* (Manchester: Manchester University Press, 2000); National Fairground Archive, Vanessa Toulmin's notes on Margaret Shufflebottom Collection, www.shef.ac.uk/uni/projects/nfa

70. Benjamin Truman, *History of the World's Fair* (New York: Arno Press, 1976 [1893]); Robert Rydell, *All the World's A Fair* (Chicago: University of Chicago Press, 1984), 65–65; David Nasaw, *Going Out: The Rise and Fall of Public Amusements* (New York: Basic Books, 1993), 67–88, chs. 2, 3; Bogdan, *Freak Show*, 50–51; David Burg, *Chicago's White City of 1893* (Lexington: University Press of Kentucky, 1976); Reid Badger, *The Great American Fair* (Chicago, Nelson Hall, 1979); and Robert Rydell, *World of Fairs: The Century-of-Progress Expositions* (Chicago: University of Chicago Press, 1993), chs. 1, 4, and 5.

71. "The Great Wheel at Chicago," *Scientific American* 69 (July 1, 1893): 21 and Adams, *Amusement Park*, 31–35.

72. James Sizer, *Commercialization of Leisure* (Boston: Richard Badger, 1917), 49. Mangels, *Outdoor Amusement*, 32–33.

73. Michele Bogart, *Public Sculpture and the Civic Ideal in New York City, 1890–1930* (Chicago: University of Chicago, 1989), 243.

74. John Glanfield, *Earls Court and Olympia: From Buffalo Bill to the Brits* (Stroud: Sutton, 2003); Paul Greenhalgh, *Ephemeral Vistas* (Manchester: Manchester University Press, 1988), 41–44.

75. Andreas Theve, Mats Wickman, and Ove Hahn, *Folkets Gröna Lund* (Stockholm: Lind & Co., 2003); www.tivoligardens.com (accessed January 3, 2004).

76. Kyriazi, *American Amusement Parks*, 34–42.

77. Kyriazi, *American Amusement Parks*, 47–57; *New York World*, July 20, 1902, Special Section, 2; Quotation from Reginald Kauffman, "Why is Coney," *Hampton's Magazine* 23 (August 1909): 224.

78. NYT, July 29, 1907, 1; and July 30, 1902, 1–2.

79. NYT, December 29, 1907, 7; and August 16 1908, X6.

80. Adams, *American Amusement Park*, 20–28; and F.D. Millet, "The Designers of the Fair," *Harpers' Monthly Magazine* 85 (November 1892): 878.

81. Oliver Pilat and Jo Ranson, *Sodom by the Sea, An Affectionate History of Coney Island* (Garden City, NY: Doubleday, 1941), 144–46; Woody Register, *The Kid of Coney Island:*

Fred Thompson and the Rise of American Amusements (New York: Oxford University Press, 2001), 92, 132–33; *New York World*, July 25, 1909, 24.

82. On opening day of Luna Park in 1903, gate admission was ten cents. Entrance to all the attractions would have cost $1.95, a sum almost equal to a day's wage for manual workers. Mangels, *Outdoor Amusement*, 46–47; Jeffrey Stanton, "Luna Park" (1998), 7–8, http://naid.sppsr.ucla.edu/coneyisland/histart.htm.

83. Adams, *Amusement Park Industry*, 48. Register; *Kid of Coney Island*, 121; *New York Herald* May 6, 1906, part 3, 14 .

84. NYT, May 7, 1905, 9; June 11, 1905, 9; Register, *Kid of Coney Island*, 121; Stanton, "Luna Park," 6–22; and Immerso, *Coney*, 71.

85. Register, *Kid of Coney Island*, 141; Stanton, "Luna Park," 22–23.

86. 1904 newspaper guide *Brooklyn Daily Eagle*, May 8, 1904; and Weinstein, "Nickel Empire," 249.

87. Barr Ferree, "The New Popular Resort Architecture, Dreamland, Coney Island," *Architects' and Builders' Magazine*, 36 (August 1904): 499; Weinstein, "Nickel Empire," 220–23.

88. *History of Coney Island*, 12, 22; Rem Koolhaas, *Delirious New York: A Retroactive Manifesto for Manhattan* (New York: Monacelli Press, 1994), 55.

89. *Scientific American*, July 5, 1905, 29–30; NYT, May 22, 1904, 9; Kyriazi, *American Amusement Parks*, 67–70; Jeffrey Stanton, "Coney Island—Dreamland," April 1998, 1–11, http://naid.sppsr.ucla.edu/coneyisland/histart.htm.

90. Stanton, "Coney Island—Dreamland," 1–22; *Brooklyn Daily Eagle* May 7, 1911 for Dreamland owners' disappointment in failing to attract a middle-class crowd.

91. Walton, "Social Development of Blackpool," 332.

92. Ibid., 87, 326–7; Peter Bennett, *A Century of Fun* (Blackpool: Blackpool Pleasure Beach, 1996), 16–17.

93. Walton, "Social Development of Blackpool," 327; Bennett, *Century of Fun*, 12–14.

94. Bennett, *Century of Fun*, 18.

95. Ibid., 18–25; Walton, "Social Development of Blackpool," 328–29; Pleasure Beach Archive, folders 6, 9, and 41.

96. Walton, "Social Development of Blackpool," 87–89; Bennett, *Century of Fun*, 18–36.

97. Pilat and Ranson, *Sodom by the Sea*, 98–99.

98. Walton, "Social Development of Blackpool," ch. 6.

99. Elmer Blaney Harris, "Day of Rest at Coney Island," *Everybody's Magazine*, 19 (July 1908): 34; NYT, July 30, 1907, 1–2; May 5, 1925, S1.

100. Kyriazi, *American Amusement Parks*. 79–81

101. Frederic Thompson, "The Summer Show," *Independent* 62 (July 6, 1907): 1463; *New York World*, 4 July 1897, 32.

102. Walton, "Social Development of Blackpool," ch. 8; F.M.L. Thompson, *The Rise of Respectable Society* (London: Penguin, 1988).

103. Weinstein, "Nickel Empire," 62–65; Photo of Oriental Hotel, Brooklyn Historical Society, V1974.22.4. 157 (1900); *Coney Island and the Jews*, 20–30; Sterngass, *First Resorts*, 88–95; Immerso, *Coney*, 34.

104. Sterngass, *First Resorts*, 230–34; Brighton Beach Hotel photos, Brooklyn Historical Society, v 1974. 22.5. 140 and 142; Lyman Weeks, *The American Turf* (New York, 1898), 471–75; Walter Vosburgh, *Racing in America, 1866–1921* (New York: Jockey Club, 1922), 26–31; Weinstein, "Nickel Empire," 74–80. For details of gambling restrictions, see NYT, June 12, 1908; July 3, 1908; May 27, 1910; and September 2, 1910.

105. Walton, "Social Development of Blackpool," ch. 1; J. K. Walton, *The Blackpool Landlady: A Social History* (Manchester: Manchester University Press, 1978), ch. 3–5; Walton, *Blackpool*, ch. 4; David Cannadine, ed., *Patricians, Power and Politics in Nineteenth-Century Towns* (Leicester: Leicester University Press, 1982); Arthur Laycock, *Warren of Manchester* (London: Simpkin, Marshall & Co, 1906); Stanley Houghton, *Hindle Wakes* (London: Sidgwick & Jackson, 1912).

106. Weinstein, "Nickel Empire," 129, 133, 148–50; William Allen, "The Opportunities at Coney Island," *Charities* 12 (June 4, 1904): 582; Robert Smith, *Brooklyn at Play* (New York: Revisionist Press, 1977), 118.

107. Weinstein, "Nickel Empire," 194; Kryriazi, *American Amusement Parks*, 26.

108. Sterngass, *First Resorts*, 105–7; David Nasaw, *Going Out*, ch. 5.

109. *New York World*, July 21, 1912, 5N.

110. Maurice G. Hope, *Castles in the Sand: the Story of New Brighton* (Ormskirk: G.W. and A. Hesketh, 1982); J. K. Walton, *The British Seaside: Holidays and Resorts in the Twentieth Century* (Manchester: Manchester University Press, 2000), 188.

111. E. J. Hobsbawm, *Worlds of Labour* (London: Weidenfeld, 1984); Richard Hoggart, *The Uses of Literacy* (London: Chatto and Windus, 1957), for the latter days of this way of life in industrial Yorkshire.

2. The Industrial Saturnalia and the Playful Crowd

1. Chris Waters, *British Socialists and the Politics of Popular Culture, 1884–1914* (Manchester: Manchester University Press, 1990); Harvey Taylor, *A Claim on the Countryside* (Keele: Keele University Press, 1997); Roy Rosenzweig, *Eight Hours for What We Will* (Cambridge: Cambridge University Press, 1983); Peter Bailey, *Leisure and Class in Victorian England* (London: Routledge, 1978).

2. R. W. Malcolmson, *Popular Recreations in English Society, 1700–1850* (Cambridge: Cambridge University Press, 1973); Douglas Reid, "The Decline of St Monday 1760–1860," *Past and Present* 71 (1976): 76–101; David Underdown, *Revel, Riot and Rebellion: Popular Politics in England, 1603–1660* (Oxford: Clarendon Press, 1985); Eileen and Stephen Yeo, eds., *Popular Culture and Class Conflict: Explorations in the History of Labour and Leisure, 1590–1914* (Brighton: Harvester, 1981).

3. Harold Perkin, *The Structured Crowd* (London: Routledge, 1981).

4. The souvenir program of the 1923 Carnival laid the optimistic claim to an international public: "There are people here from everywhere: jovial Northerners, surprised Southerners, sightseeing Americans, volatile visitors from the Continent. " John Walton, "Social Development of Blackpool" Ph.D. thesis, Lancaster University, 1974, 267, table 5.4; *Blackpool Carnival: Official Souvenir Programme, June 9th to June 16th (inclusive), 1923*, in British Library 103609 47; and see also *Blackpool: Britain's Playground* (Blackpool: Blackpool Corporation, 1928), 24; James Laver, "Blackpool," in Y. Cloud, ed., *Beside the Seaside* (London: Bodley Head, 2nd ed., 1938), 176.

5. Michael Immerso, *Coney Island: The People's Playground* (New Brunswick: Rutgers University Press, 2002), 155–56; Charles Denson, *Coney Island: Lost and Found* (Berkeley: Ten Speed Press, 2002), ch. 2; Walton, "Social Development," ch. 5.

6. Immerso, *Coney Island*, 143, 149.

7. Denson, *Coney Island*, 84; Joseph Heller, *Now and Then* (London: Pocket Books, 1998), 32–33, 44; H. S. Ashbee, "A Sunday at Coney Island" (London, 1882: reprinted from *Temple Bar*), 6; Photos of Brooklyn Historical Society, V1974.22.6.33; V1974.22.6.42; V197419.1.27.

8. Immerso, *Coney Island*, 150–55; Denson, *Coney Island*, 65, 274; Heller, *Now and Then*, 51.

9. Mark Judd, "Popular Culture and the London Fairs, 1800–1860," in John K. Walton and James Walvin, eds., *Leisure in Britain, 1780-1939* (Manchester: Manchester University Press, 1983), 24–25.

10. Peter Burke, *Popular Culture in Early Modern Europe* (New York: Harper, 1978), 178–204; Mikhail Bakhtin, *Rabelais and His World* (Bloomington, IN: Indiana University Press, 1984), ch. 1.

11. Adrian Henstock, *Early Victorian Country Town* (Ashbourne: Ashbourne Local History Group, 1978); Lyn Murfin, *Popular Leisure in the Lake Counties* (Manchester: Manchester University Press, 1990), 110–14; Stephen Nissenbaum, *The Battle for Christmas* (New York: Knopf, 1996), 5-11.

12. Martin Hewitt, ed., *Unrespectable Recreations* (Leeds: Leeds Centre for Victorian Studies, 2001); Mike Huggins, *Flat Racing and British Society, 1790–1914* (London: Frank Cass, 1999).

13. These include the Blackpool Pleasure Beach Archives, Photographic Collection, (the authors thank Ted Lightbown for his generous help in providing access to this material); National Fairground Archive, Sheffield, Mitchell and Kenyon Collection, Reels 200, 201, 203, 205; and North West Film Archive, Manchester, Accession Nos. 1822 (1930s), 175 (1934), 726 (1929), 152 (1934), 149 (1924), 166 (1924), 1169 (1928), 1166 (1933), 754 (1930s).

14. María Antonia Paz has taken this approach with Madrid newsreel film from before the Spanish Civil War, paying particular attention to headgear and footwear as status mark-

ers, as well as male facial hair and smoking habits. She classifies by age, gender, and social class. The status markers she uses for this latter purpose are based on clothing, with a strong emphasis on hats (whether worn and of what sort), shoes, spectacles and (for men) tie, coat, and mustache. María Antonia Paz, "Cine para la Historia Urbana," *Historia Contemporánea* 22 (2001): 179–213.

15. Patrick Joyce, *Visions of the People: Industrial England and the Question of Class, 1840–1914* (Cambridge: Cambridge University Press, 1991), 167–69: Allen Clarke, *The Effects of the Factory System* (Littleborough, 1985: first published 1899).

16. W. K. Haselden, cartoon in *Daily Mirror* August 3, 1909, Centre for the Study of Cartoons and Caricature, University of Kent, WH 2863.

17. Arthur Laycock, *Warren of Manchester* (London: Simpkin Marshall, 1906), 103.

18. George Beaumont, *T'Trip to Blackpool: a Yorkshire Dialect Comedy in One Act* (Idle: Watmough, 1933).

19. Dave Russell, *Football and the English* (Preston: Carnegie, 1997).

20. Photos of the Bowery, Brooklyn Historical Society, V1973.5.2726 (1903); V1973.4.684 (1910); V1972.1.1106 (1900); Frank Staley, *Staley's Views of Coney Island* (New York: Charles Frances, 1908) np; *New York World*, July 20, 1902, Special Section, 2; John Kasson, *Amusing the Million* (New York: Hill and Wang, 1978).

21. For more clearly "structured" crowds in which people knew their place and generally kept to it, J. K. Walton, "Policing the Alameda," in S. Gunn and R. Morris, eds., *Identities in Space* (Aldershot: Ashgate, 2001), 228–41.

22. *Blackpool: Britain's Playground* (Blackpool: Blackpool Corporation, 1928), 24.

23. Ad in *Brooklyn Daily Eagle*, May 27, 1911; Frederic Thompson, "Amusing the Million," *Everybody's Magazine* 19 (September 1908): 386; and Woody Register, *Kid of Coney Island: Fred Thompson and the Rise of American Amusements* (New York: Oxford University Press, 2001), 97.

24. Alfred Rumble, *Coney Island Frolics: How New York's Gay Girls and Jolly Boys Enjoy Themselves by the Sea* (New York: R. K. Fox, 1883), 37; and *New York Sun*, July 16, 1877, cited in Stephen Weinstein, "The Nickel Empire, Coney Island and the Creation of Urban Seaside Resorts in the United States," Ph.D. dissertation, Columbia University, 1984, 180.

25. Tom Treddlehoyle, "A Leeds Loiner's Leap inta Luv at Blackpool," *T'Pogmoor Olmenack an Bairnsla Foaks Yearly Jottings* (Barnsley, 1904), 28; "On Blackpool Shore," *John Hartley's Clock Almanack* (Wakefield, 1905), 42–3; *Teddy Ashton's Gradely Guide to Blackpool* (4th ed., Blackpool, 1908), 21; Gary Cross, ed., *Worktowners at Blackpool: Mass-Observation and Popular Leisure in the 1930s* (London: Routledge, 1990), 180–91.

26. Laver, "Blackpool," 155.

27. John Kasson, *Amusing the Million* (New York: Hill and Wang, 1978), 45–49; Register, *Kid of Coney Island*, 95; and Kathy Peiss, *Cheap Amusements: Working Women and Lei-*

sure in Turn-of-the-Century New York (Philadelphia: Temple University Press, 1986), 115–38.

28. Elmer Harris, "Day of Rest at Coney Island," *Everybody's Magazine* 19 (July 1908): 28–34.

29. Rollin Hartt, "The Amusement Park," *Atlantic Monthly* 99 (May 1907): 676–77.

30. Laycock, *Warren of Manchester* ; Walton, *Blackpool*, 72; Cross, *Worktowners at Blackpool*, 180–91.

31. Rob Shields, *Places on the Margin* (London: Routledge, 1991).

32. Ab-o'-th-'Yate, *Adventures at Blackpool* (Manchester: John Heywood, 1872). This stereotype was still strong nine years later: Ab-o'-th'-Yate, *Drop't on at Blackpool* (Manchester: Abel Heywood, 1881).

33. North West Film Archive, Accession 149; John Walton, *Blackpool* (Edinburgh: Edinburgh University Press, 1998), 123–24; Steve Humphries, *A Secret World of Sex* (London: Sidgwick & Jackson, 1988), 165–92.

34. King Vidor, *The Crowd* (1928, MGM, UA VCR, 1989).

35. Frank Tilsley, *Pleasure Beach* (London: Collins, 1944); J. L. Hodson, *Carnival at Blackport* (London: Victor Gollancz, 1937).

36. Photo collection of the Brooklyn Historical Society, V19174, 22. 6. 40; V1974.19.1.4; V1974.22.6.27; V1986.25.1.28; V1973.4.774; V1986.24.1.9; V1974.22.6.39; V1975.5.12.41.

37. E. V. Lucas, *Roving East and Roving West* (London: Methuen, 1921), 111.

38. This segregation of children from the full-size adult pleasures of the amusement park proper is confirmed by a home movie, which shows young children riding a miniature Captive Flying Machine and carousel, with some pre-teens joining in on the miniature roller coaster. *Blackpool: Britain's Playground*, 31; North West Film Archive, Accession 726; Immerso, *Coney Island*, 142; Lightbown, "Buildings and Rides," Pleasure Beach Archive.

39. "Toy Maker for Grown-Ups," *New York Journal*, May 5, 1916, 22; Elmer Harris, "The Day of Rest at Coney Island," *Everybody's Magazine* 19 (July 1908): 24. Register, *Kid of Coney Island*, 11 argues that Luna Park was invented, "for middle-class adults, not for the poor, or children, or families." We would qualify his class claim, for it reached blue-collar wage earners as well, but it is still a well-taken point. See also Gail Bederman, *Manliness and Civilization: A Cultural History of Gender and Race in the United States, 1880–1917* (Chicago: University of Chicago Press, 1995), 95–99; and William Gleason, *The Leisure Ethic: Work and Play in American Literature, 1984–1940* (Palo Alto: Stanford University Press, 1999), 100–14.

40. Thompson, "Amusing the Million," 385–87; Frederic Thompson, "Amusing People," *Metropolitan Magazine* (July 106) 602, 603; Thompson, "The Summer Show," *Independent* 62 (July 6, 1907): 1461.

41. Edward Tilyou, "Human Nature with the Brakes Off—Or: Why the Schoolma'am Walked into the Sea," *American Magazine* 94 (July 1922): 19, 92; Lindsey Denison,

"The Biggest Playground in the World," *Munsey's Magazine*, August 1905, 557–559 makes the same point. See also Colin Campbell, *The Romantic Ethic and the Spirit of Modern Consumerism* (Oxford: Blackwell, 1987), 77–95 .

42. Register, *Kid of Coney Island*, 12, 16; Thompson, "Summer Show," 1462; Jon Sterngass, *First Resorts: Pursuing Pleasure at Saratoga Springs, Newport, and Coney Island* (Baltimore: Johns Hopkins University Press, 2001), 272–73

43. Frederic Thompson, "Amusing the Million," 378–379; Thompson, "Amusement Architecture," *Architectural Review* 16, 7 (July 1909): 87–89; Michele Bogart, *Public Sculpture and the Civic Ideal in New York City, 1890–1930* (Chicago: University of Chicago Press, 1989), 248, 250–57.

44. *Harper's Weekly* 35 (September 12, 1891): 694. The bizarre Elephant Hotel (standing between 1884 and 1896) is described in Clay Lancaster, *Architectural Follies in America* (Rutland, VT: Charles Tuttle, 1960), 194–96.

45. Thompson, "Amusement Architecture," 88; Thompson, "The Summer Show," 1461; Kasson, *Amusing the Million*, 63; Rem Koolhaas, *Delirious New York.: A Retroactive Manifesto for Manhattan* (New York: Monacelli Press, 1994).

46. Bogart, *Public Sculpture and the Civic Ideal*, 243. On the sublimity of electric lighting see David Nye, *Electrifying America: Social Meanings of a New Technology, 1880–1940* (Cambridge: MIT Press, 1990).

47. Tony Bennett, "'Hegemony, Ideology, Pleasure—Blackpool," in Bennett et al., eds., *Popular Culture and Social Change* (Milton Keynes: Open University Press, 1986), ch. 7.

48. John K. Walton, *Blackpool Landlady: A Social History* (Manchester: Manchester University Press, 1978), ch. 3; Bennett, *Century of Fun*; Lynne F. K. Pearson, *The People's Palaces: The Story of the Seaside Pleasure Buildings of 1870–1914* (Buckingham: Barracuda, 1991).

49. Thompson, "Amusing the Million," 385; Thompson, "The Summer Show," 146.

50. Thompson anticipated an argument—that desires no longer needed to be controlled or sublimated if they were diffused—that Martha Wolfenstein would articulate in "Fun Morality: An Analysis of Recent American Child-training Literature," in Margaret Mead and Martha Wolfenstein, eds., *Childhood in Contemporary Cultures* (Chicago: University of Chicago Press, 1955), 169–74.

51. Laver, "Blackpool," 170–71.

52. Kasson, *Amusing the Million*, 59, 60; Edwin Slosson, "Amusement Business," *Independent*, 57 (July 21, 1904): 136; *History of Coney Island: Lists of Photographs by Main Attractions* (New York: Burroughs, 1904), 36–37; *New York World*, July 20, 1902, Sp. Sect., 2; and Judith Adams, *The American Amusement Park Industry: A History of Technology and Thrills* (Boston: Twayne, 1991), 45.

53. "Mechanical Joys of Coney Island," *Scientific American*, August 15, 1908, 109.

54. Adams, *American Amusement Park Industry* , 50; Kasson, *Amusing the Million*, 76.

55. Hartt, "The Amusement Park," 675; *History of Coney Island*, 16.

56. *Fun on the Pleasure Beach wi' Sally an' Sam, Jimmy an' Jane Ann, Towd by Sally Hersel*

(Blackpool: Laycock & Co., 1909). Unpaginated. See also, for example, Frank Tilsley, *Pleasure Beach* (London: Collins, 1944), 33.

57. John Urry, *The Tourist Gaze* (London: Sage, 1990).

58. See images of the Human Roulette and other such rides in "To Heaven by Subway," *Fortune* 18 (Aug. 1938); 61–68, 102–106; Gary Kyriazi, *The Great American Amusement Parks* (Secaucus, N.J.: Citadel Press, 1976), 89; Jeffrey Stanton, "Coney Island—Second Steeplechase, 1908–1964," May 1999, 6, http://naid.sppsr.ucla.edu/coneyisland/histart.htm.

59. Urry, *The Tourist Gaze* and especially *Consuming Places* (London: Sage, 1995), in which he elaborates additional versions of this concept.

60. Kasson, *Amusing the Million*, 42–43; Robert Dabney, "Gay Coney Island is a Jolly Nice Place," *New York World*, September 21, 1912, N 5; Slosson, "Amusement Business," 136, 139.

61. Immerso, *Coney Island*, 137–47; Oliver Pilat and Jo Ranson, *Sodom by the Sea, An Affectionate History of Coney Island* (Garden City, NY: Doubleday, 1941), 220–25; Todd Throgmorton, *Roller Coasters: United States and Canada* (Jefferson, NC: McFarland, 2000), 13–16.

62. Kasson, *Amusing the Million*, 70; William Mangels, *The Outdoor Amusement Industry from Earliest Times to the Present* (New York: Vantage, 1952), 165; Daniel Boorstin, *The Image: A Guide to Pseudo Events in America* (New York: Harper & Row, 1961); Dana Gatlin, "Amusing America's Millions," *World's Work* 26 (July 1913), 228.

63. *History of Coney Island*, 22, 14 and *New York World*, 20 July 1902, Sp. Sect., 2.

64. *History of Coney Island*, 12; Koolhas, *Delirious New York*, 49; Thompson, "Amusing People," 605; Slosson, "Amusement Business," 136, 139; Jeffrey Stanton, "Coney Island—Dreamland," April 1998, 1–22, http://naid.sppsr.ucla.edu/coneyisland/histart.htm; Hartt, "The Amusement Park," 673.

65. Quotations from Julian Hawthorne, "Some Novelties at Buffalo Fair," *Cosmopolitan* 31 (Sept 1901): 490–91; and a promotional brochure *Pan-American Exposition* (Buffalo, 1901), 29; Register, *Kid of Coney Island*, 71, 74–76; Albert Paine, "The New Coney Island," *Century* 68 (Aug. 1904): 544; *History of Coney Island*, 12–13; Jeffery Stanton, "Coney Island—Luna Park," May 1998, 1–2, 16, http://naid.sppsr.ucla.edu/coneyisland/ histart.htm.

66. Lucy Gillman, "Coney Island," *New York History* 3, 36 (July 1955): 280–81; Hartt, "The Amusement Park," 675–76.

67. Peter Bennett, *A Century of Fun* (Blackpool: Blackpool Pleasure Beach, 1996), 21–25, 30–35.

68. Helen Duckham and Baron F. Duckham, *Great Pit Disasters: Great Britain, 1700 to the Present* (Newton Abbot: David and Charles, 1973).

69. Callum Brown, *The Death of Christian Britain* (London: Routledge, 2000); Michael Wheeler, *Heaven, Hell and the Victorians* (Cambridge: Cambridge University Press, 1994); John Wigley, *The Rise and Fall of the Victorian Sunday* (Manchester: Manches-

ter University Press, 1980); Cross, *Worktowners*, 200; Walton, "Social Development of Blackpool," chs. 8 and 9.

70. Slosson, "Amusement Business," 138.

71. Robert Bogdan, *Freak Show: Presenting Human Oddities for Amusement and Profit* (Chicago: University of Chicago Press, 1988), 134–42, 158–60; *History of Coney Island*, 12, 24; Jeffrey Stanton, "Coney Island-Freaks," 1997, http://naid.sppsr.ucla.edu/coneyisland/histart.htm; Pilat and Ranson, *Sodom by the Sea*, 176–87; Edo McCullough, *Good Old Coney Island* (New York: Scribner's, 1957), 258–267; *New York Times* (hereafter cited as NYT), July 8, 1928, 110; Andrea Dennett, *Weird and Wonderful: The Dime Museum in America* (New York: New York University Press, 1997), 131–32; NYT, May 23, 1904, 5; and NYT, April 29, 1926, 48.

72. Kyriazi, *American Amusement Parks*, 72–74; Pilat and Ranson, *Sodom by the Sea*, 200–207; NYT, July 24, 1929, 14.

73. Public Record Office, Kew, HO45/16275/655652, September 1933; Ben Brierley, *The Nettlecrabs at Blackpool* (Manchester: Abel Heywood, 1886), 13–14; Rose Collis, *Colonel Barker's Monstrous Regiment* (London: Virago, 2001), 206–16; Cross, *Worktowners at Blackpool*, 200; Owen Davies, *Witchcraft, Magic and Culture 1736–1951* (Manchester: Manchester University Press, 1999), 253–57; Walton, *Blackpool*, 125–26.

74. Cross, *Worktowners at Blackpool*, 110–113, 117–124.

75. Leslie Fiedler, *Freaks: Myths and Images of the Secret Self* (New York: Simon and Schuster, 1978), 24–36; James Cook, *The Arts of Deception: Playing with Fraud in the Age of Barnum* (Cambridge: Harvard University Press, 2001), 73; Rachael Adams, *Sideshow U.S.A.: Freaks and the American Cultural Imagination* (University of Chicago Press, 2001), 7, 9.

76. Adams, *Sideshow*, 112–118; Bogdan, *Freak Show*, 112, 233.

77. Fielder, *Freaks*, ch. 6; C.J.S. Thompson, *History and Lore of Freaks* (London, Senate, 1976 [1930]), 88, 191, 207–8; Bogdan, *Freak Show*, 200–204, 226–228;.

78. www.neonatology.org(classics)lancet.earls.html accessed January 4, 2004.

79. Immerso, *Coney Island*, 68; and especially Pilat and Ranson, *Sodom by the Sea*, 191–200.

3. The Crowd and Its Critics

1. Maxim Gorky, "Boredom," *Independent* 63 (8 July 1907): 310–311, 315; Rem Koolhaas, *Delirious New York: a Retroactive Manifesto for Manhattan* (New York: Monacelli Press, 1994), 68.

2. William Dean Howells, "The Waters of Blackpool," *North American Review* (December 1911): 875.

3. Harvey Taylor, *A Claim on the Countryside* (Edinburgh: Keele University Press, 1997), ch. 6; Chris Waters, *British Socialists and the Politics of Popular Culture 1884–1914* (Manchester: Manchester University Press, 1990), 37–38.

4. Gustave Le Bon, *The Crowd, A Study of the Popular Mind* (New York: Ballantine Books, 1969). Note also Robert A. Nye, *The Origins of Crowd Psychology: Gustave Le Bon and the Crisis of Mass Democracy in the Third Republic* (Beverly Hills: Sage, 1975); Susanna Barrows, *Distorting Mirrors: Visions of the Crowd in Late Nineteenth-Century France* (New Haven: Yale University Press, 1981).

5. George Cutten, *The Threat of Leisure* (New Haven: Yale University Press, 1926), 89, 99, 17; Frank R. Leavis and Denys Thompson, *Culture and Environment: The Training of Critical Awareness* (1933, reprinted: London, Chatto & Windus, 1962), 30–40, and 47; Rollin Hartt, "The Amusement Park," *Atlantic Monthly* 99 (May 1907): 672.

6. José Ortega y Gasset, *The Revolt of the Masses* (1930, reprinted: New York: Norton, 1957), 7–8 and ch. 3; Oswald Spengler, *The Decline of the West* (1926–28, reprinted: New York, Oxford University Press, 1991); and Leonard Woolf, *Barbarians at the Gate* (London: V. Gollancz, 1939).

7. Sigmund Freud, *Group Psychology and the Analysis of the Ego* (1922, reprinted: New York: Norton, 1975), 5–22, 82, and 99–100.

8. Sigmund Freud, *Beyond the Pleasure Principle* (1920: reprinted: New York: Liveright, 1950), 4–5, 47, and 68.

9. Bruce Bliven, "Coney Island for Battered Souls," *New Republic* 28 (November 23, 1921): 374.

10. Richard Edwards, *Popular Amusements* (New York: Association Press, 1915), 107, 133. A similar point of view is expressed by the British observer Constance Harris, *The Use of Leisure in Bethnal Green* (London: Lindsey Press, 1927), 43.

11. Robert and Helen Lynd, *Middletown* (New York: Harcourt, Brace and Company, 1929), 251–57; George Lundberg et. al., *Leisure, A Suburban Study* (New York: Columbia University Press, 1934), 15–24, 59–72 and 142–160.

12. Bliven, "Coney Island for Battered Souls," 374.

13. Ibid.; Lindsay Denison, "The Biggest Playground in the World," *Munsey's Magazine* (August 1905): 557–59; Maurice Davie, *Problems of City Life* (New York: Wiley, 1932), 579.

14. Edward Ross, *Social Psychology* (New York: Macmillan, 1908), 54–56 cited in John F. Kasson, *Amusing the Million* (New York: Hill and Wang, 1978), 97; James Huneker, *New Cosmopolis: A Book of Images* (New York: Scribner's, 1915), 154, 156.

15. Good examples are: Frank.R. Leavis, *Mass Civilization and Minority Culture* (Cambridge: Minority Press, 1930); Clive Bell, *Civilization, An Essay* (London: Chatto &Windus, 1928); and Lewis Mumford, *Sticks and Stones* (New York: Norton, 1924). An interesting analysis of the problem is Andrew Ross, *No Respect: Intellectuals and Popular Culture* (London: Routledge, 1989).

16. Louise More, *Wage-Earners' Budgets: A Study of Standards and Cost of Living in New York City* (New York: Henry Holt, 1907), 170–180; A. Clark and Edith Wyatt, *Making Both Ends Meet: The Income and Outlay of New York City Working Girls* (New York: Macmil-

lan, 1911), 10; Peter Roberts, "Immigrant Wage-Earners," in Paul Kellogg, ed., *Wage-Earning Pittsburgh* (New York, Survey Associates, 1914), 50.

17. *Brooklyn Daily Eagle*, June 12, 1899 cited in Stephen Weinstein, "The Nickel Empire: Coney Island and the Creation of Urban Seaside Resorts in the United States," Ph.D. dissertation, Columbia University, 1984, 221–222.

18. Julian Ralph, "Coney Island," *Scribner's Magazine* 20 (July 1896): 17; William Sydney Porter, *The Complete Works of O. Henry* (New York: Doubleday, 1970), 71; "Coney Island," *New York World*, July 20, 1902, Special Section, 2; William R. Taylor, *In Pursuit of Gotham: Culture and Commerce in New York* (New York: Oxford University Press, 1992), 86–87, 109–111; James Huneker, *New Cosmopolis: A Book of Images* (New York: Scribner's, 1915), 168; *John Sloan's New York Scene*, ed. Bruce St. John (New York: Harper and Row, 1965), 141; Richard Le Gallienne, "Human Need for Coney Island," *Cosmopolitan* 39 (July 1905): 243, 245.

19. Lucas was apparently unaware that such performances *were* permitted in England, and the comparison does not convince; but the positive view of Coney Island is nevertheless arresting. H. S. Ashbee, "A Sunday at Coney Island" (London, 1882, reprinted from *Temple Bar*, copy in British Library), 6; E. V. Lucas, *Roving East and Roving West* (London: Methuen, 1921), 110–11.

20. Albert Paine, "The New Coney Island," *Century* 68 (August 1904): 542, 547, 537–47; Kasson, *Amusing the Million*, 91–94; Reginald Marsh, *Reginald Marsh: Coney Island* (Fort Wayne, IN: Fort Wayne Museum of Art, 1991).

21. Robert Neal, "New York's City of Play," *World of To-day* 11 (August 1906), 822.

22. Simon Patten, *New Basis of Civilization* (New York, Macmillan, 1907), 123.

23. Patten, *New Basis*, 125; and Daniel Fox, *The Discovery of Abundance: Simon N. Patten and the Transformation of Social Theory* (Ithaca, NY: Cornell University Press, 1967), 73–74.

24. James Sizer, *Commercialization of Leisure* (Boston: Richard Badger, 1917), 54, 66, 80–81; Patten, *New Basis for Civilization* , 128–29, 131–32.

25. J. K. Walton, "The Social Development of Blackpool 1788–1914," Ph.D. dissertation, Lancaster University, 1974, 312, 382, 423, 432–33; J. M. Golby and A. W. Purdue, *The Civilisation of the Crowd: Popular Culture in England 1750–1900*, second edition (Stroud, England: Sutton, 1999), 186–88.

26. Walton, "Social Development of Blackpool," 433–5.

27. *Blackpool 1897* (Blackpool: Corporation, 1897), 17, 29.

28. Fitton's verse is as follows: "When yo're full up wi' yo'r holiday potion,/An' wobble abeawt wi' a W motion,/Yo' then winno' think o' yo'r Nancy, or Nellies,/But bluster, an' swagger, an' fancy yo're fellies/Eh, Torry, an' Dicky, an' Harry, an' Billy,/Dunno' do that—it's so awfully silly!/That winno' do, so con this bi yo're motto, folks:/Struttin' abeawt on a prom wi' a lot o' folks/Skittin' an' chaffin', /An' yellin' an' laughin',/Cooin' and croonin',/An' smilin' an' spoonin./Bo'dyedded mashers, an' others wi' toppin' on,/Flirtin', and' doin' yo're best to be "coppin' on,"/Still if yo'r happy I'll let yo' a-be,/

Happen yo'r reet, but it winno' suit me." *Cotton Factory Times*, 5 August 1910, with thanks to Jim Pressley for this reference.

29. Arthur Laycock, *Warren of Manchester* (London: Simpkin Marshall, 1906), 92–103.

30. Allen Clarke, *The Effects of the Factory System* (first published 1899, reprinted Littleborough: George Kelsall, 1985).

31. *Blackpool Times*, May 27, 1904.

32. *Blackpool Official Guide 1924: The Home of Health, Pleasure, Fun and Fancy* (Blackpool: Corporation, 1924), 22, 34; *Blackpool: Britain's Playground* (Blackpool: Corporation, 1928), 21, 23.

33. T. H. Mawson, *The Life and Work of an English Landscape Architect* (London, n.d.), 344; and see also Helen Meller, *European Cities 1890s–1930s* (Chichester: John Wiley, 2001), ch. 5.

34. *Daily Dispatch*, August 3–7, 1934.

35. For William Holt himself, see his autobiography *I Haven't Unpacked* (London: G. G. Harrap, 1939).

36. Frank Tilsley, *Pleasure Beach* (London: Collins, 1944), 7, 19, 31–35; D. L. Murray, *Leading Lady* (London, 1947), 242.

37. Ivor Brown, *The Heart of England* (London: Batsford, 1935), 69, 20.

38. C. Delise Burns, *Leisure in the Modern World* (New York: Century, 1932), 3, 17–21, 63, 72, 77, 83, 91, 255, and 234. See also John Hammond, *The Growth of Common Enjoyment* (Oxford: Oxford University Press, 1933).

39. Gary Cross ed., *Worktowners at Blackpool* (London: Routledge, 1990), 8. See also P. J. Gurney, "'Intersex' and 'Dirty Girls': Mass-Observation and Working-Class Sexuality in England in the 1930s," *Journal of the History of Sexuality* 8 (1997): 256–90; Anthony Burgess, *Little Wilson and Big God* (Harmondsworth: Penguin, 1987), 127.

40. Harvey Taylor, *A Claim on the Countryside*, 194–95; *Labour Leader*, September 2, 1904; Waters, *British Socialists*, 37–38.

41. Taylor, *Claim on the Countryside*, 203–6; Waters, *British Socialists*, 75–76.

42. J. B. Priestley, *English Journey* (London: William Heinemann, 1934), 267.

43. Walter Greenwood, *Lancashire* (London: Robert Hale, 1951).

44. Huneker, *New Cosmopolis*, 154, 156; and Rollin Hartt, *The People at Play: Excursions in the Humor and Philosophy of Popular Amusements* (Boston: Houghton Mifflin, 1909), 53–54.

45. R. S. Neale, *Bath, 1680–1850* (London: Routledge, 1981); Peter Borsay, *The Image of Georgian Bath* (Oxford: Oxford University Press, 2000); Phyllis Hembry, *The English Spa, 1560–1815* (London: Athlone, 1991); John K. Walton, *The English Seaside Resort: A Social History 1750–1914* (Leicester: Leicester University Press, 1983); Alain Corbin, *The Lure of the Sea* (Cambridge: Polity, 1994); Hartmut Berghoff et al., eds., *The Making of Modern Tourism* (Basingstoke: Palgrave, 2002).

46. Perceval Reniers, *The Springs of Virginia: Life, Love and Death at the Waters, 1775–1900* (Chapel Hill: University of North Carolina Press, 1984), 70–88; George Waller, *Saratoga: Saga of an Impious Era* (Englewood Cliffs: Prentice Hall, 1966), 56–108; William

Dean Howells, *Literature and Life* (New York: Harper and Brothers, 1902), 172; Jon Sterngass, *First Resorts: Pursuing Pleasure at Saratoga Springs, Newport, and Coney Island* (Baltimore: Johns Hopkins University Press, 2001), 241; Weinstein, "Nickel Empire," 208–209; Cindy S. Aron, *Working at Play: A History of Vacations in the United States* (New York: Oxford University Press, 1999).

47. *The New York Times* (hereafter cited as NYT), July 16, 1866 cited in Weinstein, "Nickel Empire," 127; Eleanor Ells, *History of Organized Camping: The First 100 Years* (Martinsville IN, 1986), 1–85; Leslie Paris, "The Adventures of Peanut and Bo: Summer Camps and Early-Twentieth-Century American Girlhood," 12, no. 4, *Journal of Women's History* (Winter 2001): 47–88.

48. Henry Curtis, *The Play Movement and Its Significance* (New York, 1917), 60–65; Clarence Rainwater, *The Play Movement in the United States* (Chicago: University of Chicago Press, 1922), 100–105. For an assessment, see Dom Cavallo, *Muscles and Morals: Organized Playgrounds and Urban Reform, 1880–1920* (Philadelphia: University of Pennsylvania Press, 1981), 46–48.

49. Herbert May and Dorothy Petgen, *Leisure and its Uses: Some International Observations* (New York: A.S. Barnes, 1928), 174.

50. Ann Holt, "Hikers and Ramblers: Surviving a Thirties' Fashion," *International Journal of the History of Sport*, 4 (May 1987): 157–67; Taylor, *Claim on the Countryside*, 251–55.

51. Taylor, *Claim on the Countryside*; Helen Walker, "The Popularisation of the Outdoor Movement," *British Journal of Sports History* 2 (September 1985): 140–53; Holiday Fellowship pamphlets (British Library WP15115) and T.A. Leonard, *Adventures in Holiday Making* (London: Holiday Fellowship, 1934).

52. Taylor, *Claim on the Countryside*, 259–60.

53. For an example of the British group holiday see Mass-Observation Archive, Worktown Project, Box 2/G, reports on the Butlin camps, 1947.

54. Sylvester Baxter, "Seaside Pleasure," *Scribner's* 23 (June 1898): 677, 686; Rollin Hartt, "The Amusement Park," *Atlantic Monthly* 99 (May 1907): 667; O. Henry (William Sydney Porter), "The Greater Coney Island," in *Sixes and Sevens* (Garden City, Doubleday, 1919), 221–23.

55. George Lansbury, *My England* (London: Blount's Topical Books, 1934), 15; George Bourne (George Sturt), *Change in the Village* (London: Duckworth, 1911). Note also "The Holiday Dream," in Cross, *Worktowners at Blackpool*, ch. 3.

56. David Matless, *Landscape and Englishness* (London: Reaktion, 1998); Georgina Boyes, *The Imagined Village* (Manchester: Manchester University Press, 1993); Frank R. Leavis, *Mass Civilisation and Minority Culture* (Cambridge: Minority Press, 1930); John K. Walton, *Tourism, Fishing and Redevelopment: Post-War Whitby, 1945–1970* (Cambridge: Wolfson Lectures, 2005).

57. Cyril Joad, *Diogenes or the Future of Leisure* (New York: Dutton, 1928), 65.

58. George Soule, *A Planned Society* (New York: Macmillan, 1932), 283.

59. R. and H. Lynd, *Middletown*, 251–57.

60. Jay Anderson, *Time Machines: The World of Living History* (Nashville: American Association for State and Local History, 1984), 17–30; Quotation from Mike Wallace, "Visiting the Past: History Museums in the United States," *Radical History Review* 25 (1981): 68; Tony Bennett, "Museums and the People," in Robert Lumley, ed., *The Museum Time-Machine* (London: Comedia, 1988), 63–86; C. B. Hosmer, *Presence of the Past: A History of the Preservation Movement in the United States before Williamsburg* (New York: Putnam, 1965); Thomas Taylor, "The Williamsburg Restoration and its Reception by the American Public: 1926–1942," Dissertation, George Washington University, 1989, ch. 2; Warren Leon and Margaret Piatt, "Living-History Museums," in Warren Leon and Roy Rosenzweig, eds., *History Museums in the United States: A Critical Assessment* (Urbana: University of Illinois Press, 1989), 64–97.

61. J. D. Rockefeller, Jr., "The Genesis of the Williamsburg Restoration," *National Geographic* 71, no. 4 (April 1937): 401 cited in Anderson, *Time Machines*, 30; David Lowenthal, "The American Way of History," *Columbia University Forum* 9 (Summer 1966): 31 cited in Leon and Piatt, "Living History Museums," 73; Kevin Walsh, *The Representation of the Past* (London: Routledge, 1992), 96–97; Barbara Kirshenblatt-Gimblett, *Destination Culture: Tourism, Museums, and Heritage* (Berkeley: University of California Press, 1998), 194–95; and especially James Weeks, *Gettysburg: Memory, Market, and an American Shrine* (Princeton: Princeton University Press, 2003).

62. For example, Jennifer Jenkins and Patrick James, *From Acorn to Oak Tree: The Growth of the National Trust 1895–1994* (London: Macmillan, 1994); Graham Murphy, *Founders of the National Trust* (London: Christopher Helm, 1987).

63. John Sears, *Sacred Places: American Tourist Attractions in the Nineteenth Century* (New York: Oxford University Press, 1989), 28, 185–88; and Sterngass, *First Resorts*, 7–74.

64. Colin Ward and Dennis Hardy, *Goodnight Campers!* (London: Mansell, 1986); Ward and Hardy, *Arcadia for All* (London: Mansell, 1984).

65. Dan L. LeMahieu, *A Culture for Democracy: Mass Communications and the Cultivated Mind in Britain between the Wars* (New York: Oxford University Press, 1988), 66–69 and 82–99; Jeffrey Richards, ed., *The Unknown 1930s: An Alternative History of the British Cinema, 1929–39* (London: I. B. Tauris, 1998).

66. Denys Harding, "The Place of Entertainment in Social Life," *Sociological Review* 26 (October 1934): 393–406; Mark Pegg, *Broadcasting and Society* (London: Croom Helm, 1983), 92–109 and 195–215; Paddy Scannell and David Cardiff, *A Social History of British Broadcasting* (Oxford: Blackwell, 1991).

67. John Dewey, *Democracy and Education* (New York: The Free Press, 1966 [1916]), ch. 19; Benjamin Hunnicutt, *Work without End: Abandoning Shorter Hours for the Right to Work* (Philadelphia: Temple University Press, 1988), 116–20; Joan Rubin, *The Making of Middlebrow Culture* (Chapel Hill, N.C.: University of North Carolina Press, 1992), ch. 1, 3, 4 and 5.

68. William Leach, *Land of Desire: Merchants, Power, and the Rise of a New American Culture* (New York: Vintage, 1993), 70, 202–210; Jackson Lears, *Fables of Abundance: A Cultural History of Advertising in America* (New York: Basic, 1994), 139.

69. Donald Meyer, *The Positive Thinkers* (New York: Pantheon, 1980), ch. 8; Stanley Coben, *Rebellion Against Victorianism: The Impetus for Cultural Change in 1920s America* (New York: Oxford University Press, 1991), esp. ch. 3; Rubin, *Middlebrow Culture*, 25, 31–32.

70. Jeffrey Stanton, "Coney Island—Second Steeplechase, 1908–1964," May 1999, http://naid.sppsr.ucla.edu/conisland/articles/steeplechase2.htm, 7.

71. NYT, September 7, 1906, 5; September 18, 1922, 20; May 18, 1923, 22; September 14, 1926, 16; September 16, 1928, 37; September 15, 1929, 24.

72. Gary Cross, *The Cute and the Cool: Wondrous Innocence and Modern American Children's Culture* (New York: Oxford University Press), ch. 4.

73. NYT, March 18, 1928, 71; April 22, 1928, 125; July 5, 1928, section 1, 3; Woody Register, *The Kid of Coney Island: Fred Thompson and the Rise of American Amusements* (New York: Oxford University Press, 2001), 300–303. William Mangels, *The Outdoor Amusement Industry from Earliest Times to the Present* (New York: Vantage, 1952), 27–28; "New $5,000,000 Playground is Opened at Rye, " *New York Tribune*, May 27, 1928; "The Kiddie Park," *Showman*, May 30, 1925, 24; www.ryeplayland.org/.

74. Pleasure Beach Archives, folder 9.

75. "Circus and Museum Freaks, Curiosities of Pathology," *Scientific America Supplement*, 65(April 4, 1908): 222 cited in Robert Bogdan, *Freak Show* (Chicago: University of Chicago, 1988), 64; Leslie Gilliams, "Side-Show Freaks as Seen By Science," *Illustrated World* 38 (1922): 213–15; Hannah Lees, "Side Show Diagnosis," *Colliers* 99 (1937): 224.

76. NYT, September 21, 1924, X13; Lawrence Levine, *Highbrow/Lowbrow: The Emergence of Cultural Hierarchy in America* (Cambridge, Mass.: Harvard University Press, 1988).

77. Bertram Reinitz, "Coney Enters its Steel Age," NYT, June 16, 1929, XX2; and Jan and Cora Gordon (English artists), "Coney Island as a World Showplace," NYT, June 3, 1928, SM 7.

78. Cross, *Worktowners at Blackpool*.

79. The decline of the legitimacy of the freak show was a long process. In 1906, prominent New York African Americans protested against the featured display of an African in the Bronx Zoo's monkey house. In the 1910s, the Society for the Prevention of Cruelty to Children protested the display of underage "Siamese Twins." A curious combination of new sympathy for the humanity of freaks, but also disgust at their abnormality and, even almost embarrassment at how the popular audience gaped at their condition led to a negative middle-class reaction. A Florida law of 1921 outlawed freak shows (even though in 1972 the Florida Supreme court overturned this prohibition as an infringement on the self-employment rights of the disabled.) The 1933 movie *Freaks* by Todd

Browning, was a critical and audience failure. Both the Nazis and Soviets prohibited freak shows in the 1930s. Racial freaks (often dark-skinned people displayed in "native costume" as African savages or East Asian cannibals) became taboo by the 1950s. NYT, October 14, 1971, 31; Leslie Fiedler, *Freaks: Myths and Images of the Secret Self* (New York: Simon and Schuster, 1978), 24–36; C.J.S. Thompson, *History and Lore of Freaks* (1930: reprinted, London, Senate, 1976), 207–8.

80. Bogdan, *Freak Show*, 67. Rachel Adams, *Sideshow U.S.A: Freaks and the American Cultural Imagination* (Chicago: University of Chicago Press, 2001), 212–228.

81. J. K. Walton, "The National Trust Centenary: Official and Unofficial Histories," *Local Historian*, 26 (1996): 80–88; Peter Mandler, *The Fall and Rise of the Stately Home* (New Haven, 1997).

4. Decline and Reinvention: Coney Island and Blackpool

1. *Built Environment* 18 (1992), themed issue on seaside resorts, S. Agarwal, "Restructuring Seaside Tourism: the Resort Lifecycle," *Annals of Tourism Research* 29 (2002): 25–55; John K. Walton, *The British Seaside: Holidays and Resorts in the Twentieth Century* (Manchester, UK: Manchester University Press: 2000), 21–22.

2. William A. Douglass and Paullina Raento, "The Tradition of Invention: Conceiving Las Vegas," *Annals of Tourism Research* 31 (2004): 7–23.

3. Stephen Weinstein, "The Nickel Empire: Coney Island, and the Creation of Urban Seaside Resorts in the United States," Ph.D. dissertation, Columbia University, 272–74; Charles Denson, *Coney Island: Lost and Found* (Berkeley: Ten Speed Press: 2002), Parts 2 and 3; Jon Pareles, "Meet the New Boss," *The Observer Review* (London), July 21, 2002, 5.

4. G. Shaw and A. Williams, eds., *The Rise and Fall of British Coastal Resorts* (London: Mansell, 1997); N. Morgan and A. Pritchard, *Power and Politics at the Seaside* (Exeter: University of Exeter Press, 1999), chs. 6 and 7; John K. Walton, *Blackpool* (Edinburgh: Edinburgh University Press), chs. 6 and 7; Walton, *British Seaside*, 126–31.

5. Dana Gatlin, "Amusing America's Millions," *World's Work* 26 (July 1913), 331; Rem Koolhas, *Delirious New York: A Retroactive Manifesto for Manhattan* (New York: Monacelli Press, 1994), 70. Details of the park proposal of 1899 can be found in the *New York Times* (hereafter NYT): June 6, 1899, 14; June 14, 1899, 14; letters to the editor, June 14, 1899, 6; July 11, 1899, 12; and July 13, 1899, 14.

6. Michael Immerso, *Coney Island: The People's Playground* (New Brunswick: Rutgers University Press, 2002), 125–28; Denson, *Coney Island*, 26–29, 40–44; *Brooklyn Eagle*, January 24, 1915; Oliver Pilat and Jo Ranson, *Sodom by the Sea: An Affectionate History of Coney Island* (Garden City, N.Y.: Doubleday, 1941), 311–14.

7. Eric Ierardi, *Gravesend, Brooklyn: Coney Island and Sheepshead Bay* (Dover, NH: Arcadia, 1996), 82–128; *New York Times*, July 8, 1925, 1; Denson, *Coney Island*, 49–52.

8. Edouard Herriot, "America, The Land of Joy," NYT, 17 August 1924, SM1.

9. NYT, May 31, 1926, 2; March 18, 1928, 71; August 26, 1928, 1; September 1, 1929, SM 1; July 25, 1937, 14; August 16, 1925, RE 1; J. A. Hassan, *The Seaside, Health and the Environment in England and Wales since 1800* (Aldershot: Ashgate, 2003), ch. 5.

10. The parallels and contrasts with Central Park are interesting here. See Roy Rosenzweig and Elizabeth Blackmar, *The Park and the People: A History of Central Park* (Ithaca: Cornell University Press, 1992).

11. NYT, May 5, 1925, S1; August 13, 1925, 34; April 4, 1926, RE 1.

12. Robert Caro, *The Power Broker: Robert Moses and the Fall of New York* (New York: Vintage Books, 1975), 318–19.

13. Immerso, *Coney Island*, 137–41.

14. Immerso, *Coney Island*, 141–47, 160; Caro, *Power Broker*, 335; Henry B. Lieberman, "Nickel Empire," NYT, July 16, 1939, D89; James Onorato, *Another Time, Another World, Coney Island Memories* (California State University, Fullerton: Oral History Program, 1988), 5–6.

15. Joseph Heller, *Now and Then: From Coney Island to Here* (New York: Knopf, 1998), 30–31 and ch. 2.

16. Caro, *Power Broker*, 687; Denson, *Coney Island*, 66–67, 72; NYT, October 1, 1932, A29; June 17, 1934, 12.

17. NYT, June 30, 1934, 13; Edo McCullough, *Good Old Coney Island* (New York: Scribner's, 1957), 250–83; Pilat and Ranson, *Sodom by the Sea*, 333–34.

18. NYT, December 1, 1937, 27; August 14, 1938, 13; July 25, 1939, 36; Immerso, *Coney Island*, 159–60.

19. New York City Parks Department, *The Improvement of Coney Island* (New York: City of New York, 1939), 1–3.

20. Walton, *Blackpool*, 126–31; Walton, *The British Seaside*, ch. 4; Helen Meller, *European Cities, 1890–1930s: History, Culture and the Built Environment* (Chichester: John Wiley, 2001), 197–207.

21. Laura Chase, "Social Tone in Clacton and Frinton in the Inter-War Years," *International Journal of Maritime History* 9 (1997): 149–69; John K. Walton, "Consuming the Beach: Seaside Resorts and Cultures of Tourism in England and Spain from the 1830s to the 1930s," in E. Furlough and S. Baranowski, eds., *Being Elsewhere: Tourism, Consumer Culture and Identity in Modern Europe and North America* (Ann Arbor: University of Michigan Press, 2001), 272–98.

22. Walton, *Blackpool*, ch. 5; S. O'Connell, *The Car in British Society: Class, Gender and Motoring, 1896–1939* (Manchester: Manchester University Press, 1998).

23. Walton, *British Seaside*, 110; Public Record Office, Kew, HO45/16725/655652.

24. Bennett, *Century of Fun*, 58–84; Ted Lightbown, "Buildings and Rides," 5–7, Pleasure Beach Archives.

25. Rosemary Ind Emberton, *Joseph Emberton 1889–1956* (London: Scolar, 1983).

26. Lieberman, "Nickel Empire," D88–9.

27. Immerso, *Coney Island*, 164–65; Denson, *Coney Island*, 67–74.

28. Immerso, *Coney Island*, 163; Heller, *Now and Then*, 52–59.

29. NYT, August 13, 1944, S1, 1; September 18, 1944, 21:1.

30. NYT, August 18, 1946, S1, 2.

31. Henry Gilroy, "Everything's Atomic in Screamland," NYT, August 7, 1949, S 1, 14.

32. Immerso, *Coney Island*, 163, 165–66; Miles Barth *et al.*, eds., *Weegee's World* (Boston: Bulfinch, 1997); NYT, May 3, 1941, 17; October 29, 1946, 22.

33. NYT, April 6, 1953, S1: 1; NYT, May 4, 1949; Gilroy, "Atomic in Screamland."

34. NYT, May 18, 1947, S1: 4; Onorato, *Another Time*, ix; "Coney Island," *Life*, August 6, 1945, 65.

35. NYT, April 6, 1953, S1.

36. In the 1940s, Moses banned burlesque shows even though he had become more relaxed than Coney Island Chamber of Commerce about the wearing of beach attire in the streets. NYT, May 27, 1942, 25; June 17, 1942, 1; October 7, 1948, S7, 8.

37. Denson, *Coney Island*, 67; NYT, May 3, 1941, 17.

38. Denson, *Coney Island*, 67–76; NYT, May 19, 1940, 14; October 6, 1949, 33; April 2, 1953, 1; April 3, 1953, 3; April 6, 1953, 31; New York City Parks Department, *Coney Island Improvement* (New York: City of New York: October 24, 1954).

39. Denson, *Coney Island*, 135, 152–54; Weinstein, "Nickel Empire," 290–96; NYT, April 19, 1964, SMA 30; April 21, 1965, 37; August 14, 1979, B3.

40. James Onorato, *Steeplechase Park: Sale and Closure, 1965–66 Diary of J.J.* Onorato (Bellingham, WA: 1998), xii–xvi; Onorato, *Then and Now*, 37, 58; M. Tilyou's citations in Denson, *Coney Island*, 135.

41. NYT, April 19, 1964, SMA 30; Onorato, *Steeplechase Park*, 1–2.

42. NYT, November 30, 1963, 3; June 16, 1987, 3; Richard Snow, *Coney Island: A Postcard Journey to the City of Fire* (New York: Brightwaters Press, 1984), 11.

43. NYT, April 21, 1965, 37; August 14, 1979, B3, 1. Denson, *Coney Island*, 162, 200–14, 231–33; Onorato, *Then and Now*, 11, 25, 27–28.

44. J. Demetriadi, "The Golden Years: English Seaside Resorts 1950–1974," in Shaw and Williams, eds., *Rise and Fall*, 49–75; Paul Axel Lund, cited in Rupert Croft-Cooke, *Smiling Damned Villain* (2nd ed., London: Four Square, 1961), 81.

45. *Ward Lock's Guide to Blackpool* (n.d., *c.* 1956), 7–8.

46. Lightbown, "Buildings and Rides," 8–9.

47. Walton, *Blackpool*, 152; Gary Cross, ed., *Worktowners at Blackpool* (London: Routledge, 1990), 61.

48. *Ward Lock's Guide to Blackpool*, 37–38; Peter Marsden, *Lighting the Waves* (Blackpool: Corporation, 2004), 15–16.

49. National Fairground Archive, Smart Family Collection, Harold Tunstall to Captain Phayre, October 7, 1961.

50. Ibid., Mr Betts to Capt. Phayre, August 25, 1961; Mr Billy Smart, undated press state-

ment, late 1961; Graham Turner, *The North Country* (London: Eyre and Spottiswoode, 1967), 137–38.

51. Pleasure Beach Archive, photographs from late 1950s and early 1960s; Alfred Gregory, *Blackpool: a Celebration of the'60s* (London: Constable, 1993), 15.

52. Gregory, *Blackpool*, 62.

53. Turner, *North Country*, 133–7.

54. Lieberman, "Nickel Empire."

55. Denson, *Coney Island*, Part 3.

56. Walton, *Blackpool Landlady* (Manchester: Manchester University Press, 1978), ch. 7; Walton, *Blackpool*, 138–45, 152–3; Sue Arthur, "Crested China, Pineapple Chunks and Cherry Red Velvet: A History of Shopping in Blackpool Town Centre from 1881 to 1958," M.A. dissertation, University of Central Lancashire, 2003; Demetriadi, "The Golden Years."

57. Lancashire Record Office (LRO), CBBl 32/4, Traffic and Transport Plan, 1969, 4–6, 8–9.

58. *West Lancashire Evening Gazette* (hereafter WLEG) June 25, 1973.

59. LRO CBBl 118/2 and 118/3, Minutes of Evidence on Blackpool Corporation Bill, 1969.

60. WLEG, July 20, 1977. Thanks to Karen Guerin for research assistance with this material.

61. Ibid.

62. WLEG, July 21, 1977.

63. WLEG, January 6, 1972, December 2, 1974.

64. Walton, *Blackpool*, 145.

65. North West Civic Trust, *Renaissance North West: A Plan for Regional Renewal* (Manchester: North West Civic Trust, 1987), 50–51.

66. Ibid., 145–48, 168–69.

67. Ibid., chs. 6 and 7.

68. G. Sternlieb and J. Hughes, *The Atlantic City Gamble* (Cambridge: Harvard University Press, 1983); Roger Munting, *An Economic and Social History of Gambling in Britain and the U.S.A.* (Manchester: Manchester University Press, 1996), 147–49; Bryant Simon, *Boardwalk of Dreams: Atlantic City and the Fate of Urban America* (New York: Oxford University Press, 2004), 132-217.

69. "Journey into the Future: The Blackpool Masterplan," *WLEG Special Publication*, March 13, 2004.

70. C. Beatty and S. Fothergill, *The Seaside Economy: The Final Report of the Seaside Towns Research Project* (Sheffield: Sheffield Hallam University, 2003); idem., *A Case Study of Blackpool* (Sheffield: Hallam University, February 2003); Nicholas L. Ribis, "Cashing in on Casino-Led Regeneration," paper presented at the British Urban Regeneration Association (BURA) conference on resort regeneration, Imperial Hotel, Blackpool, March 2004.

71. Shaw and Williams, *British Coastal Resorts*.

72. Paul Flynn, "Why I Love: Blackpool Pleasure Beach," *The Guardian*, G2, February 26, 2004, 23.

5. The Disney Challenge

1. Lawrence Mintz, "Simulated Tourism at Busch Gardens: The Old Country and Disney's World Showcase, Epcot Center," *Journal of Popular Culture*, 32, no. 5 (Winter 1998): 47–58; Jean Baudrillard, *The Ecstasy of Communication* (New York: Semiotext(e), 1988), 56, 104; Aviad Raz, *Riding the Black Ship: Japan and Tokyo Disneyland* (Cambridge: Harvard University Asia Center, Distributed by Harvard University Press, 1999), 30–40, 188–91; Margaret King, "Disneyland and Walt Disney World: Traditional Values in Futuristic Form," *Journal of Popular Culture*, 15, no. 1 (Summer 1981); Alexander Moore, "Walt Disney's World: Bounded Ritual Space and the Playful Pilgrimage Center," *Anthropological Quarterly* 53 (October 1980): 207–18; Daniel Boorstin, *The Image: A Guide to Pseudo-Events in America* (New York: Harper, 1964); Umberto Eco, *Travels in Hyperreality* (San Diego: Harcourt, Brace, 1986); Stephan Fjellman, *Vinyl Leaves: Walt Disney World and America* (Boulder, CO: Westview, 1992).

2. George Ritzer, *The McDonaldization of Society* (Thousand Oaks, CA: Pine Forge Press, 1993); Ritzer, *The McDonaldization Thesis: Explorations and Extensions* (London: Sage, 1998); Ritzer, *The Globalization of Nothing* (Thousand Oaks, CA: Pine Forge Press, 2003); Barry Smart, ed., *Resisting McDonaldization* (London: Sage, 1999); Edward Relph, *Place and Placelessness* (London: Pion, 1976).

3. From Derrick Jones's interview with George Ritzer, "The Disenchanted Kingdom: George Ritzer and the Disappearance of Authentic American Culture," *The Sun Magazine*, June 2002.

4. Alan Bryman, *Disney and His Worlds* (New York: Routledge, 1995), 96–97; Hugo Hilderbrandt, "Cedar Point," *Journal of Popular Culture* (1981): 87–88; Elizabeth and Jay Mechling "The Sale of Two Cities: A Semiotic Comparison of Disneyland with Marriott's Great America," *Journal of Popular Culture* 15 (Spring 1981): 166–79.

5. Letter to editor, *Nation*, June 28, 1958, cited in Walt Disney Productions, *Walt Disney Imagineering: A Behind the Dreams Look at Making the Magic Real* (New York: Hyperion, 1996), 19; Ray Bradbury, "The Machine-Tooled Happyland," *Holiday* 38 (October 1965): 104.

6. John M. Findlay, *Magic Lands: Western Cityscapes and American Culture after 1940* (Berkeley: University of California Press, 1992), 66–67.

7. *Disneyland, the First Quarter Century* (Walt Disney Productions, 1979), 15

8. At first, Walt Disney was contented with thinking about transforming an empty lot across the street from his Burbank California studio into a park with pony rides and statues of Mickey Mouse so that small kids visiting the area could see where "Mickey lives."

9. Walt Disney cited in "Insights to a Dream," *News From Disneyland* (hereafter cited as NFD), 1979, Anaheim Public Library, Disneyland Collection (hereafter cited as APL).

10. Neil Harris, "Expository Expositions: Preparing for the Theme Parks," in Karal Ann Marling, ed., *Designing Disney's Theme Parks* (New York: Flammarion), 26; Beth Dunlop, *Art of Disney Architecture* (New York: Harry Abrams, 1996), 26, 36.

11. Karal Ann Marling, "Imagineering the Disney Theme Parks," in *Designing Disney's Theme Parks*, 35, 39; Dunlop, *Art of Disney Architecture*, 27.

12. Quotes from "Building a Dream," NFD, 1956, "Insights to a Dream," NFD, 1979, APL; "Walt Disney Imagination Unlimited," *Readers' Digest*, November 1964, 273; Marling, "Imagineering," 40–41, 45–47; Martin Sklar, *Walt Disney's Disneyland* (Anaheim: Walt Disney Productions, 1969), np.

13. Philip Santora, "Disneyland Captures Hearts of Youngsters and Elders' Respect," *New York Daily News*, October 1, 1964, 12c.

14. Peter Bailey, *Leisure and Class in Victorian* England (London: Routledge, 1978); Martha Wolfenstein, "Fun Morality: An Analysis of Recent American Child-training Literature," in M. Mead and M. Wolfenstein, eds., *Childhood in Contemporary Cultures* (Chicago: University of Chicago Press, 1955), 169–70, 172–74.

15. *Disneyland: The First Quarter Century*, 11; *Walt Disney's Guide to Disneyland* (Anaheim: Walt Disney Productions, 1964), 2.

16. Harris, "Expository Expositions," in Marling, *Designing Disney*, 27.

17. Walt Disney Productions, *Walt Disney Imagineering*, 14.

18. *Disneyland: The First Quarter Century*. 17; *Walt Disney's Guide to Disneyland* (1964), 16–18, 22; "New Disneyland Attractions," NFD, May 13, 1956, APL; Date Line USA, 1955 opening of *Disneyland* TV show; "Walt Disney's Guide to Disneyland," Disneyland file, 1956, APL; "Story of Disneyland," Disneyland, 1955 file, APL.

19. "Dateline Disneyland," and "Disneyland Diary, 1957," Disneyland, 1957 file, APL; "Visit to Disneyland," NFD, 1956, APL; "A New Tomorrowland," NFD, 1959, APL; "The Disneyland Story," October 27, 1954 episode of *Disneyland*, in *Disneyland USA* (DVD recordings, 2001), and *Disneyland, the First Quarter Century*, 17.

20. David Harvey, *The Condition of Postmodernity* (Oxford: Blackwell, 1990), 300.

21. *Disneyland: The First Quarter Century*, 12–13.

22. "Adults Outnumber Kids 4 to 1," *Oakland Tribune*, March 21, 1965, 2B, Disney Publicity Book, p. 59, APL.

23. Walt Disney Productions, *Walt Disney Imagineering*, 11; Erica Doss, "Making Imagination Safe in the 1950s: Disneyland's Fantasy Art and Architecture," in Marling, *Designing Disney*, 180–81.

24. "The Disney Theme Show: From Disneyland to Walt Disney World" (no publication information, 1975?), 8, MS.R. 77 Box 2, file 3, University of California at Irvine, Special Collections.

25. Bryman, *Disney and His Worlds*, 157; Dunlop, *Art of Disney*, 25, 37; Alexander Moore, "Walt Disney World: Bounded Ritual Space and the Playful Pilgrimage Center," *Anthropological Quarterly* 65 (1980): 207–18.

26. Marling, "Imagineering," 81; and Sklar, *Disney's Disneyland*, np.

27. Gary Cross, *The Cute and the Cool: Wondrous Innocence and Modern American Children's Culture* (New York: Oxford University Press, 2004), ch. 3.

28. "News release," NFD, April 1973, APL.

29. Cross, *The Cute and the Cool*, ch. 3.

30. Konrad Lorenz, *Foundations of Ethnography* (New York: Simon and Schuster, 1981), 164–65; Steven Jay Gould, "Mickey Mouse Meets Konrad Lorenz," *Natural History*, 88, no. 5 (1979): 30–36; "It's a Small World," 1963 by Richard and Robert Sherman, in Disneyland brochures, MS R 77 B 1/1, University of California at Irvine Library, Special Collections.

31. Bryman, *Disney and His Worlds*, 157; *Disneyland: The First Quarter Century*, 1. Examples of ads are in Disney "Publicity Books," vols 1–4, APL.

32. Cross, *The Cute and the Cool*, ch. 3, 4.

33. Note, for example, Elizabeth and Jay Mechling, "The Sale of Two Cities," 116–79; *Disneyland, the First Quarter Century*, 3; and *Walt Disney's Guide to Disneyland* 4; and "A Visit to Disneyland," NFD, 1956; "Disney Gazetteer," 1965, APL.

34. *Walt Disney's Guide to Disneyland*, 4.

35. King, "Disneyland and Walt Disney World,"116–40; Jean Starobinki, "The Idea of Nostalgia," *Diogenes* 54 (Summer 1966): 81–103; and Peter Fritzsche, "Specters of History: On Nostalgia, Exile, and Modernity," *American Historical Review* 106 (December 2001): 1587–1618.

36. Eric Smoodin, *Disney Discourse* (New York: Routledge, 1994), 10 and David Nye, *American Technological Sublime* (Cambridge: MIT Press, 1994).

37. Walt Disney Productions, *Project Florida: A Whole New Disney World* (Burbank, Ca: 1967), 5.

38. William Hollingsworth Whyte, *The Organization Man* (New York: Simon and Schuster, 1956); Kenneth Jackson, *Crabgrass Frontier: The Suburbanization of the United States* (New York: Oxford University Press, 1985).

39. In 1964, Disney managed to block the construction of a planned 18–22 story Sheraton hotel that would have intruded the real world into the sky backdrop to Disney's artifice. A rule was enacted that imposed a 150-foot height maximum on buildings near Disneyland; it was extended in 1980. See especially, "Does the Magic Kingdom Run a Company Town?" *Orange County Register*, December 18, 1992; and "Building Height Limits in Disneyland Area Revisited," *Los Angeles Times* (hereafter LAT), April 26, 1980.

40. Quoted in "New Disneyland Attractions," NFD, May 13, 1956.

41. "Sequence of Opening Pay Attractions at Disneyland, August 29, 1974," Disneyland 1955 file; "New Disneyland Attractions," NFD, May 13, 1956; "Matterhorn," NFD, 1959; all APL.

42. "Disneyland Gazetteer," NFD, 1965, APL.

43. "Walt Disney's Guide to Disneyland," Disneyland 1960 file; "Disneyland Will Continue to Grow," NFD, 1960; "Disneyland Gazetteer," NFD, 1965, all APL; John Urry, *The Tourist Gaze* (London: Sage, 1990).

44. Among the sources at the APL Disney collection are: "Disneyland: World's Fastest Growing Ten-Year Old," NFD, 1965; *Anaheim Gazette*, December 5, 1963, Disneyland 1963 file; "Disneyland Gazetteer," NFD, 1965; "Tencennial," NFD, 1965; "Biographical Sketch," NFD, 1965; "Disneyland Diary," Disneyland 1972 file; "Attractions for Summer 67," NFD, 1967; *Anaheim Bulletin*, August 12, 1969, Disneyland 1969 file; "Disneyland Diary," *Disney News*, Summer 1985.
45. "The New Tomorrowland," NFD, 1967, APL.
46. Walt Disney Productions, *Project Florida*, 4.
47. Prices went up a lot over the course of the last nearly fifty years. When first opened the price of admission for 15 attractions was $4 for adults, $3.50 for 12–17 year olds, and $3 for children under 12. NYT, February 2, 1958, C1.
48. "Fathers of Invention," *Disney Magazine*, Fall 1996, 65; B. Shapiro, "Adults Outnumber Kids," *Oakland Tribune*, March 21, 1965, 58; John Hench cited in "In Fairy Dust, Disney Finds New Realism," NYT, February 20, 1989, C1.
49. Disney Employee Training Manuals, 1984–87, MS R 77B, University of California at Irvine Library, Special Collections.
50. Robert Ferrigno, "Personal Impression from the First Trip to Disneyland," *Orange County Register*, November 7, 1982, 1 Accent Section; "Crime Takes No Holiday at Disneyland," *Anaheim Bulletin*, August 17, 1983, 1; "Soft Arm of the Law," LAT, January 12, 1981, part 11 A 1.
51. "Disney Report, 1958," Disneyland 1958 files, APL; "Disney Isn't Only for the Kids," NFD, Fall 1971, APL; "The Never-Never Land Khrushchev Never Saw," NYT, October 4, 1959, 11; and note also "How Disney Does it," *Newsweek*, April 3, 1989, 5; Bryman, *Disney and his Worlds*, 87.
52. Although on August 6, 1970 a group of radical hippies, the self-styled "Yippies," demanded entrance, forcing the early closure of the park that day, Disney kept the place clear of long-haired, drug-using youthful "troublemakers" in this era. *Anaheim Bulletin*, July 16, 1971, 1. From the APL collection: "Disneyland Diary: Year Five," (1973), Disneyland 1960 file; "Special Events" NFD, 1965; "Big Bands," NFD, May 1967; "Performers at Disneyland," NFD, May 1968; "Senior Citizen Days," NFD, Spring 1974; "Disneyland Spring Program, 1988," Disneyland 1988 file; "Today at Disneyland," Show Schedule file, July 8, 1989.
53. "Letter from a Guest," *Disneyland Line*, July 18, 1969, 6; "Disneyland Guide to Happiness"; "Disneyland Names Ambassador for 1966," NFD, 1966, all APL.
54. Sources from APL Disney Collection include "Summer Opening," NFD, 1972; Publicity Disneyland Vols. 1–4, 1966–67; Disneyland ad, LAT, October 23, 1988, 24, Disneyland 1988 file; "Theme Parks," *Disney News*, Fall 1987, 4; "America on Parade," NFD, August 17, 1975; "First Annual Report to Disneyland Lessees," April 1956, Disneyland 1956 file; "Gala St. Patrick's Day Parade," NFD, 1969; "Viva Mexico Celebration," NFD, April 29, 1973.

55. From the APL collection: "Disney Diary 1961," Disneyland 1967 file; "Disney Diary, Year 2," Disneyland 1957 file; "Disneyland Readies All Nite Parties," NFD, 1968; "Disneyland Diary, Year Fifteen," Disneyland 1970 file; "Summer '67," NFD, 1967.

56. "Disneyland Story, 1980" Disneyland 1980 file; "Disneyland," *Anaheim Bulletin*, January 3, 1985, A1, Disneyland 1985 file, both APL.

57. See Cross, *Cute and Cool*, especially chs. 3 and 5.

58. "Southland Thrill Rides," LAT, June 20, 1987, F, 1; "Cheap Thrills," LAT, December 9, 1987, F 32; "Batman vs. Mickey," LAT, April 20, 1987, Disneyland 1987 File, APL. Also "Variation on a Theme," *Westways* (August 1991): 34–40, Disneyland 1991 file, APL; Susan Davis, *Spectacular Nature: Corporate Culture and the Sea World Experience*, (Berkeley: University of California Press, 1997).

59. "New Thrill Ride," LAT, August 21, 1978, F 1.

60. "Disneyland at 30," LAT, July 14, 1985, 3; and "Magic Kingdom," *Orange County Register*, August 14, 1985.

61. "Captain Eo," *Disneyland Gazetteer*, October 1985, MS R 77 2/4 University of California at Irvine Library, Special Collections; From the APL Disney Collection: "Captain Eo," *Disney News*, Fall 1986, 7–10; "Disneyland Today," December 20, 1986; Show Schedules, vol. 1: "Theme Parks," *Disney News*, Winter 1986.

62. "Mickey's Toontown is Open," *Disney News*, Spring 1993, 22, APL.

63. At APL: "Let's Get Small," *Disney News*, Winter 1994, 56–57; "Uncovering the Indiana Jones Adventure," *Disney Magazine*, Spring 1995, 18–21.

64. Sources from ALP include: "Disneyland Report, 1958," Disneyland 1958 file; "Disneyland Will Open Teen Night Club," LAT, April 23, 1985, F 1; Disney Ad, LAT March 25, 1994, F31; "Disneyland and Orange County," *Orange County Register*, December 25, 1987, 1, Disneyland 1987 file; "Disneyland and Teens," LAT, August 23, 1992, A1; "Disney Poll," LAT, March 2, 1994, D1, 9.

65. "A New Disney World is Rising in Central Florida," NYT, December 29, 1970, 27; "New Florida Countdown," NYT, October 1, 1971, 26; "Disneyland Story, 1980," NYT, March 7, 1994, D7; "Disney Theme Show, (Disneyland 1980 File, APL; Eve Zibart, *Disney: The Incredible Story of Walt Disney World and the Man behind the Mouse* (Foster City, CA: IDG Books, 2000), 72–112; Richard Fogelsong, *Married to the Mouse: Walt Disney World and Orlando* (New Haven: Yale University Press, 2001).

66. "Booming Amusement Parks: The Theme is Extreme," *Newsweek*, March 30, 1998, 12.

67. Fred Guterl, and Carol Truxal, "The Wonderful World of Epcot," *IEEE Spectrum* 19, no. 9 (September 1982): 46–55; Irwin Ross, "Disney Gambles on Tomorrow," *Fortune*, October 4, 1982, 62–69; Walt Disney Productions, *Project Florida*, 10–11.

68. Walt Disney Productions, *Walt Disney Imagineering*, 31, 92–93; "Epcot's International Pavilions Operate as True Global Village," LAT, March 25, 1990, 4; "Close Encounters with Epcot," NYT, November 14, 1982, 10; M. Sorkin, "See You in Disneyland," in M. Sorkin, *Variations on a Theme Park* (New York: Noonday, 1992), 216.

69. "A Tour is Born," *Disney News*, Summer 1989, 17, APL; "In Fairy Dust, Disney Finds New Realism," NYT, February 20, 1989, C1; and "Nastiness Is Not a Fantasy in Movie Theme Park War," NYT, August 13, 1989, 1, 2.

70. At APL: "History of the World," *Disney News*, Fall 1981, 3–5; "Lake Buena Vista," *Walt Disney World News*, Summer 1975, 1–2.

71. Joe Flower, *Prince of the Magic Kingdom: Michael Eisner and the Re-making of Disney* (New York: Wiley, 1991); "Fanfare as Disney Opens Park," NYT, October 2, 1982, 1,2; Michael Eisner (with Tony Schwartz) *Work in Progress* (New York: Hyperion, 1999); Disney Company, *Annual Report*, 1971, 7, APL.

72. "Who We Are, Where We Go," *St. Petersburg Times*, September 29, 1996, 1E; "Broadening the Mind into the Magic Kingdom," *The Economist*, March 23, 1991, 20; "Body Wars," *Disney News*, Spring 1989, 36, APL.

73. "Disney World to Open Another Thrill Ride," *Chicago Tribune* September 3, 1989, 8; "General Motors Corp.: Plans for Overhaul of Ride at Epcot will be Unveiled," *Wall Street Journal* February 13, 1996; quotes from "On Track," *Disney Magazine* (Fall 1998): 44–47, APL.

74. Craig Wilson, "New Attractions in Honor of Mickey," *USA Today*, June 1, 1988, 4d.

75. "Walt Disney Co. to Build a Roller Coaster in Disney-MGM Studios," *The Orlando Sentinel*, 1C; "Rock 'n' Roller Coaster," *Eyes and Ears* (WDW in-house newsletter), April 23, 1998, 1, 3, APL.

76. "River Country," *Walt Disney World News*, July 1977, 2; "Theme Parks," *Disney News*, Summer 1987, 4; "Water Works," *Disney Magazine*, Spring 1999, 44–47, APL.

77. "Disney World to Grow with 5 New Attractions," *Chicago Tribune*, December 6, 1987, F1; "New Attractions in Honor of Mickey," *USA Today*, June 1, 1988, 4d; At APL: "Grand Floridian," *Disney News* (Fall 1986): 4; "Dolphins and Swans and More," *Disney News* (Winter 1989): 29; "Downtown Disney," *Disney Magazine*, Spring 1998, 2; "Disney's Board Walk," *Disney News*, Winter 1995, 19–23; "Sports Complex," *Eyes and Ears*, February 27, 1997, 1. See also Dave Smith, *Disney A to Z* (New York: Hyperion, 1998).

78. At APL: "New Wedding Pavilion," *Eyes and Ears*, July 13, 1995, 1; "Magical Matrimony," *Eyes and Ears*, October 16, 1997, 3.

79. "Magic Kingdom Where Adults Can Go Goofy," *The Times of London*, January 13, 1996; "At ALP: Learn and Live," *Disney Magazine*, September 1996, 36–43; "Disney Institute," *Disney Magazine*, March 23, 1995, 1; APL, 8.

80. At APL: "Making Magic," *Disney Magazine*, Spring 1997, 48–53; "Imagineers Put Castaway Cay on the Map," *Eyes and Ears*, October 16, 1997, 113.

81. "Disney to Expand in Florida," *The Globe and Mail*, November 14, 1994, B4; "Disney World Tries to Stem Tourist Drop," November 14, 1994, *Orange County Register*, A3; "Time Off: Taking the Mickey as Disney Unveils a New Animal Kingdom," *The Guardian*, January 15, 1998, T20.

82. "Beauty and the Beasts Stocked with Real Creatures and Fantastic Images," *Time Magazine*, April 20, 1998, 66; "Disney Introduces New Animal Kingdom," *The Orlando Sentinel*, April 22, 1998, 1A.

83. "Family Vacations: Florida; Creature Feature; Exploring Disney's Animal Kingdom, Where Faked Reality Reigns," LAT, May 17, 1998, 17.

84. *Brandweek*, October 24, 1994, 22–29; *The Independent*, January 17, 1999, 10; *St. Petersburg Times*, October 16, 1996, 23; "California Dreaming," *Disney Magazine*, (Spring 2001): 36–61; LAT, April 9, 2001, C1; *Minneapolis Star Tribune*, April 8, 2001, 1G; LAT, September 20, 2001, C1.

6. "Enrichment through Enjoyment": The Beamish Museum in a Theme Park Age

1. Christopher Harvie, "Engineer's Holiday: L.T.C. Rolt, Industrial Heritage, and Tourism," in Hartmut Berghoff et al., eds., *The Making of Modern Tourism* (London: Palgrave, 2002), 203–21.

2. The direct influence of Scandinavian practice weighed more heavily than that of Beamish's one British precursor, the Welsh Folk Museum at St Fagan's, Cardiff, founded in 1946, which in any case also looked to Scandinavia. Frank Atkinson, *The Man Who Made Beamish: An Autobiography* (Gateshead: Northern Books, 1999), 9, 85–86; Tony Bennett, *The Birth of the Museum: History, Theory, Politics* (London: Routledge, 1995), 115. There was also the Ulster Folk Museum at Cultra, founded in 1958.

3. Atkinson, *The Man Who Made Beamish*, 9.

4. C. Williams, "Museums: Centres for Learning, or Disneyland?," *Labour History Review* 57 (1992).

5. Stacy Warren, "Cultural Contestation at Disneyland Paris," in David Crouch, ed., *Leisure/Tourism Geographies* (London: Routledge, 1999), 109–25.

6. National Fairgrounds Archive (hereafter NFA), Smart Family Collection, "Themeland" file, W. Butlin to R. Smart, telegram of March 27, 1961.

7. Ibid., C. James to Ronald Smart, April 13, 1961.

8. For months thereafter, Ronald Smart was still trying to make contact with an elusive Walt Disney and still hoping to use the word "Disneyland" for the Blackpool venture. Even after those plans were abandoned and renamed "Themeland," it was referred to informally as "the Disneyland proposition" in Blackpool. Ibid., R. Smart to C. Bernstein, June 28, 1961; R. Smart to C. Bernstein, October 4, 1961; site plans, Roy Thomson to Ronald Smart, May 1, 1961; memorandum, August 25, 1961.

9. Ibid., Ronald Smart to Cecil Bernstein, October 4, 1961; draft plans for "Themeland"; ibid., draft plans for "Themeland"; Harold Tunstall to Capt. Phayre, October 7, 1961.

10. Steve Mills, "American Theme Parks and the Landscape of Mass Culture," *American Studies Today Online*, http://www.americansc.org.uk/disney.htm, 3.

11. NFA, Smart Family Collection, Ronald Smart to H.R. Henshall, August 31, 1961; undated press statement from Mr. Billy Smart, late 1961.

12. Ibid., press statement; Kenneth G. Higgins, Quantity Surveyor to Butlin, forwarded to Ronald Smart, April 19, 1961; Mr Betts to Capt. Phayre, August 25, 1961.

13. Ibid., L.V. Phayre to Billy Butlin, May 23, 1961.

14. Colin Ward and David Hardy, *Goodnight Campers* (London: Mansell, 1986).

15. Martin Parr, ed., *Our True Intent Is all for Your Delight: The John Hinde Butlin's Photographs* (London: Boot, n.d.).

16. Mills, "American Theme Parks," 3.

17. Kevin Moore, *Museums and Popular Culture* (London: Continuum, 2000), ch. 7.

18. Mills, "American Theme Parks," 6.

19. Michael J. Fisher, *Alton Towers: A Gothic Wonderland* (Stafford: M.J. Fisher, 1999), 9.

20. Ibid., 11–12, 160–64; and www.alton-towers.co.uk accessed March 18, 2004.

21. NFA, Smart Family Collection, "Themeland" file; "Calico Ghost Town, Southern California's Greatest Silver Camp" (Knott's Berry Farm, 1959); Knott's Southern California and related websites: http://www.knotts.com/coinfo/history/index/shtml accessed February 4, 2003; www.knotts.com/park/index.shtml accessed March 19, 2004; www.narrowgauge.org/nge/html/kbfarm/kbfarm-main.html accessed March 19, 2004.

22. Peter Mandler, *The Fall and Rise of the Stately Home* (New Haven: Yale University Press, 1997), 217–21.

23. Ibid., Part IV; David Cannadine, *The Decline and Fall of the British Aristocracy* (New Haven: Yale University Press, 1990), 645–56.

24. Merlin Waterson, *The Servants' Hall* (London: Routledge, 1977).

25. Harvie, "Engineer's Holiday: L.T.C. Rolt, Industrial Heritage and Tourism," in Berghoff et al., eds., *The Making of Modern Tourism*, 212.

26. Ian Carter, *Railways and Culture in Britain* (Manchester: Manchester University Press, 2001), ch. 9; Becky Conekin, "'Here is the Modern World Itself:' The Festival of Britain's Representations of the Future," in Conekin et al., eds., *Moments of Modernity* (London: Rivers Oram Press, 1999).

27. Michael Freeman, *Railways and the Victorian Imagination* (New Haven: Yale University Press, 1999), 244–45.

28. Nicholas Whittaker, *Platform Souls: The Trainspotter as Twentieth-Century Hero* (London: Victor Gollancz, 1995).

29. Freeman, *Railways*, 242–43.

30. Raphael Samuel, *Theatres of Memory* (London: Verso, 1994).

31. It also has American counterparts, although it was spread more thinly. Harvie, "Engineer's Holiday," 211–12.

32. Kevin Walsh, *The Representation of the Past* (London: Routledge, 1992), 100.

33. Julian Barnes, *England, England* (London: Cape, 1998); Barbara Korte, "Julian Barnes, *England, England*," in Berghoff, et al. eds., *The Making of Modern Tourism*, 285–303.

34. Michael Rawlinson, "Cadbury World," *Labour History Review* 67 (2002): 101–19.

35. Site visit, Hershey, April 2003.

36. Rawlinson, "Cadbury World," 102, 115; T. Friedman, "The World of *The World of*

Coca-Cola," *Communication Research* 19 (1992); M. Wallace, "Making Mickey Mouse History: Portraying the Past at Disney World," in W. Leon and R. Rosenzweig, eds., *History Museums in the United States* (Urbana: University of Illinois Press, 1989).

37. For an early critique of Ironbridge see B. West, "The Making of the English Working Past: A Critical View of the Ironbridge Gorge Museum," in R. Lumley, ed., *The Museum Time Machine* (London: Routledge, 1988), 36–62.

38. Martin Wiener, *English Culture and the Decline of the Industrial Spirit* (Harmondsworth: Penguin, 1985); Bennett, *Birth of the Museum*, 114.

39. Bennett, *Birth of the Museum*, 110–14; Walsh, *Representation of the Past*, 97–100; Robert Hewison, *The Heritage Industry* (London: Methuen, 1987), 93–95. Walsh, *Representation of the Past*, 95–96, points out that Artur Hazelius, the Swedish founder of the open-air museum movement, sought to "use the idea of heritage and understanding of the past as a steadying influence in the face of violent influences of modern life" (quoting E. P. Alexander, *Museums in Motion* [Nashville: American Association for State and Local History, 1979], 85). The racial dimension to such perceptions in the United States, as (for example) critics rightly pointed out that slaves were rendered invisible at Williamsburg, carries less immediate purchase in Britain outside old slave ports like Liverpool, Bristol, and Lancaster; but the points about class and gender, and more broadly about the legacy of empire, do need to be addressed: W. Leon and M. Piatt, "Living-History Museums," in Leon and Rosenzweig, eds., *History Museum*. Walsh, *Representation of the Past*, 141–42, critiques the presentation of the slave trade at the Maritime Museum at Liverpool's Albert Dock.

40. Hewison, *The Heritage Industry*; Patrick Wright, "Restoration Tragedy," *Guardian Review* (London), September 13, 2003, 16–17; Peter Mandler, *History and National Life* (London: Profile Books, 2002), 126–27.

41. Leon and Piatt, "Living-History Museums."

42. Kevin Moore, *Museums and Popular Culture* (London: Continuum, 1997), ch. 7; Hewison, *Heritage Industry*, 93–95; Walsh, *Representation of the Past*, 98; Bennett, *Birth of the Museum*, 113.

43. Hewison, *Heritage Industry*, 93–95.

44. Walsh's hostility may be colored by his erroneous belief that Beamish was a "private heritage attraction" rather than a "public museum." Hewison at least got this right. Walsh, *The Representation of the Past*, 100, 182; Hewison, *Heritage Industry*, 93.

45. Walsh, *Representation of the Past*, 97–100.

46. Bennett, *Birth of the Museum*, 110–14, 117–20.

47. Moore, *Museums and Popular Culture*, 137–43.

48. Martti Puhakka and Solveig Sjoberg-Pietarinen, eds., *The Luostarinmaki Handicrafts Museum: Guide Book* (Turku: Turku Provincial Museum, 2000).

49. For the Bowes Museum see Charles E. Hardy, *John Bowes and the Bowes Museum* (Newcastle: Frank Graham, 1970).

50. Atkinson, *Autobiography*, 23–24, 73, 85–87; Beamish Museum Archive (BA), Box labeled "F. Atkinson's Early Correspondence, to 1966" (hereafter "1966 Box"), Atkinson to Jim Boyden, September 8, 1965.

51. Atkinson, *Autobiography*, 90–92. It may be significant that Beamish's emergence coincided with a general "turn against urban modernisation" in Britain in the 1970s: Peter Mandler, "New Towns for Old," in Conekin et al., eds., *Moments of Modernity*, 226.

52. Mark Clapson, *Invincible Green Suburbs, Brave New Towns* (Manchester: Manchester University Press, 1998); Jeremy Alden and Robert Morgan, *Regional Planning: a Comprehensive View* (Leighton Buzzard: Leonard Hill, 1974), for a view from the planners of Peterlee and nearby Newton Aycliffe.

53. These aristocrats included Sir Humphrey Noble of Humshaugh, Viscount Gort of Hamsterley Hall, and the Earl of Rosse, a member of the Standing Commission on Museums and Galleries. BA, 1966 Box, Atkinson to J. Boyden, M.P., Sir Humphrey Noble, Viscount Gort, Councillor Dan Smith, and the Earl of Rosse, September 8, 1965; Atkinson to Lord Fleck (of Imperial Chemical Industries), September 6, 1965; Atkinson, *Autobiography*, 92–93.

54. BA, 1966 Box, Report on St Fagan's visit, October 25–27, 1965; Agenda for Museums Sub-Committee, November 24, 1965; Report to Museums Sub-Committee, November 24, 1965; Brian Shallcross to Atkinson, November 23, 1965; Atkinson to Earl of Rosse, December 13, 1965.

55. Atkinson, *Autobiography*, 99–103; BA, Newspaper Cuttings, "1970" Box File (hereafter "1970 Box"), *Journal*, July 12, 1967.

56. BA, 1970 Box, *Stanley News*, April 1967.

57. BA, North Regional Industrial Museum Working Party, October 4, 1966, Site Report.

58. Atkinson, *Autobiography*, 103–7; BA, 1966 Box, Memorandum about the availability of Beamish Hall, September 8, 1966; Atkinson to Ian Swanson, August 30, 1966; notes of conversation between John Walton, Rosemary Allan, and John Gall, Beamish, August 20, 2002.

59. BA, 1966 Box, correspondence between Atkinson and Councillor McMillan, especially November 22, 1966.

60. BA, 1970 Box, *Northern Echo*, January 23, February 18, 1969; *Evening Chronicle*, February 25, March 13, March 15, 1969; *Guardian*, March 24, 1969; *Daily Mail*, March 24, 1969; *Sunderland Echo*, June 3, 1969.

61. Local garage proprietor Eric Hall spoke out in favor of the museum in April, and denounced the opposition as "social climbers" and comparative newcomers to the district. BA, 1970 Box, *Northern Echo*, April 9, 1969; *Sunderland Echo*, April 19, 1969; news cuttings dealing with ministerial acceptance, May 28, 1969.

62. Finally, a bitter, if isolated, attack from the Left came from W. Walker of Ryton, objecting to plans to "help in the desecration of Beamish Park, or to spoil the beauty spots of

the North-East with tawdry commercialism for the enrichment of vested travel interests." BA, 1970 Box, *Evening Chronicle*, March 15, 1969; *Sunderland Echo*, July 9 and 10,
1969; *Evening Dispatch*, August 8, 1969.

63. BA, 1970 Box, *Morning Advertiser*, December 12, 1970.

64. BA, 1970 Box, *Daily Telegraph*, March 6, 1969.

65. For Wharton see M. Wharton, *The Missing Will, and a Dubious Codicil: A Double Autobiography* (London: Hogarth Press, 1992), and Dave Russell, *Looking North* (Manchester:
Manchester University Press, 2004).

66. BA, 1970 Box, *Northern Echo*, June 29, 1968; *Evening Chronicle*, July 19, 1968.

67. Within ten days it had recruited 50 members, but much more important was the issue
of a glossy public relations and recruitment pamphlet at a press conference, and the
making of a national BBC2 television program on the museum and its philosophy,
which generated further free publicity. By the second Annual General Meeting the
Friends had 334 members, with two affiliated societies. By the end of 1971 there were
873 individual members and 18 affiliated societies. British Library (hereafter cited as
BL), P423/57, *Friends of the Northern Regional Open-Air Museum, Newsletter One* (June
1968); P421/193, *Annual Reports for 1969 and 1971*.

68. BA, 1970 Box, *Northern Echo*, February 16, 1971; BL J/X0410/105, Miscellaneous
Beamish Pamphlets, *Living History*, version 2.

69. BA, 1970 Box, *Northern Echo*, August 24, 1970.

70. BL P421/193, *Minutes of Fourth Annual General Meeting*, April 17, 1971; *Annual Report
for 1971*.

71. The museum's collections of old everyday objects became overwhelmingly large, and
washing mangles became particularly numerous because Atkinson once incautiously
mentioned in an interview that the Museum was looking for them. This story is almost
a Beamish legend, but John Walton's colleague Stephen Caunce, who was working at
Beamish at the time, confirmed it in conversation, March 25, 2004.

72. BA, North Regional Industrial Museum Working Party: Report of Clerk of Durham
County Council (Meeting, October 4, 1966).

73. Atkinson, *Autobiography*, 133; Peter Johnson and Barry Thomas, *Tourism, Museums and
the Local Economy: The Economic Impact of the North of England Open Air Museum at
Beamish* (Aldershot: Edward Elgar, 1992), 20.

74. BA, Development Strategy 2001, p. 26, Appendix 1, "Visitor Numbers"; Johnson and
Thomas, *Tourisms, Museums and the Local Economy*, 21.

75. BA, 1966 Box, Beamish: 1973 and Beyond, June 1973, 8, 12; Johnson and Thomas,
Museums and the Local Economy, 23–24.

76. BA, 1966 Box, Typescript of Atkinson's Presidential Address to the Museums Association, Durham, 1975, 5–6.

77. Ibid., 6–8; BA, 1966 Box, Discussion Paper for Joint Committee, February 1976, 8.

78. BA, 1966 Box, Joint Committee, February 1976, 8–10, 13.

79. This decline in visitor numbers followed a doubling of admission prices to a more realistic £1.50 (which meant that visitor income year on year had actually grown) and a rainy summer. Johnson and Thomas, *Museums and the Local Economy*, 25–30; BA, 1966 Box, Atkinson's Report to Joint Committee on "Marketing Beamish," March 6, 1981. By 2001 the local authorities' contribution had fallen to around 5 percent of the £3 million per year running cost, the remainder coming from the European Development Fund, English Tourist Board, Countryside Commission, National Heritage Memorial Fund and Heritage Lottery, together with the Beamish Development Trust which encouraged support from local industry: http://www.beamish.org.uk/digest.htm, accessed August 7, 2002.

80. BA, 1966 Box, "Marketing Beamish," and report by Kenneth Robinson, November 24, 1980.

81. Informal interview: John Walton, Rosy Allan and John Gall, August 20, 2002; BA, Development Strategy 2001, 26, Appendix 1; http://www.beamish.org.uk/digest.htm, accessed August 7, 2002.

82. Walsh, *Representation of the Past*, 99–100.

83. http://www.beamish.org.uk accessed April 4, 2004.

84. Ibid.

85. Ibid.

86. Informal interview, above, note 81, and site visit. See also Alan Doyle, *Mining: the Beamish Collection* (Newcastle: Centre for Northern Studies, 2001); John Gorman, *Banner Bright: An Illustrated History of the Banners of the British Trade Union Movement* (Harmondsworth: Penguin, 1976; 2nd ed. 1985).

87. BA, Handbooks for Demonstrators, Pockerley Manor, 1995.

88. BA, Staff Training Manuals, Interpretation, 2002; Rosy Allan to John Walton, e-mail communication, September 17, 2002; and see Atkinson, *Autobiography*, 211–12.

89. Compare Leon and Piatt, "Living History Museums," for American practice.

90. E-mail, Rosy Allan to John Walton, September 17, 2002.

91. Jill Liddington and Jill Norris, *One Hand Tied Behind Us* (London: Virago, 1978).

92. Val Williamson, "Regional Identity: A Gendered Heritage," in S.A. Caunce et al., eds., *Relocating Britishness* (Manchester: Manchester University Press, 2004).

93. Beamish, interview notes, August 20, 2002.

94. BA, 1976–77 Newspaper Cuttings Box, *Durham County Advertiser*, April 16, 1976, 30 September 1976; *Stanley News*, April 7, 1977.

7. The Crowd Transformed?

1. Norbert Elias, translated by Edmund Jephcott, *The Civilizing Process: Sociogenetic and Psychogenetic Investigations*, Revised Edition (Oxford: Blackwell Publishers, 2000); J. M. Golby, *The Civilization of the Crowd: Popular Culture in England, 1750–1900* (New York: Schocken Books, 1985).

2. Eric Leed, *The Mind of the Traveler: From Gilgamesh to Global Tourism* (New York: Basic Books, 1991).

3. Raymond Weinstein, "Disneyland and Coney Island: Reflections on the Evolution of the Modern Amusement Park," *Journal of Popular Culture* 26 (Summer 1992): 131–42.

4. T. J. Jackson Lears, *Fables of Abundance: A Cultural History of Advertising in America* (New York: Basic Books, 1994); Roland Marchand, *Advertising The American Dream: Making Way for Modernity, 1920–1940* (Berkeley: University of California Press, 1988); William Leach, *Land of Desire: Merchants, Power and the Rise of a New American Culture* (New York: Vintage, 1993)

5. Gary Cross, *The Cute and the Cool: Wondrous Innocence and Modern American Children's Culture* (New York Oxford University Press, 2004), ch. 3.

6. Jacqueline Rose, *The Impossibility of Children's Fiction* (London: Macmillan, 1984), 1–9.

7. Pleasure Beach Archives, folder 6.

8. As Stacy Warren argues, Disneyland Paris soon became a cultural hybrid. The French workforce successfully resisted attempts to impose the full Disney agenda, especially as regards dress codes, while "Tomorrowland" was replaced by a "Discoveryland" that was based on the works of Jules Verne, including a re-creation of his imagined Trip to the Moon. Warren suggests that Disneyland Paris is a "site of postcolonial struggle," as the multinational corporation seeks to impose its culture on the nation state: hence, in part, the attacks on Disney icons and identifiable Disney personnel that disturbed and threatened the early days of the theme park. The "struggle" is genuine, and has consequences: the local can still assert itself in ways that modify the global, affecting the nature of the crowd's experience of the site. Stacy Warren, "Cultural Contestation at Disneyland Paris," in David Crouch, ed., *Leisure/Tourism Geographies* (London: Routledge, 1999), 109–25; Andrew Lainsbury, *Once upon an American Dream: The Story of Euro Disneyland* (Lawrence: University Press of Kansas, 2000).

9. Aviad Raz, *Riding the Black Ship: Japan and Tokyo Disneyland* (Cambridge: Harvard University Asia Center, Distributed by Harvard University Press, 1999), 30–40, 61; Sharon Kinsella, "Cuties In Japan," in L. Skov and B. Moeran, eds *Women, Media and Consumption in Japan* (Richmond, England: Curzon, 1995), 220–50; *Financial Post*, October 25, 1995, 62.

10. Disney Collection, Anaheim Public Library: Disney Company, *Annual Report*, 2002, 24; "Vive la Difference!: Euro Disneyland," *Disney News*, Fall 1990, 35–39.

11. Judith Adams, *The American Amusement Park Industry* (Boston: Twayne, 1991), 57, 112–36; Susan Davis, *Spectacular Nature: Corporate Culture and the Sea World Experience* (Berkeley: University of California Press, 1997), 20–26

12. Margaret King, "New American Muse," *Journal of Popular Culture*, Spring 1991, 56–62; Lainsbury, *Once upon an American Dream*, 170, 174; Hugo Hildenbrandt, "Cedar Point," *Journal of Popular Culture*, 1981, 87–107; Davis, *Spectacular Nature*, 9–10, 34, 37, 161–162, 169.

13. The Disneyfication of Las Vegas may not be so profitable. According to a 1997 survey, adults spent 500 dollars per day at the luxury casinos, but only 100 dollars when the kids tagged along. MGM dropped its "Wizard of Oz" theme, replacing the Emerald City entrance with slot machines and a night club. *Rocky Mountain Daily News*, January 19, 1997; *Tampa Tribune*, October 13, 1997.

14. John Terrell, "Disneyland and the Future of Museums," *American Anthropology* 93 (1991): 149–52.

15. "In Disney Mold Firm Takes Animation to Museums," *Los Angeles Times* April 16, 1985, 5A.

16. "Aquariums Hooking Visitors," *USA Today*, December 19, 2003, D6; "Disney wishes upon B'way," *USA Today*, November 13, 2002, D8; "A Plague on the Quarter," *New Orleans Times-Picayune*, December 16, 1998, B1; "The Future Is Foggy On Fisherman's Wharf," *New York Times*, February 4, 2001, 5; "The Mouse that Roars on Broadway," *Boston Globe*, April 27, 1997, D1; "Times Square Transformed from Porn Mecca to Mickey Mouse," *Houston Chronicle*, June 30, 1996, 9.

17. Margaret King, "McDonald's and Disney," in Marshall Fishwick, ed., *Ronald Revisited and the World of Ronald McDonald* (Bowling Green: Bowling Green State University Popular Press, 1983), 117. For a full treatment, see Henry Giroux, *The Mouse that Roared: Disney and the End of Innocence* (Lanham, Maryland: Rowman & Littlefield, 1999).

18. "Lower Attendance, Budget Deficit Trouble Colonial Williamsburg," *St. Louis Post-Dispatch*. September 28, 2003, T.5; "Where Jefferson and Henry Strode, There's an Anxious Turn to Trendy," *Washington Post*, November 30, 2003, F.01. The promise and perils of living history museums that try to dramatize the past with staff acting as if they actually live in the past is discussed in Warren Leon and Margaret Piatt, "Living-History Museums," in Warren Leon and Roy Rosenzweig, eds., *History Museums in the United States* (Urbana: University of Illinois Press, 1989), 64–97, quotation on p. 75.

19. "Universal's Parent is Pushing Big-Budget Plans for Expansion in the Tourism Industry," *Los Angeles Times*, June 3, 1990, 7 "Duel in the Florida Sun," *Marketing News*, January 6, 1992, 1.

20. Peter Stearns, *American Cool: Constructing a Twentieth-Century Emotional Style* (New York: New York University Press, 1994).

21. Significantly, new rides focused on superhero comic book characters that had since the late 1930s symbolized separation from the worlds of the cute and the improving culture of the middle class. Amy Nyberg, *Seal of Approval: The History of the Comics Code* (Jackson: University Press of Mississippi, 1998), 5–6, 37–38; Bradford Wright, *Comic Book Nation* (Baltimore: The Johns Hopkins University Press, 2001), 201–25; and Cross, *The Cute and the Cool*, ch. 6.

22. "Virginia, Say No to the Mouse," *New York Times*, February 24, 1994, A22.

23. "America Loves to Hate the Mouse; Behind the Fantasy Walt Disney Built Looms a Dark Reality," *Washington Post* December 5, 2001, C1.

Index